D. H. Lawrence

# D. H. Lawrence

## Fifty Years on Film

Louis K. Greiff

Southern Illinois University Press

*Carbondale and Edwardsville*

Library of Congress Cataloging-in-Publication Data
Greiff, Louis K., 1938–

    D.H. Lawrence : fifty years on film / Louis K. Greiff.

      p. cm.

    Includes filmography (p.) and videography (p.).

    Includes bibliographical references and index.

    1. Lawrence, D. H. (David Herbert), 1885–1930—Film and video adaptations. 2. English fiction—Film and video adaptations. I. Title: David Herbert Lawrence. II. Title.

    PR6023.A93 Z63113 2001

    791.43'6—dc21                 00-061225

    ISBN 0-8093-2387-7 (alk. paper)

The paper used in this publication meets the minimum requirements of American National Standard for Information Sciences—Permanence of Paper for Printed Library Materials, ANSI Z39.48-1992. ♾

For my wife, Sandy, and my son, Luis

Alas, I could not be filmed.
I should feel, like a savage, that they had stolen my "medicine."
    —D. H. Lawrence, letter to Lady Cynthia Asquith (1920)

Here's to ol' D. H. Lawrence.
    —Jack Nicholson as George Hanson in *Easy Rider* (1969)

# Contents

# Illustrations

# Preface

Ten feature-length films based on the life and works of D. H. Lawrence were released over the second half of the twentieth century, beginning with *The Rocking Horse Winner* in 1949. When I began this book, my goal was to chronicle the fifty-year history of the Lawrence feature film and likewise to interpret and evaluate its results. A complication I encountered early on, however, was the tendency of my subject matter to expand beyond just ten films. There are short Lawrence films as well as features, for example, including a new *Rocking Horse Winner,* which appeared near the end of the century to beg comparison with its fifty-year-old predecessor.

There are also Lawrence-related television productions, more of them in fact than large-screen films, so that they probably deserve a book of their own. All the same, I found it impossible to keep them out of this book, even though I assured myself that "officially" they were not my major concern. In addition to all the feature films, then, fifteen Lawrence television productions are listed at the end of this volume in a separate videography. Also, a third of these are included for discussion in the chapters that follow on the basis of their interconnectedness with the feature films under primary study. An examination of Ken Russell's 1993 *Lady Chatterley* for BBC Television, therefore, introduces my seventh chapter, devoted to the long and erratic relationship between Lawrence's final novel and the movies. Similarly, the televised *Rainbow* and the televised *Sons and Lovers* are taken up in the chapters devoted to those texts and their adaptations for the large screen. Peter Barber-Fleming's *Coming Through,* a 1985 television production, is included in the chapter devoted to Christopher Miles's *Priest of Love* (1981), since both are Lawrence biographies by the same writer, Alan Plater. Finally, a little-known television adaptation of "The Horse-Dealer's Daughter," made for PBS Television in 1984 by the American Film Institute, figures in the conclusion of this study. Its experimentally effective adaptation of the short story provides some indication of where Lawrence may be leading filmmakers in the future or where they may be taking him.

Anyone studying film or film adaptation faces the daunting problem of availability of source material, with television posing an even greater complication and challenge than standard cinema. Almost all of the Lawrence feature films have been available on commercial videotape. While many of them no longer remain in print, at least this means that copies continue to exist in quantity and can be tracked down for viewing in libraries, specialized film collections, and commercial outlets like Facets Video. On occasion, some even appear as televised reruns that can be recorded on VCR. It's a different (and sadder) story with the adaptations made for television, where only four of the fifteen Lawrence productions have ever been released on tape: *The Trespasser* (now out of print), *The Horse Dealer's Daughter, Coming Through,* and *Lady Chatterley.* The only extant videotape copies of the remaining television productions are those made by private individuals for their own use when the programs originally aired. Today such copies are not only few in number but extremely difficult to trace and obtain for viewing. Also, of course, no such copies exist of any production released before VCR technology became available to the public.

More than half of the fifteen Lawrence video productions are the work of BBC Television. Of these, only two have been released on tape, and only one *(Lady Chatterley)* remains on the market today. Since BBC-TV regularly makes its programs available on commercial videotape, it's both disturbing and puzzling that it has not seen fit to do so with the Lawrence productions—particularly the major productions like Stuart Burge's serialized adaptations of *The Rainbow* and *Sons and Lovers* or Claude Watham's version of "The Captain's Doll," in which Jeremy Irons appears as Captain Hepburn. The release of such productions would be of significant value to students of Lawrence and film adaptation alike. I also believe BBC would profit from the ongoing interest, on the part of general audiences, in Lawrence-related material on screen.

An altogether separate problem facing students of fiction into film involves text rather than film availability. I am referring to the question of which editions—in this case, of Lawrence's novels, novellas, and stories—to work with in examining their adaptations for the screen. One possible answer here is to use the Cambridge University Press editions of Lawrence, a definitive scholarly series in the process of being released volume by volume until the complete works have been made available. A major drawback to this answer, however, is that the Cambridge project came too late for any of the Lawrence filmmakers to have benefited from its results. Even the most recent Lawrence feature film and television production—Ken Russell's *Rainbow* (1989) and *Lady Chatterley* (1993)—appeared simultaneously with the Cambridge editions of those texts, which therefore could not have figured in either production.

A second and seemingly straightforward answer on text is to use the editions the filmmakers used when they made their adaptations. This is not as simple as it sounds, however, since filmmakers, unlike scholars and critics, don't tend to worry about the differences between one edition and another and don't necessarily remember which edition (or editions) they used. Larry Kramer, for example, recalled working with a 1960 paperback in writing his screenplay for *Women in Love* but after checking further wrote me that instead he relied on a hardcover "edition of WIL that I really and mostly used when writing the screenplay." Kramer used this hardcover edition as the basis for his script but also worked with the paperback edition on the set, underlining it to identify the "actual lines of dialogue that we used in the film."

For the purposes of this study, I've decided to rely on two separate Lawrence editions, each of which fulfills a different purpose. When my references are exclusively textual—that is, to an unfilmed Lawrence work, or to his letters, or to biographical information—the Cambridge editions are generally cited. When my references are to the filmed texts, however, the Viking Press editions of the 1960s are generally cited instead, since these editions enjoyed wide distribution during the years the Lawrence films were produced. The Viking editions were readily available, worldwide, both to filmmakers and to their audiences—to viewers who went to the movies already familiar with the book, as well as to viewers inspired to read the book by having first seen the film.

The major exception to this division of labor is *Lady Chatterley's Lover*. Not counting pornographic rip-offs, Lawrence's final novel has been filmed three times. The first production, *L'Amant de Lady Chatterley*, was adapted in 1955 from a French stage play rather than directly from the novel. The second and third productions, released in 1981 and 1993, are both more dependent on Lawrence's two earlier versions (*The First Lady Chatterley* and *John Thomas and Lady Jane*) than on *Lady Chatterley's Lover* itself. As a result of this complex and uniquely indirect filming history, no earlier edition of *Lady Chatterley's Lover* presents itself as a logical choice for this study, so the Cambridge edition is cited throughout.

# Acknowledgments

To write a book is to discover how dependent we all are on the kindness of strangers and friends alike. No author works alone, and no book gets finished without the participation of dozens, sometimes hundreds, of people even when only one name finally appears on the title page. For this book, I owe debts of gratitude to dozens of strangers and friends, although I already know that I won't remember all of them. Some are right next door in Alfred, New York, and others halfway around the world. I'll try to mention everyone, but I apologize in advance to all whose help I eagerly accepted then somehow managed to forget.

First, I must thank Marlin Miller, member and former chair of Alfred University's board of trustees. A generous gift from Marlin to Alfred University several years ago established the Fred H. Gertz Chair in English, which allowed me to jump-start my Lawrence on film project by way of release time from teaching. Without the precious morning hours Marlin's endowed chair gave me to write, this book could never have been started, let alone finished. Also, I need to thank the staff of Alfred University's Herrick Memorial Library, especially Gary Roberts, formerly its interlibrary loan specialist, whose patience with me and my requests for obscure material never ended—at least not until he received a promotion and moved to a different department. One other Alfredian I need to thank is Barbara Greil of Hinkle Library, Alfred State College. Despite working for the "other" college library in town, Barb gave generously of her time and expertise to put me in touch with the fascinating world of film and film study in Australia. Barb made this connection for me cheerfully and efficiently at a point in my project when I was stuck and no one else seemed able to assist.

Beyond Alfred, I visited a number of research libraries and special film collections across the country. Their staffs all deserve my heartfelt thanks for their professionalism, their kindness, and their consistent willingness to give of their time in the interests of my project. Thanks, then, to the staff of the Bobst Library at my own alma mater, New York University, for their assistance with film script research. Also in New York, thanks to the staff of the Celeste Bartos International Film Study Center at the Museum of Modern Art, particularly to three resourceful and generous individuals: Charles Silver and Ron Magliozzi of the Film Study Center, and Mary Corliss of the Film Stills Archive, Museum of

Modern Art, for most of the book's illustrations. Moving west to Bloomington, Indiana, sincere thanks to the staff of Indiana University's Lilly Library, especially to Sue Presnell for seeming to give everyone she works with 100 percent of her attention and concern. Finally, in Los Angeles, thanks to the staffs of three libraries, all invaluable resources on the subject of film: the Los Angeles Public Library, the Louis B. Mayer Library at the American Film Institute, and the Margaret Herrick Library at the Academy of Motion Picture Arts and Sciences.

Within the select community of Lawrence filmmakers, I owe special thanks to Michael Almereyda for making his experimental adaptation of "The Rocking-Horse Winner" available to me shortly after its debut at the New York Film Festival, and to Larry Kramer for providing me with detailed information on the filming of *Women in Love* and on his writing of the screenplay for that film. Along with the Lawrence filmmakers, many Lawrence scholars and critics also deserve my thanks, both collectively and individually. First, I wish to thank the D. H. Lawrence Society of North America for being a uniquely welcoming and supportive community of scholars and for sponsoring the most exciting professional conferences I've attended in more than thirty years of academic life. Beyond this, I need to thank a number of individuals within this organization for their friendship and support of my project over the past several years: Gary Adelman, Jay Gertzman, Barbara Miliaras, and Mark Spilka. And I would like to extend special thanks to Jay, who shares my passion for film, for also being willing to share his video collection with me. Without his help, I'm sure I'd still be chasing after copies of scarce Lawrence productions such as BBC Television's *The Rainbow* or *The Boy in the Bush*.

Other members of the Lawrence community of scholars need to be thanked for extending their help in different ways. Thanks to Dennis Jackson for being enthusiastic about this project when it was just getting started and for offering me his support at the Ottawa Lawrence conference in 1993. Thanks also to Lori Linderman Clovis for her careful efforts as a proofreader and for her willingness to take on the daunting job of copyright detective on my behalf. And, most of all, thanks to Keith Cushman for taking my project as seriously as if it were his own. Over the past year, Keith has offered me invaluable editorial advice and has shared with me his truly impressive fund of knowledge and insight on Lawrence and all matters Lawrentian. The end result of my effort has been strengthened by Keith's interest and participation, and I remain permanently in his debt.

Finally, and most deeply, I owe a lifetime of thanks to my wife, Sandy, for her loving and patient willingness to share her husband with his book for the past several years. The job of being the writer's spouse is probably the most thankless and frustrating of any, since it entails all the burdens of authorship with very few of the rewards.

D. H. Lawrence

# 1
# D. H. Lawrence on Film

D. H. Lawrence's condemnation of the movies may not be as famous as some of his other polemics, yet it has been established clearly enough in accounts of his life and in his writings. One tale is that in 1926 he tried to watch *Ben-Hur* but left in a rage instead. According to his American friend Achsah Brewster, he was sickened by the falseness and inhumanity of the film and had to leave.[1] This incident proves revealing because the same charges—falseness and inhumanity—seemed to crop up whenever Lawrence wrote about film. He wrote about it as a poet in "When I Went to the Film" and "Let Us Be Men," both from the *Pansies* collection. In the first of these verses, Lawrence suggests that going to the movies must be like going to heaven—only a sterile heaven, where human vitality has been bled dry, leaving a white void

> upon which shadows of people, pure personalities
> are cast in black and white, and move
> in flat ecstasy, supremely unfelt,
> and heavenly.[2]

The indictment is even stronger in "Let Us Be Men," where Lawrence grabs us by the collar and yells in our collective faces:

> For God's sake, let us be men
> not monkeys minding machines
> or sitting with our tails curled
> while the machine amuses us, the radio or film or
> gramophone.[3]

"Monkeys minding machines"—how potent and yet how unfair. It's a safe bet that the man who wrote these lines saw very few films. It's also no surprise that neither do the fictional people he created; with few exceptions, D. H. Lawrence characters don't go to the flicks. John Thomas Raynor and Annie Stone do in the short story "Tickets, Please," but the film breaks partway through, and they're both interested in other things anyway. "The pictures danced and dithered" for Paul Morel and Clara Dawes just once in *Sons and Lovers* when they attended "the cinematograph . . . for a few minutes before train-time."[4] Constance Chatterley doesn't actually see a film but notices its title in what turns out to be a critical moment in *Lady Chatterley's Lover.* When Connie takes her famous ride through Tevershall, she passes the cinema among the other familiar eyesores of modern life. Her reaction, although more sad than angry, is much the same as Lawrence's in the poems:

> The car ploughed uphill through the long squalid struggle of Tevershall, the blackened brick dwellings, the black slate roofs glistening their sharp edges, the mud black with coal-dust, the pavements wet and black. It was as if dismalness had soaked through and through everything. The utter negation of natural beauty, the utter negation of the gladness of life, the utter absence of the instinct for shapely beauty which every bird and beast has, the utter death of the human intuitive faculty was appalling. The stacks of soap in the grocers' shops, the rhubarb and lemons in the greengrocers', the awful hats in the milliners', all went by ugly, ugly, ugly, followed by the plaster-and-gilt horror of the cinema with its wet picture-announcements, "A Woman's Love!"[5]

What's playing in Tevershall as Connie rides by forms a strange and unintended prediction of D. H. Lawrence on film. The title *A Woman's Love!* on the marquee brings to mind any number of his own titles: *Women in Love, Sons and Lovers,* "A Modern Lover," and *Lady Chatterley's Lover* itself. The invented film title seems to offer an acknowledgment on Lawrence's part that modern mass culture shares his deepest preoccupations yet somehow vulgarizes them, making what he took so seriously seem mechanical and even inhuman.[6]

If Lawrence disliked the movies, it is a troublesome irony that in many important ways he shouldn't have. He was, after all, a visual artist as well as a writer. Among his peers, the great figures of early modern fiction, he was possibly the most sensitive to the potentialities of image and scene, the most adept at empowering the word by making it visible and vitally active. In addition, he was interested in finding a source of beauty and a suitable art form for the mass of modern men and women, not just for the cultural elite. This preoccupation is expressed several times by Oliver Mellors, the hero of the very novel that stops short at the "plaster-and-gilt horror" of the cinema's exterior and that sees nothing of value within. Mellors and Lawrence, in fact, would have the common people of Tevershall scrap the cinema, along with every other twentieth-century "improvement," in favor of a neoprimitive revival: "If the men wore scarlet trousers . . . they wouldn't think so much of money: if they could dance and hop and skip, and sing and swagger and be handsome, they could do with very little cash. And amuse the women themselves, and be amused by the women."[7]

No doubt this strange lot isn't about to line up for the next screening of *A Woman's Love!* Lawrence, by all that is logical, should have been sensitive at least to the promise of film, but for the most part he wasn't. This paradox is made even plainer by recalling James Joyce, Lawrence's equal in creative achievement yet his intellectual and artistic opposite in so many important ways. It was Joyce and not Lawrence who logically should have been revolted by the movies or at best indifferent to them. His gifts as a writer, in contrast to Lawrence's, were always more essentially auditory and linguistic than visual. Also, Joyce had no interest in the aesthetic needs of modern humankind en masse. In fact, he used his art defensively to keep the world—and Ireland in particular—at some safe distance from himself.

Yet it was Joyce who broke exile in 1909 to help establish the Volta, Dublin's first cinema. The vision of Lawrence attempting something similar for Eastwood or Nottingham is downright laughable. Also laughable is the vision of the two great writers, separated by nearly twenty years of history, yet brought together in the mind's eye. Joyce, in the company of two Italian businessmen, rushes about Dublin to make sure the Volta will be open in time for Christmas 1909. His eyesight is poor and getting worse, so probably he won't be seeing many films himself. Yet he works feverishly on the project, staying up until 3:00 and 4:00 A.M. night after night, until finally he falls sick with exhaustion.[8] Lawrence also falls sick, some two decades later, not from trying to establish a cinema but merely from trying to remain inside one long enough to sit through *Ben-Hur.* Ramon Novarro and Francis X. Bushman make his efforts impossible, and Lawrence walks out.

Biographers like Richard Ellmann and Brenda Maddox have suggested that more than a pure love of film motivated Joyce's efforts on behalf of the Volta project. He was deep in poverty in 1909, with a family to look after, and saw the prospect of bringing the movies to Dublin (not to mention Cork and Belfast) as his chance for financial success.[9] A more complex suggestion is that Joyce may also have seen in film the potential for releasing serious artists from the clutches of the crowd. If the public at large could satisfy its hunger for fictions at the cinema, it would cease to trouble writers with the temptation to compromise. They might remain poor as a result yet be artistically free as well.[10]

One thing appears certain despite the complexity and perhaps ultimately the obscurity of Joyce's motivations in 1909. He committed himself to the Volta with an enthusiasm that would have been unthinkable had he shared Lawrence's reaction against the movies. Joyce sensed potential in film because, despite his dim eyesight, he regarded it essentially as image and as image holding popular, financial, and even artistic promise. Lawrence, on the other hand, seems to have been blocked from receiving film as image at least partly because of its relationship to technology.[11] Lawrence's distrust of machines surely began with his awareness of the Eastwood pits and of his father's entrapment within them. It ended with such telling symbols as Sir Clifford's typewriter, wheelchair, and radio in *Lady Chatterley's Lover*. Lawrence always could transform the burden of his obsessions into artistic treasure, yet that burden may have cost him something as well. In film he could see only cold mechanical process—physically and metaphysically sickening, ultimately even pornographic. Despite his vision in so many senses of that word, he could not see beyond process to image—to an artistic end result, in film, not all that different from his own.[12]

It is an altogether appropriate irony, then, that the film industry has repaid Lawrence's hostility with a great deal of attention to his work. The first stirring of interest came in 1922 when an American company offered $10,000 for the screen rights to *Women in Love*. The film was never made, however, because Lawrence's American publisher, Thomas Seltzer, demanded twice that amount, and the offer was withdrawn.[13] Lawrence's death in 1930 may have prompted several new film proposals. Jesse Lasky toyed with the prospect of filming *The Plumed Serpent* partly because Mexican footage was available as a result of Sergei Eisenstein's unreleased work on *Que Viva Mejico*. This project came to an end once Lasky actually read the novel. Harry T. Moore made some headway in bringing *The Boy in the Bush* to Hollywood's attention. He also wrote to Frieda Lawrence about filming *Lady Chatterley's Lover*, only to learn that she had just sold the rights to a movie company in the Soviet Union. This outburst of cinematic interest soon ended, however, with no Lawrence film going into production as a result.[14]

Filming Lawrence has not been a steady effort but instead has occurred in several measurable waves, beginning in the late 1940s. The first film was completed in 1949 in Lawrence's homeland—Anthony Pelissier's *Rocking Horse Winner*. Six years later, *Lady Chatterley's Lover* was released not in Russia but in France, as *L'Amant de Lady Chatterley*. Its director, Marc Allegret, preserved some measure of the novel's original Englishness by casting Leo Genn as Sir Clifford. The final film of this first wave came in 1960—at the exact transition between two very different decades. It was once again a British production, Jack Cardiff's *Sons and Lovers,* yet with an American producer, Jerry Wald, and the anomaly of a young American actor, Dean Stockwell, starring as Paul Morel.

Despite the commercial and critical success of *Sons and Lovers,* large-screen Lawrence filming temporarily stopped after 1960, not to resume for nearly a decade. During this fallow period, however, Lawrence came to the small screen for the first time by way of England's Granada Television Network. Granada's first effort was a 1961 production of *The Widowing of Mrs. Holroyd* followed by a televised anthology of Lawrence short stories released in 1966 and 1967. The Granada series presented sixteen stories, including some of the most prominent ("The Blind Man," "The Prussian Officer," and "Tickets, Please"), along with several lesser-known works ("The Blue Moccasins" and "None of That").

The second wave of theatrical films began in 1968 with the release of Mark Rydell's controversial American adaptation of "The Fox." This was followed by two British productions—Ken Russell's *Women in Love* (1969) and Christopher Miles's *The Virgin and the Gypsy* (1970).

Ten years elapsed before the next feature productions appeared, with the third wave proving to be the most prolific to date. In 1981, Christopher Miles coproduced and directed *Priest of Love,* a British adaptation of Harry T. Moore's biography, and Just Jaeckin cowrote and directed a second *Lady Chatterley's Lover,* a British-French collaboration as well as a somewhat cautious excursion into softcore pornography.[15] These efforts were followed, in 1986, by Tim Burstall's *Kangaroo,* an Australian production. The final film of the decade, once again from England, was Ken Russell's *The Rainbow,* released in 1989. This quartet of feature films was supplemented by a burst of television programs in the 1980s, with small-screen productions far outnumbering theatrical films. The first were Colin Gregg's *The Trespasser* and Stuart Burge's *Sons and Lovers* (in seven episodes), both appearing on BBC Television in 1981. Burge went on to direct a three-episode version of *The Rainbow* for BBC in 1988, just one year before Ken Russell's large-screen *Rainbow* was released. A fourth British production called *Coming Through* dramatized D. H. Lawrence's early years. This was written by Alan Plater, who also provided the scripts for Miles's *Priest of Love* and *Virgin. Coming Through* was directed by Peter Barber-Fleming and first aired on Central Independent Television in 1985. In the United States, a thirty-minute version of "The Horse-Dealer's Daughter" was made for public television by the American Film Institute and shown in 1984 as part of its "Short Story Collection."

As this summary reveals, the 1980s also proved to be the decade of repeat directors, with Stuart Burge, Ken Russell, and Christopher Miles each enjoying another attempt at Lawrence. Russell's second Lawrence film was his sequel to *Women in Love,* completing the Brangwen saga in two installments. Lawrence himself had done the same thing, only with *The Rainbow* coming first both in fictive chronology and in order of composition. Christopher Miles's efforts at putting Lawrence on screen outdid even Russell's in the 1980s, at least potentially. Beyond *Virgin* and *Priest,* Miles picked up where Jesse Lasky had left off in the 1930s and attempted a version of *The Plumed Serpent* that was never completed because of production problems and the opposition of the Mexican government. Russell has since overtaken Miles by way of his 1993 production of *Lady Chatterley* for BBC. This was the third attempt to capture *Lady Chatterley's Lover* on screen (not counting the pornographic spin-offs), making this novel the second most filmed of Lawrence's works. The most filmed, surprisingly enough, is "The Rocking-Horse Winner." After Anthony Pelissier's full-length production, three short versions of this story were released in as many decades. The first, in 1977, was directed by Peter Medak and intended for use as a classroom supplement to the text. The second, in 1982, was directed by Robert Bierman for Paramount Pictures in England. The third was a twenty-three-minute experimental adaptation, directed by Michael Almereyda, which premiered at the New York Film Festival in 1997.

No book dealing with all the Lawrence films has previously been published, but two partial studies have appeared, both deserving attention. The first is a casebook devoted exclusively to one story and its film translation: *From Fiction to Film: D. H. Lawrence's "The Rocking-Horse Winner,"* edited by Gerald R. Barrett and Thomas L. Erskine and published in 1974.[16] The casebook presents the original text along with the shooting script for the film. These primary sources are followed by a collection of essays, some devoted to the story and others to the screen adaptation. The second study, Jane Jaffe Young's 1999 *D. H. Lawrence on Screen,* focuses on three adaptations: *The Rocking Horse Winner, Sons and Lovers,* and *Women in Love.*[17] Jaffe Young pursues a formal analysis of these text-film combinations, arguing that successful adaptation occurs when filmmakers find close cinematic equivalents to the distinctive patterns of Lawrence's prose style within these three works. Her analysis will be taken up again in the concluding chapter of this study during discussion of recent developments, critical as well as creative, relative to D. H. Lawrence on film.

Several books on screen adaptations, published during the watershed 1980s, contain one or more chapters devoted to Lawrence movies. Most prominent are *The English Novel and the Movies,* a 1981 anthology edited by Michael Klein and Gillian Parker, Joy Gould Boyum's *Double Exposure: Fiction into Film* (1985), and Neil Sinyard's *Filming Literature* (1986).

Lawrence on film has also been discussed in dozens, and possibly hundreds, of scholarly, critical, and popular articles and reviews. The journal *Literature/Film Quarterly* debuted in 1973 with an issue devoted entirely to Lawrence. At the other end of the periodical spectrum, even *Playboy* was inspired to offer a "pictorial essay" on *The Fox,* published just before the 1967 film was released. With its photo spread of Anne Heywood appearing as March, nude and in an autoerotic ecstasy, the *Playboy* piece provided its readers with something unique in the way of coming attractions.

In all, then, filming Lawrence seems to emerge as an artistic and cultural phenomenon of some magnitude. Any critic examining this phenomenon today has a complex issue at hand yet, thanks to the development of the videocassette recorder and the digital videodisc player, a smoother road to travel than most of his or her immediate predecessors, the film scholars and students of film adaptation writing two or more decades ago. A work like George Bluestone's groundbreaking *Novels into Film,* published in 1957, makes clear that before the VCR, film analysis was inconvenient well past the point of frustration. In his preface, Bluestone acknowledges that his selection of novel-film combinations for study was predicated on which films could be viewed (and re-viewed) under conditions suitable for close examination.[18] Bluestone thanks a long list of individuals, studios, and museums for making his work possible and states that the analysis of just six films took him to five U.S. cities.

Any child of the 1990s would be amazed at Bluestone's travels and, remaining at home, would be strides ahead of him, at least in Lawrence's much-detested technology. Today, viewers and critics don't need to go to the movies at all; the movies come to them, neatly packaged up in little boxes. Nearly all the D. H. Lawrence films have been released on videotape. As I write, they sit in front of me, arranged on a shelf and outwardly resembling the books they were based upon. I can insert any one of them into my VCR and view it "normally," from start to finish. Using auto search and a digital counter, I can also isolate specific scenes, examine them, rewind, and examine them again, ad infinitum. This activity is different—yet not so different—from reading and then returning to a specific scene within a novel. An evolving technology, in short, has caused film analysis and textual analysis to begin merging as a process. The main thing missing when "reading" a film is the opportunity to scribble in the margins.

A new and more convenient technology, however, can go only so far in helping the critic. It has eased the process of studying film adaptation, although the critical substance of that study remains as challenging as it was thirty-five years ago. Most of the same basic questions raised by Bluestone are still raised today— answered and discussed many times over and from differing perspectives, then asked and answered again. Is a film adaptation of a fictional work, for instance, a reinscription of the text—a second strike on the author's original mark by way of the new medium? If so, fidelity to its literary source would seem to be a critical measure of the film's artistic merit. Or, conversely, is the film that is based on a novel or short story a fresh inscription rather than a reinscription? Is it really like the palimpsest, which layers and ultimately obliterates the undertext with something new? And do these two alternatives completely define the field, or are there additional aesthetic possibilities to be discovered between or beyond the symmetrical either/or?

Applied to the Lawrence films, the familiar "either/or" of cinematic adaptation breaks down or rather merges before the viewer's eyes into "and." In more concrete terms, a film like *The Virgin and the Gypsy* takes serious liberties with the original text, yet seems to remain faithful, in artistic spirit, to Lawrence as well as to itself. Simply departing from the source, however, affords the filmmaker no guarantees of any kind. Mark Rydell's *The Fox,* for example, rewrites Lawrence far more radically than *Virgin* does. Yet, while watching it, the viewer feels somehow doubly cheated, missing both the glow of the familiar and the brightness of the truly new.

These examples begin to provide an aesthetic model not only for the two Lawrence films just mentioned but for all of them. Taken together, these films seem to form a structure with two opposing borders and a mediating point between them. If one ineffective extreme is linear fidelity to the text, then its equally unsuccessful opposite is radical departure. What remains is an intricate equilibrium, whereby both fidelity and imaginative freshness are attained together—whereby the text is displaced and yet preserved in a single artistic coup. While Aristotle and Derrida might seem unlikely critical partners, their combined formulations help to construct this model and to clarify the complex interaction that constitutes fiction into film. The transformation from page to screen is from one perspective an Aristotelian process that repeats the seemingly inescapable lessons of *The Poetics.* Centers are safer than edges; mediations are more successful than attempts to go too far. Derrida and deconstructionists, however, are generally much more concerned with margins than with centers. Despite this, the dynamic balance of the effective Lawrence film seems to invite discussion in terms of their playfully seductive metaphors and concepts. Perhaps the Lawrence filmmakers are like a team of textual surgeons whose cut is also a cure.[19] Or perhaps these filmmakers are like deconstructive writers—not rewriters so much as "double writers"—whose end product offers an improvement upon the palimpsest. The traditional palimpsest covers what it reinscribes, if not to the point of complete disappearance, then at least to the point of illegibility. All writers, as understood by Derrida, destroy in this way as they create—erase prior inscription by the very act that inscribes again. Yet, since erasure can never be total, they always make their new mark so that an impression of the original permanently remains.[20] So, too, with the successful Lawrence filmmaker and with all successful filmmakers who use literature as the basis for their art. By way of this "double gesture," they can find a means of saving the text through the very act that transforms it into something new.[21]

In *Double Exposure*, Joy Gould Boyum introduces another level to the discussion by suggesting that if filmmakers are writers of a complex sort, they are also readers. Boyum concludes her third chapter on theory with the following definition of the film adaptation:

> In assessing an adaptation, we are never really comparing book with film, but an interpretation with an interpretation—the novel that we ourselves have re-created in our imaginations, out of which we have constructed our own individualized "movie," and the novel on which the filmmaker has worked a parallel transformation. For just as we are readers, so implicitly is the filmmaker, offering us, through his work, his perceptions, his vision, his particular insight into his source. An adaptation is always, whatever else it may be, an interpretation.[22]

The filmmaker not only writes over the text, then, but reads over it with a critical eye as well. Boyum suggests that one specific way film adaptation can parallel literary criticism is by making implicit judgments upon the text. She illustrates this with reference to Hemingway's dialogue in *The Sun Also Rises*, "which on the printed page had always seemed so strikingly lifelike. On screen, in startling contrast, it sounded mannered, artificial, lifeless. (Thus can an adaptation sometimes turn a discomforting magnifying glass on a novel, revealing, if not quite its flaws, at least the inaccuracy of our impressions. Hemingway's dialogue may have energy and precision. But lifelike? Clearly, it's anything but.)"[23] Of course, critical judgment cuts at least two ways, as Boyum acknowledges, "not only to magnify faults, but also to reveal virtues" within the original text.[24]

Such insights apply to the Lawrence films and help reveal their implicit function as criticism and evaluation. Boyum's remarks on the Hemingway illusion, as exposed on screen, recalls a parallel situation when Lawrence's "The Fox" is similarly "magnified." The reader of this work might be tempted to regard Henry Grenfel's killing of Banford as acceptable because on paper the deed seems bloodlessly figurative. Through Henry, Lawrence is exploring the image of man as a natural hunter—in relation to the woman he pursues sexually and also in relation to his enemies. When Banford's death is made visible, however, we don't see a subtle metaphor so much as a brutal act. The scheming Keir Dullea murders Sandy Dennis with a large tree. A productive result of this scene, and its nastiness, is to return us to Lawrence questioning the complexity of the moral issue that lies behind the seductive and perhaps ultimately dishonest imagery of the text.

A very different return to the text takes place when the film, as a critical reading, makes evident a stroke of brilliance on the part of the author. The swinging

scene in *Sons and Lovers,* involving Paul Morel and Miriam Leivers, offers a striking instance of this experience. In the film version, this scene is made almost
meaningless. The effect of watching it on screen is, at once, to regret its absence—
to be driven back to the novel by failure in hopes of reconfirming the power of
the original and perhaps discovering what made it work so well in the first place.
The interesting fact behind film experiences like this one, which recall the triumph of the text, is that they occur when the filmmakers stumble—when they
appear guilty of misinterpretation or serious misreading.

In one sense, however, reading is always misreading in film adaptation and
meaningful misreading at that. Whenever a novel or story is filmed years after
the original publication of the text—from a changed historical and cultural perspective—movie makers and audiences alike approach the film as mirror. They
read within it the book of themselves, the inscription of their own age. Such
cultural misreading is clearly at issue within the present study, since every one
of the Lawrence films appeared in an era far different from his own. The creators
and viewers of even the earliest Lawrence film—*The Rocking Horse Winner*—
knew the burden of a depression and a world war that he did not live to see.

Any examination of these films as cultural artifacts will, of necessity, go beyond individual works to question the distinct periods or "waves" of Lawrence
filmmaking and the differences among them. An innocent surface seems to char-
acterize the initial films of the postwar period, for example, and to contrast sharply
with the sexual bravado and overt rule breaking of later productions. This early
innocence softens the erotic, even in the first version of *Lady Chatterley's Lover,*
in favor of the didactic and presents the films as moral critique, particularly regarding European values in the aftermath of World War II. The Lawrence films
seem to make a Blakean leap from this period to the next one—from Innocence
between 1949 and 1960 to Rebellion in the late 1960s and early 1970s. If so,
they skip Blake's second stage of Experience altogether but do make a transition
of sorts in *Sons and Lovers,* which appeared exactly at the border between decades.
While not reflective of Experience in Blake's sense, this bridge film does project
an image torn between youthful innocence and youthful rebellion and, in fact,
remains an ambiguous production partly as a result of this conflict. Although
*Sons and Lovers* was the last black-and-white Lawrence film, it was also the first
to appear in Cinemascope. The film's transitional nature, then, seems reflected
even in its mixture of older and newer technology.

If the Blakean pattern were to fit the Lawrence films exactly, those of the third
wave, developing in the 1980s, would reflect the mystical and enlightened stage
of Higher Innocence. No description of these near-contemporary Lawrence films
could, however, be more misleading. An ambivalent era invites a like reflection
of itself in popular art, and surely gets it in the Lawrence productions released

during the 1980s and 1990s. As suggested earlier, the 1980s are the most pro-lific years for Lawrence adaptations, with four feature films and twice as many television productions. At least part of the reason was historical and biographi-cal, since 1985 marked the centennial of Lawrence's birth. Whereas the first- and second-wave productions focused exclusively on his works, the third-wave film-makers turned much of their attention toward his life, providing us with two official film biographies: Christopher Miles's 1981 *Priest of Love* and Peter Bar-ber-Fleming's 1985 *Coming Through*. A third production, Tim Burstall's *Kanga-roo* (1986), also proves to be biography flimsily packaged as fiction, with Rich-ard Lovat Somers writing the novel (or movie) he is in, even as he appears on screen, and Harriet speaking in a German accent about her cousin, a highly deco-rated pilot during the Great War.

There is more, however, to this developing interest in Lawrence and the Lawrences than merely historical tribute. It is partly a case of interest bordering on wonder at the absolute otherness of Lawrence, as the inhabitants of a com-fortable and self-satisfied decade look back sixty years at their opposite number—an individual who never was comfortable and never even wanted to be, and who possessed the uncanny ability to discomfort others, whether in person or on the printed page. Along with fascination, the Lawrence revival of the 1980s may also imply a certain degree of hostility, or at least a desire to get Lawrence under con-trol, through the very cinematic processes of familiarization and diminishment. He is, after all, both safely dead and safely enclosed within the four borders of the media screen, large and small alike. More specifically, the biographical and semibiographical film productions of the 1980s present a conflicted vision of Lawrence, showing him as volatile and dangerous, yet as not so different from the rest of us today—even as partly domesticated or tamed.

Along with all of this, these Lawrence films of the 1980s also appropriate him, as both artist and man, for their own purposes. Beneath the decade's yuppified surface of upward mobility, materialism, and self-congratulation, it was an age of difficult self-assessment over tangled human issues that are still far from re-solved or even sorted out. One such issue involves women and work, how they fare in "The Man's World," as Lawrence called it eighty years ago and as it prob-ably remains today. A second issue, again as Lawrentian as it is postmodern, in-volves the men themselves in "their" world, still burdened by outworn codes of masculinity and in dire need of sensible and sensitive alternatives. It is no won-der, then, that in the 1980s and 1990s more Lawrence films came before the public, in theaters and on television, than during all the previous decades com-bined. Lawrence's far-sighted fiction, written well over a half century ago, struggled with all of the same questions that now worry an entire generation. The answers Lawrence provided in that fiction were emphatically different from ours, yet they have made for valuable and productive misreading. Together, contemporary filmmakers and their audiences have searched Lawrence while really looking for themselves. They have transformed his image in order to confront their own.

The D. H. Lawrence film then, like every film adaptation, accomplishes many paradoxical results in a single artistic act. As it erases, it also preserves; as it writes, it also reads and misreads. My hope for the present study is to approach the Lawrence feature films with this diversity of achievement in mind and to account for as many sides of it as possible. An organization based on film chronology seems best suited to my purpose. On one hand, it allows for examination of each separate film, in turn, as "double inscription" on the base text and as critical interpretation of that text. On the other hand, chronology allows for a clear vision of the films, in sequence, as a single yet ever-changing artifact, as a mirror reflecting our own cultural image in flux.

Although chronology provides the spine of this book, there are points where departure from the time line seems called for by common sense. For example, I'll look at *Women in Love* and *The Rainbow* in sequence even though two decades separate their release. Both films are by Ken Russell, and both novels spring from a single vision within Lawrence's own imagination. I'll also examine all three chronologically distant Lady Chatterley films in a single chapter, including the 1993 television production, since it completes Ken Russell's Lawrentian film trilogy. Finally, I'll disturb chronology once more by saving *Priest of Love* (1981) for last. This will focus my conclusions on a film different from the rest, by virtue of its "factual" or biographical approach, yet remarkably typical of the entire effort, now fifty years old, to capture Lawrence on screen.

# 2
# *The Rocking Horse Winner:*
# Expansions and Interpolations

$T$*he Rocking Horse Winner,* released in 1949, represents the moviegoer's introduction to Lawrence. Director Anthony Pelissier wrote the screenplay and therefore did most of the work of transforming Lawrence's words into visual drama. John Mills also did double duty as producer and as the actor portraying Bassett, a character far more prominent on screen than in the original story. The major actors (including Mills himself) all had had recent experience in films adapted from literature. Valerie Hobson—who portrayed Hester Grahame, Paul's mother—had worked with Mills just a few years earlier in David Lean's adaptation of *Great Expectations* (1946). The child actor who played Paul, John Howard Davies, had the title role in Lean's 1948 adaptation of *Oliver Twist.*[1]

Some fifty years after its release, *The Rocking Horse Winner* remains available on videotape, even though several more recent Lawrence films have been withdrawn from circulation.[2] Beyond this, Pelissier's *Rocking Horse* is unique among all the Lawrence feature films in that its shooting script has been published. The script remains accessible thanks to the Dickenson Literature and Film Series of casebooks, which includes a volume on the process of bringing Lawrence's story to the screen. A bit of irony about the 1949 *Rocking Horse* production involves the mark of the censors upon it—censors much like those who chased Lawrence himself across an entire lifetime. They required that the following biblical passage (Luke 17:1–2) appear superimposed across the film's final shot:

> It is impossible but that offences will come:
> but woe unto him, through whom they come!
> It were better for him that a millstone were

hanged about his neck, and he cast into the sea,
than that he should offend one of these little ones.[3]

This biblical postscript does not, however, appear on the print of the film presently in release on videocassette.

The passage seems superfluous on the original print as well, given the already heavy moralizing evident throughout the film. At least on its surface, Pelissier's *Rocking Horse* seems to reduce Lawrence's subtle narrative to a naive cautionary tale about materialism. This has been most apparent to the film's critics in Pelissier's final scene, which has no counterpart in the text and which follows Uncle Oscar's (and Lawrence's) closing words: "My God, Hester, you're eighty-odd thousand to the good, and a poor devil of a son to the bad. But, poor devil, poor devil, he's best gone out of life where he rides his rocking-horse to find a winner."[4] The film preserves Oscar's speech word for word, then continues beyond it to a scene in which Bassett, following Hester's orders, burns the rocking horse. As this takes place, Hester joins him "to see the end of it," and Bassett asks her what to do with Paul's winnings. She tells him to burn the money as well, suggesting melodramatically that she has at last rejected materialism and greed as a result of her son's death. Bassett refuses, telling Hester that as a poor man he knows the value of money too well. Instead, he'll turn Paul's fortune over to Hester's lawyer, who perhaps can put it to good use and make up for some of the evil it has caused. The film closes with Bassett's departure and with a shot of the burning horse, which finally disappears in the smoke of its own destruction.

Many critics, skeptical about Hester's conversion, have focused on this scene as typical of the major flaw in Pelissier's film. It transforms the story, they suggest, into a Ben Franklinesque moral lesson that surely would have disappointed Lawrence. Neil Sinyard refers to the scene in *Filming Literature* as "a cosy ending" that "dilute[s] the irony and harshness" of the original story.[5] In a more extensive treatment of the final scene and the film as a whole, Joan Mellen comments on the heavy presence of melodrama and the damage that results when the director "succumb[s] . . . to an ill-advised temptation to include moral commentary in the dialogue."[6]

Despite the film's creaky ending and generally brittle surface, it is surprising to discover how much of the original Lawrence survives unharmed. Besides Uncle Oscar's closing words, several dialogues from the story appear more or less verbatim in the film—Paul's conversation with his mother, for example, about why the family doesn't keep a car and also their critical exchange about luck. The first conversation is carried over exactly from story to film, while the second omits only Paul's confusion over the words *lucre* and *luck* and his assumption that they mean the same thing.

Beyond words, the film uses visual means to preserve some of the less tangible material within the story. An example of this would be Lawrence's suggestion that human will and human knowledge become especially dangerous when combined. Pelissier's film makes this visible in two scenes where Paul compulsively insists that he must "know for the Derby!" He first speaks these words to himself while walking rigidly toward Bassett and Oscar, his betting partners, and later just before his final ride. In the first scene Paul appears to be performing a mechanical dance—almost "rocking" without the horse. In the second scene, the toy horse, with its fixed gaze mirroring Paul's, seems a fitting image for a boy who by now has lost his childhood to the lifeless process of willing and knowing.

Two additional sequences in the film convey Lawrence's rejection of knowledge by presenting the mechanical instruments of close examination: a telescope and a pair of binoculars. In the first scene, as Hester and her son stroll through an expensive antique shop, the boy picks up two objects that foretell his bleak future: the statuette of a horse (again inanimate) and a long telescope through which he attempts to see. In the second scene, when Paul attends his first and last horse race, the film audience sees most of the action on the track from within the confining frames of Uncle Oscar's binoculars. Earlier in this sequence Paul himself looks through these binoculars, only backwards—a mistake suggestive of Lawrence's association, in this story and in most of his writings, between intense scrutiny and distortion.

Equally well translated into film images is the haunted and whispering house from Lawrence's story. We learn early on in the text of "The Rocking-Horse Winner" that

> the house came to be haunted by the unspoken phrase: *There must be more money! There must be more money!* . . .
> It came whispering from the springs of the still-swaying rocking-horse, and even the horse, bending his wooden, champing head, heard it. (791)

Although Pelissier alters a few details of this passage, its essential spirit and effect remain graphically preserved. The words *"There must be more money!"* don't go "unspoken" but originate with Hester during one of the family's frequent quarrels. Once uttered, her words are transformed into music that accompanies the camera's ascent up the staircase of the Grahame household. The camera's focus is not on the stairs but on the railings, which offer the viewer a suggestion of imprisonment. Somewhere on the journey upward, perhaps halfway between the living room and the nursery, the music transforms itself back into Lawrence's words, now echoed by the house. The words reach the nursery, and Paul hears them for the first time not from the swaying springs of the rocking horse but directly from the horse's mouth. Also at variance with the original, the other children in the film, Paul's two sisters, seem not to have heard the choral complaint of the house. As Paul listens to it, they go on playing undisturbed.

Beyond verbal and visual preservations, even some of Lawrence's unheard and unseen material finds effective expression in the film. A major example of this is the sexual, and specifically Oedipal, issue within "The Rocking-Horse Winner," first discussed by W. D. Snodgrass in a 1958 article for the *Hudson Review.*[7] At least one critic of the film disputes any such sexual reading, however, claiming instead that Pelissier deliberately "remove[s] the suggestions of masturbation and oedipal love" in order to focus more directly on the theme of materialism.[8] This judgment remains questionable, however, in that sexual and materialistic issues seem conflated in the film, exactly as they do in Lawrence's story. Paul, in both, cares little (and knows little) about money, acting only out of love for his indifferent mother and from a desire to capture her attention by making her happy. Responding to this element in the film, S. E. Gontarski reaches the following conclusion:

> "Rocking-Horse Winner" is finally a strongly masturbatory and Oedipal film. . . . The visual images, which exclusively carry the film's sexual level, are memorable: a young boy, Paul, on his toy horse—a dual symbol of childhood innocence and emerging sexuality—massages his genitals against the horse in a revery until he falls satisfied to the floor. The film's Oedipal level focuses on Paul's replacement of his ineffectual father as the family's economic support. In short, Paul satisfies his mother's need better than his father can.[9]

A conflation of textual ideas or themes such as sexuality and materialism can be rendered on film through montage. A revealing sequence of this sort occurs just after Paul's first major win and birthday present to his mother of five thousand pounds. The scene shows Valerie Hobson as Hester in a series of fashion poses, each time wearing a different lavish outfit—in effect squandering the love tribute Paul has just paid her. Superimposed upon this sequence is Paul on his horse, furiously rocking in an effort to generate more winners. What the viewer sees is Paul rocking across or really through Hester's body—the boy seeming to merge with his mother as he rides in pursuit of her love and attention.

The original Lawrence, then, is very much alive and present in this film. Nevertheless, what may remain most tempting in Pelissier's *Rocking Horse* is not the preservation of Lawrence so much as the intrusion of seemingly alien material. Those points in the film which rewrite or distort the text stand out as perhaps its most fascinating assets, even including Pelissier's trite and brittle ending. A plausible speculation is that the people who made *Rocking Horse* had no choice but to expand Lawrence's text and to fill in the blanks with invented interpolations. How else could a ninety-one-minute feature film be crafted from a story that can be read in fifteen minutes or less? One of Pelissier's most effective and relatively straightforward techniques of rewriting is simple expansion. Time and again, the film will seize on a single sentence from the text and deliberately, often ingeniously, blow it out of proportion.

Hester, for example, tells Paul at one point in the story that her "family has been a gambling family, and you won't know till you grow up how much damage it has done" (801). In Pelissier's film, Hester's vague statement becomes an invitation to transform her husband, Richard—all but invisible in the text—into a habitual and inept cardplayer who loses large sums of money he doesn't really have. "You know people send mother writs, don't you, uncle?" (798) This single line of Paul's engenders not one but two scenes in the film, both involving Hester in confrontations with unpleasant men who don't merely send her writs but show up in person at her doorstep demanding to be paid. "And, in spite of himself, Oscar Cresswell spoke to Bassett, and himself put a thousand on Malabar: at fourteen to one" (803). By this point in the story, Paul is dying, so Oscar is under no illusions about how much it costs to win. "In spite of himself," his complicity in Paul's destruction, and his guilt, the urge to profit becomes too tempting for this reasonably likable man, so he bets. In the film, Lawrence's terse words lead to a scene that becomes one of Pelissier's minor triumphs. Oscar doesn't speak to Bassett but contacts his bookmaker directly over the telephone—another instrument of mechanical process. The scene takes place in the Grahame living room, shot from a low camera angle with the telephone always in the foreground between the viewer and Oscar Cresswell. He paces the room, looks at the phone, hesitates, and finally makes the call. As Oscar speaks, the camera does not allow us to see his face, perhaps suggesting his sense of shame. Instead, it focuses on his comfortable midsection, his expensive clothes, and his nervous hands, constantly in motion.

The whispering house "frightened Paul terribly. He studied away at his Latin and Greek with his tutor. But his intense hours were spent with Bassett" (800). In the original story, any intensity Lawrence has in mind relates to the race after winners—to Paul and Bassett's fixation on the track and the wager. In the film, this single sentence offers an excuse to transform material intensity into emotional intensity and to make the relationship between the boy and the servant something far deeper than it is in the text. Lawrence's Bassett is primarily a catalyst, an instrumental character who involves first Uncle Oscar and then Paul in the world of horse racing. Beyond this, the only complication between Bassett and Paul, Lawrence suggests, is the servant's intuition that some mystery surrounds the boy's "luck"—some mystery important enough to be approached with reverence. "'It's Master Paul, sir,' said Bassett in a secret, religious voice. 'It's as if he had it from heaven'" (797).

In Pelissier's film, Bassett's awe at Paul's clairvoyance is preserved but diminished by something far stronger—his love for the child and concern for his welfare. It is tempting to suggest that when Bassett joins the Grahame household he becomes a father to Paul, replacing the ineffectual and irresponsible Richard. But this is not the case. It is the film's Uncle Oscar who plays the role of Paul's surrogate father, introducing him to the wider world and initiating him into its complexities. In every scene where Paul ventures beyond his home, with the one exception of the shopping trip for antiques, Uncle Oscar accompanies him as guardian and mentor. By contrast, and completing a uniquely male version of the nuclear family, Pelissier's Bassett is more of a mother to Paul than a father or a friend—certainly more of a mother than Hester has ever been. Where Oscar's scenes with Paul occur in the outer world, Bassett's scenes with him are invariably domestic, taking place either within or just outside the Grahame house. Also, where Oscar's involvement with the boy is intellectual and educational, Bassett's relationship with Paul is fundamentally emotional, based on the strong intimacy that has sprung up between the servant and the child. The film includes several scenes in which Bassett, and no one else, senses Paul's unhappiness, perhaps because of something as subtle as a look on the boy's face. Like a mother, Bassett immediately becomes concerned and tries to comfort Paul, although he remains baffled at the cause of the boy's agony. Such incidents seem to oppose the many film scenes that show Hester as ignorant of Paul's feelings and ultimately indifferent to them. In one, Hester cruelly rejects Paul's offer of money, thinking he's playing a game, and thereby seriously hurts him, all the while unaware of what she has done. Perhaps the film's contrast between Bassett and Hester reaches its climax at Paul's deathbed, where they appear together and juxtaposed. Although his real mother tries, it is the male servant whose voice awakens the child just before the end.

The issue of Bassett and Hester as maternal counterparts is not only confirmed at a more covert level of the film but revealed to be an ongoing and important preoccupation. Bassett and Hester are paralleled by a series of identical images and objects associated with both of them. Some of these objects—such as a suitcase, for example, or a dwelling—clearly imply feminine associations, ultimately maternal and womblike. Hester has a suitcase, and so does Bassett. We see Hester's when she desperately fills it with clothing she hopes to sell to pay off an overdue bill. Although the clothes and the case originally cost hundreds of pounds, a disreputable tailor offers Hester only forty pounds for everything—just enough to pay the bill and get rid of the bailiff who brought it. The tailor, Mr. Tsaldouris, aptly refers to Hester's suitcase as a "fancy case." It is like the woman and mother who owns it—an elegant shell that finally contains nothing very valuable inside. Bassett's suitcase exactly reverses Pelissier's image of Hester. Outside it isn't fancy at all, just a "cheap" model as described in the shooting script.[10] Inside, it contains treasure—Paul's winnings, which here represent significant material value and human value as well. The boy trusts the servant completely, and so gives over every penny of the winnings to his care.

As with suitcases, so too with dwellings. Hester has one home, and Bassett has another of an opposite sort. Even though he is the Grahames' full-time servant, he doesn't sleep in their house. Rather, he chooses to live in an outbuilding that, aptly enough, once served as a stable. It is here that Paul and Bassett meet at the very start of the film, the boy first watching the servant's arrival out of curiosity, then quickly becoming his friend. As they talk, Hester appears and asks Bassett if he wouldn't rather give up these modest quarters and move in with the family. He tells her he is content, and the conversation turns, playfully, to Paul's preference of homes. Would he rather remain in his mother's house, with its "fancy" nursery, or move out to Bassett's converted stable? When Hester—along with the film audience—realizes the answer Paul is about to give, she silences him, then quickly removes him from Bassett's dwelling place and back into her own.

Beyond the enclosing imagery of cases and houses, even the film's own enclosures seem to imply a parallel between Bassett and Paul's mother, especially so if the original text is recalled. Lawrence begins and ends his story with Hester, moving from "There was a woman" (790) to Uncle Oscar's closing words or, more exactly, back to the same woman, now hearing "her brother's voice saying to her: 'My God, Hester, you're eighty-odd thousand to the good, and a poor devil of a son to the bad'" (804). In contrast, yet obliquely repeating Lawrence, Pelissier starts and stops his film with Bassett, the covert maternal figure in Paul's life. The film's initial sequence, the "dwelling scene," is really a record of Bassett's arrival at the Grahame household—something Lawrence casually mentions (794) but does not depict in the text. Bassett's departure never occurs in Lawrence's story at all, yet it closes the film and provides some complication to the otherwise clichéd horse-burning scene. In the undertext of this scene, Bassett and Hester once again appear juxtaposed, confirming their maternal parallel by agreeing that they will carry the memory of Paul's tragedy for life. Entirely absent from the scene, however, is any explanation of why Bassett is now leaving the Grahames' employ. A plausible answer is that he has become rich from his winnings and no longer needs to work as a servant. A more compelling answer, and one which accords with the emotional dynamics of the film, is that Bassett leaves because

Paul is dead. With the boy gone, his deepest service to the Grahame family is no longer possible. He departs, suitcase in hand, to end the film.

A question raised by Bassett's maternal presence is whether any of the film's Oedipal intensity spills over and redirects itself from Hester to her masculine counterpart. Is there a homoerotic component to the relationship between the manservant and the child? My own answer to this question tends to be a yes, but one that is both qualified and cautious. For the most part, Bassett and Paul seem loving toward one another but without any suggestion of sexuality. The man's love for the boy is essentially nurturing and protective—again, maternal. The child's love for the man appears equally innocent and filial—a combination of trust, admiration, and emotional dependency. Only once does a border of some sort seem to be crossed into love of a more ambiguous coloration. During an early scene, absent from the text, Bassett presides over Paul's first ride on the rocking horse and shows him how it is properly done. He assists the child in mounting the horse, urges him to ride faster, and even joins in an imaginary race, doubling Paul's rocking motion with his own. If critics like Snodgrass and Gontarski are right about the sexuality of rocking in the text and on screen, then surely this scene requires explanation even though nothing like it occurs anywhere else in the film. Bassett and Paul's ride together, being unique, can't be equated with overt, ongoing homoerotic love between man and boy. It can, however, be understood as an image of sexual awakening or, perhaps more delicately, as Pelissier's acknowledgment that in any relationship this warm and loving Eros has got to intervene.

*The Rocking Horse Winner,* then, seems to establish a complex film structure upon a remarkably simple textual foundation: "But his intense hours were spent with Bassett" (800). If this is so, to distort Lawrence through cinematic expansion is ultimately to recover him unharmed. A loving all-male relationship superimposed upon "The Rocking-Horse Winner" surely blots Lawrence's writing in this particular story where no such thing exists. As the film erases one text, however, it reinscribes several others and in fact articulates a preoccupation central to Lawrence's writing as a whole. It is not difficult to recall several male couples in Lawrence whose relationships are like that of Bassett and Paul in the film—warm, intense, erotic, yet just short of overtly sexual. Gerald and Birkin, in *Women in Love,* are one such pair, as are Mellors and his dead commanding officer in *Lady Chatterley's Lover.* Even Lawrence's other Paul—Paul Morel in *Sons and Lovers*— and Baxter Dawes briefly seem to fit this pattern. Of the six characters mentioned, only Paul Morel and Baxter are a youth and an older man. And Baxter, in contrast to Pelissier's Bassett, becomes not a mother figure to his Paul but a substitute father in *Sons and Lovers.* The mothering male, however, is an original Lawrence character, too, and can be found vividly depicted in Rawdon Lilly from the novel *Aaron's Rod.* Lilly establishes an intimate connection with his friend

Aaron Sisson by becoming a mother to him in crisis, even though Aaron is a grown man. In a chapter Lawrence calls "Low-Water Mark," Aaron arrives at Lilly's doorstep sick in body and spirit but intuitively seeking help from the "right" person. "I'm going to rub you with oil," Lilly suddenly tells Aaron. "I'm going to rub you as mothers do their babies whose bowels don't work."[11] He does this, and the intimate touch between men—not sexual but erotically maternal—effects a miracle. As Lilly watches, his "child" and patient comes back from the dead:

> He rubbed every speck of the man's lower body—the abdomen, the buttocks, the thighs and knees, down to the feet, rubbed it all warm and glowing with camphorated oil, every bit of it, chafing the toes swiftly, till he was almost exhausted. Then Aaron was covered up again, and Lilly sat down in fatigue to look at his patient.
>
> He saw a change. The spark had come back into the sick eyes, and the faint trace of a smile, faintly luminous, into the face. Aaron was regaining himself. But Lilly said nothing. He watched his patient fall into a proper sleep.[12]

In Pelissier's film, Bassett's mothering is also a healing force, yet ultimately insufficient to bring about a similar miracle. It fails, finally, to displace Hester's destructive presence as the major influence in Paul's life, and the boy perishes as a result.

In all, then, the image of male mother and child stands as a central example, in Pelissier's *Rocking Horse,* of expansion as film strategy. By magnifying a character and a relationship in one story to the point of distortion, the film seems to achieve a complex intertextuality with much that is essential in the general body of Lawrence's writing. Beyond expansion, a second film strategy at work can be identified by the term *interpolation.* This occurs when the film commits violence upon the text, rather than merely expanding it, by introducing material for which there is no basis whatsoever in Lawrence's story.

A relatively simple example of interpolation involves what Pelissier does with the imagery of climbing and descending stairs. Such actions hardly occur in Lawrence's original text and serve no meaningful function whatsoever, yet they seem prominent and significant in the film, especially during scenes involving Hester. Given the sexual and Oedipal undercurrents of *Rocking Horse,* one might be tempted to interpret the film's stairways as Freudian, along with the imagery of cases and houses. The cinematic stairs, however, seem not to be sexually suggestive, as at least one other critic, Joan Mellen, has noted, but instead monetary and social.[13] When Hester climbs a staircase, she dances out her aspirations toward the wealth and prestige of British upper-class life. The audience sees this at several points in the film as Hester and Richard discuss their financial plans and needs while climbing the stairs to their bedroom. Also, late in the film Hester and Richard are shown together mounting a grand staircase at the charity ball she has organized—an event she hopes will mark her full acceptance into polite society.

When Hester goes down a staircase, the action implies a setback, usually an embarrassment of some kind over money. Thus on one occasion Hester descends the stairs of her home to encounter a derby-hatted man waiting to serve a writ. This comedown is interesting because it leads, almost immediately, to another effort on Hester's part to climb back up. She accepts the writ and, to console herself, takes Paul along on an impulsive and ultimately costly shopping trip. Mother and son are shown arriving at a posh antique store, where Hester is clearly a familiar customer and at once ascending a staircase, presumably to view the more expensive pieces. At this upper level Paul toys with the telescope and the horse figurine while his mother buys a miniature painting she can't afford, thereby perpetuating the cycle of purchase and debt. Specifically, because the new painting can't be paid for, it causes the arrival of another, even nastier, stranger in the Grahame home, a bailiff who insists he will remain there for as long as it takes Hester to raise forty pounds. This second financial crisis again brings Hester to a set of stairs—leading not upward to the consolations of shopping but downward to a squalid basement and to Hester's deepest humiliation in the film.

This episode, in which Hester lowers herself by selling off some clothing and her "fancy case," is pure interpolation on Pelissier's part. In Lawrence there is no such scene at all, no questionable shop into which Hester descends and no Mr. Tsaldouris—tailor, foreigner, and dealer in used goods. Although occupying less than five minutes of screen time, Pelissier's basement interpolation merits study as possibly the most controversial point in the film. It takes place while Paul attends his first horse race, so the camera alternates between the two very different experiences of mother and son—both, however, intended to generate more cash. As Hester enters Mr. Tsaldouris's already darkened shop, he lowers the window shade, suggesting that he understands her visit to be somehow covert or at the very least embarrassing. Tsaldouris has a strong accent of indeterminate European origin and is peculiarly attired. He also possesses a tiny, incongruous dog, wrapped in a blanket and completely passive except for the piglike grunts it makes. The animal sounds continue as surreal chorus throughout the scene. As Hester and the tailor haggle over her goods, it becomes clear that he somehow knows everything about her—that she has obtained his name for just such an emergency, that she needs a certain amount of money immediately and in cash. Tsaldouris makes Hester an outrageously low offer for her fancy stuff. They argue back and forth, but finally the tailor imposes his will upon her by forcing Hester to relinquish everything for just enough cash to pay the debt. Hester's only small triumph, within defeat and humiliation, is her refusal to count the money Tsaldouris hands her. She leaves the shop to return to her waiting taxi, and the odd little scene ends.

Beyond squalor taken to the point of surrealism, perhaps the most unsettling element in Pelissier's shop episode is its antiforeign cast and, ultimately, its anti-Semitism. The sequence implies that Hester's obsession with money and things, revealed raw and undisguised in Tsaldouris, belongs not to British culture but instead to the ghettos of middle Europe. The contention that this basement scene is anti-Semitic may be questioned, since the film never identifies Tsaldouris as a Jew. His name, in fact, isn't recognizably Jewish at all but more likely Greek or Turkish. If not the name, however, Tsaldouris's persona comes dangerously close to the stereotypical image of "the Jew" as depicted in Nazi propaganda. Tsaldouris's multiple professions, for example—tailor, dealer, and provider of cash to the desperate—all play upon common fascist clichés. His physical appearance and particularly the fact that he wears his hat indoors suggest Jewishness as well. A final bit of evidence for Tsaldouris as Jew, and as anti-Semitic portrayal, comes from a line of dialogue cut from the finished film but present in the shooting script. When Tsaldouris offers Hester thirty pounds for everything, she responds, "You're trying to cheat me!" The same line in the shooting script reads, "You're trying to do me down."[14] This change from script to screen suggests that "do me down"—echoing the familiar "Jew me down"—was too overt a revelation of the filmmakers' intent and had to be omitted or "repressed."

If Mr. Tsaldouris is an anti-Semitic caricature, then Pelissier's tailor shop scene is a descent into darkness not just for Hester but for the entire film. Pelissier's dark passage leads directly back to Lawrence and to a low point in his work as well. Like the film expansion, this interpolation, which seems at first to violate Lawrence, proves to mimic him instead and to appear before us like the shade of his own anti-Semitism. There may not be a greedy shopkeeper in the Lawrence canon, hatted and bespectacled like Tsaldouris, but there are equally derogatory and unpleasant portrayals of Jews scattered throughout his work. There is Loerke in *Women in Love,* a subterranean and surrealistic figure like Tsaldouris himself but of a far more complicated and dangerous sort. There is the potentially smothering Ben Cooley in *Kangaroo.* There is Mrs. Simon Fawcett in *The Virgin and the Gipsy,* a better sort than the first two characters, but to Lawrence a "little Jewess," as he repeatedly describes her.[15] And, finally, there is "Mr. Nosey Hebrew" in *Studies in Classic American Literature,* not a flesh-and-blood character but an abstraction and an appalling idea—exactly what Mr. Tsaldouris represents in the film.[16]

The anti-Semitic image of Tsaldouris may indict Lawrence, but ultimately its suggestions go beyond just one writer and his blind side. The portrayal also reveals a truth about the period in which the film was made, about the filmmakers themselves, and about the audience they envisioned. This becomes especially clear if the Tsaldouris episode is understood in relation to two additional antiforeign, if not anti-Semitic, interpolations present in Pelissier's shooting script but likewise ultimately "repressed" or cut from the finished film. In both cases, the excised scenes have some slight basis in Lawrence's text. In both, the targets of prejudice are the French—Great Britain's allies in a war scarcely over when Pelissier began work on his script. The initial anti-French scenario takes place precisely as the Tsaldouris scene is unfolding—at the track, where Paul watches his first race. Its textual origin is Lawrence's description of a Frenchman also attending the race. "A Frenchman just in front had put his money on Lancelot. Wild with excitement, he flayed his arms up and down, yelling, *'Lancelot! Lancelot!'* in his French accent" (796). In what was to have been the film expansion of these relatively innocuous lines, Pelissier describes the same figure as "an excitable Frenchman, a patriot having difficulty in understanding how apparently sane people can be so mad as to run any sort of animal against Lancelot. In an extremely serious voice, and in very halting English, he tells Paul that Lancelot is the only horse in the race."[17] Later, when it becomes clear that Lancelot has lost, Pelissier's caricature Frenchman is "sunk in Gallic gloom."[18] Still later, when Paul returns home from the race, he excitedly reports to Hester and Bassett everything he has seen, including "a froggy Frenchman next to me, and he shouted and screamed and said we were all a lot of 'imbeciles' to back anything but Lancelot."[19]

A second instance of anti-French bias in the script (also cut from the film) involves Pelissier's planned expansion of the following lines from Lawrence's text:

> [Paul's] . . . mother went into town nearly every day. She had discovered that she had an odd knack of sketching furs and dress materials, so she worked secretly in the studio of a friend who was the chief 'artist' for the leading drapers. She drew the figures of ladies in furs and ladies in silk and sequins for the newspaper advertisements. The young woman artist earned several thousand pounds a year, but Paul's mother only made several hundreds, and she was again dissatisfied. She so wanted to be first in something, and she did not succeed, even in making sketches for drapery advertisements. (799)

In the script, this aside of Lawrence's is transformed into a major scene involving Hester's attempt at a career, her failure, and—repeating the tailor-shop episode—her ultimate humiliation at the hands of a foreigner. Hester has taken work as a fashion artist at "Sergine et Alix," a French dressmaking establishment. When she exceeds her humble role by attempting to give advice on design, she is publicly and nastily rebuked by the owner, Madame Alix, another foreigner in caricature. The film script initially describes Madame Alix as "fat, French and unpleasantly tough."[20] Where Pelissier's sporting Frenchman was simply a fool, his pasteboard couturiere is an egomaniac and an ogre who ends her verbal assault on Hester by shouting, "*Alix! Alix!* That is the only person who matters here. Me. Madame Alix. You? Once you come into this house you are nothing. You have no identity, no personality: you have no authority, no standing, nothing. But me, I am everything—and don't forget it."[21]

That a British film made just after World War II would reflect anti-Jewish and anti-French sentiments is not really too difficult to understand. In the aftermath of the ordeal, a residue of bitterness and resentment had to remain— surely toward former enemies but perhaps also toward the Continent as a whole, including former allies and friends. Put somewhat less negatively, the film's anti-Semitic and antiforeign implications may have provided its postwar audience with a kind of ritual for casting the war and its memory away for good. Part of this ritual might well involve an exorcism of European Jews, Frenchmen, and foreigners in general—their symbolic dismissal in favor of characters and values perceived by audience and filmmaker alike as essentially British. If such a nationalistic rite of self-affirmation is taking place within *Rocking Horse,* then the figure of Bassett, once again, remains at the very center of the issue. This minor Lawrence character, as expanded by Pelissier's script and John Mills's portrayal, emerges here as the film's protagonist twice over. As masculine mother to Paul, he was hero, first, of the familial and psychological drama in *Rocking Horse.* As British common man—decent and even noble by nature—he is hero, again, of the social and political drama also playing itself out within the film. Julian Smith has singled out the on-screen Bassett as idealized Englishman and worker and has commented on him as follows:

> The expansion of Bassett's character beyond the mere outline sketched in the source . . . did more than provide a suitable vehicle for John Mills, who was both the producer and the chief box office attraction. (In those days Mills was known for playing working-class characters of a sensitive bent—honest, candid, simple-hearted. . . .) No, the expansion of Bassett's role and the casting of Mills reflect the fact that a large portion of England's population (and the film-going public) in those days of Clement Attlee's Labour government was avowedly proletarian.[22]

Smith suggests that this vision of Bassett as noble British working man verges the film on "classic Marxist fable." He also suggests that "John Mills's portrayal of humble Bassett resembles . . . Joe Gargery in David Lean's adaptation of *Great*

*Expectations,*" as well as several other on-screen Dickens characters, some of whom had recently been played by Mills himself. Based on these Marxist and Dickensian parallels, Smith's overall assessment of *Rocking Horse* and its working-class hero is that they are not "Lawrentian" at all in concept and in spirit.[23]

With regard to Bassett, this conclusion deserves some attention because it may not be entirely correct. As a postwar ideal for the British public, a pacified and proletarian John Bull, Bassett certainly emerges as anti-Lawrentian. As an individual human being, and not a patriotic image, he also seems to lack the essential strengths of the positive Lawrence man. Most basically, except for the oblique intimacy with Paul, Bassett is asexual—as is, in fact, every other adult character in the film. Also, unlike Lawrence's dynamic male figures, he is altogether too servile—too deferential to his employers and everyone else above his social station. Because of this, Oliver Mellors, had he met Pelissier's Bassett, might well have regarded him as one of the tame ones: "You say a man's got no brain, when he's a fool; and no heart, when he's mean; and no stomach, when he's a funker. And when he's got none of that spunky wild bit of a man in him, you say he's got no balls. When he's sort of tame."[24]

Although the description partly fits, a more accurate truth is that Bassett also somewhat resembles the very man who makes this speech. Like Mellors and the gypsy Joe Boswell, Pelissier's Bassett has been hurt by a great industrial war but has survived it. Bassett's crippled leg comes directly from the text, yet the film gives it an additional and very Lawrentian twist. Like Mellors and Joe Boswell, the on-screen Bassett used to have something to do with horses. He had planned to become a jockey, but World War II has made this impossible. So instead he now serves the social classes above his own just as Mellors and Boswell did twenty fictional years earlier. Bassett works in several capacities within the Grahame household. Yet his most interesting job, from the standpoint of Lawrentian intertextuality, comes to him late in the film when, thanks to Paul, Hester and Richard have gained enough financial ground to own a car. Once this occurs, Bassett is transformed into their chauffeur, complete with uniform and cap. His life's journey, then, begins to resemble Lawrence's prophetic tracing of the century's progress in general—from organic wholeness to a wound, a partial castration inflicted by the machinery of modern war, and from there (if he survives) to some form of mechanical servitude.

It is true that Mellors and Joe Boswell fight body and spirit against this dehumanizing process and that Bassett accepts it. To this degree, if his situation is recognizably Lawrentian, his personal response to it is not. It is docile or "tame" rather than defiant and, given the nature and function of popular film, more or less socially acceptable or normal. To his ultimate credit, however, at least Bassett ends his servitude at the close of the film and departs entirely alone. Like Mellors, he quits his employers. Like Joe Boswell he fades out of the picture at the very end and disappears—perhaps to begin an equally tame middle-class life on his new winnings, but perhaps to find some measure of Lawrentian spunk and freedom instead.

# 3

# Sons and Lovers: Flight from the [S]mothering Text

The 1960 screen version of *Sons and Lovers* appeared over a decade after *The Rocking Horse Winner*, yet resembles its predecessor in a number of ways. Like Anthony Pelissier's effort, it is another relatively short, careful British production filmed in black and white. Yet the challenges of adaptation facing its director, Jack Cardiff, were absolutely the reverse of those Pelissier encountered. Pelissier needed to spin out and finesse a fifteen-page short story into a feature-length film. Cardiff, on the other hand, confronted a heavyweight novel, well over four hundred pages long, with the prospect of squeezing it into a movie about the same length as Pelissier's. This, in fact, is exactly what he did. The finished print of *Sons and Lovers*, including a scene excised by the censors, amounts to ninety-nine minutes of film—a paltry eight-minute increase in running time over *Rocking Horse*.[1]

The skills that Cardiff brought to this project—and to the challenge of effective adaptation—were primarily camera-related. *Sons and Lovers* was only his third directorial assignment, but he had a series of major successes behind him as director of photography, with credits including *The Red Shoes*, *The African Queen*, and *War and Peace*. Cardiff's official director of photography for *Sons* was Freddie Francis, an equally prominent and experienced cinematographer. Despite this, Cardiff was preoccupied with the photographic challenges of *Sons*, as a 1960 interview with *Films and Filming* reveals. Here, he discusses his decision to use black-and-white film with the Cinemascope camera, a combination suggestive of ambivalent transition between old and new technology. His remarks, however, reveal that he was experimenting with technique even in his choice to shoot in black and white. The film he used was new high-speed Tri-X. Its effect was to increase depth of focus and, as a result, to allow more "freedom of movement" while filming indoors or in subdued light.[2] Cardiff also talks about "pushing" the Cinemascope camera by exploring its potential for extreme close-up work when normally it is brought no nearer than six feet from its subject.[3] The more familiar Cinemascope panoramas are present in *Sons and Lovers* as well and may have provided a visual means of offsetting the condensation process and attempting to preserve some of the novel's original resonance and sweep.

Except for one comment on Dean Stockwell's "burning intensity" as an actor, Cardiff remains silent in his interview about his diverse cast.[4] They included distinguished veterans Trevor Howard and Wendy Hiller, appearing as Mr. and Mrs. Morel, and newcomer Heather Sears as Miriam Leivers. Just one year earlier, Sears had appeared as a girl somewhat similar to Miriam in Jack Clayton's *Room at the Top,* a film in which Freddie Francis worked as director of photography. Susan Brown—the character Sears portrayed in *Room*—paralleled Miriam in innocence, naivete, and eventually lost virtue. She offered up her virginity to Laurence Harvey's Joe Lampton, and would do so a second time in *Sons,* making the identical sacrifice to Dean Stockwell's Paul Morel.

For Stockwell, this film represented the beginning of an adult acting career and a short-lived brush with stardom in his emergence as a young romantic lead. He had been a prominent child-actor in the 1940s. After leaving the profession for several years, he returned to enter what was to be, in Cardiff's words, the brief "burning intensity" phase of a very long and varied career—a career which remarkably would take him from the innocence of *The Boy with Green Hair* in 1948 to the perversity of *Blue Velvet* nearly forty years later. Stockwell burned intensely but all too briefly, starring in *Compulsion* (1959), *Sons and Lovers* (1960), and *Long Day's Journey into Night* (1962) as Edmund Tyrone, a figure similar to Paul Morel in sensitivity and youthful artistic inclinations. He then went into eclipse a second time, only to reappear two decades later as a character actor specializing in quirky and menacing roles.

Two more members of the cast who deserve mention here are Mary Ure, appearing as Clara Dawes, and Donald Pleasence as Pappleworth. Ure's career met an untimely end with her death in 1975 at the age of forty-two. Pleasence's career (like Stockwell's) took a turn toward the grotesque at about the same time with his appearance in such films as the Beatles' *Sgt. Pepper's Lonely Hearts Club Band* (1978), *Escape from New York* (1981), and the apparently endless *Halloween* series. Before their separate fates overtook them, Ure and Pleasence had enjoyed success on the British stage. Both were closely involved with the dramatic emergence of the Angry Young Men in the late 1950s and had acted together just one year before *Sons and Lovers* in the film version of John Osborne's *Look*

*Back in Anger.* Ure, who was married to Osborne, brought her role from stage to screen. Four years later, Pleasence did the same with his part in Harold Pinter's *The Caretaker.* Recalling Heather Sears and Freddie Francis's recent involvement in *Room at the Top,* what all of this amounts to is the definite presence, in spirit, of the Angry Young Men among the cast and crew of *Sons and Lovers,* a spirit surely not identical to that of Lawrence's novel, yet parallel in its preoccupation with youth, sexual discovery, rebellion, and escape from the British working class.

As measured by the initial responses of critics, *Sons and Lovers* was a great success. Cinematography, direction, and acting all received favorable notices, with the greatest praise going to Trevor Howard. Stockwell got a somewhat less enthusiastic reception but largely among English reviewers who questioned the presence of an American (in fact, the cast's only American) as the star of a British film based on a British book.[5] This is not to suggest, however, that subjective opinions were limited to England. *Time* announced that the film included "everything important in Lawrence's 500-page novel."[6] Reviewing *Sons and Lovers* for the *New Yorker,* Whitney Balliett used his praise for the film and book as an excuse to attack *Lady Chatterley's Lover,* which he described as one of Lawrence's "lamentable later efforts" by comparison.[7] Largely unconscious of the irony, Stanley Kauffmann combined his comments on *Sons and Lovers* for the *New Republic* with a very nasty review of *Psycho,* leaving any specific comparison of Paul Morel and Norman Bates as devoted sons to the perverse imaginations of his readers.[8] Among the early reviewers, the most perceptive was Pauline Kael, who pointed out the strengths of the film but also understood its limitations, suggesting that at best it represented a cautious approach to the novel's potent and dynamic material.[9]

A second measure of the film's initial success came in the form of nominations and awards. *Sons and Lovers* went to the Cannes Film Festival as Great Britain's official entry in 1960. In America, the film received an Academy Award for cinematography and a half-dozen additional Oscar nominations—to Trevor Howard for best actor, to Mary Ure for best supporting actress, and to Jack Cardiff for best director. It was also nominated for best art direction, script, and picture. The best script nomination seems somewhat curious in that, almost immediately, the screenplay was singled out by critics as the weak point of the film. Writing for *Films in Review,* Henry Hart expressed praise for every element in *Sons and Lovers* except the screenplay, even suggesting that any apparent lapses in the performances of Stockwell and Sears were really the result of a defective script. Similarly, John Gillett in a *Film Quarterly* review suggested that a weak script resulted in compression "into a kind of *Reader's Digest* version" of the novel. Hart and Gillett also pointed out that Cardiff had to seek screen writing reinforcements well into the production process. T. E. B. Clarke and possibly others joined the project late to assist Gavin Lambert, Cardiff's original scriptwriter and a man whose prior experience had been more critical and editorial than creative.[10]

What most troubled initial reviewers about the script was omission of detail and compression of the story as a whole. They called attention to this in order to criticize the film. Forty years later, it is possible to view the same condensation process somewhat more objectively and to regard it as a useful example of what tends to happen when a feature-length film grapples with a massive and powerful text. In *Sons and Lovers,* plot clearly suffers during this struggle. Despite losses, however, the screenwriters' strategies for adapting and compressing Lawrence's material are both interesting and enlightening to observe. In relation to the novel, for example, the beginning of *Sons and Lovers* on film is *in medias res* with a vengeance. Utterly absent are the Morels' courtship, young Gertrude Coppard's aspirations before meeting her future husband, and the reasonably happy early stages of their marriage. Also missing is Lawrence's vivid chronicle of Paul Morel's childhood and of the family's daily life as he and his siblings are growing up.

A second screen version of *Sons and Lovers* was released in 1981. Directed by Stuart Burge, with a screenplay by Trevor Griffiths, it appeared in seven episodes on BBC television. In contrast to Cardiff's ninety-nine minutes, Burge's adaptation takes up six and a half hours, allowing for a more expansive production as well as more opportunities to preserve detail from the text. As a result, much of the early novel cut in Cardiff's version now resurfaces. Gertrude's relationship with John Field, for example, along with her first encounter with Morel, their courtship, and their early married life all appear on television—not chronologically, as might be expected, but as flashbacks that occur as Gertrude has plenty of time to consider her past, having been locked out of the house by her husband. It is noteworthy that despite this wealth of time and opportunity, at least compared with Cardiff's film, the BBC screenwriter, Trevor Griffiths, still complains of having felt constrained. In his introduction to the published screenplay for the televised production, he writes that "there are the differences born of trying to incorporate a 500-page novel into a six-and-a-half-hour time slot. Much that is rich and textured has gone, where it has not been needed to support the narrative or serve the social relationships of the characters."[11]

Griffiths's introduction reveals several other points of contrast between the television production and the feature film. One is that Griffiths intended his screenplay as social and economic protest, far more emphatically than his predecessors Gavin Lambert and T. E. B. Clarke did, as well as a celebration of the working class. As a result, the mine scenes in the television production clearly suggest exploitation of labor for profit. Similarly, the scenes portraying Miriam, Mrs. Leivers, and Gertrude Morel in domestic circumstances all imply the constraints placed upon women in general by late Victorian society. Partly because of the more overt class issue in the 1981 *Sons and Lovers,* Walter Morel (played by Tom Bell) and Baxter Dawes (played by Jack Shepherd) take on special prominence. Griffiths and his colleagues have deliberately conceived Morel to seem "as much victim as anyone else and, incidentally, much closer [than in the text] to the 'father' that Lawrence revalued towards the end of his own life."[12] The 1960 feature filmmakers also depict a "revalued" father through Trevor Howard's compelling performance as Morel but, as I hope to show, by way of a far less deliberate process. Baxter's friendship with Paul Morel, born of their struggle over Clara, is especially prominent in the television series, whereas it is virtually ignored on film. In fact, the 1981 Paul (played by Karl Johnson) seems to feel a grudging admiration for Baxter long before he decides to visit the older man in the hospital. This more developed and complex friendship becomes another way for the BBC filmmakers to explore their social and economic concerns while indirectly returning to the textual issue of fathers and sons.

With less than two hours of screen time at their disposal, Cardiff, Lambert, and Clarke were challenged by the demands of compression and acceleration in place of exploration. Thus, when *Sons and Lovers* opens on the large screen, Paul is already a young adult. During the first fifteen minutes, the 1960 film seems to be set in fast-forward, at least with regard to the text. Within three minutes, the audience hears of Miriam and learns that Mrs. Morel is troubled by the girl's relationship with Paul. Within six minutes, we see Miriam and Paul together in an affectionate, idyllic meeting at the farm. Their postadolescent "lad and girl" lovemaking is interrupted, nine minutes into the film, by an explosion at the mine where Paul's father and brother Arthur are both working. Arthur's corpse is brought up from the mine shaft two minutes later, and, one minute after that, Paul's elder brother, William, comes home from London for the funeral. Paul finds work at Jordan's in Nottingham immediately afterwards and William begins courting Louisa Western. The fifteen-minute "overture" ends with William presenting Louisa's photograph to Paul and Mrs. Morel as his train departs for London.

It would be absurd and, in fact, impossible to attempt such a pace much beyond the film's first few scenes. With Arthur's death and William's departure, viewing speed returns to normal, and for the next hour the audience is given a sustained account of one critical year in Paul Morel's life—the year of his and Miriam's sexual initiation, his affair with Clara Dawes, and his mother's death. Time and the need for compression still drive the filmmakers, but now their methods shift from fast-forwarding to the technique of condensation. Several major incidents within the film behave like Freudian dream structures in relation to the book. They are actually conflations of two or more textual events taken from different parts of the novel and melded together into a single screen episode.

Arthur's death at the mine, which completes the film's introduction, is the first such reconfiguration of the text. In Lawrence's novel it is not Arthur who suffers a mine accident but his father who is seriously but not fatally injured. Also, it is not the younger brother, Arthur, who dies in the novel but the elder brother, William. In effect, the screen version of *Sons and Lovers* merges the father's injury with the brother's death, so that the one film event resonates with the implications of both catastrophes. Arthur's death, like Walter's injury, suggests the ugliness and danger of work in the mine and confirms Mrs. Morel's resolve to keep Paul away from it. At the same time, Arthur's death, like William's, is much more than merely an injury, even a critical injury. It is a "death in the family" and, in text and film alike, the first tragic event that Mr. and Mrs. Morel have had to endure together.[13]

In the text, William's death is most of all a loss to Gertrude Morel, who has always favored her first-born son. She nearly follows him to the grave but is saved when Paul falls ill, reminding her of other maternal responsibilities and recalling her to life. An interesting shift in modulation on screen is that Arthur's death is most essentially a loss to his father and not to his mother. The emotional symmetry established in the film's initial scenes suggests that, of the two Morel boys remaining at home, Paul is his mother's child and Arthur is his father's. Arthur's death, then, has the early effect of isolating Walter Morel within his own household. This sets up a lonely and essentially defensive battle that Walter will be fighting against his family until the end and that will become one of the film's major achievements of both plot and character.

A second instance of film conflation involves a violent domestic quarrel and provides an example of failure rather than qualified success. Like Arthur's death, the quarrel is a composite of two textual episodes—the incident in which Morel strikes his wife with a drawer and the earlier incident in which he locks her out of their home. Where meaning is saved in the film reconstruction of "Death in the Family," it seems to be lost in this quarrel, leaving only the ugly and empty event before us. In the text, meaning within both confrontations of man and wife depends on Paul's intimate participation—as an infant and, even before that, as part of his mother's pregnant body. In the drawer scene, Paul is literally baptized in parental conflict and with his mother's blood. In the locking-out, he is likewise symbolically conceived amid the violent struggle of his progenitors.

On screen, Trevor Howard's Morel flies into a drunken tantrum at not getting his dinner. He throws a kitchen drawer to the floor, but does not strike his wife, then quickly puts her out of the house. Since Paul is already grown when this happens, none of the text's complexity of implication is possible. Instead, the scene climaxes with Paul's return home, rescue of his shivering mother, and confrontation with Morel, which nearly results in blows. Even this exchange of melodrama for meaning fails to work. In the Oedipal standoff between father and son, Dean Stockwell's Paul looks too delicate to fight. In turn, Trevor Howard's Morel looks too gentle, beneath his pit dirt and grimaces, to be capable of hitting anyone, least of all his son.

In the final fifteen minutes of the film, an abrupt reversal of plot strategy takes place again. The technique of conflation is dropped, and the film returns to the fast-forward pace of its beginning. It is not difficult to understand why this happens, since the filmmakers' concluding challenge is to get Paul quickly out of everything he has gotten himself into, particularly his relationships with the three women in his life: Miriam, Clara, and Gertrude.

Clara and Miriam are disposed of with one brief scene of farewell apiece. Gone is the slow, agonizing process by which Paul frees himself from Miriam's stifling yet not wholly unwelcome embrace. Gone also is Paul's near-filial friendship with Baxter Dawes, which springs up after they lay violent hands upon one another. Since this is missing from the film, so too is Paul's ambiguous involvement in the reconciliation between Baxter and Clara, his actions as ex-lover and go-between in returning the strayed wife to her husband. Cardiff's Paul says a clean farewell to both women, and the former lovers simply move off screen.

While Paul and his mother cannot be parted quite this easily, Mrs. Morel's death is also melded into the rush of the film's final quarter hour. As a result, it is far more peaceful and free of suffering than was Gertrude's death in Lawrence's text. Her slow, wasting cancer is transformed into a quick series of heart attacks, again as a concession to time but also as a way of sparing the imagined sensibilities of the audience. Similarly, Paul does not play a part in his mother's death as he does in the novel. Paul as mercy killer, like Paul as matchmaker to Clara, disappears in the filmmakers' reluctance to darken his image in any way or to complicate the straightforward goodness of the young hero.

Really, the only complication surrounding Mrs. Morel's film death has to do with Paul's painting and the interest she has always taken in his art. While ill, Mrs. Morel has told Paul she would like to see the springtime daffodils, the implication being that she won't live long enough to do so. Paul resolves to paint the daffodils in order to grant her wish. He does, but she never sees them, dying just as he attempts to place the unfinished (and somewhat van Gogh-like) canvas in front of her. Although melodramatic, the scene manages to convey a suggestion interesting in part because of its opposition to the text. Lawrence's Paul speeds his mother's journey with morphine, giving her the final gift of death. The filmmakers' Paul gives her springtime flowers instead of the drug, as if trying to hold his mother back with images of renewal and life. Mrs. Morel's film death is also interesting for biographical reasons. Like Paul presenting his canvas, Lawrence gave his own mother an advance copy of his first book, *The White Peacock,* when she was fatally ill.[14]

It seems logical to expect that a major reduction of plot is bound to overtake the film's characters as well. In fact, it does, yet with two exceptions significant enough to warrant special attention: Mary Ure's portrayal of Clara Dawes and Trevor Howard's portrayal of Walter Morel. The shrinkage of character on screen, however, is far more immediately evident to an observer than any expansion or gain. For example, one misses several important figures in the novel who have simply been dropped from the film: Paul's sister Annie, his childhood playmate and adult accomplice in their mother's death, and Miriam's older brothers, who for a time become Paul's closest friends.

Other memorable characters may be physically present yet absent in spirit, since they are reduced to flatness. The women who work with Paul at Jordan's suffer this fate, losing their distinctive personalities as they are merged into a comic chorus of observers to Paul's workplace courtship of Clara. Baxter Dawes is similarly flattened and cut. No trace remains of his softer side or of his paternal resemblance to Walter Morel. He survives in the film merely as a kind of prop—a threat to Paul and a clichéd image of the violently jealous husband. In fact, Baxter's reduction to one or two qualities provides an insight into the filmmakers' general strategy for adapting a novel that contains a remarkably full cast of round characters. With Baxter and several other major figures in *Sons and Lovers,* the film tends to maintain focus on a single human issue, omitting or else backgrounding all the rest.

This is very evident in the screen conception of Paul and Miriam. Their original complexity as a couple is largely absent, especially their ability to fuel their relationship by a unique synthesis of feelings and ideas. One cannot, for instance, conceive of Dean Stockwell and Heather Sears, in their portrayal of Paul and Miriam, discussing Paul's painting as these same characters do in the text and transforming words and impressions into erotic, ultimately mysterious energy:

> "Why do I like this so? . . ."
> "Why *do* you?" he asked.
> "I don't know. It seems so true."
> "It's because—it's because there is scarcely any shadow in it; it's more shimmery, as if I'd painted the shimmering protoplasm in the leaves and everywhere, and not the stiffness of the shape. That seems dead to me. Only this shimmeriness is the real living. The shape is a dead crust. The shimmer is inside really."[15]

With such intricacies removed, what's left of the original Paul and Miriam is simply the sexual obstacle between them. Otherwise they are perfectly matched—both youthful, optimistic, artistically inclined, and ordinary. Paul is a pleasant young man who paints (indifferently) and who yearns for his first sexual relationship. Equally pleasant and colorless, Miriam neither paints nor wishes, under any circumstances, to have a sexual experience—not with Paul, not with anyone. He must have sex, and the very idea of it scares her to death. No question that this is a real issue between Paul and Miriam in the text, yet it is their one and only issue on screen. Like Baxter, this critical couple is pared down to a single conflict that serves as their raison d'être throughout the film.[16]

As with sons and their would-be lovers, so too with mothers. Wendy Hiller's Mrs. Morel is referred to as Gertrude just once in the film, the virtual disappearance of her given name accidentally suggesting her simplification as a human being. What remains of her is, again, a single trait—her obsessive, overprotective devotion to Paul. Actually, three mothers are present in the film, just as they are in the text: Paul's, Miriam's, and Clara's. The filmmakers, however, have called attention to them as a trio far more insistently than Lawrence ever did in the novel, so that the single human quality in each mother stands out boldly to create a sharp three-sided contrast of characters. Mrs. Morel's excess of maternal love is opposed by Mrs. Leivers's coldness to all of her children, especially Miriam. Rosalie Crutchley portrays her as a forbidding religious fanatic whose harshness is largely responsible for Miriam's inhibition and fear of sexuality. In contrast to these opposite extremes, the film presents the healthy normality of Clara Dawes's mother and implies that Clara's independence of body and spirit is at least in part the gift of maternal influence.

Clara's mother and Miriam's mother remain flat characters in their limited appearances. Far more visible, however, Mrs. Morel does eventually undergo a slight rounding-out before the film ends. Despite her failed marriage and obsession with Paul, Mrs. Morel occasionally and wistfully reminisces. In her happy monologues about the past, the film audience is allowed to glimpse what little spark remains of her youthful sexuality and once-passionate love for Walter. Plot also gains, or regains, dimensionality through Mrs. Morel's on-screen memories. They afford the filmmakers an opportunity to put back a little of what was cut from the beginning chapters of *Sons and Lovers*.

A final pair of characters who suffer the simplification process are Paul's brother William and his fiancée, Louisa Western. The older brother never dies on screen, like his textual counterpart, but just fades away, returning to a London career and an eventual marriage to the attractive but shallow Louisa. Lost from the film, with the absence of William's death, is Lawrence's submotif of suffocation. In the novel, William dies of erysipelas, which begins with a chafing at the throat and spreads through his entire body. The suggestion is that William has been stifled, eventually strangled, by the dual constrictions of modern employment and modern romance. His workday collars have always seemed too tight, and in his final delirium he speaks to his mother about a ship's cargo of sugar which, like his engagement, has turned to rock (135). His love affair with Louisa has been something like an addiction, sexually euphoric yet debilitating in every other way. This is because although William compulsively desires Louisa's body, he detests the rest of her and holds no regard for her as a future wife or a human being. In Lawrence's hands, this minor but fascinating relationship becomes an ominous paradigm for the hazards of modern existence and also a specific prophecy for Paul, who could, by the very different agencies of his mother and Miriam, be hopelessly smothered himself.

What remains of William and Louisa is their visible sexuality, which becomes the film's simplified prophecy of Paul's future. William and Louisa serve as bridge characters, helping Paul cross from sexual frustration in his relationship with Miriam to sexual satisfaction in his impending affair with Clara. When William brings his fiancée home for the Christmas holidays, they kiss erotically, using the mistletoe as an excuse. Earlier in the film, when Paul attempted to kiss Miriam with similar fire, he succeeded only in angering and revolting her. He now watches his brother and Louisa carefully, and the difference between her response to the kiss and Miriam's is clear to audience and protagonist alike. Since the on-screen Louisa directs Paul, sexually at least, from Miriam toward Clara, the filmmakers have altered her appearance to suit her function. Whereas Lawrence's Louisa is dark-haired and dark-eyed, her on-screen counterpart resembles and anticipates the blonde and fair-skinned Clara Dawes.

Any similarity between Louisa and Clara, however, begins and ends with this physical resemblance. William's superficial fiancée is the flattest character in a film largely peopled by flat characters. Mary Ure's Clara, on the other hand, is one of the few to escape being reduced to a single human dimension. She strikes the audience as a figure we don't know everything about and, in fact, can't know everything about—this quality tied in part to the skill of Ure's performance.

Beyond her ambiguity, yet related to it, Clara Dawes may be the only character in the film to strike the truly Lawrentian note—to survive cinematic transformation as a figure still his own in conception and spirit. The on-screen Clara effectively conveys a mixture of vulnerability and strength, a combination of qualities found not only in the original Clara but generally in the Lawrentian sisterhood. Ursula Brangwen, Ellen March, Yvette Saywell, and Connie Chatterley are all similarly conflicted figures. Also like her textual counterpart, Ure's Clara Dawes seeks to achieve a balance among three familiar Lawrentian forces—selfhood, sexuality, and the will to power. She is more than eager to be lost in the erotic moment so long as she can regain herself whole and intact afterwards—not merged with another or, worse, sacrificed to his needs. Beyond this, Clara Dawes in the film successfully projects the human urge to exert authority—to hold and apply power somehow and somewhere in the world. In text and film alike, this need informs Clara's political activity as a feminist and also explains her refusal to cut the tie with Baxter, a man to whom she does not belong but who clearly belongs to her.

It is not surprising, then, that the one film sequence which seems most Lawrentian in spirit and tone centers on Clara. This is the same scene that caught the censors' attention in 1960 by way of its postcoital intimacies between Clara and Paul. Their conversation takes place at a seaside hotel and has no exact counterpart in the novel. It is another cinematic conflation in which the filmmakers have combined several textual dialogues between the lovers into a single concentrated exchange. Speaking many of Lawrence's lines word-for-word, Clara accuses Paul not of sexual failure but of failure to acknowledge her as a separate being and failure to yield anything of himself: "About *me* you know nothing,—about *me!*" "But is it *me* you want, or is it *it?*" "You've never given me yourself." The words of this indictment fall like hammer blows. Clara speaks them while lying on the bed, her appearance suggestive of nudity under the covers. Paul stands over her, bare-chested. Despite these sensuous details, the lovers appear sundered from one another by way of their angry words and also by way of the filmmakers' visual composition of the scene. As Clara speaks, her face is framed by the brass bars of the bedstead, a pose suggesting imprisonment in the now-oppressive love affair and also inevitable alienation from Paul. The scene achieves an interesting intertextuality not only with *Sons and Lovers* but also with the later and darker *Women in Love* as well. As these lovers struggle with their dying relationship, they come to resemble Gudrun and Gerald in "Snowed Up," confined together in even more dangerous circumstances. At the outset of that chapter, Gudrun and Gerald also struggle in a shared hotel bedroom, physically close yet hopelessly separated and destined for a far more drastic parting than Clara and Paul.

Clara, then, gives us Lawrence whole, while most of the other characters in this film give us less. Curiously enough, Trevor Howard's rendering of Walter Morel somehow manages to go beyond Lawrence to give us more of a father than we have in the original text. The on-screen Morel is a many-sided figure, whereas Lawrence's coal miner seems simpler by comparison, flattened a bit, ironically a little like one of the characters in the film. Despite some winning qualities, the original Morel remains a negative presence and a negative force within the family. In the film, Morel's better nature and sensitivity show through, along with his coarseness and occasional brutality. As with the accurate rendering of Clara, this expansion of Morel can be understood partly in relation to the actor playing the role. While Trevor Howard effectively expresses both the dark and bright sides of Morel, he actually seems more convincing in his warm vitality than in his rages, as if there were an attractive human being slightly hidden under the pit dirt and nastiness. Seen from the past perspective of *The Rocking Horse Winner*, there is a clear relationship between this performance and John Mills's interpretation of Bassett. While Bassett is surely more wholesome than Morel, as well as more passive and deferential, both men represent a similar film tribute to unpolished and natural decency or, in other words, to a popular and idealized image of the British working man.

Beyond Trevor Howard's performance, the expansion of Morel also represents the work of the film's director and screenwriters, who gave this figure qualities that Lawrence deliberately held back. The cinematic Morel is clearly the most vital member of his family, reflecting a gaiety and enjoyment of life on screen that mainly survive in Gertrude Morel's memories in the text. These warm qualities are especially evident in the film's Christmas Eve scene, where Morel sings a music-hall song and creates a memorable image that has no counterpart in the novel. In only one important respect does this expanded figure fall short of the original. The filmmakers, regrettably, have denied Morel any trace of his natural talent in the text as a teller of wonderful tales. With the omission of Paul and his siblings as young children, no opportunity remains in the film for their father to gather them about and fascinate them with stories of Taffy, the clever pit pony, stories which Lawrence wrote "would go on interminably" and which "everybody loved" (64).

What the on-screen Morel may lack in narrative gifts, he more than makes up for in sensitivity and intelligence. He is very aware, for example, of all the undercurrents and tensions within his family and often of the unexpressed feelings of his wife and son. This is revealed through several scenes in the film during which Morel confronts either Paul or Mrs. Morel—not physically but with words and emotions. In one such scene between father and son, the morning after Mrs. Morel has been locked outside, Morel correctly suggests that Paul's view of his parents' marriage is far bleaker than the reality itself, pointing out that it has endured many such crises and will continue to do so. In a later scene, after Mrs. Morel's death, this same father perceives the suicidal potential in Paul's grieving and manages to turn him round in the direction of life—something which Paul, in the text, has to do entirely on his own. Morel tells his son that rather than "letting things slide," Paul owes himself and his dead mother a good struggle with life's possibilities. Morel even advises Paul to seize his independence by going to London in pursuit of his artistic career.

Given Lawrence's original conception of Morel, as an avoider and repressor of awareness, neither of these scenes would be possible in the text. Nor would the bedroom confrontation between Mr. and Mrs. Morel in which they argue over Paul's involvement with the married Clara Dawes. During this exchange Morel blames his wife for the affair, claiming that her intense possessiveness has prevented any relationship between Paul and a more eligible woman that might have led to marriage.

The Morel of Lawrence's text is not altogether unaware of the Oedipal triangle within his family, as implied by his less-than-sober question, "At your mischief again?" when he discovers mother and son in a moment of intimacy (213). Yet the original Morel's awareness always remains largely inarticulate and subconscious:

> "H'm—h'm! h'm—h'm!" he sneered.
>
> He went into the passage, hung up his hat and coat. Then they heard him go down three steps to the pantry. He returned with a piece of pork-pie in his fist. It was what Mrs. Morel had bought for her son. (213)

In the film, it is Mrs. Morel, instead, who seems the unconscious one, her husband having to explain to her that any son can escape the effects of a low father far more easily than he can avoid suffocation at the hands of a mother who loves too well. That Lawrence could have written a parallel scene into his novel, with a parallel explanation from Morel, seems difficult to imagine.

The film version of Morel is a mature and finished human being. Lawrence's Morel, by contrast, remains incomplete in many respects—still somewhat of a child despite his robustness and physical courage. This childishness becomes most evident just after Gertrude Morel's death when Paul suddenly realizes that his father is frightened by the presence of her corpse—afraid to look at his own dead wife, afraid even to remain in the same house with her: "His father looked so forlorn. Morel had been a man without fear—simply nothing frightened him. Paul realised with a start that he had been afraid to go to bed, alone in the house with his dead. He was sorry" (400).

The response of the on-screen Morel to death and to his own dead is very different: he is resigned as a result of the past experience with Arthur and in no way frightened. This Morel, like his original counterpart, also fails to see his wife's body but not out of cowardice. In her last illness Mrs. Morel has asked that they not see one another again—not obliterate what good memories remain of their marriage with more bitter ones. By refusing to view her in death, Morel is simply honoring his wife's final wishes.

Of the film's pair of fully realized characters, then, only Clara Dawes remains true to her textual counterpart. Morel the father does not because he proves to be deeper and more complete than the original. In a strangely prophetic way, however, Trevor Howard's Morel does remain true to Lawrence himself—not to the Lawrence of *Sons and Lovers* but to the more mature author and man who, ten years later, honestly reassessed his parents' marriage and his father's worth as a human being. Calling attention to this now well known reassessment, one of Lawrence's biographers, Jeffrey Meyers, writes as follows:

> In the late 1920s Lawrence . . . told his friends Rhys Davies and
> Achsah Brewster that he now understood and respected his father—
> "a piece of the gay old England that had gone"—much more than
> he had when he wrote *Sons and Lovers.* He thought his parents'
> quarrels were caused more by his mother's malicious taunts than by
> his father's drunkenness. He believed he had not done justice to his
> father, grieved over the hostile portrait and felt like rewriting the
> novel.[17]

Mark Kinkead-Weekes indicates that Lawrence's reassessment of his father may have begun much earlier than 1920, during the writing of *Sons* and even because of it. "As he grew more critical of his mother in writing *Sons and Lovers,* the sense may have grown of how much in his father's world had only been glimpsed in its pages."[18] It would seem from these biographical insights that an interesting relationship exists between the on-screen Morel and the unwritten Morel of Lawrence's evolving imagination. If the film character erases the original text of *Sons and Lovers,* he also inscribes a Lawrence text that never quite got written. Trevor Howard's Morel—vital, sensitive, and essentially good—emerges as a strange ghost, thirty years after the author's death, of the father Lawrence regretted not having created himself.

Beyond plot and character, a less literary film element needs to be discussed here. This can be described as the visual achievement of *Sons and Lovers* on screen—the extent to which it realizes itself as effective cinematic art. Here it would seem that Lawrence's original text has a great deal of direct help to offer the filmmakers. As raw material to be turned into film, the novel is already visually energized—not in a fixed way, like painting, but kinetically, something like accomplished motion picture art itself. Any reading of *Sons and Lovers* is surely an experience measured in dynamic scenes—each one startling when first encountered in the text, each one moving and memorable in the way that first-rate film should be and sometimes is.

The memory, at liberty within this novel and among such scenes, might take a reader back to William Morel's first haircut, or to Paul's sacrifice of the doll "Missis Arabella," an act which prefigures so much about his future relations with women of flesh and blood. The reader might also recall bread baking at the Morel household and how such a seemingly simple activity can be supercharged with human emotion and significance. Beyond these examples, there are several vivid scenes throughout *Sons and Lovers* exploiting nature as a means of revealing character and relationship. Paul Morel, for instance, repeatedly stabs at the earth with a stick, acting out the conflict within himself between sexual desire and sexual rage. Or Miriam Leivers, with equal frequency, embraces the flowers she finds so beautiful—roses, sweet peas, daffodils—all crushed and stifled, as Paul fears he will be, against her loving breast. Or Clara Dawes, more controlled in her admiration, caresses a stallion, expressing by the single gesture both her will to dominate the creature and her susceptibility to its power. Perhaps the most startling thing to be said about the film, at least in regard to its visuality, is that all of these scenes are absent—as if the filmmakers had refused outright Lawrence's generous gifts.

The swinging scene between Paul Morel and Miriam Leivers is one exception. Here Jack Cardiff and his associates have attempted to preserve a luminous moment from the text and to present it on screen. Despite the movement and intensity of Lawrence's original scene, the result of this effort proves to be a failure. In the novel, the swinging scene takes up only two compressed pages of text, yet reveals so much about Paul and Miriam as separate people and as a couple in conflict. When Paul swings, he loses his single, fixed being within the activity itself, within sensations powerful enough to dissolve him into the wider experience. This is something Miriam knows she can never do: "Away he went. There was something fascinating to her in him. For the moment he was nothing but a piece of swinging stuff; not a particle of him that did not swing. She could never lose herself so, nor could her brothers. It roused a warmth in her. It were almost as if he were a flame that had lit a warmth in her whilst he swung in the middle air" (151).

When Paul swings Miriam, the implications of the scene turn directly erotic and predict their future incompatibility as lovers—their insoluble conflict between sexual searching, on his part, and sexual fear, on hers: "She felt the accuracy with which he caught her, exactly at the right moment, and the exactly proportionate strength of his thrust, and she was afraid. Down to her bowels went the hot wave of fear. She was in his hands. Again, firm and inevitable came the thrust at the right moment. She gripped the rope, almost swooning" (151).

None of these implications survives in the film. Only the external shell of Lawrence's scene remains. On screen, the sequence occurs just after Paul learns that a wealthy man has purchased one of his paintings and plans to become his patron. He rushes to the Leivers farm to tell Miriam the news and finds her sitting on the swing. After a few halfhearted efforts at pushing Miriam back and forth, Paul suddenly takes her place and begins boasting about his recent achievements as he stands up and swings. Any sense of eroticism is lost from the scene, as is Lawrence's suggestion about more intense realities and a meaningful freedom from self. What the film scene proves to be about, in fact, *is* self and nothing much else: Paul's egotistical celebration of his success and his ambition to become not a great artist so much as a famous and wealthy one. While he swings, he crows to Miriam, now standing beneath him, "I'm going to the top of the world. You coming with me?" He then disappears, leaving the swing empty as he jumps into a hayloft above it and deliberately hides from Miriam. As she looks for him, confused by the whole performance, he showers her with money—the four five-pound notes he has just received for his painting. Finally he reappears, sliding down from the hayloft, back to Miriam, and proclaims, "Women are all the same. They always want to drag a man down to their own level."[19]

Lawrence's memorable scene, then, is hopelessly damaged in the film and made to reflect materialism in place of human complexity, as well as a male smugness in Paul nastier than anything similar in the novel's original character. One conclusion that could be drawn from this failure is that the filmmakers were correct to omit virtually all of the major Lawrence scenes from *Sons and Lovers*. Despite their visual impact, these scenes are really inward visions and therefore impossible to film realistically without externalizing them and thus violating their essential spirit.

If many of Lawrence's visionary scenes in *Sons and Lovers* are either botched or avoided on screen, it also appears that none of the film's truly effective moments owes very much to the text at all. This is exemplified by several memorable sequences already mentioned here: the strong and honest confrontations between Morel and Paul or between Mr. and Mrs. Morel, the father's music-hall performance on Christmas Eve, and the censored bedroom exchange between Paul and Clara. Not one of these scenes has a textual counterpart in *Sons and Lovers*, suggesting that visually the filmmakers have gotten farther on their own than on anything derived from Lawrence. In addition, the film's visual or artistic unit of measure is not ultimately the kinetic scene at all, as it is in the novel, but something far more fixed. In an ironic reversal, the original text appears to be more cinematic than the movie, a work of literature in constant flux and motion as opposed to a film essentially static, "painterly," or even "textual" in its artistic accomplishments.

A simple instance of the still quality in Jack Cardiff's *Sons and Lovers* involves a trio of sketches and paintings employed in the film as literary symbols might be employed in a text. The works in question are three portraits done by Paul Morel during the film: one of his mother, the second of his father, and the third of Clara Dawes. In quite literary terms, what Paul portrays here are his own strong feelings—images of people in his life who rouse his love, or hate, or both. Where no such intense emotions exist, as with Miriam Leivers, the corresponding portrait is absent from the film. Paul's three portraits are purely the filmmakers' invention, their only textual basis being a sketch done by Lawrence's Paul not of Clara's face as in the film but of her hand and arm.[20]

The portraits of Paul's parents are also interesting as a related pair of images, behaving independently from the text yet in a purely literary way. Paul's drawing of his mother is idealized, depicting her as younger than her actual years and wearing a seductive bonnet in place of her usual dour one. The portrait of Paul's father is more naturalistically conceived and remarkably evocative of Lawrence's own *Contadini* painting in its general composition and in the central figure's pose. Where the *contadino* looks down and away, however, Walter Morel looks defiantly out at the viewer, his face blackened by mine dust except for his eyes.[21]

In one of the film's earliest scenes, Morel and his son Arthur notice Paul's sketch of Mrs. Morel as they come down to breakfast. Arthur makes good-natured fun of it, but his father ruins the portrait when he lays his greasy bacon fork upon it. The hostile gesture here strikes at wife and son together—at Paul's adoring tribute to his mother, and at Mrs. Morel's own superior and ladylike image. Morel then tries to repair the damage by rubbing the drawing with his handkerchief. He succeeds only in blackening Mrs. Morel's face, thus making it resemble his own. These hostile actions in the film, then, may have a touching side to them as well, by mutely expressing Morel's wish that he and his wife might be more alike.

An altogether separate visual metaphor, and one which proves to be more pervasive than the three portraits, involves the turning wheel. Wheels appear frequently in *Sons and Lovers* and provide the film with an image more capable of movement and change than a picture enclosed within a frame. The first wheel suggests mechanism and industry, but soon expands in meaning to involve death as well. The film's opening scene is of a rural landscape at dawn. The camera pans across this landscape until it reaches what the script describes as "an alien element; a coal mine," and in particular a large wheel that operates the mine shaft elevator.[22] As the camera pauses here, the wheel begins to rotate, frightening away a flock of pigeons roosting nearby. The audience sees this same wheel just a few scenes later when the mine elevator brings Morel up from the pit with his son's dead body.

A different cinematic wheel seems opposed to the industrial wheel—now rural, natural, and sexual in its connotations. This is the water wheel at the Leivers farm, an object prominent in Paul's first scene with Miriam and associated, throughout the film, with her and with the couple's evolving courtship. When they first become lovers, the camera focuses on this wheel turning in the water as the scene dissolves to black. Later, when Paul ends his relationship with Miriam on Christmas morning, the camera shows this same wheel now frozen in the winter stream.

A third wheel, introduced late in the film, complicates matters by bringing together the opposite suggestions of the first two and conflating sexual passion with dead mechanical process. This wheel appears at the close of the fire-side scene in which Paul and Clara first make love. As this warm and living image fades from the screen, it is replaced by a close-up of spinning bobbins at the factory where Paul and Clara work, an image suggesting furious yet utterly lifeless activity.[23]

No mine wheels, mill wheels, or bobbin wheels operate within the pages of *Sons and Lovers*. They are purely cinematic interpolations, yet provide Cardiff's film with a way back to the novel and to Lawrence's own reaction against industry as ultimately an agent of death. A more problematic implication in the film's turning wheels, however, is that mechanical cycle and sexual cycle may somehow be related. A wheel appears somewhere on screen during every one of Paul's passionate adventures, perhaps implying that his initial sexual euphoria will eventually give way to mechanical repetition. Departing from Lawrence here into a kind of existential misogyny, the film counsels Paul to save himself by utterly rejecting the sexual go-round. The film's closing message to its hero and audience alike is to climb straight to the top of the world alone—go as a man on your own, unencumbered by women who will drag you down into a vicious erotic spin. This is precisely what Dean Stockwell's Paul does to bring *Sons and Lovers* to a close. As the credits appear, he replaces the film's sexual turnings with a straight and narrow line of march. The film audience sees him approaching from a distance, walking toward the Bestwood railroad station swiftly, directly, and with very little baggage. He boards the waiting train, which will accelerate his linear journey to London, conveying him to likely success as a man within a man's world.

The film seems to end here on a blatantly reductive note, especially so if we recall the poetic ambiguity of Paul Morel's "quickly" moving figure in the scene that closes the novel (420). Yet the screen imagery that prepares for this anticlimax is neither blatant nor reductive. It juxtaposes Paul's linear and exclusively masculine escape at the end with sexual convolution, ultimately feminine convolution, in that the film's turning mill wheels and spiraling bobbins always imply either Miriam or Clara. Such film imagery seems provocative in a way closer to current feminist discourse than to Lawrence's text. The film's closing combination of inventive metaphor and questionable suggestion provides a revealing statement about its own mixed results as a work of cinematic art. This final paradox therefore also raises the inevitable question of judgment. How is the reader/viewer ultimately to assess a filmed work of fiction as conflicted as *Sons and Lovers* is on screen between the compelling and the embarrassing? My own answer here is that Jack Cardiff's film achieves a marginal success or, perhaps more accurately, amounts to an interesting failure. Its embarrassments, counted up and tallied, far outnumber its handful of breakthroughs: the general shrinkage of Lawrence's characters and plot, for example, to suit the restrictions of ninety-nine minutes on screen—or the scenic opportunities offered by the text either muffed or simply ignored by the filmmakers.

On the credit side of cinematic reckoning, the film's achievements are few yet memorable when they do occur. Among the successes within *Sons and Lovers*, only Mary Ure's Clara Dawes pays direct tribute to the filmmakers and to D. H. Lawrence at the same time. In every other instance, the film soars, albeit briefly, only when it resists Lawrence, either altering his text or else leaving it out of the picture entirely. On the level of plot, Arthur Morel's mine death provides an example of such radical and artistically effective resistance. The same can be said, regarding character, of Trevor Howard's Walter Morel, a cinematic figure who actually complicates Lawrence's original. As to visual achievement, the film's most telling images are derived not from the text but from the filmmakers' own artistic resources—that curious grouping of still portraits, turning wheels, and linear progressions, for instance, absolutely uncinematic in conception yet effective on screen just the same.

By breaking free from Lawrence, then, the film manages a few moments of confident flight. Yet by eluding the writer, this film obliquely recovers him, too, as when Trevor Howard suddenly reminds us of a father Lawrence never acknowledged in his novel but eventually wished he had. There is a broader sense, as well, in which the film recovers Lawrence by the very act that rejects him. His text concerns the human need to throw off many kinds of dominations, especially the overwhelming maternal urge, which, if not resisted, smothers in the cause of nurturing and cripples in the name of love. Paul Morel is a young man who cannot move "quickly"—in the double-edged sense of vitally and fast—until he liberates himself from this force, as difficult and prolonged as the struggle might be. Like the novel's protagonist, the film *Sons and Lovers* moves "quickly" only in moments of successful escape from its parental and potentially smothering text.

The "shining modern rocking-horse" seems to interrupt a conversation between Bassett (John Mills, *left*) and Master Paul (John Howard Davies) in Anthony Pelissier's *The Rocking Horse Winner*. Copyright ©2001 by Universal City Studios, Inc. Courtesy of Universal Studios Publishing Rights, a Division of Universal Studios Licensing, Inc. All rights reserved.

The major cast of Jack Cardiff's *Sons and Lovers* pose for a formal portrait never used in the film. *Left to right:* Trevor Howard as Walter Morel, Heather Sears as Miriam, Wendy Hiller as Mrs. Morel, Mary Ure as Clara Dawes, and Dean Stockwell as Paul. *Sons and Lovers* ©1960 Twentieth Century Fox Film Corporation. All rights reserved.

Yvette (Joanna Shimkus) seems preoccupied with her troubles, while the Gypsy (Franco Nero) looks on in the background, his image deliberately unfocused—perhaps to suggest Yvette's daydreams about him. Christopher Miles's *The Virgin and the Gypsy.*

Rupert Birkin (Alan Bates, *left*) and Gerald Crich (Oliver Reed) exchange firelit gazes after their gladiatorial encounter in Ken Russell's production of *Women in Love*. Still photograph from the Brandywine–United Artists production of *Women in Love* used by permission of Larry Kramer.

Ursula Brangwen (Jennie Linden) and Rupert Birkin (Alan Bates) smile triumphantly at one another against a background of idyllic nature in Ken Russell's *Women in Love*. Still photograph from the Brandywine–United Artists production of *Women in Love* used by permission of Larry Kramer.

In the close quarters of the Alpine lodge, Gudrun Brangwen (Glenda Jackson) and Gerald Crich (Oliver Reed) contemplate the end of their relationship, already over yet not quite finished, in Ken Russell's production of *Women in Love*. The lamp in the foreground and the clock in the background suggest the inescapable presence of knowledge and of time, two of Lawrence's major preoccupations in the novel. Still photograph from the Brandywine–United Artists production of *Women in Love* used by permission of Larry Kramer.

A smiling Winifred Inger (Amanda Donohoe) and a pouting Ursula Brangwen (Sammi Davis) regard the camera in Ken Russell's *The Rainbow.*

Now lovers, Mellors (Erno Crisa) and Connie (Danielle Darrieux) embrace by the firelight in the gamekeeper's hut. Marc Allegret's *L'Amant de Lady Chatterley.*

At sea in marriage and apparently content to be there, Harriet (Judy Davis) and Richard (Colin Friels) begin the only love scene in Tim Burstall's *Kangaroo*. Courtesy Ross Dimsey.

Seeming to pose for their formal portrait, Lawrence and two of his ladies in waiting (dressed alike) contemplate the ruins of Monte Alban, in Oaxaca, Mexico. *Left to right:* Ian McKellen as D. H. Lawrence, Penelope Keith as Dorothy Brett, and Janet Suzman as Frieda Lawrence. Christopher Miles's *Priest of Love.*

# 4
# Foxes and Gypsies on Film:
# They Steal Chickens, Don't They?

At least in theory, Lawrence's short novels should offer the optimum starting point for successful cinematic transformation. Their genre seems to promise a balance between two difficult extremes for filmmakers: an opportunity to avoid the expansions and interpolations of *The Rocking Horse Winner* and the condensations of *Sons and Lovers*. In his review of Christopher Miles's film of *The Virgin and the Gipsy*, John Simon reaches the same conclusion when he writes, "The novella may be just about the only form of fiction that readily lends itself to cinematic adaptation: it is long enough to offer the filmmaker a sufficiency of material to use, expand, or drop; but it is not so long as to oblige him to cut ruthlessly and disfiguringly, nor so short as to force him into wholesale inventions and additions."[1] This reference to the cinematic advantages of the short novel is a familiar one, echoed by numerous critics yet surprisingly put into practice by few of the Lawrence filmmakers. The exceptions are two directors, Mark Rydell and Christopher Miles, whose screen adaptations of Lawrence novellas were released close together and during a renaissance period for Lawrence filming in which three high-profile productions appeared in as many years: *The Fox* in 1968, *Women in Love* in 1969, and *Virgin* in 1970.[2]

Mark Rydell's version of *The Fox*, which began this cinematic outburst, was the first Lawrence film to be directed by an American. Rydell's producer, Raymond Stross, maintained the British presence in Lawrence filming, however, as did Anne Heywood, the female lead in *The Fox*, who was also Stross's wife and a former Miss Great Britain. Heywood, as March, was joined by two better known American actors, Sandy Dennis as Banford and Keir Dullea as Paul Grenfel, a renamed version of Lawrence's Henry Grenfel. (After *Sons and Lovers* and *Rocking Horse,* perhaps filmmakers assumed that any Lawrence screen hero had to be named Paul.) Heywood, Dennis, and Dullea were virtually the film's entire cast. Rydell's screenplay for the production was written by Lewis John Carlino and Howard Koch—the same Howard Koch who cowrote the script for *Casablanca* with Julius J. and Philip G. Epstein. Photography was by William Fraker and musical score by Lalo Schifrin.[3]

The second novella on film was a British production of Lawrence's *The Virgin and the Gipsy,* released forty years after the text's posthumous publication with the slightly edited title *The Virgin and the Gypsy.* This film was directed by Christopher Miles, a member of a well-known theatrical family. Like Mark Rydell two years earlier, Miles was using Lawrence to make his debut as a director. Miles's title characters were played by Joanna Shimkus, a Canadian model-turned-actress, and the Italian actor Franco Nero, both new faces and potential stars in the mid-1960s. *Virgin* surrounded its young leads with veterans of the British stage and screen, including Fay Compton as Granny (a diminished version of Lawrence's formidable Mater), Kay Walsh as Aunt Cissie, Maurice Denham as the Rector, and Norman Bird as Uncle Fred. Honor Blackman and Mark Burns appeared as Mrs. Simon Fawcett and Major Eastwood. Kenneth Harper produced the film, with script by the British playwright Alan Plater, who would later write the screenplays for *Priest of Love* (1981) and *Coming Through* (1985). Photography for *Virgin* was by Bob Huke and musical score was provided by Patrick Gowers.

Several similarities in cast and crew link *The Fox* and *Virgin,* not the least of which is that both films were the work of first-time directors. In addition, both female leads were models with little acting experience beforehand and short-lived careers after their appearance in the Lawrence films. Anne Heywood's film career ended almost immediately after *The Fox.* After *Virgin,* Joanna Shimkus played a series of promising roles in unpromising films before marrying Sidney Poitier in 1976 and ending her acting career.[4] By contrast, both male leads went on to enjoy long-term if artistically mixed careers. They came to their roles in *The Fox* and *Virgin* already having enjoyed prominence in successful productions. Dullea starred in Frank Perry's *David and Lisa* in 1962 and in the 1964 screen adaptation of James Jones's *Thin Red Line.* Nero portrayed Sir Lancelot in the 1967 musical *Camelot,* so trading sword and armor for his raggle-taggle outfit may have seemed a comedown. After *The Fox,* Dullea continued in a series of roles, frequently offbeat, that stood him in good stead well into the 1980s, with his best-known work as David Bowman, the astronaut in Stanley Kubrick's *2001: A Space Odyssey* (1968) and again in its unfortunate sequel, *2010* (1984). Nero appeared in dozens of films, many made in his native Italy. In the 1990s, he costarred with

Bruce Willis in *Die Hard 2: Die Harder,* a title which unintentionally applies less to Willis than to Nero's own survival skills within the film industry.

A final figure deserving mention here is Sandy Dennis, who played Jill Banford in *The Fox.* She had previously starred in *Splendor in the Grass* (1961), *Up the Down Staircase* (1967), and the screen version of *Who's Afraid of Virginia Woolf?* (1966), where as Edward Albee's vapidly nasty Honey she won an Oscar for best supporting actress. Despite Pauline Kael's damning and disconcertingly apt comment that Dennis "made an acting style out of postnasal drip," she continued on in several significant if not stellar roles before her death in 1993.[5] Among the best known of Dennis's later films were *The Four Seasons* (1981), *Come Back to the Five and Dime, Jimmy Dean, Jimmy Dean* (1982), and *Parents* (1989).

When *The Fox* and *The Virgin and the Gypsy* first appeared, both films received mixed responses with most of the praise directed at *Virgin* and much of the criticism aimed at *The Fox.* Reviewers tended to stress *Virgin's* fidelity to the text or to "the Lawrence quality," in Hollis Alpert's words, which he suggests "comes through clearly, gracefully, and tellingly."[6] Penelope Gilliatt, writing for the *New Yorker,* concluded by observing that "If you care for Lawrence . . . the film is likely to strike you as truthfully done and satisfying."[7] Initial reviewers tended to praise Joanna Shimkus's performance as Lawrence's Yvette (with the most extreme, almost adoring tribute coming from John Simon) and to condemn Franco Nero's rendering of the gypsy.[8] The major exception to this came from Stanley Kauffmann, who referred to Shimkus in his review for the *New Republic* as "an Anglo-French Candice Bergen: a pretty girl who, by trying to act and failing, makes herself unpretty."[9] Beyond the reviews, *Virgin* went on to receive further recognition by winning the United Kingdom Film Critics Award for Best British Film and the U.S. Film Critics Award for Best Foreign Film.[10]

*The Fox,* by contrast, received no awards, nor were its reviewers as kind to the director, the cast, or the production as a whole. John Simon's comments reflected the reviewers' general disappointment with the film. He offered lukewarm praise for its minor elements, such as photography and musical score, but viewed the film's explicit sexuality as sensationalist, commercially motivated, and reductive of Lawrence's text. Atypically Simon praised Anne Heywood's performance as March (and, curiously, that of the fox playing himself). He described Keir Dullea as an indifferent Paul Grenfel who merely looked right for the part and damned Sandy Dennis as abominable. Simon's savaging of Dennis, in fact, makes Pauline Kael's comment about postnasal drip seem almost complimentary. Simon quoted Kael and then added that Sandy Dennis "balances her postnasal condition with something like prefrontal lobotomy, so that when she is not a walking catarrh she is a blithering imbecile." Unwilling to leave ill enough alone, Simon continued by cataloging Dennis's facial expressions and gestures in *The Fox* as "a sick smile befitting a calf's head in a butcher shop, an embryonic laugh that emerges as an aural stillbirth, and an epic case of the fidgets." He concluded by suggesting that Dennis's rendering of Banford offers the film audience "not so much a performance as a field trip for students of clinical psychiatry."[11]

By far the most balanced and thoughtful review of *The Fox* came from Pauline Kael, whose *New Yorker* article discussed it along with the screen adaptation of Carson McCullers's *Reflections in a Golden Eye*. Here Kael expressed disappointment with the Lawrence film that parallels Simon's, yet without his subjectivity or nastiness. Typically, Kael also used her review to pursue larger issues than merely the judgment of one or two particular films. Movies adapted from books tend to fail, she suggested, at the point where they "attempt to modernize or clarify the author and to 'fill out' the author's material" for a supposedly up-to-date or "savvy" movie audience. Thus for Kael, "Making Lawrence More Lawrentian" (the title of her review), or trying to, was Rydell and his colleagues' fatal mistake—one which always "has the odd result of making . . . movies seem novelistic when they depart most from the novels" upon which they are based.[12]

In the years following their release, *The Fox* and *Virgin* have continued to invite discussion among film scholars and literary critics, especially those committed to Lawrence studies. Among the earliest of such discussions were two review-essays by G. B. Crump published in the *D. H. Lawrence Review*, focusing separately on each film (1968 and 1971). These studies were followed by a second pair of essays appearing in the 1973 premier issue of *Literature/Film Quarterly*: Joan Mellen's "Outfoxing Lawrence: Novella into Film," and Julian Smith's "Vision and Revision: *The Virgin and the Gypsy* as Film." Breaking with the pattern of parallel essays, Michael Klein and Gillian Parker's 1981 anthology, *The English Novel and the Movies*, ignored *The Fox* but offered a detailed examination of *Virgin* in S. E. Gontarski's essay "An English Watercolor." One limitation of many of these studies, and others like them, is that they seem text-bound and, as a result, tend to approach the films with the single purpose of measuring fidelity to the original. Studies of these films from the literary rather than the cinematic perspective, especially the two Crump essays, fall most readily into this pattern—not an error exactly, since trueness to text does count, but rather an unwillingness to see possibilities beyond this single standard of evaluation. Two worthwhile exceptions to such critical nearsightedness are the Gontarski and Smith studies of *Virgin*, with both critics demonstrating an impressive depth of understanding and sensitivity to the films and source texts alike.

It is somewhat surprising, in reviewing the critical literature on *The Fox and Virgin* films, to realize that they have never been examined together or compared—surprising because many connections seem evident between the two films as well as the two Lawrence novellas upon which they are based. G. B. Crump positions himself for a comparative analysis of *The Fox* and *Virgin,* as one writer publishing on both films for the same journal and within a relatively short period of time. Crump's article on *Virgin,* however, never looks back at *The Fox* but instead compares Christopher Miles's film to Ken Russell's recently released *Women in Love.* A second commentator, Neil Sinyard, also seems about to study *The Fox* and *Virgin* together in his book *Filming Literature,* which contains a discussion of Lawrence on screen and which refers to *Virgin* in its general introduction as the only successful movie based on a Lawrence work.[13] Sinyard's subsequent chapter on Lawrence ("Another Fine Mess: D. H. Lawrence and Thomas Hardy on Film") offers a brief discussion of *The Fox* yet (inexplicably given his earlier praise) never returns to *Virgin* at all.

In addition to the "English Watercolor" article on *Virgin,* S. E. Gontarski has contributed a major resource to students of both films—not a direct comparison yet a uniquely implicit one. In the early 1980s, Gontarski published interviews with Christopher Miles and Mark Rydell, asking specific and parallel questions about their films and inviting them to look back fourteen years and attempt to assess their achievements. What's clear from these interviews, if not an overt contrast between films, is a revealing juxtaposition of filmmakers, a view of their creative awareness during the cinematic process and of their accomplishments recollected in tranquillity well over a decade later. Christopher Miles continues to be proud of *Virgin,* but Mark Rydell adopts a somewhat defensive tone in explaining to Gontarski that what had seemed sexually daring in 1968 might seem heavy-handed and obvious in 1982.[14] It is also revealing to learn from these interviews that censorship continued to track the Lawrence filmmakers even into the late 1960s. For Rydell, the effort to alter and suppress came from his own studio rather than from governmental committees as it did with Cardiff in 1960 and Pelissier in 1949. Rydell reveals to Gontarski that *The Fox* was filmed in Canada "to get away from the controlling interest" of the studio, which feared public outcry at the movie's explicit sexuality and was especially worried about a scene in which Anne Heywood, as March, masturbates before her bathroom mirror.[15] In the changed cultural climate of the 1960s, Rydell won the battle that both of his more restricted predecessors had lost in making the earlier Lawrence films. *The Fox,* unlike either *Rocking Horse* or *Sons and Lovers,* reached the screen and public untouched by anyone except the filmmakers themselves.[16]

More generally, in relation to censorship and the late 1960s, it is clear from the Gontarski interviews that in filming Lawrence Miles and Rydell consciously saw themselves as cultural visionaries, using their work to articulate, and even to help create, the values of what seemed to them a revolutionary era. This self-perception on the part of both directors is important because *The Fox* and *Virgin* lay claim to an identity as artifacts of a particular historical moment. Separate from the question of any universal or enduring significance these films may possess, both survive as period pieces of a unique point in our century—rereadings and rewritings of Lawrence shaped by radical perspectives that were challenging America and the West at the turn of a troubled decade. In 1968, Mark Rydell took sexual liberation from among such perspectives as his special cause and singled out a Lawrence text to transform into what he still insisted, fourteen years later, was "a very brave film; a kind of blow for freedom and against censorship." Rydell described *The Fox* to Gontarski as "the first in this move toward sweeping aside conventional concepts of what can or can not be articulated on film. Certainly, the film industry had never seen anything so daring, and so I feel happily responsible for reflecting the need of our period to tell the truth about sexuality and stop hiding and stop glamorizing and artificializing sexuality at the very least."[17]

Telling the truth about sexuality might seem a tall order for a 110-minute film, yet to anyone viewing *The Fox* Rydell's goal of challenging sexual limits is certainly achieved and even overachieved. The heavy-handedness in the film, finally even to Rydell himself, results partly from his attempt to turn *The Fox* into an erotic show-and-tell of sorts, a graphic demonstration of several sexual options available to humankind. The on-screen catalog includes heterosexuality (Heywood and Dullea in the barn), lesbianism (Heywood and Dennis in bed or in the snow), and masturbation (Heywood and her bathroom mirror). Reversing the studio's worries about such explicitness, the film's promoters seemed concerned that 1968 audiences might wrongly assume from its title that *The Fox* was a nature movie and remain at home. As a result, Rydell's film gained an unofficial subtitle shortly after its release, being billed in newspaper ads and on theater marquees as *The Fox—Symbol of the Male.* The film became notorious, probably without needing a subtitle, and movie audiences lined up around the block to see it.[18] Its visibility and impact were also evident in the immediate attention it received from commentators at distant and opposed quarters of the cultural spectrum. Kate Millett took note of *The Fox* in *Sexual Politics* (1970) as one of many examples of "the woman as homosexual . . . today as decidedly a [male] sexual object [just] as other women" are. "Hollywood's *The Fox* and other productions of popular cinema [which present lesbian or exclusively feminine relationships] are . . . likely to be directed at masculine audiences."[19] Seeming to bear out Millett's contention, *Playboy* magazine had recently treated its largely male readership to a photo-essay on *The Fox* in which Heywood's lesbian and auto-erotic scenes were graphically and colorfully displayed.[20]

Also sexually daring by 1970 standards, Christopher Miles's *Virgin* was not as methodically explicit as *The Fox* nor was Miles deliberately championing eroticism as the film's major cause. In his 1983 interview with Gontarski, he emphasized a preoccupation separate from sexual liberation yet equally reflective of the changing values of the period. Miles's stated intention in *Virgin* was to speak out for youth through his film—to represent the discontent of young people, particularly their sense of entrapment within an aging social structure and behavioral code. He told Gontarski, "The whole point of the film is to establish the Virgin herself in the rectory, to establish the frustration of the young people." Miles justified his decision to change Lawrence's ending in accord with this central theme. Whereas Lawrence's Yvette remains at home after the flood and her rescue by the gipsy, Miles felt it essential to conclude by severing her family ties and allowing her to escape. "I'm saying that I wanted to give her complete freedom," he told Gontarski. "I did not want to trap her back under the family wing in the movie. I wanted to give her total freedom to go off with this fun couple, the Eastwoods, to London or wherever they were going, and let her find her liberation with this charming couple."[21]

Miles's revised ending and the film's general insistence on youth over age must have moved young audiences at the time of its release. In fact, *Virgin* still has its electrifying moments for such audiences thirty years later. In one of the film's many collisions between Yvette and her elders, the Rector delivers an ultimatum that all her rebellious behavior must cease at once. "It can't go on, Yvette," he tells his daughter. "Of course it can," she replies. "It will go on. Because one day I'll be alive and you'll all be dead."[22] Yvette's deadly counterthrust is pure screen interpolation, Miles's or Plater's line and not Lawrence's. It is also one point in the film that continues to touch young viewers. College seniors watching *Virgin* today, in their habitual poses of sophistication and detachment, applaud, cheer, and even stand up when Yvette condemns Daddy, Granny, and Cissie to death.[23]

Perhaps Yvette's verbal violence is especially meaningful to today's crop of twenty-somethings and indicative of their frustrations because so many of them finish school only to reoccupy the stale nest—exactly what Yvette and her sister Lucille do in the film and in Lawrence's text. Despite some striking moments like Yvette's killer line, however, both *The Fox* and *Virgin* can easily strike contemporary viewers of all ages as dated and therefore as nothing more than relics of an interesting but remote decade. A valid question, then, is whether these films survive their own youthful and once-radical timeliness in any major way, either by capturing Lawrence's enduring substance on screen or else by establishing some measure of universality on their own.

The surfaces of the two films, story line and plot, seem to offer little by way of a positive answer here, only added evidence of the late 1960s period piece or else of that most dismal universal, two hours of erotic entertainment on screen. Plot development in *The Fox,* and even in the more sedate *Virgin,* all too often becomes merely a vehicle for sexually provocative scenes. Regardless of the motives behind this, radical ideals or box office profits, the results are similar: a reduction of Lawrence's two texts or an externalization of their unique and artistically compelling erotic inwardness.

In light of Mark Rydell's deliberate sexual agenda, *The Fox* is an especially easy target for this charge and a rich source of embarrassing examples. Rather than dreaming out her stifled erotic wishes like Lawrence's heroine and in sleep imagining a brilliant, singing fox, March plays her guitar and sings a song of her own, "Roll It Over," a bawdy ballad obviously directed at Paul Grenfel. Rather than the quick, brushing kiss Lawrence's Henry offers March to seal his inept proposal, the film's more mature and experienced Paul locks her in a prolonged and passionate tongue twister, Hollywood's erotic trademark. A change of clothing for March becomes a moment of transformation both in Rydell's film and in Lawrence's novella. In the text, however, March's discarding of her sexually ambiguous "land girl's uniform" in favor of "a dress of dull, green silk crape" has the effect of quelling Henry's passion rather than exciting it and of predicting the responsibilities and complications that a permanent union with her will involve.[24] In the film, when Anne Heywood's Ellen makes her entrance wearing a dress for the first time (its color changed from green to passionate pink), the effect on Paul Grenfel is instant, predictable, and utterly opposed to the complex implications of the text. He spirits her off to the barn, and they consummate their relationship audibly if not visibly.

Even Banford falls victim to the filmmakers' urge in *The Fox* to externalize Lawrence and his characters.[25] Her lesbianism is made overt in the film, whereas in the text it remains latent or even uncertain. The film also seems compelled to explain the causes of Jill's "abnormality," and it has her describe a traumatic date rape or near rape to March, an experience which we are to understand has permanently changed her life and her feelings about men. Beyond this outing of Banford, the film is also responsible, ironically enough, for her re-normalization soon afterwards. In two consecutive exchanges, March and Paul both suggest that, deep down, Banford might find him attractive and that her "real" problem is simply that she lacks a man:

> *Banford:* I hate the sight of him.
> *March:* Do you? I'm not so sure.

In the scene with Paul, immediately following this exchange, the same suggestion turns ugly, sexist, and downright dangerous when Keir Dullea takes hold of Sandy Dennis as he speaks his lines and seems about to attempt another rape:

> *Paul:* How come you never got married, Miss Banford? You're not bad looking. Features are good. Nice legs. But you never had a man.

I think that's really your problem. That's really what you want, isn't it? Isn't that what you need?

Always more delicate, Christopher Miles's *Virgin* never falls into sexism and sexternalization this blatant, yet it still disturbs Lawrence's erotic indeterminacy by forcing it to the surface. In the text, Lawrence's suggestive yet evasive description of the virgin's final encounter with the gipsy continues to raise controversy and debate among critics over whether sexual consummation actually occurs: "And though his body, wrapped round her strange and lithe and powerful, like tentacles, rippled with shuddering as an electric current, still the rigid tension of the muscles that held her clenched steadied them both, and gradually the sickening violence of the shuddering, caused by shock, abated, in his body first, then in hers, and the warmth revived between them. And as it roused, their tortured, semi-conscious minds became unconscious, they passed away into sleep."[26] While some readers insist that what this passage describes is the end of Yvette's maidenhood, others suggest that her loss of innocence is an emotional transformation, not necessarily physical at all. Since the power of Lawrence's passage lies precisely in its balanced ambivalence, this debate like many other textual debates will never be resolved.

Miles, however, has resolved it too easily with a film convention as familiar as the Hollywood kiss in *The Fox*. This convention is Yvette's "morning after" scene in which her appearance and behavior form a code well known to movie audiences across several generations. It tells us indirectly but in no uncertain terms that the screen heroine has enjoyed a night of sexual fulfillment. The scene shifts Lawrence's textual setting from Yvette's bedroom to her father's—the change implying that her sexual awakening is partly a rebellion against his moral priggishness and hypocrisy. What the camera reveals as this scene opens is pure film cliché: the heroine smiling in her sleep, her face radiant (with the help of makeup), and her hair beautifully spread upon the pillow in a new style—all of this despite her life-and-death struggle in the flood just a few hours earlier. These details are the standard tropes of filmmaking, employed here by Miles as visual conceits for Yvette's loss of virginity and sexual transformation.[27]

While such contrived imagery does not saturate *Virgin*, instances of the sexually obvious, or again of cinematic externalization, do crop up. Miles, for example, insists on establishing his gypsy's machismo and sexual credentials early on as preparation for his final possession of Yvette. Thus the gypsy and the Saywells' chambermaid, Mary, are depicted as covert lovers during much of the film, and the couple eventually are discovered *in flagrante delicto* by a shocked and somewhat envious Yvette. Likewise, and in parallel to *The Fox*, this film also tinkers with Lawrence's textual colors in order to allow its heroine a scarlet scene. A "dress

. . . of blue silk velours" (44) in the novella leads to a violent quarrel with Aunt Cissie and, finally, to the Mater's blurted insult that her granddaughters "come of half-depraved stock" (48). This scene is preserved, only with Yvette gaining both the last word in the quarrel ("you'll all be dead") and the chance to show off her legs in an unfinished and revealing red dress.

*Virgin* can even lay claim to its own masturbation scene, again following the dubious lead of *The Fox*. Unlike March's mirror sequence, this scene is thinly symbolic rather than overt and perhaps even clumsier as a result. It occurs just after the Eastwoods appear at the gypsy camp and Yvette meets them for the first time. As in the text, she agrees to ride home in their car, interrupting a flirtation with the gypsy that is clearly leading toward seduction. In the novella, Yvette and the Eastwoods simply leave to end Lawrence's sixth chapter. In the film, as their car pulls away, the camera focuses on Franco Nero's gypsy, who sits with his legs apart, holding a small wooden twig in a position and at an angle which can only be described as penile. He also holds a knife, and we see his hand moving back and forth, whittling the twig until it has been reduced to almost nothing. He suddenly throws the mutilated bit of wood away to complete the scene and the film's weakest moment in a gesture of sexual anticlimax and frustration.[28]

A separate link between the two film plots deserves attention here because it helps account for the problem of externalization by seeming to oppose it. Both films foreground Lawrence's sexual writing in these texts, so that his covert eroticism becomes simplified and fully visible, often reductively visible. Reversing this, a different body of Lawrence's writing in "The Fox" and *The Virgin and the Gipsy* suffers censorship in the films simultaneous with their overexposure of his sexual material. The censored writing in both texts is that having anything to do with war. Lawrence wrote World War I deeply into this pair of short novels, to the point that it functions as an absent yet crucial component of plot. Banford and March, for example, wouldn't even be on the land, trying to run a farm in place of the missing men, if it weren't for the war. Beyond this, Henry Grenfel is a soldier just returned from overseas, awaiting discharge and sick nearly to death of military life. Major Eastwood and the gipsy are both veterans. They served together in the same unit and, in an even deeper bond, were both near-fatal casualties of the war—resurrected men, in the Major's words, who were almost killed yet who clutched so tightly to life that they came through.

Potentially dramatic as this material might be, it is suppressed within the two films and, in fact, erased entirely from *The Fox*. Unlike Henry Grenfel, his screen counterpart Paul is purely a civilian, transformed from a soldier to a merchant seaman on leave because his ship is home for a refit. No war or aftereffect of war plays any part in this film. War is at least implied in Christopher Miles's *Virgin*. Major Eastwood retains his rank, and the Window Fund, as in the text, is meant for a stained-glass memorial to the fallen. Beyond these scant references, however, Miles's film, like Rydell's, has been virtually demilitarized. Except for his rank, Major Eastwood is as much a civilian as Paul. No reference is made to his military background, nor is any hint given that he has experienced combat and become its victim. The same is true for Franco Nero's gypsy, so that when he and Eastwood meet they can talk only about horses and not about the ordeal they shared in the text.[29]

It seems no mystery that two films made near the turn of a decade in turmoil would be this consistent in their inconsistency, flaunting sexuality during a sexual revolution and concealing war from a public already poisoned by it in real life. In 1968, when *The Fox* was released, Americans were becoming familiar with place-names like Hue and Khe Sanh and with grim celebrations like Tet. By the time *Virgin* appeared in 1970, *My Lai* and *Vietnamization* had been added to our vocabularies, and Vietnam veterans were coming home in ever-increasing numbers. Like Henry Grenfel, Americans had "seen enough of rifles" to last a lifetime—real rifles for some and, for the rest of us, rifles on television every night at six.[30] We did not need to go to the movies for more.[31]

Such similarities of plot in *The Fox* and *Virgin* seem to return us to the same fact about these films—their shared identity as pieces of cultural history. Perhaps the first hint of what is beyond this, and the first measure of artistic distinction between the films, presents itself in the very issue now under study: the on-screen distortion of text. In *The Fox*, Rydell's erasure of Lawrence's war material proves to be consistent with a tendency to cut in all areas except the sexual. Also omitted from the film, for instance, is Henry Grenfel's intense scene with his captain as he pleads for a leave he doesn't deserve, a miniature but remarkable battle of wills that Henry wins in anticipation of his larger victories over Banford and March. The loss of this exchange is, of course, a result of the film's demilitarization, yet some version of it surely could have been worked back into the script. Gone as well is Lawrence's tragicomic involvement of Banford's parents in the episode of her death, a curious development of plot that both complicates and humanizes the event. What remains after Rydell's cuts is Lawrence's stark triangle and little else, with the film's single focus creating a sense of entrapment as the audience watches Banford, March, and Paul fighting it out alone in their isolated farmhouse.

In *Virgin*, by contrast, Christopher Miles's omission of war from the plot runs counter to his general strategy of expansion. Several major changes add rather than subtract through film interpolations based on very slight material in the text or even upon no material at all. Leo Wetherell's proposal to Yvette at a casual party and her equally casual response are broadened, for example, into a major confrontation between the couple during the overblown celebration of Leo's twenty-first birthday. Unlike her textual counterpart, Yvette explicitly denounces Leo and declares her independence from his conventional, middle-class world. Similarly, Lawrence's one-sentence reference to *Mary in the Mirror* (36–37), a show the sisters produce to raise money for the Window Fund, emerges as a major event in the film. The performance itself, converted into a "daring" Continental revue, appears in detail, along with rehearsals, a family critique the next day, and even a scene in which the Eastwoods arrive at the hall only to be turned away and insulted by the Rector. The ongoing affair between the gypsy and Mary the chambermaid is purely a celluloid invention, having no original basis in the text at all.

Looking back at the two Lawrence films discussed in previous chapters, I'm inclined to suggest that *The Fox* pursues a general cinematic strategy like that of *Sons and Lovers,* Jack Cardiff's strategy of condensation, while *Virgin* adopts the techniques of expansion and interpolation first seen in Anthony Pelissier's *Rocking Horse Winner.* If such a four-way comparison is valid, it is somewhat surprising to realize that filming a novella, frequently identified as the optimum genre for screen adaptation, doesn't seem to offer any particular advantage to Miles or Rydell or to place constraints on their inclination to manipulate the text. Two Lawrence works of middle length—close, actually, to film script length—remain cinematic starting points no more privileged than his short story or long novel. They are simply raw material for two filmmakers to shrink or expand as they see fit.

Without question, the key instance of Mark Rydell's shrinkage of text is his decision to omit March's dreaming from *The Fox.* In Lawrence's original, two dreams serve as clear windows to March's otherwise bolted-and-shut personality. Through one, the reader first sees her sexual longing in the vision of the brilliant, singing fox, a bearer of pleasure and pain combined. In the second dream, as March prepares Banford's coffin, the reader glimpses beyond Eros toward a darker desire, March's wish to be rid of her companion even if this can only be accomplished through death.[32] The erasure of these two dreams from *The Fox* on film represents a major mistake as well as a major condensation, since they could have provided Rydell a revealing and cinematically effective inward view of his central character. Without such a perspective, the filmmaker is forced to fall back on plot, as has been seen, and its purely external demonstrations of human motive and personality—a bawdy song to express sexual invitation or, more blatant, masturbation to act out sexual need. In his 1982 interview with S. E. Gontarski, Mark Rydell acknowledged the general influence of Ingmar Bergman on his career as a film director, and he specifically mentioned *The Silence* as the source and inspiration for March's masturbation scene.[33] One can only wonder why Rydell was not equally inspired by Bergman's ability to incorporate powerful dream sequences into his own films. Bergman's success with this technique, in fact, seems to guarantee that literary and cinematic expression could have been reconciled in *The Fox* had Rydell used his mentor to guide him creatively back to the text.

As with most erasures, Rydell's obliteration of March's dreams is not complete, so a faint trace of the original remains—too faint, unfortunately, to be very meaningful or effective. Early in the film, March and Banford's pursuit of their escaped cow, Eurydice, allows Rydell his first opportunity to establish the lesbian relationship between the two women. Their chase after the cow leads to a playful tumble in the snow, with snow serving throughout the film as the objectification of lesbianism as Rydell sees it, white-cold and sterile. As the snow fight progresses, the scene takes an openly sexual turn. March climbs astride Banford and begins pouring snow into her friend's mouth. At this point, a rare shift occurs in Rydell's routinely realistic approach to *The Fox*—a cautious venture into something beyond it that suggests at least the impulse, if not the resolve, to follow Bergman and Lawrence's artistic lead into dreaming. The shift begins with a stop-action view of March's face as she looks down at her companion. The screen then flashes to red, then to four separate stopped views of Banford's face, each preceded by a flash-to-black. The effect of this sequence is exactly as if the audience were viewing four separate color slides of Banford lying in the snow. The fourth and final "slide" is followed by another flash to red, after which realistic action resumes with March telling Banford, "You're getting cold."

On one level, the four views of Banford, lying open-mouthed, suggest sexual arousal and thus reinforce the realistic intention behind this homoerotic scene. On a less overt level, Banford's appearance is also just slightly corpselike, hinting (with help from Rydell's stopped action) that she has experienced death rather than orgasm in the snow. This suggestion becomes a prophecy of Banford's death, exactly as March's second dream is in the text. Also, since the entire stop-action scene begins and ends with March staring down at Banford, it implies that we are seeing what March sees (Banford aroused) but perhaps also what March wishes to see (Banford dead). This too places Rydell's brief departure from realism into close parallel with Lawrence's textual dreaming and in particular with March's darker dream, the wish-fulfillment vision of Banford's corpse. Unfortunately, this scene remains an isolated example of what might have been possible by way of transformative fidelity to the text. After it ends, Rydell resumes his strategy of minimalism and sexual naturalism virtually until the close of the film. He does return to the stop-action mode once more and at a critical moment that bears out the suggestions just provided. When Banford lies in the snow a second time, now really dead, the scene again ends with a freeze-frame close-up of March's face.

March's dreaming in Lawrence's text serves a wider purpose than the exposure of her humanity from within. Beyond this, it also reinforces the "Sleeping

Beauty" subtext of "The Fox," a familiar Lawrence motif that he never seems to tire of weaving into his works. It is not entirely surprising then to discover that *The Virgin and the Gipsy* and "The Fox" are both variations on this theme. March and Yvette are entranced maidens, asleep in spirit and in sexual body. They slumber and sometimes dream in a prison where men are either absent or diminished and where controlling yet essentially sterile women preside—women like Banford, Aunt Cissie, or the Mater. This prison is penetrated by a male intruder, the gipsy or Henry Grenfel, a stranger who challenges the controlling figures and attempts to steal the maidens away. If he succeeds, Sleeping Beauty may awaken from her trance. Her female captors will be defeated in the ensuing struggle and possibly destroyed.

In "The Fox," Lawrence makes use of his Sleeping Beauty motif effectively to reveal and develop March's paralysis of resolve, her unwillingness to choose between the limitations of the familiar and the hazards of the unknown. Thus her typical response to Henry and Banford is no response at all—a spellbound silence, as Lawrence repeatedly calls it, in the face of their conflicting and strident demands. In Mark Rydell's film of *The Fox,* all trace of this entranced and conflicted quality disappears from March's personality along with her two vivid dreams. Anne Heywood's portrayal of Lawrence's heroine never achieves her complexity of character or conveys her ambivalence of will. Quite the opposite, March comes across as a fully alert and powerful woman, decisive in her actions and aware of her desires and how to fulfill them.

With *The Virgin and the Gypsy,* by contrast, an interesting reversal of emphasis occurs as the Sleeping Beauty story moves from text to screen. In the original, Lawrence identifies Yvette as his entranced maiden, yet far less insistently and less frequently than he does with March. Yvette's particular trance is associated primarily with her youth rather than with any deep ambiguity of being. Not a child anymore, nor yet an adult, she seems to be waiting passively and rather heedlessly for the transition to occur. Being very young, she is usually unaware of her own feelings and always unaware of those of others. She remains detached and vague, as Lawrence describes and redescribes her. Unlike Mark Rydell, who cancels March's inwardness, Christopher Miles takes Yvette's spellbound vagueness as the starting point for her characterization and eventually develops it beyond the text. Her passive, waiting state is conveyed through a series of vivid close-up sequences, the most compelling of which occurs as Yvette stares silently and bemusedly alongside a massive leaking dam, a precursor of the flood that will eventually liberate her.

Moving inward from such scenes, Miles permits Yvette to dream, as if salvaging and putting to effective use what Mark Rydell had discarded from Lawrence's "The Fox." Yvette's dreams have no basis in the text and thus provide strong examples of Miles's tendency to interpolate—to inscribe upon *The Virgin and the Gipsy* rather than simply erase. Unlike March's dreams in "The Fox," Yvette's do not occur as she sleeps. Instead, they are waking fantasies, closer to consciousness than dreams, yet still capable of providing vision and entrance into Yvette's hidden self. Both of her fantasies involve the gypsy and are grounded in memories of past encounters with him.

The first, some thirty-eight minutes into the film, allows Yvette's imagination to reconfigure their initial meeting during an excursion in Leo Wetherell's car. In the real scene Franco Nero's gypsy leaves his cart after it has blocked Leo's motorcar and begins walking toward him. He climbs on the car's running board, at first seeming to menace Leo, then suddenly invites both couples to have their fortunes told. What the film audience sees in Yvette's fantasy re-vision of this incident is, first, an altered repetition of the gypsy's movements, initiated with a flash-to-white. In the dream version, he does not pause to confront Leo but continues to the rear of the car and to Yvette. Where in reality she wears a long overcoat and wide hat, concealing her hair and face, she now sits bare-headed and dressed only in a thin white gown. The dream gypsy opens Yvette's car door, and she steps to the ground, leaving her companions behind. The entire fantasy sequence plays with every figure frozen except Yvette and the gypsy, who move in slow motion. The sequence is also wordless, the original dialogue having been replaced by a musical theme that matches the movements of the two central figures. As Yvette joins the gypsy, this music and the entire fantasy are broken by the sound of a domestic bell that returns the dreamer and the film audience to the dull realities of Saywell life.

Yvette's second fantasy, nearly an hour into the film, follows this first one closely in style and form. The screen flashes to white again, intruding upon a family discussion of the stained-glass window and allowing Yvette her own window of opportunity to repeat and improve upon the past. This time she returns to the moment when she and the gypsy were interrupted by the Eastwoods' arrival at his camp. He has just removed her overcoat and now goes on, in fantasy, to remove her dress and slip as well. Yvette stands nude, her arms concealing her breasts and then turns toward the gypsy as they embrace. As before, the dream scene plays in slow motion and to the same musical theme. Now, however, Miles adds a variation to the fantasy by including traces of the Saywells' real conversation as voice-over, barely audible during Yvette's dream. This detail strengthens the suggestion that she has left routine consciousness behind and entered a transfixed state in which all physical senses except hearing have been suspended. Finally, and again as in the first fantasy, both trance and wish-fulfillment are shattered by the ringing of a servant's bell. Yvette is suddenly returned to her family amid their breakfast-table talk of window prices and marmalade.

It is possible but by no means certain that Christopher Miles had "The Fox" and March's dreams in mind when he created these fantasies for Yvette. Whether by accident or design, she experiences two distinct visions, just as March has two distinct dreams in Lawrence's text. Both of Yvette's visions, however, are really screen counterparts or allusions only to March's initial dream, erotic wish-ful-fillments and not death fantasies as March's second dream surely is. Also, Yvette's daydreams about the gypsy are simple and sexually open, almost blatant in comparison to the rich and artistically embroidered dreams that Lawrence wrote into the fabric of "The Fox." Even so, it remains true that Christopher Miles's decision to mix visible and hidden realities in *Virgin* offers him an inroad to Lawrence generally neglected by the other filmmakers examined thus far. Yvette's on-screen fantasies also offer an implicit yet severe critique of Mark Rydell's *The Fox* by demonstrating that human motivation and desire need not be limited to external representation. Character can be penetrated and presented to film audiences and readers alike from inside. We are returned to Yvette's inner visions near the end of *Virgin* and during her actual love scene after the flood. Interspersed amid views of her encounter with the gypsy are momentary flashbacks to the initial car fantasy, then to the fantasy at the encampment, again set to music and shown without accompanying dialogue. Given Miles's insistence that Yvette loses her physical virginity, his reprise of the two fantasies during this scene may be intended to suggest that dream and reality have finally become one.

Unfortunately for *Virgin* as a whole, no character in the film except Yvette is presented from the inside, nor is any major figure developed with an equal degree of originality by the filmmakers. With several other characterizations, in fact, Miles relies heavily on externals, much as Rydell does, to the extent that their two films begin to resemble one another and to disappoint in similar ways. The two heroines, for example, are matched with male leads, or male "intruders," who prove to be remarkably alike and remarkably predictable as lovers. An opposition of sorts does exist between the men, however, involving language and somewhat resembling the reversal of female dreams discussed above. Just as Yvette seems to borrow her dreams from March, or from the "wrong" work, Paul Grenfel seems to steal a tongue from the gypsy and to leave him mute in the process.

Lawrence's textual original, *Henry* Grenfel, possesses little of the gift of gab. Not at all stupid or by any means inarticulate, he is, however, a listener by nature rather than a talker, more eloquent and powerful by far in his silence than in his speech. By contrast, language plays a much greater part in the gipsy's original conception, not in its quantity perhaps but in its resonance. His warning and prophecy to Yvette, late in the work, is speech about speech as metaphor. "Listen for the voice of water" (101). Lawrence also chooses to end the work and provide Yvette her final contact with the gipsy purely through language in the abstract, disembodied note he sends her:

"Dear Miss, I see in the paper you are all right after your ducking, as is the same with me. I hope I see you again one day, maybe
at Tideswell cattle fair, or maybe we come that way again. I come
that day to say goodbye! and I never said it, well, the water give no
time, but I live in hopes. Your obdt. servant Joe Boswell."
And only then she realised that he had a name. (120)

The deceptively simple message is couched in language containing multiple and interrelated references to language. Yvette, reading the note, reads about the gipsy reading about her in the newspaper. Reading further, she learns that his purpose in seeking her out just before the flood was to *say* good-bye. Reading to the close, she learns his name, which demystifies and de-objectifies the gipsy, thus humanizing both him and Yvette through a final stroke of language, the simple but penetrating inscription "Joe Boswell," which ends emotional virginity in hu-man recognition.

Not only does such innocent complexity disappear from *Virgin* on film but any trace of the gypsy as a person with a name and a voice. While some of his orig-inal dialogue is preserved, it is always beaten flat by Franco Nero, who mumbles in a dazed monotone. Rather than words, Nero's primary means of expressing and interpreting his character are gestures and gazes directed mostly at Yvette. In the text when Yvette asks, "How many children have you?" Lawrence's gipsy responds with the odd and linguistically suggestive reply, "Say five" (69). In the counter-part scene on screen, Nero's response typifies the film's muting of the text by omitting the words and replacing them with a silent and meaningless sweep of his hand.

Reversing this silencing process, Mark Rydell loosens his hero's tongue, mak-ing Paul Grenfel resemble Lawrence's gipsy more than he does his own textual counterpart, the quiet listener Henry Grenfel. Paul's discourse, however, is not in-nocent yet meaningful like Joe Boswell's but smooth, flowery, and ultimately dis-honest. Whether flattering March's looks or Banford's cooking, he comes across through Keir Dullea's performance as a dangerous manipulator of language, an emo-tional con man using words to his advantage and as a weapon against both women.

In an important sense, however, this linguistic turnabout doesn't make much difference in the long run. Beneath the gypsy's cloddish silence and Paul Grenfel's sly palaver, the two men are fundamentally alike: sexual and sexist predators. True to the reputations of foxes and gypsies alike, they make off with the chickens every chance they get. Their fixed and frequent gazes at Yvette and March come finally to resemble not the lover beholding his beloved so much as the carnivore about to seize his prey. When he hears of the special way the gipsy gazes at Yvette, Major Eastwood observes, in both the text and film, that "A cat may look at a king" (87). On screen, however, Nero's unnaturally green eyes seem to be locked upon a helpless canary.[34]

It could be maintained that to film both Henry Grenfel and the gipsy as sexual predators is to translate Lawrence quite accurately from page to screen. After all, a great deal of male gazing was written into the text of *The Virgin and the Gipsy* long before anyone thought of making the film. Also, Lawrence's Henry is not a soldier or a farmer at heart but a hunter. The predator-prey relationship is fundamental to his life, informing his erotic pursuit of March as well as his mortal struggle with Banford. What complicates and humanizes both of these Lawrence figures, however, is that deliberate sexual conquest is not their single and simple motive in either text. Both men follow their attractions toward Yvette and March, yet for reasons deep enough to remain partly closed to our understanding as readers and to their own conscious awareness as well. If this were not the case, there would be no critical debate over Yvette's loss of virginity or any hesitation on Henry Grenfel's part when he has the chance to possess March.

By contrast, this degree of complication disappears from the two films where the single and simple issue is deliberate sexual conquest, with *deliberate* proving to be the operative word. Keir Dullea's Paul and Franco Nero's gypsy emerge as calculating seducers, losing all trace of their original spontaneity and ambivalence. During one screen addition to *Virgin,* for instance, the gypsy pressures Yvette insistently to "go riding" with him in a downpour on his "stallion" and toward certain "warm places" that he knows. Despite her fascination, even the virgin seems to look clearly into her gypsy at this point in the film. Finding nothing beyond his transparent sexual demand, she dismisses him—temporarily but with considerable force of character and resolve.

A particular scene in *The Fox* similarly exposes Paul Grenfel's premeditation, yet less directly and in symbolic terms uncharacteristic of this film as a whole. In Lawrence's story, Henry Grenfel kills his animal counterpart almost by chance. He leaves the farmhouse in anger "looking for something to shoot" after overhearing part of a bedroom conversation between Banford and March.[35] Once outside in the winter night, Henry suddenly remembers the fox. "Why not watch for him, anyhow!" he asks himself, in keeping with the impulsive and spontaneous nature Lawrence gives him.[36] When Keir Dullea's Paul Grenfel acts out this incident, he also leaves the farmhouse with murder in his eye but, unlike Henry, already knows exactly what he'll kill and how. Paul selects one of the women's domestic fowl and beheads it, spreading the hen's blood around the barnyard as bait. When the fox appears a few moments later, falling easily into this trap, Paul shoots him to complete his plan. In contrast to Henry Grenfel's skilled yet almost casual conquest of the fox, Paul's stratagem involves entrapment and deliberate cruelty. If there is little spirit of the chase in the death of the fox, surely there is none at all in the execution of the hen. Here, in fact, Lawrence's natural hunter of birds and women seems to give way to a far more sinister figure, the cold-blooded lady killer, practiced in his craft and essentially passionless. During this scene Paul first cradles the hen in his arms, stroking and comforting it so that it won't be afraid. Once certain that the bird trusts him, he calmly chops off its head.[37]

In Lawrence's *Women in Love,* Birkin explains to Gerald that all murder involves consent or at least complicity between victim and killer. "It takes two people to make a murder: a murderer and a murderee. And a murderee is a man who is murderable. And a man who is murderable is a man who in a profound if hidden lust desires to be murdered."[38] Birkin's complete truth presumably includes murderable women, too. One such murderable female, Banford, is felled outright by Henry Grenfel, and the Mater falls victim to nature itself in the form of a flood. The gipsy isn't responsible for this yet may be implicated anyway, since he makes little effort to save her. In these two texts, Lawrence presents both Banford and the Mater to readers as "murderees," women who are so willfully negative in spirit as to invite (and deserve) their own destruction. Outwardly soft and vulnerable, Banford and the Mater are nasty customers at heart who use their cover to manipulate and control others. Banford is Lawrence and Henry's "Evil" and "queer little witch," with "tiny iron breasts" hidden beneath "her soft blouses and chiffon dresses."[39] "Under her old-fashioned lace cap, under her silver hair, under the black silk of her stout, forward-bulging body," the Mater has "a cunning heart, seeking forever her own female power." Her "stony, implacable will-to-power" is slowly devouring the entire family, including Yvette. Like the lipless "old toad," which Yvette discovers emptying the beehive into its gullet, the Mater can't be deterred, only destroyed.[40]

In both texts Lawrence uses these women as images or embodiments of many things he came to detest in human existence: repression, mental will, the urge to control and smother natural vitality. Because of Banford and the Mater's abstract function, their violent deaths in print seem welcome, liberating, and even celebratory events. Another medium, however, presents an entirely different impression of these characters and of what befalls them in the end. It is one thing for Lawrence to write symbolically of Banford's tiny iron breasts. It is quite another to consider Sandy Dennis actually having them. Nor can the Mater be visually likened to a destructive toad or shown graphically as anything but what she is in the flesh, a fragile old lady. Both characters lose all trace of their destructive and largely abstract power on film and tend to strike the viewer as, at worst, minor annoyances to the major characters. Lawrence's queer and evil witch Banford emerges as a whiner, a nag, and a lesbian. While she's still queer, although not in Lawrence's sense of the word, Banford's only evil seems to be affection for March and, because of it, opposition to the menacing Paul. Her crimes on film seem hardly deserving of the cruel, ugly death he brings down upon her. Similarly diminished and defanged, Lawrence's potent Mater is transformed into "Granny," an all but helpless figure whose mortal sins are deafness, extreme old age, and a tendency to pester Yvette and her young friends. Ironically enough, as the films fail to translate these characters from page to screen, they reveal Lawrence's extremes more than their own limitations. In disembodied print, a character may serve brilliantly as vessel for the author's bile—as mental-lifer, power-seeker, witch, toad, and sacrificial scapegoat or murderee. To flesh all this out on screen, however, and present it in ordinary human form is to define its irrational excess—to expose not Banford or the Mater but Lawrence himself.

While hardly inviting her own murder, one figure in *Virgin* does come through as approximating Lawrence's willful female. This is Aunt Cissie, played so strongly by Kay Walsh as to replace Fay Compton's Granny as the Saywells' true dictator and as Yvette's most dangerous antagonist. Walsh's interpretation of Cissie even intensifies Lawrence's character and demonstrates that her poison is nothing but the corrosive overflow of a blocked emotional and physical life. Cissie pounces on Yvette over the Window Fund after several scenes in which she watches the girl's activities through shut and latticed windows, as if from inside a prison. This visual expansion of the window image, along with the nasty delight evident in Cissie's attack, establishes her as a repressed repressor in very Lawrentian terms, a woman whose only remaining pleasure in life is denying others what she herself has been denied.

Beyond the Sleeping Beauty triangle of maiden, oppressor, and male intruder, there are no other characters in *The Fox*. In *Virgin,* however, the central trio is surrounded by a lively chorus of minor figures, some expanded from the text, others invented for the film, and all worthy of notice. In developing his chorus, Christopher Miles may have taken inspiration from *Mary in the Mirror,* the casual title Lawrence gives the Window Fund show produced by Yvette. Miles drops the title but seems to seize the idea behind it, transforming several minor characters (Mary among them) into reflections of the major figures and central issues of the work. Mary, the Saywells' chambermaid and a film addition, serves as a reversed image of Yvette. The two girls are about the same age, but otherwise they live opposite lives, especially in relation to the important human constants of love and labor. Mary is frequently shown performing unpleasant domestic tasks, fetching coal for the Saywells' fire and scrubbing out their kitchen pots, or worse, their chamberpots. Yvette, by contrast, does nothing because she has nothing to do. Finished with school, the youngest daughter of Colgrave's respectable Rector lies dormant, presumably until an appropriate bridegroom turns up. Despite her domestic enslavement, however, Mary possesses a measure of sexual freedom utterly impossible for Yvette. Exempt from middle-class constraints, Mary is more or less at liberty to explore the gypsy's warm places with him whenever she can get away.

A minor male character, Norman Bird's Uncle Fred, also reflects the issue of sexuality in a repressed climate but from a somewhat different perspective. Completely nondescript and neuter in the text, Uncle Fred is expanded into a man of strong appetites barely concealed, a church organist who sings bawdy songs, a chaser of chambermaids and strange women on the street. Uncle Fred as lively closet satyr affords the film a bit of comic relief. In keeping with the traditions of comic relief, his personality and behavior also provide an amusing variation on a serious matter in text and film alike—Eros versus civilization, and Victorian civilization specifically. Yvette's father, as played by Maurice Denham, is represented as sexually dammed-up and damned, much more like Aunt Cissie than Uncle Fred. This portrayal is essentially faithful to the text, yet Miles and his colleagues also develop mirroring qualities in the Rector beyond Lawrence's intention and in accord with the artistic agendas of their own time. One original film scene, for example, brings Reverend Saywell and his daughter face to face during the Window Fund performance. It is here that he insults the Eastwoods and argues with Yvette over children and money. She has allowed some scruffy coal miners' sons into the hall, all clearly Nonconformist rather than Church of England. The Rector is at first annoyed, but consoles himself with the thought that chapel pence will increase high church pounds. When he hears that Yvette hasn't asked the children to pay, his annoyance turns to nastiness and anger. The mirroring here reflects the film's generational rather than sexual oppositions. Miles idealizes the social consciousness and natural virtue of youth by placing it in sharp contrast to the materialistic mean-spiritedness of middle age.

The filmmakers' late 1960s social values are also responsible for the suppression of Lawrence's anti-Semitism in *Virgin*. Although Lawrence insists every chance he gets that Mrs. Simon Fawcett is "probably a Jewess," "a spoilt Jewess," "a bourgeois Jewess: a rich one, probably," every trace of his diatribe is erased from the film.[41] Despite this, John Simon manages to see in Honor Blackman's portrayal of Mrs. Fawcett "a certain Semitic intensity and slightly overrouged vitality," a description which may reveal more about Simon's perceptions than about the film he is reviewing.[42] Ironically, the film actually suffers some loss through the omission of Mrs. Fawcett as "Jewess." More exactly, it misses a good opportunity to use minor figures as mirrors, this time an opportunity which Lawrence takes advantage of in the text. One implication of Mrs. Fawcett's Jewishness is her ethnic opposition to her lover, who is blond, light-skinned, and Nordic. Lawrence's Eastwoods become a gender-reversed reflection of the gipsy and Yvette, with both couples implying an erotic union of opposites—northern light combined with exotic darkness and warmth, privileged race joined with marginalized pariah. The gipsy engulfs Yvette in passionate and humanizing flood just as Mrs. Fawcett melts Major Eastwood, a man associated with snow and ice like Gerald Crich in *Women in Love.*

Unfortunately, all of these reflections disappear on screen along with Lawrence's racial preoccupations. While still depicted as light-skinned and blond, Mark Burns's Major Eastwood is no longer the ice-bound and frozen figure who has experienced resurrection. If anything, he's the more passionate lover, warmer and less repressed than Mrs. Fawcett herself. In a sense, he has been pre-melted on film, not by a Jewish mistress but by his director, Christopher Miles, who associates him with water rather than with Lawrence's snow and ice. Eastwood is shown leading Mrs. Fawcett and Yvette toward a beautiful lake, rowing them across, swimming nude, and discussing love with them while artfully tying fishing flies. With the loss of their Nordic/Semitic opposition, the Eastwoods cease to be minor-key doubles for Yvette and the gypsy, functioning instead as role models and spiritual parents to Yvette who eventually lead her toward freedom.

It is at the conclusion of this film, and of *The Fox* as well, that Lawrence and his screen interpreters seem to part company altogether. In both texts, Lawrence chooses to close with disembodied language that describes and also exemplifies human ambivalence. Joe Boswell's letter ends *The Virgin and the Gipsy,* its uncertain yet hopeful message applying as much to the woman who reads it as to the man who writes it. Perhaps he and Yvette will meet again at Tideswell. Perhaps she has lost her innocence in favor of something better. Having climbed down a ladder alone, perhaps she is now brave enough in body and spirit to begin an independent life. Having fainted in her father's arms, however, perhaps she isn't ready and will continue to languish at home. "The Fox" ends with a lecture instead of a letter, Lawrence's own "long tail" appended to the work with some difficulty in 1921.[43] Hardly flesh and blood, or flesh and fur, this tail also turns out to be pure discourse. It suspends plot and direct presentation of character in favor of a five-page essay on human indeterminacy. Henry Grenfel may have violently "won" March, Lawrence informs us, but he has "not yet got her."[44] For her own part, March wishes to be happy and at peace with Henry. Yet she is of at least two opposing temperaments: active and passive, masculine and feminine, restless and exhausted. Satisfying one temperament will always frustrate the other, so that her complete fulfillment remains impossible. In terms of Lawrence's closing metaphors, March resembles a child demanding two contradictory things at once and struggling, much like Yvette herself, somewhere between wakefulness and sleep.

Discussing this ending during his 1982 interview with S. E. Gontarski, Mark Rydell commented, "You can't in film lecture people" or "end a film with an essay."[45] The same apparently holds true for a letter, especially since Christopher Miles insisted in his interview that it was "a well-known fact . . . gypsies could not write. It is extremely unlikely that in 1922 he would have penned a letter in those eloquent terms to Miss Yvette. Rubbish, rubbish!"[46] What then replaces Lawrence's original rubbish (the ambiguous refuse heap of language) on screen? The reliable automobile, for one thing, which in a strange coincidence conveys both heroines, March and Yvette, out of the picture in the closing scene. Implicit in this all-too-familiar movie vehicle is a journey for both of them away from sexual freedom or youthful independence and back to the safe limits of middle-class life. March has had both her lesbian fling and her premarital roll in the hay with Paul. Now it is time for them to settle down and get serious, the film seems to assure us near the close. We see March and Paul at the end of *The Fox* involved in the trivial pursuits of materialism, an inventory of household goods, with both of them transformed by way of a second change of clothing. March has traded in her mannish farm duds and her seductive pink gown for a conservative tailored outfit. And Paul emerges in a coat and tie for the first time in the film, appropriate attire for taking care of business and, with husbandly yet firm authority, of March herself.

As Yvette rides away in the Eastwoods' convertible to end *The Virgin and the Gypsy*, she may be escaping rather than embracing such constraints with the help of her newly adopted spiritual parents—"this fun couple," as Christopher Miles calls them.[47] Yet perhaps all three are really on the road toward a version of middle-class life only slightly more interesting than the Saywells' and toward another movie ending that gives up rebellion at the eleventh hour in favor of a return to the fold. Like March and Paul, Miles's Eastwoods are going to be married as soon as possible. Their little touring car, so jaunty and free-spirited in appearance, will eventually convey them to London, where employment and respectability await.

Fortunately, Rydell's and Miles's screen endings are not as reductive nor as repentant as they seem. Both are complicated by the late introduction not of Lawrentian discourse but of an alternative imagery that confounds and partly deconstructs the vehicles of convention. Rydell develops his subversive images at the close by reaching back to the beginning of *The Fox*. The frozen landscape of its opening scene reappears at the end, only now transformed by heavy spring rains and melting snow. This transformation, at least theoretically, should reinforce the film's overt, conventional resolution. March herself has also been released from the deep winter of Banford's lesbianism and is about to experience a warmer and more fertile season with Paul. To the film audience, however, such symmetry does not accord with visible reality, since the frozen landscape at the beginning was far more striking and attractive than the sodden landscape at the end. What we see before us as *The Fox* concludes is windswept rain, mud, and darkness, all indicating continued turmoil for Paul and March in place of the happily ever after. A second early image preserved and transformed for Rydell's ending is the fox itself. The film's initial sequences involve a confrontation between March and this animal in which woman and beast stare one another down and in which the fox's intense and vitally alert expression is captured in a long close-up shot. The camera focuses down on the fox again, just as the film closes, only now he is a dead shell of his former presence, the pelt which Paul Grenfel has nailed to the barn door. What we see in this final frame is not ugly but hideous, the creature's once-living face now grinning in death, rainsoaked and rotting. Such an image, upon which Rydell chooses to close, bodes ill for March, Paul, and the future. Combined with the bleak and turbulent weather of the final scene, it mocks the film's complacent surface and restores a bit of Lawrence's long, ambiguous tail to the production just before the screen goes dark.

*The Virgin and the Gypsy* also concludes with a partial, oblique return to its own earlier imagery. As Yvette climbs down the rescue ladder from her father's window, the entire Saywell clan awaits her below. Granny is gone, but the rest of them stand together absolutely motionless as if posing for a photograph. This movie still is, in fact, a reference back to the scene of Yvette's homecoming in which a similarly arranged and slightly menacing family group confronts her as she first returns from school. Yvette's arrival and departure, then, are presented in deliberate juxtaposition. In the closing scene, as Yvette reaches the foot of the ladder, her father attempts to help her down. Instead of fainting like Lawrence's Yvette, she walks away, leaving all the frozen Saywells behind as she begins moving toward the Eastwoods' car. At this point, Miles introduces a second imagistic déjà vu that, like Rydell's rotting fox skin and foul weather, seems to belie what is overtly taking place. Yvette's final exit is called into question as a real event in the film because it looks and sounds exactly like one of her own past fantasies. Yvette departs dressed in white and with her hair down, appearing much as she did in her initial dream encounter with the gypsy. She also remains mute from the point of her awakening in her father's bed until the end of the film. As she walks from the ladder to the car, everyone else remains mute as well, all dialogue having been silenced by music just as it was in the two earlier fantasies, silenced and replaced by the now-familiar theme of Yvette's imaginary life.[48] All such closing images conspire to foil the heroine's escape into movie cliché, regardless of which cliché we choose to believe—total freedom with a "fun couple," or merely an exchange of bad parents for better ones. Christopher Miles, in short, seems to scrap his own *ex machina* (really, *ex auto*) contrivances at the last minute in favor of a covert return to the text. To end his film in a dream is, ironically, to end it in pure realism and to admit, exactly as Lawrence does, that Yvette may not be going anywhere just yet and that her future, like all human affairs, remains uncertain.

Both Christopher Miles and Mark Rydell, then, end their films in a dispute between easy cliché and ambivalent image. In many ways this closing mismatch forms an apt emblem of the two films in general and of their own ambivalent achievements as cinematic art. If such art ideally evades time, these films are similarly impeded by their directors' self-proclaimed roles as spokesmen for a particular age and culture. The deliberate late-sixties-style "daring" in *The Fox* and *Virgin* productions recalls Pauline Kael's caveat to filmmakers against bringing a work of literature "up to date" and "attempt[ing] to modernize or clarify an author and to 'fill out' the author's material."[49] Such efforts, she suggests, are doomed to fail and have the odd result of making a film seem more bookish and dated than the text upon which it is based. We see the "Kael effect" working all too well in *The Fox* as Lawrence's complex eroticism is streamlined for the sexual revolution, primarily through the macho figure of Paul Grenfel and his hot pursuit of March. Ironically, as Mark Rydell cries "freedom" in *The Fox* from one sort of sexual intolerance, he unwittingly falls victim to another, as yet invisible to him but painfully clear with hindsight to anyone viewing *The Fox* today. Paul Grenfel, erotically liberated by the standards of his decade, seems little more than a conniving and nasty sexist by our standards, his homophobia and misogyny ill concealed at best by a practiced smile and smooth line of talk to the girls. Paralleling *The Fox, Virgin* also exchanges one kind of cultural prejudice for another rather than escaping outright. As Christopher Miles champions the young (censoring out Lawrence's unabashed anti-Semitism in the process), he happily and blindly trashes the old—so well, in fact, that Yvette's "you'll all be dead" remark to Granny and the Rector still gets a rise out of college crowds today. The sexism of one film is fully matched by the ageism of another, with both directors remaining innocent of words and ideas that had not yet penetrated the culture as a whole.

It is also true, however, that some of the strongest work in *The Fox* and *Virgin* films, as well as what is most embarrassing and dated, results from tampering with Lawrence. Their successes come not so much from keeping the author "up to date" as from keeping him in harmony with the film medium itself. Effective cinema, in other words, occurs in both *The Fox* and *Virgin* when they manage to achieve what I have referred to earlier as "transformative fidelity to the text." Looking back on these films, it's fair to say that their most compelling and resonant material finds no counterpart in the novellas at all. This is true of the deconstructive imagery that closes both productions, as well as March's waking vision of Banford dead in the snow and the several fantasy sequences involving Yvette and running throughout *Virgin*. All of these examples constitute meaningful and original cinema, entirely independent from the letter of Lawrence's text yet remarkably faithful to its spirit.

What finally allows us to judge *The Fox* and *Virgin,* as potentially enduring cinema, and to distinguish between them, is the extent to which such creative yet faithful transformation takes place. I believe that *The Fox* is largely a failure in this regard and probably the weakest Lawrence production in the first two decades of attempting to capture him on film. This is because transformative fidelity proves to be the rare exception for Mark Rydell rather than the rule. Beyond March's stop-action daydream and the film's provocative closing images, there is nothing further that reminds us of Lawrence by erasing him, only the director's ongoing (and commercially driven) emphasis on sexuality and on the eternal and eternally predictable triangle of March, Banford, and Paul. *The Fox,* however, remains an intriguing failure, because its rare artistic breakthroughs are sufficient to hint that it might have been a better film than it turned out to be. It leaves us wishing that Mark Rydell had learned more from Ingmar Bergman about how Lawrence's text might have been imaginatively yet loyally undone.

If *The Fox* is an interesting failure, then *The Virgin and the Gypsy* is an imperfect success, at least if judged by the same standards of measure. For me it emerges, along with *Women in Love,* as one of the two best Lawrence productions in the first twenty years of filming his work. It is probably true, however, that *Virgin* succeeds in part because it does not face overwhelming competition from the author himself. Unlike "The Fox," *The Virgin and the Gipsy* is more bittersweet fairy tale than masterpiece. It is also Lawrence's unrevised sketchbook for *Lady Chatterley's Lover.* Along with this, its central character, Yvette, is less complicated than March and therefore easier to present from the external perspectives of the camera eye. Acknowledging all this, however, Christopher Miles, unlike Mark Rydell, still finds ways to reach his heroine's hidden life that stand him in good stead for an entire film. Yvette's fantasies become a unifying leitmotif within *Virgin* and a means of regaining Lawrence by seeming to abandon him. The original Yvette experiences no textual fantasies at all, yet their cinematic addition provides Miles with exactly the Lawrentian element missing from Rydell's production of *The Fox,* with something resembling the writer's inner vision of covert and ambivalent humanity. Yvette's fantasies are the rhythmically beating heart of *Virgin* on film and, in a separate metaphor, the artistic gesture of successful cinematic adaptation. It is through such a gesture, as we have seen and will see again, that an author's text can be betrayed and remade in a single stroke.

# 5
# Ken Russell's Women in Love: Repetition as Revelation

Less than three minutes into *Women in Love,* one suspects that Ken Russell may have taught Christopher Miles how to open a D. H. Lawrence film. Start off with two sisters, attractive and vital women of the 1920s. Contrast their energy and color to the deadly surroundings of industrial England and to the stale, repressed lives of their parents. Have the sisters immediately discuss their prospects, romantic and otherwise: careers, the pros and cons of being "adored," the possibility of marriage or not. As begins *The Virgin and the Gypsy* in 1971, so precisely began Russell's screen adaptation of *Women in Love* just two years earlier.[1] Yet Miles's cinematic debt to Russell may only be external. Beneath nearly identical opening settings and situations, many differences remain to keep the two films distinct. Missing from *Women in Love,* for example, is Miles's celebration of the very young. In comparison to the youthful Lucille, Yvette, and their circle of friends, the principals of *Women in Love* seem middle-aged, especially as portrayed by Alan Bates, Glenda Jackson, and Oliver Reed. Among the film's major characters, only Jennie Linden's Ursula appears young both in spirit and in years. Also, the more youthful minor figures in *Women in Love,* like Gerald's younger sister, Laura, and her new bridegroom, Tibby, are not idealized as they might have been in a Miles film but instead presented as trivial and shallow, a self-absorbed and ultimately self-destructive couple.

Russell's *Women in Love* is similarly distinguishable from *The Fox,* Mark Rydell's contribution to this late 1960s trilogy of Lawrence films. Gone, along with Miles's cult of youth, is Rydell's self-conscious cataloging and celebrating of human sexuality. *Women in Love* is hardly a prudish film, yet its several explicit scenes seem far less designed for erotic excitation than Rydell's. This is probably because Russell's love scenes, unlike Rydell's, are less suggestive of un-inhibited ecstasy and pleasure than of suffering. This is most evident during Gerald's revenge-rape of Gudrun at the Alpine lodge. Yet it is also evident in the initial sexual encounters of both couples (just after a drowning and then a fu-neral), and even in the screen translation of "Gladiatorial," which combines homoerotic exploration between the two men with deadly serious combat.

Examined from certain perspectives, *Women in Love* and *Virgin* seem to align themselves together and in contrast to *The Fox*. This is most apparent in rela-tion to "periodicity," in that both Miles and Russell opt to remain roughly con-temporaneous with Lawrence, whereas Rydell updates his textual source to some unspecified time much closer to his own. This relationship, again, might present only a superficial parallel that really conceals the uniqueness of *Women in Love*. Regardless of period, both *Virgin* and *The Fox* demilitarize their source texts, as has already been shown, in keeping with a war silence that was common to Anglo-American film during the late 1960s. By contrast, *Women in Love* is laden with specific reminders of a specific war, this to the point of violating Lawrence's own wishes as expressed in the 1919 foreword to the American edition of his novel: "This novel was written in its first form in the Tyrol, in 1913. It was altogether re-written and finished in Cornwall in 1917. So that it is a novel which took its final shape in the midst of the period of war, though it does not concern the war itself. I should wish the time to remain unfixed, so that the bitterness of the war may be taken for granted in the characters."[2]

Rather than "unfixed," Russell's film time is precisely 1920, and the bitter aftermath of the Great War is neither absent nor implied but always visibly present.[3] The film's beginning is constructed around a full-dress military wed-ding, a purely cinematic expansion of Lawrence's terse description of the groom, Tibby, as "a typical naval officer" (16). When Birkin explains to Hermione that the groom arrived late because he would discuss the immortality of the soul, she replies that the subject seems more appropriate for an execution than a wed-ding. Her comment (which again alters the text) predicts the death of the new-lywed couple at Shortlands. Yet it also looks ahead to another scene that seems to conflate a soldier's funeral with a military ceremony of some obscure sort. As a man in uniform lies motionless in a coffinlike box and a priest mouths all of the expected clichés, the statue of a Tommy in heroic pose is unveiled before the public.[4] This sequence creates a grotesque and distorted mirror of the military wedding, and perhaps in so doing provides a useful clue to Russell's reliance on repetition as a major cinematic and artistic technique in this film.

Beyond such overtly military scenes, several of the civilian sequences in *Women in Love* are also heavily peopled by men in uniform who wander on and off as visible background chorus. Some of them are maimed combat veterans, finally home but wounded, blinded, gassed. As the British director of a British picture, Ken Russell may not have deliberately intended contemporary implications in these figures, since his homeland had been at peace for some time. Yet for Russell's American film audience and for Larry Kramer, his American producer and screenwriter, these soldiers, helpless and pathetic in their military trappings, must have carried a painfully immediate resonance in 1969, the year of the film's release.

During Russell's unsettling scene of the military ceremony, Alan Bates's Birkin initially reveals himself as an upstart, a social critic, and a passionate, if slightly scattered, man of ideas. He becomes enraged as the priest intones truisms about love and, to Ursula's extreme embarrassment, launches into a loud countersermon about hate, all the while pushing his way through the crowd of spectators. We see in this outburst, for the first time, a Birkin far less intellectually complex (yet also somewhat more likable and amusing) than Lawrence's original. We also see Russell's major relationship to the "periodicity" of his own decade—his celebration not of Miles's youth or Rydell's sexuality but of a historically recognizable attitude, style, and way of life. In external appearance, Alan Bates's Birkin is made to resemble D. H. Lawrence himself. Internally, however, he is made to resemble the more contemporary and familiar figure of the hip 1960s man—a bohemian and a rebel, a deeply serious reformer, and a lovable eccentric. By coupling the external image of Lawrence with the internal image of the idealized hippie, Russell may be suggesting that Lawrence himself was such a figure, well ahead of his time, or that he would have been such a figure had he lived in the 1960s. This suggestion seems highly questionable in light of Lawrence's biography as well as the text itself—the "Creme de Menthe," "Totem," and "Pompadour" chapters of *Women in Love,* for example, which ridicule and bitterly condemn figures like Halliday, Libidnikov, and Pussum—figures who come uncomfortably close to predicting the beat and hip of future decades.[5]

Watching *Women in Love* thirty years after its release, one can't help wondering about the question of intent. Just how conscious were these Lawrence filmmakers of articulating and displaying the spirit of their own age? Fortunately, some light can be shed on this matter because Russell and Kramer were quite vocal about their accomplishments during the late 1960s and early 1970s, and Russell continues to discuss his film.[6] About war—or specifically about an intended allusion to Vietnam through the veteran-chorus of *Women in Love*—neither man has a thing to say. Nor on Birkin as hippie or Lawrence as hippie either, although in a 1970 interview with Gene Phillips, Russell does comment on his use of period films to express contemporary concerns. "I generally select period material because all of the stories I do are about the relationships of people to their environment and to each other . . . which we are just as concerned about today as people were in the past." Russell adds, "To see things of the past from the vantage point of the present is to be able to judge what effect they have had on the present."[7] This last observation could suggest that Russell consciously envisioned Lawrence and Lawrentian values as leading toward the spirit of time-present in 1969.

Russell's comments just after the film's release are somewhat more specific on the subjects of youth and sexuality—oddly enough more Miles's and Rydell's central preoccupations than his own. On youth, Russell confirms his unwillingness to celebrate adolescence in *Women in Love,* during an interview with John Baxter, when he criticizes Jennie Linden for playing Ursula as less mature than the original character:

> Although Jennie Linden was good in the film I think, having since worked with a couple of the people I saw but passed over at the time, they might well have been better, especially from a physical point of view. I think she was really too "pert" for the part. This was probably all my fault. I foolishly allowed her to see the rushes. She told me at the end of the film that because she thought she looked much younger on screen than Gudrun she decided secretly to play Ursula much younger than we'd originally intended. I suppose I should have noticed this in the rushes, but as it was quite subtly done I didn't twig until the rough-cut stage when it was too late to do anything about it. Her best scenes were the first ones she did in the corn field with Birkin, before she'd seen any rushes at all. Since then I've never allowed actors to see rushes.[8]

Ken Russell's remarks on sexuality and sexual explicitness in *Women in Love* convey nothing of Mark Rydell's erotic bravado, as expressed in the Gontarski interview, nor anything resembling a deliberate intention to shock or arouse an audience. What does recall Rydell's interview, however, is Russell's awareness and fear of the censor, by now a seemingly inescapable presence in Lawrence filming, especially of the censor's potential reaction to the "Gladiatorial" scene during which Alan Bates and Oliver Reed wrestle and display their full frontal nudity. The director confides to one interviewer, with what seems like a mixture of pride and relief: "In England the film passed the censors without a cut, and went on to win film awards. Lord Harlech, president of the British Board of Film Censors, defended the wrestling match as one of the finest scenes ever filmed."[9] Russell shares with another interviewer his amused surprise, a few years after the release of *Women in Love,* to learn that in machismo-conscious Latin America the same scene may have been permanently disappeared, although with results exactly counter to what the censors intended:

A while back I met a girl from South America playing the guitar in a Pizza Express restaurant, a student at the film school of the Royal College of Art. She'd seen *Women in Love* in England, quite liked it, but was amazed on returning to her country to find that her friends considered it sexually the most daring film ever made because of "that scene with the two men." So she saw it again and what had happened was that the censor had cut out the entire wrestling match. In the South American version Gerald simply locked the door, then there was a direct cut to the two men lying naked on the carpet side by side, panting. It became known as The Great Buggering Scene and filled the cinemas for months. So much for the subtleties of censorship.[10]

Another productive insight arising from Russell's uninhibited and abundant commentary concerns the degree of conflict during the making of *Women in Love,* particularly between Russell and Kramer. On a superficial level this conflict takes the form of petty squabbling between creative colleagues over who deserves credit for what. In several interviews, and in downright hostile tones, Russell insists that he did most of the final script writing and revision on *Women in Love,* work for which Kramer received exclusive screen credit and exclusive praise, including an Academy Award nomination:

By the time we got back to London the script had been printed, and when I opened it up there was "Screenplay by Larry Kramer." I immediately rang him and said, "What's this? We wrote the script together." (Actually Lawrence wrote 90% of it and we did the rest.) "But I wrote it down," Larry said. "I regard myself as your pencil, Ken." "Whoever heard of giving a pencil full screen credit?" "Well," he said, "I'm very upset that this is the way you feel." I asked my agent to get in touch with Rosen [the film's coproducer], who said, "I didn't have the heart to tell Larry [that Russell had requested co-credit as screenwriter]; I knew he'd be so upset he wouldn't go ahead with the film." I'd done an enormous amount of work on the script—for nothing incidentally; I didn't get a penny for all that writing and preparation—but I couldn't see any way to get recognition for it, nor could my agent. By then a lot of my friends, like Billy Williams and Luciana Arrighi, the designer, were involved, and Larry kept saying, "But Ken, you're directing the film. What more do you want? Can't you do the big thing and give me a break? It's my first major screen credit." So I just gritted my teeth and got on with it.[11]

Russell is especially vocal about his unrecognized work on "Class-Room," claiming that he transformed Kramer's clumsy opening sequence into a compelling flashback of Ursula's as she and Gudrun watch the Crich wedding. He insists that this change condensed *Women in Love* sufficiently to win approval from United Artists for the film's release.[12]

There's more to the Russell/Kramer conflict, however, than simply competition between artistic temperaments. Beneath this, it's an instance of two strong-willed, talented filmmakers working together, yet possessed of utterly opposed sensibilities and worldviews. Russell, by his own admission, is a director who rejects content, especially abstract content, in favor of dynamic visuality and sound.[13] By contrast, Kramer defines his view of "film as a medium for words and ideas. . . . I don't agree with the directors who say everything in a film must be expressed visually. If film is to be a serious artistic form, it has to deal with abstract ideas and deal with them in words."[14] Kramer also expresses a much more reverential attitude toward Lawrence and toward the text than Russell does. His interviews suggest that he understood *Women in Love* in part as a tribute to Lawrence, achieved by projecting the author's work and words onto a new medium. "We wanted a visual and philosophical re-creation of a great novel. The film isn't mine, it isn't really anyone's. It's D. H. Lawrence's film."[15] This opening to a *Los Angeles Times* interview leads Kramer to reveal his exploration of Lawrence's work even beyond the primary text. "Slightly more than half the film is exactly from Lawrence. Not all is from the novel—some of it is from his letters, essays, and plays. I had the right to use random excerpts. The sequence where Alan Bates, the Lawrence character, discourses on eating a fig is an abridged version of a Lawrence poem."[16]

To exploit texts in this fashion, one first has to read them, and Russell seems proud of not having done so. In what could be a counterthrust to Kramer's interview, he tells John Baxter, "I don't know Lawrence's work well enough to say how close the film is to its spirit. I'd read some of his books twenty years earlier and they hadn't meant a thing to me. . . . Anyway I purposely didn't read any more of his books after I started [filming] *Women in Love,* though I did read a couple of biographies. A lot of the book seemed pretentious and repetitive, and I left a lot of it out because films lasting twenty-four hours are frowned on by distributors and partly, as I say, because Lawrence simply repeated his themes."[17]

Ironies large and small lurk among Russell's words here and within the two filmmakers' failure to agree. One irony is the contradiction between this attack on Lawrence and another Russell comment, quoted above, that the novelist really deserves credit for 90 percent of the disputed script. A related but larger irony is that in condemning Lawrence for repetition, Russell seems unaware of his own inclination to do the same thing on film and to do it successfully. A third and possibly major irony emerges with the reader/viewer's growing suspicion that this theoretical conflict between Russell and Kramer may not have been a burden, as one might logically expect, but rather an asset in the creation of an effective Lawrence film. The opposition between visuality and Logos or between creative bravado and reverence to text seems to capture a measure of Lawrence's own paradoxical complexity of vision and to hint that the making of *Women in Love* may itself have been a gladiatorial among the filmmakers, an angry battle yet a dynamic and vital one as well.[18]

Russell has continued to bring D. H. Lawrence to the large and small screens and has never been reluctant to talk about his work. In discussing his 1989 film of *The Rainbow* and his 1993 version of *Lady Chatterley* for British television, he has invariably returned to the subject of *Women in Love,* providing an ongoing footnote of sorts to his thirty-year-old project and its attendant controversies. With time, Russell seems unconsciously to have accepted some of Kramer's perspectives, at least regarding the film's function as a celebration of the text and its author. Russell's repeated observation in recent statements is that *Women in Love* is a distinguished film which could have been even better with more screen time to explore Lawrence's original vision. "I couldn't really do justice to *Women in Love* in two hours [he tells an interviewer who is more interested in discussing *The Rainbow*], so it wasn't as good as it could have been."[19] Russell says the same thing even more emphatically in *The Lion Roars,* a book-length collection of witty, disorganized, and unashamedly subjective pronouncements on film in our time, including his own productions:

> But it's impossible to film a 600-page novel and be true to the author's vision. Two hours is about all anyone can take at a sitting. Many great scenes had to be sacrificed. I particularly regret the omission of the Brangwen girls' sojourn in London where they sample *la vie boheme.* It helped form their characters and explains their subsequent behavior.
>
> . . . That was my problem with *Women in Love.* It was impossible to do justice to the 600-page original in 120 minutes of screen time. An extra 80 minutes would have made all the difference.[20]

Unless he's thinking of "Gudrun in the Pompadour," the omitted episode Russell mentions here is his own rather than Lawrence's, since the sisters don't sample *la vie boheme* in the text either. Despite this odd error, Russell seems to retract his earlier dismissal of the author's vision and spirit and also his claim of having saved the film, through textual cutting, from the blunders of Lawrentian repetition.

The retrospective on *Women in Love* provided by Russell's more recent writings cannot be left without noting the director's grudging admission that the public considers it his best film. Russell is certainly proud of this, yet disappointed as well, because he would prefer his audiences to regard new work rather than past work as his greatest. "We all love to be loved, but, when love is blind, it gets a bit wearing. I've made better films than *Women in Love,* but obviously it had something that tickled the public's fancy. . . . People still come up to me in the street and say it changed their lives. Complete strangers at film festivals stop me and say, 'I'm a great fan of yours, and I simply love . . .' (you wait for it, hoping against hope that it will be your last movie they are about to extol, but no, it's always) . . . '*Women in Love.*' I nod and smile, but maybe I should react like that superb jazz trumpeter, Miles Davis, who always replied to unsought opinions, from friends and foes, with a cryptic 'So what?'"[21]

Miles Davis's "So what?" seems a less appropriate response in today's climate of admiration than in 1969 when *Women in Love* was Ken Russell's newest work yet by no means universally well received. In the year of its release, and immediately after, reactions to the film were violently mixed, although with some indications of long-term recognition already beginning to emerge. To the extent that nominations and awards are a measure of achievement, *Women in Love* did well at once, at least in the United States. Glenda Jackson won the Academy Award for best actress in 1969 for her performance as Gudrun. Russell received an Oscar nomination for best director, as did Larry Kramer for script and Billy Williams for cinematography. In keeping with the ambivalent first response to *Women in Love,* the film was not nominated for best picture.

Initial reviews, including those written by usually balanced commentators, tended to be strident, contradictory, and oddly ad hominem. Even when such critics agreed to disparage the film, they did so for wildly conflicting reasons. Pauline Kael used the word *purple* to describe both Russell's picture and Lawrence's text, claiming, however, that Lawrence wrote purple prose for honest artistic reasons whereas Russell simply wanted to "excite the senses" of his audience and bring "a bash of a movie" to the screen.[22] Equally negative yet in blatant contradiction to Kael, others took *Women in Love* to task for not being purple enough. Writing for *Hudson Review,* Stephen Farber claimed that any screen version of Lawrence's novel required "a more extravagant and evocative romantic imagery" than Russell was capable of providing.[23] Robert F. Knoll similarly referred to Russell's "filmic visualizations" as "rather flat and unimaginative" in a *Film Heritage* article.[24] It was almost as if these critics had not seen the same film.

The academic community began discussing *Women in Love* sooner after its release than with earlier Lawrence films, reaching conclusions no less in conflict than those of the journalists. Harry T. Moore was stirred by the film, claiming that despite some serious flaws it was "in many ways a moving-picture masterpiece"[25] F. R. Leavis was also stirred by *Women in Love* or, more exactly, stirred up to angry condemnation of the entire undertaking. When Larry Kramer invited Leavis to write a commentary on the film adaptation of Lawrence's novel, the critic responded with strikingly Lawrentian rage: "It's an obscene undertaking to 'write it again' for the screen. . . . No one who has any inkling of the kind of *thing* the novel is, or how the significance of a great work of literature is conveyed, or what kind of thing significance is, could lend himself to such an outrage. Great writers even where they're dead ought to be protected."[26] While Leavis's reaction was probably the most extreme of any, his claim that the novel was unfilmable and had been violated in the attempt was taken up by several other commentators and echoed in their reviews. After creating a long list of the film's textual violations, Elliott Sirkin suggested in *Film Quarterly,* "Maybe *Women in Love* can't be made into a movie at all."[27] John Simon, recapturing Leavis's outraged tone, claimed that "a film version of *Women in Love* must fail" and that "the only safe and wise thing to do with a novel like *Women in Love* is not to make a film of it at all." Based on such assumptions, Simon declared Russell and Kramer's project to be "a profound betrayal" of novel and novelist alike.[28]

A most peculiar side-effect of these intense reactions, or really of the surprising anger stirred up by Russell's film, was a tendency among critics and reviewers to attack the cast of *Women in Love* in a most personal way, taking them to task not so much for their performances as for their looks. Probably the best known of these attacks was the claim that Jennie Linden, playing Ursula, resembled Debbie Reynolds so closely as to be ineffective in a serious role. This damning observation was first made by Robert F. Knoll in a *Film Heritage* review, then taken up by several other commentators including Harry T. Moore, who inadvertently complicated the show-business comparison by mistakenly identifying Linden as "Jennie Jones."[29] One can only speculate on these same critics' reactions had they known that two decades later Ursula Brangwen was again to appear on screen, still burdened by Hollywood coincidence. In *The Rainbow,* Ken Russell's Debbie Reynolds look-alike was replaced by an actress named Sammi Davis.

Even stranger than the Debbie Reynolds issue was a tendency among commentators to remark on the unattractiveness of certain members of the cast, with the late Oliver Reed as Gerald probably emerging as their primary target. Many were satisfied merely to note that Reed's Gerald, unlike Lawrence's, was not Nordic in appearance or even blond, while others felt the need to go from objective observation to personal insult. Robert F. Knoll referred to Reed as imparting "a heavy-lidded Neanderthal quality to the character."[30] Generally, however, botanical rather than anthropological metaphors turned up as critics sought the exact words to describe Reed's unacceptability as Gerald. Elliott Sirkin, for instance, at least saw his "massive, eggplant-shaped face" as "intriguing" if at the same time ugly and inappropriate to the role.³¹ John Simon described Reed as a "pear-faced, sinisterly mustachioed skulker." Not content to stop with Reed, Simon added Glenda Jackson to his critical salad when he referred to "her much-revealed breasts, [as] shaped like collapsing gourds," unaware, in all probability, that Jackson was pregnant for much of the filming.³² These critics seemed to take perverse inspiration from Lawrence himself in such attacks, not merely in their level of rage but in the very language used to express it, in metaphors resembling parodies of Lawrence's own imagistic vegetation, the catkins, primroses, and pine burrs of *Women in Love*.

Predictably, the shrillest critical voices died down after the early 1970s, making way for a more thoughtful and balanced appraisal. Occasional outcries still could be heard well into the next decade, such as Neil Sinyard's subjective condemnation of the film, expressed as follows in *Filming Literature,* his 1986 study of screen adaptation: "Funnily enough, Ken Russell is one of those directors who one feels might have the necessary daring and devil to scale the Lawrentian heights. But his highly acclaimed film of *Women in Love* (1970) [*sic*] has always seemed to me one of Russell's most tepid and visually boring movies, of what I have always found to be one of Lawrence's most unpleasantly tendentious and misogynistic novels."³³ Perhaps a critic who discards the textual baby along with the tepid cinematic bathwater need not be taken all too seriously. Sinyard, in fact, turns out to be strongly biased against all attempts at Lawrence filming, as indicated by his dismissive chapter title on Lawrentian adaptation, "Another Fine Mess." His rather heated judgments are, however, the exception among later commentators on *Women in Love,* including those who ultimately see the film as falling short of success. More representative of such commentators is Theodore Ross, examining the film in a late 1970s article for *College English.* Ross concludes a largely negative analysis by agreeing with F. R. Leavis, yet in an argument free of Leavis's anger and open to debate precisely because it is based on reasoned judgment rather than emotional reaction:

> In part the incoherence [of *Women in Love*] results from the film's blankness concerning the interplay of social institutions and the psychodynamics of class. Its "texture" in this respect is exceedingly thin. Yet the novel's range of social observation and its prophetic notations on character in the modern world depend precisely on its realism: F. R. Leavis has taken pains to stress the sweep and accuracy of the novel's social and historical perspectives. The flattening of such perspectives, together with the transformation of the characters into hard-edged character types leads to the more abstract canvas of Russell as compared to the Lawrentian representation.³⁴

Students of *Women in Love* in the 1970s and 1980s began to take the film's measure artistically as well as historically, with many of them reaching conclusions more favorable than these. Serious examination of Russell's film as potential art object probably began with G. B. Crump's review essay "*Women in Love:* Novel and Film," written for the *D. H. Lawrence Review.* Crump may well have been the first critic to notice Russell's heavy reliance on dance sequences and dance images in *Women in Love* and to conclude that in dance Russell may have discovered a "proper objective correlative" by which the novel's rhythms could be made manifest.[35] Both of these issues—dance and the challenge of filming Lawrentian rhythm in general—were taken up by a later critic, Joseph A. Gomez, and explored in greater detail within *The Adaptor as Creator,* his 1976 book on Russell and again five years later in a more condensed study of *Women in Love* written for Michael Klein and Gillian Parker's anthology, *The English Novel and the Movies.* Gomez's somewhat overlapping studies discuss Ken Russell's interest in Isadora Duncan and his 1966 television documentary on the dancer as the basis and inspiration for the director's choreographic approach to *Women in Love.* Gomez also widens out discussion of the film by suggesting that dance is just one of several devices employed by Russell to project Lawrence's novel on screen. Gomez introduces the term *counterpointing* to describe Lawrence's essential literary method in *Women in Love* as well as Russell's analogous technique of cinematic transformation.[36]

The technique of counterpointing is taken up in two other noteworthy studies: Ana Laura Zambrano's article "*Women in Love:* Counterpoint on Film," written for the 1973 premier issue of *Literature/Film Quarterly,* and Joy Gould Boyum's "*Women in Love:* Style as Daring," the portion of *Double Exposure,* her 1985 book on screen adaptation, devoted to Russell's film. Both of these critics suggest that Russell and Kramer turn cinematic counterpointing into an effective means of reconciling fidelity to the text with expression of the filmmakers' original and independent vision. This shared judgment leads Zambrano and Boyum to reach remarkably similar conclusions expressed in almost identical terms. For Zambrano, "Russell's *Women in Love* is one artist's interpretation of another. . . . Russell's *Women in Love* is not a pure translation from the novel, nor is his treatment of the characters completely unaltered; but the film provides masterful and penetrating insight into Lawrence's themes, and it enriches our appreciation of the beauty and complexity of the style of both artists."[37] For Boyum, in exact parallel, "Russell's *Women in Love* seems . . . less a betrayal than an appreciation of Lawrence, and an adaptation that (whatever its flaws) emerges an ideal instance of its kind—an adaptation, that is, which manages to be a commentary on one work of art by another, a celebration of one artist by another, and a work of art in its own right, all at the very same time."[38]

It's safe to say that Russell's *Women in Love* remains the most discussed and most famous of all the D. H. Lawrence films. This degree of exposure raises the question of whether there is anything left to say thirty years after the film's release. One necessary piece of unfinished business, I believe, is to explain how the critical voices, in conflict across three decades, have all fundamentally been right—how their very oppositions reveal the complex paradox of what Russell and Kramer achieve. The film adaptation of *Women in Love* does indeed celebrate Lawrence as it simultaneously betrays him. Moreover, it achieves its most respectful tribute to his art, as I hope to show here, through the very techniques that appear to erase it and replace it with something new.

The film's most serious erasure of text occurs as the formidable intellectual complexity of the original is all but lost, this despite Larry Kramer's hope of paying tribute to Lawrence by filming his ideas. The filmmakers' diminishment of ideas in *Women in Love* leads to an even more fundamental loss, since the novel's individual characters always serve to articulate and demonstrate Lawrence's thinking. As the ideas shrink on screen, so too do the fictional figures who bear their textual burdens. Such loss is more than made good, however, through the film's intricate tribute to Lawrentian repetition—through its flattering yet original imitation of his own most striking technique. In the final paragraph of his foreword to *Women in Love,* Lawrence reveals his reliance on repetition as the essential artistic principle that governs the text. "In point of style, fault is often found with the continual, slightly modified repetition. The only answer is that it is natural to the author; and that every natural crisis in emotion or passion or understanding comes from this pulsing, frictional to-and-fro which works up to culmination" (viii). Lawrence's statement may easily be misunderstood as referring simply to repetition of language—words, phrases, even ideas—in *Women in Love*. Rather than this, however, it constitutes a much deeper and rarer invitation from author to reader to listen for the novel's heartbeat, to understand that its vital rhythm is achieved and maintained through a progressive series of ever-similar yet ever-varied artistic pulses—images, scenes, symbolic objects, and symbolic actions in constant replication yet in constant flux. Russell's *Women in Love* comes to life, as an adaptation and an original work, through a similar heartbeat, yet rarely through exact repetition on screen of Lawrentian repetition in the text. More typically, the film realizes itself in a double artistic gesture of embrace and rejection at once, exactly as did *The Rocking Horse Winner, Sons and Lovers,* and *The Virgin and the Gypsy* in their most successful moments. While rejecting Lawrentian substance, the film embraces Lawrentian methodology, adapting the "pulsing, frictional to-and-fro" to newly created content and reconciling it, through transformation, with the demands of cinematic art.

Since the reduction of mind-content in *Women in Love* is difficult to overlook, it makes a useful starting point for detailed discussion of the film. The novel's flow of ideas both large and small may not have been considered manageable on screen, and so diminishes, as has been suggested, with serious consequences for character development. A clear instance of this relates to Lawrence's concern in *Women in Love* with time or, more exactly, with the dangers of being permanently entrapped by time. Of the novel's four major figures, Gudrun Brangwen runs the greatest risk of this eventuality, finally falling victim to it just as Ursula and Birkin seem to be breaking free of temporal constraints by way of their strengthening relationship. By the middle of the "Continental" chapter, these two have begun to live in an ongoing eternal moment, feeling little worry about their specific futures and wishing they were "pastless" or born anew in one another. Shortly before the couple suddenly decides to leave the Alps and move southward, Ursula muses to herself:

> She wanted to have no past. She wanted to have come down the slopes of heaven to this place, with Birkin, not to have toiled out of the murk of her childhood and her upbringing, slowly, all soiled. She felt that memory was a dirty trick played upon her. What was this decree, that she should "remember!" Why not a bath of pure oblivion, a new birth, without any recollections or blemish of a past life. She was with Birkin, she had just come into life, here in the high snow, against the stars. (399)

In contrast to Ursula's sense of release, her sister Gudrun begins to fear that she is becoming entombed in time—this impression growing much stronger, ironically, just as she breaks free of her ties with Gerald and really with everyone else in her past life. Gudrun suspects that whatever she decides to do, stay with Gerald, go to Dresden with Loerke, or disappear by herself, she will be equally condemned to linear chronology, one day leading to an endless sequence of similar days: "The thought of the mechanical succession of day following day, following day, *ad infinitum,* was one of the things that made her heart palpitate with a real approach of madness. The terrible bondage of this tick-tack of time, this twitching of the hands of the clock, this eternal repetition of hours and days— oh God, it was too awful to contemplate. And there was no escape from it, no escape" (456). To the outward view, Lawrence's Gudrun is a powerful figure, growing even stronger toward the novel's end, as she strikes the last blow and wins her life-and-death struggle with Gerald. Inwardly, however, Lawrence also allows us to look into the abyss of Gudrun's vulnerability and dread. As this woman comes to dominate Gerald and to make him suffer, she suffers invisibly and painfully herself—in some sense like Milton's Satan, who deals out punishment yet also receives it in return.

The idea of enslavement to time and the view of Gudrun as experiencing private agony during her triumph come across in the film of *Women in Love* only once. This occurs during the "Death and Love" sequence when Gerald gains covert entrance to the Brangwen household and sleeps with Gudrun for the first time. In the aftermath of sex, as in the novel, Gerald sleeps the refreshing and deep sleep of early childhood while Gudrun, in absolute contrast, finds herself "wide awake, destroyed into perfect consciousness" (338). In the film scene depicting this, Glenda Jackson as Gudrun lies on her back with the full weight of Oliver Reed's Gerald upon her. Gudrun's eyes are wide open, and her ears, along with those of the audience, are fully attuned to the repetition of the ticking clock in her bedroom and of the church bells tolling the early morning hours outside. Except for this single brilliant vignette, Gudrun is depicted as essentially one-dimensional—uniformly decisive, certain of purpose, and, in relation to Gerald, powerful to the point of invincibility. She lacks her textual counterpart's secret deficiency of spirit—an existential sense of insignificance and entrapment that could have deepened and completed Gudrun's portrayal on film.

The disappearance of time as Gudrun's master and the resultant flattening of her humanity provide a clear but limited example of loss that typifies *Women in Love* on film, often involving issues more far-reaching than this one. In the novel, Lawrence's exploration of Gudrun's time-entrapment is really the minor variation of his major temporal concern: humanity in evolution or, more exactly, his four major characters as modern instances of the ancient yet ongoing organic process. This issue is lost on film with Russell and Kramer's decision to omit Lawrence's "Moony" chapter. Gone, along with Birkin's hopeless yet fascinating attempt to stone the female moon to oblivion, are all of his agonized speculations about the human race and its potential future. In the aftermath of the moon scene, Birkin's mind wanders to the primitive carvings in Halliday's London flat, realizing that they speak to him of at least one line of human development moving toward extinction. For Birkin, the African statues reflect cultures that have taken the path of purely physical and sensual exploration and that have reached a final dead-end: "There is a long way we can travel, after the death-break: after that point when the soul in intense suffering breaks, breaks away from its organic hold like a leaf that falls. We fall from the connection with life and hope, we lapse from pure integral being, from creation and liberty, and we fall into the long, long African process of purely sensual understanding, knowledge in the mystery of dissolution" (246).

Birkin's epiphany expands when he turns from this tropical process of counter-evolution to its apparent opposite. For the fair-skinned races, as opposed to the dark, the pathway involves mechanical, abstract exploration in place of hot, biological sensuality. Yet the result of such colder Nordic process is equally entropic and in the long run uncannily similar to the African way. "There remained this way, this awful African process, to be fulfilled. It would be done differently by the white races. The white races, having the Arctic north behind them, the vast abstraction of ice and snow, would fulfill a mystery of ice-destructive knowledge, snow-abstract annihilation" (246).

As a result of these musings, Birkin thinks suddenly of Gerald, who seems to offer a perfect modern instance of evolution toward Nordic ice-destiny. Externally, he is blond, blue-eyed, and powerful. Internally, he tries to smother all sensual impulse, spontaneity, and emotion, in favor of the cooler pursuits of technology and scientific mining. Yet while Gerald appears to walk the twentieth century's high road to the future, he is really moving toward much the same cul-de-sac as the primitives, only by an alternate route. Gerald's closeness to his apparent cultural opposites is, in fact, implied through his attraction to tropical exploration—of the Amazon when he was younger and, more recently, of Pussum, Halliday's companion and a living example of what the primitive carvings tell Birkin about sensual knowledge and corruption.

Gerald and in truth many in the Crich family are also the novel's examples of what Rupert Birkin conceives of as the "murderee"—that person whose secret and yet most central purpose in life is self-annihilation. "There's one thing about our family, you know," Gerald tells Birkin in the aftermath of Diana Crich's drowning at Shortlands. "Once anything goes wrong, it can never be put right again—not with us. I've noticed it all my life—you can't put a thing right, once it has gone wrong" (176). Gerald's words seem to offer a profound if unaware admission that his evolutionary line is doomed and that he himself will eventually be caught in its downward spiral. As if all this were not enough, Lawrence's Gerald also bears the mark of Cain, having shot and killed his brother in a childhood accident.

As suggested earlier, to omit all such thought-adventuring from the film is also seriously to limit the mental adventurer. Alan Bates's attractively lighthearted yet intellectually lightheaded interpretation of Birkin does not allow for this much complexity of vision or for any potentially unfilmable pondering of "murderees," African fetishes, or the future of the human race. This diminishment of character doesn't end with Birkin either, since as he speaks for Lawrence on regressive evolution, Gerald Crich gives the text its living example. On screen, however, all references to Gerald as murderee are removed, as is the significant background fact of his brother's violent death. A single line of dialogue about the mark of Cain survives in the film, delivered by Birkin, yet far more in relation to Gudrun than to Gerald. This occurs during Russell's "introduction scene" at Hermione's estate as all of the film's major figures, and several minor ones, sit together at an elegant outdoor table. They discuss the peculiarity of their names, with Glenda Jackson commenting (beyond the text) that Gudrun was a figure from Norse mythology who murdered her husband. Responding to this, Alan Bates's Birkin wonders if all of them might be "cursed with the mark of Cain."

Until Gerald freezes to death in the mountains, the film of *Women in Love* offers little to suggest his symbolic association with cold or any foreshadowing of his ice-destruction such as Lawrence amply provides in the text. This omission was, of course, responsible for the hue and cry among the film's early critics that Oliver Reed, neither blond nor blue-eyed, had been hopelessly miscast as Gerald. With the filmmakers' decision to omit the issue of negative evolution from the film, in both its Nordic and tropical manifestations, no reason remains to portray Gerald physically in this way. And to Reed's credit—despite his bad press, and despite the loss of all supporting images and ideas—he does interpret Gerald with remarkably self-destructive fidelity to the text. All through the film, Reed's Gerald seems to be imposing a polished, conservative, comme il faut exterior upon himself, by pure force of will, in an effort to cover the hidden chaos within. At moments of crisis, this effort fails and Reed allows a truly hysterical, frightened, and frightening Gerald to emerge, dangerous to others and to himself in equal measure. His sadomasochistic rape of Gudrun comes immediately to mind here, as does his wild yet helpless struggle to rescue Laura from drowning, a struggle which nearly brings about his own death. Both of these moments on film are, in fact, so revealing of Gerald's implosive nature as to cause the scene of his actual death to seem less dramatic by comparison.

In Lawrence's text, escape from the deadly either-or of counter-evolution occurs to Birkin when he remembers that human development need not be limited only by these binary choices of nightmare—Nordic or tropical extinction. At a moment of mental and spiritual exhaustion, Birkin suddenly makes his central epiphany complete:

> There was another way, the way of freedom. There was the paradisal entry into pure, single being, the individual soul taking precedence over love and desire for union, stronger than any pangs of emotion, a lovely state of free proud singleness, which accepts the obligation of the permanent connection with others, and with the other, submits to the yoke and leash of love, but never forfeits its own proud individual singleness, even while it loves and yields. (247)

Here Birkin is returning to a hopeful vision for humanity he has earlier described as "an equilibrium, a pure balance of two single beings:—as the stars balance each other" (139) and as "two single equal stars balanced in conjunction" (142). His description, poetic rather than empirical, does not imply a reconciliation of tropical fire and arctic ice to create a new and perfected way of life. Rather, it is a separate option altogether that rejects both the sensual African way and the mind-abstract Nordic way as equally death-driven and, in the long run, lethal to the human race. Instead of such terminal possibilities, Birkin struggles to clarify a mode of existence and relationship moving men and women toward renewal rather than disintegration, an evolutionary path that opens out toward the future rather than freezing over or choking in jungle growth. Such a path, according to Birkin and Lawrence alike, will be walked mainly by couples who can sustain a balance between integrity of relationship and freedom of individual spirit. This is the "star balance" that Birkin proposes to Ursula beyond marriage, a concept she first rejects as dishonest and then accepts only reluctantly at best and never fully even by novel's end.

All such promising yet uncertain prophecies for the human future are lost as *Women in Love* moves from page to screen. Birkin's struggle to articulate and understand his "star balance" is omitted, as is his less cloudy, flesh-and-blood struggle with Ursula to realize the ideal through their relationship. We see instead a couple engaged in a far simpler romantic conflict, one immediately recognizable to the audience because it has been reduced to cinematic cliché. Jennie Linden makes the standard film heroine's demand for commitment from Alan Bates: love and marriage or nothing at all. He, in turn, proves reluctant to go along for fear of losing his freedom and male independence. With this all-too-familiar movie simplification, *Women in Love* inadvertently overturns Ursula's provisional acquiescence to Birkin in the text, her willingness to find out if he truly wants a star to balance his own rather than merely a female satellite. On screen it is Birkin and not Ursula who seems to give in, or give up, to her conventional and insistent demand for love alone. As the loss of entropic evolution from the film proved costly to character, here the disappearance of Lawrence's "star balance" has a parallel effect on human relationship. The text's positive couple and their fluid marriage, ever-turbulent because ever-evolving, begin to resemble the typical lovers and love conflicts of Hollywood romance.

In the novel itself, both evolutionary processes—Birkin's hoped-for "star balance" as well as Nordic/tropical loss—are imaged in works of art and discussed in aesthetic terms. This association is based on Lawrence's profound belief that art always reflects life and humanity—not just progressive humanity, unfortunately, but humanity in decay as well. As a result of this belief, an aesthetic debate takes place throughout *Women in Love*, erupting at times into violent argument over whether art should serve the vital principle or not. This is why Halliday and his carvings are present in the text, and why they ultimately function to anticipate Loerke, a character Lawrence introduces late in the work to move the evolutionary and aesthetic issues toward final convergence.

In the "Continental" chapter of *Women in Love*, Birkin immediately recognizes Loerke as Dresden's counterpart to Halliday's disintegrative London world, describing him to Gerald as living "like a rat, in the river of corruption, just where it falls over into the bottomless pit. He's further on than we are. He hates the ideal more acutely. He *hates* the ideal utterly, yet it still dominates him" (418–19). If Loerke repeats Halliday and his entropic sculpture, however, he also reflects some portion of Gerald Crich as well, thus confirming Lawrence's implication that the Nordic and tropical pathways eventually merge into one. Loerke is at work on "a great frieze for a factory in Cologne" (413) and further reveals his allegiance to the mechanical principle when he tells Ursula and Gudrun that "machinery and the acts of labour are extremely, maddeningly beautiful." And "Art should *interpret* industry as art once interpreted religion" (414–15). To conceal from himself and from others that as artist he serves the law of entropy, Loerke insists that art and life have nothing to do with one another—that they exist in separate, irreconcilable worlds. In Loerke's argument with Ursula over his statue of a nude on horseback, he lectures her patronizingly on this subject, in terms uncomfortably close to those of James Joyce or, more precisely, of Stephen Dedalus as he similarly lectures Lynch on the streets of Dublin. Loerke tells Ursula that his statue

> is a work of art, it is a picture of nothing, of absolutely nothing. It has nothing to do with anything but itself, it has no relation with the everyday world of this and other, there is no connection between them, absolutely none, they are two different and distinct planes of existence, and to translate one into the other is worse than foolish, it is a darkening of all counsel, a making confusion everywhere. Do you see, you *must not* confuse the relative . . . [world] of action with the absolute world of art. That you *must not do*. (421)

But Ursula does, becoming a spokeswoman for Lawrence on the issue of art by delivering a rebuttal to Loerke and indirectly to Stephen Dedalus as well. Ursula, in contrast to her sister, is not an artist, nor is she normally preoccupied with aesthetic questions. Yet like many of Lawrence's nonartists, she grasps more clearly than they do that, for good or ill, their work only extends and projects their humanity—so that, universally, art and life are of one organic substance and can never be separated at all. In *Lady Chatterley's Lover* another Lawrentian nonartist, Mellors, perceives Thanatos as the inspiring presence behind Duncan Forbes's mechanical and metallic paintings, characterizing one of them to the artist's face as "a pure bit of murder."[39] In *Women in Love*, Ursula similarly grasps the mean destructiveness of Loerke's life and art in equal measure, giving him back the truth about both in a brilliant outburst of clairvoyant speech:

"It isn't a word of it true, of all this harangue you have made me," she replied flatly. "The horse is a picture of your own stock, stupid brutality, and the girl was a girl you loved and tortured and then ignored. . . .

"As for your world of art and your world of reality . . . you have to separate the two, because you can't bear to know what you are. You can't bear to realise what a stock, stiff, hide-bound brutality you *are* really, so you say 'it's the world of art.' The world of art is only the truth about the real world, that's all—but you are too far gone to see it." (422)

While art objects add a compelling and meaningful imagery to the film, Russell and Kramer have clearly decided to minimize Lawrence's more abstract aesthetic discussions, no doubt for sound cinematic reasons but once again at cost to complexity and depth of character. To his credit, Vladek Sheybal manages an effective and faithful (although critically ignored) portrayal of Loerke—one which captures this character's decadent and squalid nature, both as artist and as human being, while managing to preserve most of Loerke's original speech to Ursula about the inviolable world of art. What's utterly and regrettably lost, however, is Ursula's powerful response, an omission that shrinks her presence on film both mentally and spiritually and, likewise, that silences Lawrence's own voice in the artistic debate. Rather than repeating any portion of Ursula's brave reply, Jenny Linden simply quits the field of battle, uttering one desperate line of dialogue over her shoulder as she retreats: "Well, love has no place in your world of art." It's no doubt already clear that all four of the principal characters in *Women in Love* undergo some degree of flattening as a result of the film's diminishment of ideas. Ursula, however, is probably the figure who suffers most from this process—here, for example, demonstrating an intellectual passivity and weakness of resolve which, while always forgivable in film heroines, utterly denies her admirable toughness of mind and heart in the text. Also, of course, Ursula's one-liner to Loerke as she exits his bedroom further confirms her commitment to what might have to be termed the Doris Day (or Debbie Reynolds) principle, the romantic leading lady's shrill demand for love, love, nothing but love, and surely nothing without it.

No one would claim that Lawrence's ideas in *Women in Love*—whether on art, on evolution, or on the future of the human race—constitute a fully consistent body of thinking, either philosophical or scientific. This, however, by no means dismisses the novel's intellectual substructure as either incoherent or unimportant. *Women in Love* remains, in the best sense, a thought-burdened novel, one which offers neither an anthropologist's monograph nor a theoretician's aesthetic to its readers, but instead a poet's thought-adventure and visionary chart for the course of humankind. It is precisely this—Lawrence's thought-exploring and imaginative mapping in *Women in Love*—that is most sadly betrayed on film as Russell, Kramer, and company entirely cut, or else shrink to movie cliché, idea after idea. Ironically, however, even their betrayal of Lawrence has a Lawrentian spin to it, as if these filmmakers had taken too seriously all of Birkin's railings, during the novel, against Hermione's intellectualism and intellectualism in general—against the submission of human experience to the searching eye and brain—a process which, for author and protagonist alike, transforms life into mere knowledge, reducing it to sterile yet pornographic mind-content. To betray Lawrence by his own hand is to create an interesting paradox, yet one easily enough avoided had the filmmakers remembered his caveat against believing what the artist says rather than what he does. At the outset of *Studies in Classic American Literature,* Lawrence declares, "An artist is usually a damned liar, but his art, if it be art, will tell you the truth of his day." Therefore, "Never trust the artist. Trust the tale. The proper function of a critic is to save the tale from the artist who created it."[40] Perhaps the same thing should be said about the proper function of a literary filmmaker as well. By de-intellectualizing *Women in Love*, in short, this particular group of filmmakers may have erred by paying more attention to Lawrence's preachment against human thought than to its brilliant practice in his text.

Ideas by themselves, however, do not make *Women in Love* a major work of literature. Lawrence's fundamental achievement resides not in abstraction but in visionary imagination that transforms ideas, and everything else it touches, into living art. To term *Women in Love* an organic masterpiece is to suggest, at the risk of literary cliché, that the novel provides a vital instance of its own intellectual content. In treating time thematically, *Women in Love* also exemplifies the narrative's capacity to transcend chronology—to evade what E. M. Forster referred to in *Aspects of the Novel* as "the tapeworm of time."[41] In discussing evolution, Lawrence's work itself evolves and develops before our eyes, as do its four major characters. In comparing a sterile aesthetic to a vital one, the novel ultimately emerges as its own best instance of what Lawrence thought art should accomplish. In *Women in Love,* Lawrence's insistence upon repetition serves him brilliantly as a means of bringing discourse to life and, more generally, as the novel's single most important artistic technique. Repetition itself, however, has both its own vital and sterile manifestations. We overhear the deadly tick-tock of the machine, for example, in Gudrun's ominous clock as it measures her life away, moment by insignificant moment. "But better die [Ursula thinks, not realizing that Gudrun's fate is what she foresees] than live mechanically a life that is a repetition of repetitions" (184). Much later in the novel Gudrun herself muses that "between two particular people, any two people on earth, the range of pure sensational experience is limited. The climax of sensual reaction, once reached in any direction, is reached finally, there is no going on. There is only repetition possible, or the going apart of the two protagonists, or the subjugating of the one will to the other, or death" (443). Here, of course, Gudrun is thinking about Gerald as her lover and the likeness of his sexuality—powerful yet cold—to the very machinery of the mines—the "latest improvements" he himself has introduced.

Mechanical repetition is precise but incapable of change, thus creatively dead—as when a factory stamps out one metal part, then a thousand metal parts, ad infinitum. Organic repetition, however, is another breed of cat or a horse of a remarkably different color—as when a cell makes a copy of itself, exact yet never exactly the same, and ever capable of radical departure from the pattern. Organic repetition, or Lawrence's artistic imitation of this vital process, governs the form of *Women in Love* and thereby brings the novel's own best ideas to life. A full accounting of organic repetition in *Women in Love* would require a separate book-length study, since the process is intricate and ever-present in the text, at times even spilling beyond it as when Birkin stones the moon in parallel to a scene from another novel—Ursula's moon-dance in *The Rainbow* celebrating her triumph over Anton Skrebensky and over men in general.

In this approach to *Women in Love* on film, one major area of textual repetition will suffice for comparative purposes. The original title of the novel's seventh chapter, "Fetish," was changed to "Totem" for the first English edition, presumably in direct reference to the carved statue of a woman in labor that several characters gather around and discuss at Halliday's flat. The more exact meaning of totem, however, is a living entity, usually an animal, with which a person or group chooses to identify itself. By such identification, the individual or clan becomes empowered to repeat, in human terms, the particular qualities of the chosen creature—the cunning of Henry Grenfel's fox, for example, or the remote strength of Gerald Crich's wolf. "'His totem is the wolf . . .' [Gudrun] repeated to herself" on seeing Gerald for the first time, and "'His mother is an old, unbroken wolf'" (9). In the novel, Lawrence practices a unique form of literary totemism, connecting virtually all of his characters to natural living things, animals, or even plants, and using such connections to create a rhythm that can be felt, like a heartbeat, throughout the novel. More specifically, a particular scene in *Women in Love* will involve one character with an animal or plant so as to strip away polite appearances and honestly, often cruelly, to reveal that character's inner being. Such a scene will sooner or later copy or repeat itself by involving a second character—often the lover or special counterpart to the first one—in an almost identical scene.

The mutually destructive love relationship between Birkin and Hermione, for example, comes to an end amid flora and during two scenes crafted as replications of one another. In the first, "Class-Room," Hermione turns Ursula's botany lesson into a rhapsodic analysis of the catkin plant with its male and female flowers:

> "Now I shall always see them," she repeated. "Thank you so much for showing me. I think they're so beautiful—little red flames—"
> Her absorption was strange, almost rhapsodic. Both Birkin and Ursula were suspended. The little red pistillate flowers had some strange, almost mystic-passionate attraction for her. (31)

Hermione is, of course, engaged in a symbolic action that dances out the nature of her own eroticism in vegetative tropes. As she compulsively attempts to see and know the tiny sexual flowers, so too does she subject Birkin and their lovemaking to visual and cerebral scrutiny. The connection is hardly lost on Birkin, so that he immediately flies into a rage and an act of violence against Hermione that proves shocking even though it remains purely verbal:

> You, the most deliberate thing that ever walked or crawled! You'd be verily deliberately spontaneous—that's you. Because you want to have everything in your own volition, your deliberate voluntary consciousness. You want it all in that loathsome little skull of yours, that ought to be cracked like a nut. For you'll be the same till it *is* cracked, like an insect in its skin. If one cracked your skull perhaps one might get a spontaneous, passionate woman out of you, with real sensuality. As it is, what you want is pornography—looking at yourself in mirrors, watching your naked animal actions in mirrors, so that you can have it all in your consciousness, make it all mental. (36)

Birkin's vegetative simile, "cracked like a nut," is an unconscious prophecy of Hermione's eventual experience of spontaneity and at least temporary liberation from the need to see and know. Her first truly passionate act is an effort, with a lapis lazuli paperweight, to apply Birkin's advice to his skull rather than her own. Hermione's failed "last blow" ends their relationship, driving Birkin out of her house and into the woods where, bloodied but unbowed, he dances out a botanical trope of his own in oblique but clear reply to "Class-Room." Birkin's dance of the flowers condemns and cancels Hermione's by re-creating it with a difference—by replacing her cerebral and visual rhapsody with unexamined experience and with the tactile contact of one naked organism against another. Birkin "took off his clothes, and sat down naked among the primroses, moving his feet softly among the primroses, his legs, his knees, his arms right up to the arm-pits, lying down and letting them touch his belly, his breasts. It was such a fine, cool, subtle touch all over him, he seemed to saturate himself with their contact" (100).

Gudrun and Gerald, a second dysfunctional couple, share an even more powerful pairing of scenes, only now to mark the start rather than the finish of a deadly relationship. Here the scenes in repetition involve both characters with animals rather than plants—a red Arab mare to bring out Gerald's cruelty and will to dominate the opposite sex, and a herd of wild Scottish bullocks to do precisely the same thing for Gudrun. Gerald's symbolic dance with the mare reveals that his strategy and style of mastery involve mechanism and possession. The horse belongs to him and as property must submit to use and to the will of its rider. Gerald commands it to stand near a railway crossing as a locomotive shunts coal vans to and fro; the railway equipment and the coal are, of course, his property as well. Each time the train approaches, the animal shies away in terror, and each time Gerald forces it back to the crossing, finally bloodying the mare's flanks with his spurs. The Brangwen sisters witness this event, and their reaction to it forms a study in contrasts. Ursula is reduced to hysterics by Gerald's actions and by the suffering animal, but Gudrun remains fascinated and aroused as she watches, as if seeing in Gerald a reflection of her own deepest urges.

Gudrun's turn to dance comes soon after this incident, just before Diana Crich drowns at Shortlands. She and Ursula have taken a canoe to an isolated island on the Crich estate in order to escape the water-party crowd. As Gudrun dances for her own amusement and Ursula's, a herd of Highland cattle appear, drawn to her movements out of curiosity. Despite Ursula's terror, Gudrun insists on dancing before them "as if she were confident of some secret power in herself, and had to put it to the test. 'Sit down and sing again,' she called [to Ursula] in her high, strident voice. . . . It was evident she had a strange passion to dance before the sturdy, handsome cattle" (158–59). Hermione's catkins—juxtaposed against Birkin's primroses, hyacinths, and fir-trees—establish the pair as incompatible lovers, exactly opposed in how they relate to natural life. Gerald's mare and Gudrun's bullocks establish a similar incompatibility, only now by way of a destructive likeness rather than an opposition. The style of Gudrun's animal-dance may differ radically from Gerald's, far more subtle and based on art rather than industry or the economics of ownership, yet its purpose is the same—to torture a lesser creature of opposite gender and ultimately to vanquish it by force of will. Lawrence employs a final stroke of repetition to imply the close connection between his beast and flower scenes. Hermione's blow to Birkin's head places the final period on their stricken relationship and sends him reeling into the woods for comfort. Preserving yet reversing the complex replications, Gudrun's dance leads first to an irrational quarrel with Gerald (over ownership, in fact, since the cattle, like the mare and the train, are his)—then to a second blow, anticipatory this time rather than terminal, as she transfers her hostility and urge to dominate the bullocks to the man who owns them:

> "You have struck the first blow," he said at last, forcing the words from his lungs, in a voice so soft and low, it sounded like a dream within her, not spoken in the outer air.
>
> "And I shall strike the last," she retorted involuntarily, with confident assurance. He was silent, he did not contradict her. (162)

At other climactic points within *Women in Love,* Lawrence varies and complicates his rhythm by placing couples rather than individuals in similar organic scenes, with similar repetitions designed to expose and explore their relationships. Gerald and Gudrun, for example, dance out their attitudes separately with a mare and a herd of cattle, but dance them together with a rabbit in what proves to be a most revealing and ominous duet. Repeating this repetition, Lawrence creates a parallel scene for Birkin and Ursula in which the nature of the beast changes from rabbit to cat and in which the symbolic dance remains troubled yet far more amusing to watch.

Bismarck is a large male rabbit belonging to Winifred, the youngest member of the Crich family and Gudrun's private pupil since her father's death. When Gerald attempts to remove the rabbit from its cage, so that Winifred and Gudrun can draw its portrait, Bismarck reacts in a blind combination of rage and fear until Gerald terrorizes the animal into submission:

> Swift as lightning he drew back and brought his free hand down like a hawk on the neck of the rabbit. Simultaneously, there came the unearthly abhorrent scream of a rabbit in the fear of death. It made one immense writhe, tore . . . [Gerald's] wrists and his sleeves in a final convulsion, all its belly flashed white in a whirlwind of paws, and then he had slung it round and had it under his arm, fast. It cowered and skulked. His face was gleaming with a smile. (233)

Although Gerald delivers this blow alone, the emotions behind it are his and Gudrun's together, now conspiring in sadistic alliance against the animal. As a mare and herd of cattle had previously summoned their separate cruelties and power urges, so now this lesser creature acts as the single vessel for their collective poison and for the deadly impulses they will soon turn against one another: "'Isn't it a *fool!*' she cried. 'Isn't it a sickening *fool?*' The vindictive mockery in her voice made his brain quiver. Glancing up at him, into his eyes, she revealed again the mocking, white-cruel recognition. There was a league between them, abhorrent to them both. They were implicated with each other in abhorrent mysteries" (234).

Bismarck's animal counterpart is Mino, a young male cat who brings Birkin and Ursula together in similar yet ultimately inverted circumstances. At first glance, Mino seems only to repeat the problems of sexual violence and the urge to dominate lesser creatures. As Birkin and Ursula watch, the cat encounters a wild female and dances a graceful yet cruel dance with her. Mino reminds Ursula at once of Gerald astride his mare, and she tells Birkin angrily that the animal is simply forcing male mastery upon its mate as the basis for their relationship. "'Mino,' said Ursula, 'I don't like you. You are a bully like all males.' . . . 'It is just like Gerald Crich with his horse—a lust for bullying—a real Wille zur Macht—so base, so petty'" (141, 142).

Partly in sport and partly in seriousness, Birkin takes the opposite view here, arguing with Ursula that the two cats dance out an equilibrium of free and opposite natures, his very own "star-balance," rather than a subjugation of one creature to the will of another. Mino's paws (unlike Gerald's spurs) are delicate and give no injury at all to the female. Likewise, despite her sexual submissiveness to the male cat, she retains the absolute freedom of a wild creature, leaving him and returning to the woods whenever she wishes to do so: "'I agree [Birkin replies to Ursula's accusation] that the Wille zur Macht is a base and petty thing. But with the Mino, it is the desire to bring this female cat into a pure stable equilibrium, a transcendent and abiding *rapport* with the single male. Whereas without him, as you see, she is a mere stray, a fluffy sporadic bit of chaos. It is a volonté de pouvoir, if you like'" (142).

At this stage of their relationship Ursula remains as wary of Birkin and his theories as she is of his tomcat and its lordly behavior. Her healthy skepticism and the couple's sexual sparring in general prove to be the scene's essential point and likewise the means by which Lawrence reveals these two lovers as fundamentally opposed to Gerald and Gudrun. Through Bismarck, in other words, Gerald and Gudrun expose themselves as all-too-dangerously alike, each possessing an equal measure of cruelty, power-lust, and the rabbit's own chaotic force. Through Mino, by contrast, the human dynamic brought forth in Birkin and Ursula is of an entirely opposite and far more promising sort—a playfully erotic give-and-give-back between the woman and the man, a balance of two lovers in which neither single self is compromised and in which each individual retains ultimate freedom of spirit.

Lawrence's major technique here of organic repetition—his visible juxtaposition of firs and catkins, horses and cattle, rabbits and cats—seems so inherently cinematic as to offer Ken Russell his material ready-made. At odds with the

author's potential gift, however, is what seems in the film to be a deliberate effort to obscure or simply omit the complex mirrorings within the scenes just
discussed, as if Russell were demonstrating in cinematic practice his critical rejection of Lawrentian repetition in general. The Mino incident, for example,
which so sharply defines Birkin and Ursula in relationship, disappears from the
film altogether, leaving its counterpart for Gerald and Gudrun isolated in a kind
of aesthetic vacuum and reducing it to a trivial and largely meaningless event.
Only a few seconds of film are devoted to Bismarck, which, unlike Lawrence's
explosive rabbit, scarcely moves a muscle. The animal simply gets handed by
Winifred Crich first to Gudrun, then to Gerald, as the two adults stare at one
another in mutually lustful male and female gazes. Russell's passive film rabbit
seems more related to Gerald than to the couple's relationship with its black-and-
white fur precisely matching his clothing. While this may succeed visually in
implying Gerald's erotic desire for Gudrun, the rabbit scene as a whole fails to
imply any of the far darker and more complex forces that unite this couple in
destructive alliance.[42]

Even when both of Lawrence's scenes-in-counterpoint survive within the film,
any sense of repetition or mirroring between them is frequently lost in translation. Hermione's catkins, for instance, fail to foreshadow or even relate to Birkin's
firs and primroses despite both floral scenes being preserved reasonably intact
on screen. While much of Lawrence's original language remains in "Class-Room,"
the critical bridge-line that connects this incident to Hermione's blow, and that
prepares for Birkin's subsequent actions, does not. In the film, Birkin suggests
that Hermione's skull should be cracked open not in the classroom scene but at
Breadalby, just as she lifts the paperweight to try his advice upon his own pate.
As a result, cinematic anticipation, in contrast to textual foreshadowing, is made
so short-term as to become blatantly obvious and to obscure all serious implications behind or beyond the incident itself.

In the hands of the filmmakers, Lawrence's animals seem to suffer much the
same loss of significance-in-repetition as do his flowers and trees. While both
Gudrun's encounter with the bullocks and Gerald's torture of his mare are incorporated into the film, they give no indication of being related events. This is
partly the result of a curious imbalance or lopsidedness of emphasis within the
two counterpart scenes. Russell deals with Gudrun's power-dance before Gerald's
cattle with great care and attention to detail, so that it becomes one of the film's
most effective and memorable scenes, but he gives cinematic short shrift to
Gerald's horseback ride. As with the Bismarck scene, only a very brief fragment
of film is focused on Gerald and his mare—so brief, in fact, that the event must
seem confusing and pointless to anyone viewing the film without first having
read the book. In less than a minute of screen time, Gerald races his mare against

an oncoming coal train, all the while shouting lines of dialogue made all but incomprehensible by the noise of the locomotive. He suddenly pulls up at the grade crossing where Gudrun and Ursula are standing, whips and spurs his rearing horse bloody, then rides off laughing as the two sisters look on, and as Glenda Jackson repeats Gudrun's line from the text, "I should think you're proud" (105). Regrettably lost here, along with all organic connection to the cattle incident, is any sense of how differently Gudrun and Ursula react to what they have just witnessed. While Jennie Linden is shown in tears, and Glenda Jackson is not, little else in Gudrun's behavior or facial expression remains to suggest that, in sharp contrast to Ursula, she identifies herself with what Gerald has done and, beyond this, has been powerfully aroused by it.[43]

What seems to happen, then, as *Women in Love* moves from page to screen is either a botching of Lawrentian repetition or else an overt effort to suppress it entirely. The less visible but more complete truth, however, is that Russell and company only bungle or obliterate the mirrorings when they belong to Lawrence and his text—never when they are the original creations of the filmmakers themselves. The film turns out to be a paradoxical piece of artistic business, often lapsing or failing outright when held strictly to textual account, yet recovering and ultimately achieving creative triumph through a unique gesture of homage to the text and simultaneous violence upon it. In Lawrence's own terms, the film "comes through" artistically when it preserves the author's repetitive strategy, while erasing his specific repetitions, and then applies that strategy to freshly minted cinematic material. Ironically, all of this seems to accord with Lawrence's method and spirit, despite Russell's loud protests against the writer's tendency to repeat himself in print.

One technique by which Russell erases yet retraces Lawrence can be termed "cinematic reattachment." This occurs when the film "uncouples" one of the text's originally paired sequences from its counterpart, then reattaches it to material newly made for the screen. As suggested earlier, no one watching Russell's *Women in Love* would perceive the original relationship between Hermione's soliloquy to the catkin plant and Birkin's naked walk in the woods. On screen, however, the catkin episode is reflected in and recalled by another incident occurring just a few scenes later—in fact, by another apostrophe to vegetable life, now delivered by Birkin in oblique response to Hermione.

This occurs during what I've referred to as the film's "introduction scene," an event having no basis in Lawrence's novel. In it, the guests and hostess at Breadalby are gathered around an elegant outdoor table, and at Birkin's instigation the four principal characters make themselves known to the audience by discussing the peculiarity of their names. In the midst of this, Birkin notices Hermione (who has not participated in the discussion) eating a fig. He seizes one of his own from a fruit bowl and, in what is meant to be taken as an impromptu

outburst, recites approximately half of Lawrence's poem "Figs."[44] The lines that
Birkin speaks aloud to the company elaborate upon Lawrence's comparison between the fig and "the female part," "The fissure, the yoni,/ The wonderful moist
conductivity towards the centre" and between this fruit and womankind in general.[45] It seems, therefore, to have been added by the filmmakers (with a key assist from Lawrence) as a repetition of Hermione's monologue to the similarly
personified, and sexual, catkins in Ursula's classroom. This cinematic repetition
emphasizes the opposition between Hermione and Birkin as failed lovers, exactly
as does Lawrence's juxtaposition of her catkins against his firs and primroses in
the text. In a very subtle but revealing stroke of filmmaking, Russell manages to
construct an effective bridge between these two scenes-in-repetition which, while
not verbal, functions much the same way as did Birkin's "cracked like a nut"—
Lawrence's transition between counterpart events in the novel. In the film's class-
room scene, Ursula deliberately brings Hermione's catkin monologue to an end
by ringing her school bell to dismiss the class. Repeating this detail, but appropriately reversing it, Russell has Alan Bates begin his recitation of "Figs" by ringing
a bell in order to gain the attention of Hermione and her guests.

A lesser but equally original film repetition links "Class-Room" to "Gladiatorial," the wrestling match between Gerald and Birkin, in a way independent from
the text. Here the repetition involves the very Lawrentian image of electricity and
the negative act of destroying a mood or a moment of connection between human beings by suddenly switching on the lights. In Lawrence's novel it is Birkin
who does this when he interrupts Ursula's botany lesson and startles her in the
process. The film preserves Lawrence's electric gesture, changing the light-giver
from Birkin to Hermione in order to emphasize (or perhaps overemphasize) her
destructive function and her commitment to knowing and seeing. Hermione's
intrusive illumination of "Class-Room" reveals her inward nature and also connects her to another child of light, Gerald Crich, who repeats her action later in
the film with equally negative implications. In the aftermath of his gladiatorial
with Birkin, visually compelling because of its red, fire-lit coloration, Gerald
rejects the mood of intimacy and the developing yet frightening possibility of
brotherhood with Birkin by switching on the harsh, white electric lights, an action that never takes place in Lawrence's text.

Using this technique of cinematic reattachment, the makers of *Women in Love*
bring about an equally original repetition of Gerald's abuse of his mare. This very
brief film scene is entirely disconnected from Gudrun and her cattle, but then
reconnected to a second scene involving Gerald and following almost immediately after his horseback ride. As Gerald gallops away from the railroad crossing
and the two sisters, Russell's camera suddenly shifts to the interior of a coal mine
and to the dismissal of an elderly worker, Dewhurst, who can no longer perform

up to Gerald's demanding standards. This episode is followed by a second mine sequence in which Gerald and his ailing father leave work together amid a crowd of departing miners. The elegantly dressed father and son enter their open-topped, chauffeur-driven automobile surrounded by a plodding horde of black-clad men and women. The colors of the Crich car, pure white with a plush red interior, stand out in especially sharp contrast to the drab crowd and in exact repetition of colors just seen by the film audience on Gerald's rearing horse, its pure white coat stained with blood. Unlike the textual repetition of "Coal-Dust," which mirrors Gerald's sadism in Gudrun's dance, this cinematic repetition refers back to Gerald himself, revealing his deficiencies twice over. If the colors red and white conflate a flesh-and-blood horse with an inanimate car, the film implies that Gerald sees no difference between them. Living or not, both are simply his vehicles, the organic as well as the mechanical forced to submit to every demand of convenience and use. As in the paired catkin and fig sequences, here again the filmmakers insert a connecting detail to reinforce the similarity between Gerald's ride on horseback and in his car. A steam locomotive, once again suggesting ownership and mechanical power, presides noisily in the background of both scenes.[46]

A final example of screen reattachment involves Gudrun's cattle-dance, the text's gender-reversed repetition of Gerald and his mare. On film her dance bears no similarity to his horseback ride but instead resembles an earlier dance, performed and also directed by Hermione Roddice ostensibly for the amusement of her guests at Breadalby but really to impose her will upon all of them—and upon Ursula, Gudrun, and Birkin especially. Unlike Russell's two previous reattachments, this one grows from a slight textual incident in which Hermione's guests don costumes and dance out in pantomime the biblical grieving of Orpah, Naomi, and Ruth. In the text, "Hermione loved to watch" rather than participate, and so takes no part in this dance at all (84). On film, the biblical pantomime is entirely her invention, forced upon a group of bored and tired guests. Hermione assumes the lead role of Ruth for herself and by way of the dance attempts to overwhelm the other performers, Ursula and Gudrun, and also to repossess Birkin and prolong their failed relationship. Hermione's ballet is another power-dance, much like Gudrun's performance before the cattle not only in spirit but also in style, precisely anticipating many of Glenda Jackson's exact movements and gestures. The two dances also come to an abrupt end in parallel, Gudrun's interrupted by Gerald (as in the text) and Hermione's (in a film interpolation) interrupted by Birkin, who breaks her oppressive mood by requesting a ragtime tune and then dancing with Ursula. Both masculine interruptions lead immediately to violence. Birkin's interruption of Hermione on film stimulates her failed "last blow," struck with the lapis lazuli paperweight. Gerald's similar interruption of Gudrun a few scenes later achieves both textual fidelity and cinematic invention. As it re-creates Lawrence's original scene almost exactly, it repeats the earlier and purely original film sequence as well. Gudrun slaps Gerald's face in a "first blow," far more dangerous than Hermione's final one, then warns him, "And I shall strike the last," her exact words in the text. Glenda Jackson speaks this line as she leans upon a tall tree, her arms thrust upward in unconscious imitation of Hermione and her melodramatic dance-pose against a marble column at Breadalby.

It is evident from these examples of cinematic reattachment that while Lawrence's artistic strategy survives on screen reasonably intact, a great deal of his original material undergoes change. Certainly the novel's totemism, its tendency to find human significance in the world of birds, beasts, and flowers, is both diminished and obscured on film. While several of Lawrence's animals and plants still appear and function as meaningful tropes, they are de-emphasized and partially replaced by mechanical objects or else by objects and gestures of art—dance especially but sculpture and painting as well. This modification of text holds true for a second order of repetition on film which, unlike what I'm calling "reattachment," owes no debt to the text at all. Russell and his colleagues, in fact, probably achieve their most effective repetitions not by recombining new material with old but by going outside the text altogether to mint both sides of the Lawrentian coin anew.

An early example of cinematic repetition as total rather than partial interpolation involves no images whatsoever, animal, vegetable, mechanical, or artistic, but simply human beings. I'm referring to the much discussed and, in fact, often condemned film sequence in which Birkin and Ursula first make love and in which their painful mating struggle is equated visually with the death-embrace of the drowned couple, Tibby and Laura Lupton. When the film version of *Women in Love* first appeared, this episode attracted negative attention from critics and reviewers on several fronts, the most common objection being its seemingly pointless alteration of the text. Lawrence's Tibby and Laura Lupton don't drown at the Crich water party. Laura's sister Diana drowns, along with the young doctor who attempts to save her. On film, Diana Crich is left out entirely, with the newlywed couple taking her place and the doctor's as victims at Shortlands. As their bodies are discovered at the bottom of the drained lake, Russell's camera crosscuts between Laura and Tibby in death and Birkin and Ursula, who have just achieved ambiguous and troubled sexual consummation. Playing perhaps upon the Metaphysical conceit of orgasm as the little death, the filmmakers depict the living lovers as doubles of the drowned man and wife, with Ursula and Birkin reclined and intertwined in the same position as the dead couple.[47]

In more recent discussions of *Women in Love* on film, the first objections to this repetition as pointlessly tampering with the text have given way to a more searching approach, but likewise to puzzled disagreement among the commentators. Some writers like Ana Laura Zambrano and Joseph Gomez interpret Ursula and Birkin's first sexual encounter, oddly enough, as comic while others like Joy Gould Boyum come closer to my own assessment of it as essentially a "first unhappy attempt at making love."[48] No two critics, however, among those discussing love and death as mirrored in this scene, seem to agree on its significance or on what the filmmakers may have intended by way of their visual repetition. Boyum concludes her discussion with the straightforward suggestion that both this episode and the film in general imply that "love is inextricably entwined with death."[49] Zambrano believes that the same mirror-imaging reflects self-concern rather than the universal presence of death in love, comparing Laura Crich's "killing" of Tibby in a desperate effort to save her own life with Ursula's selfish and aggressive seduction of Birkin.[50] Gomez concludes that the scene's intent is to deflate Birkin's lofty, theoretical idealism about his relationship with Ursula and literally to bring him down to earth or to the painful realities of love and death.[51] G. B. Crump, contributing an equally independent voice to this discussion, suggests perhaps more pessimistically than the others that "the crosscutting visually [between the living and dead couples] dramatizes the . . . point that Ursula's emotional possessiveness would drag Birkin to his psychic death in the same way Laura dragged her unfortunate husband to his actual death."[52]

While each of these conclusions is unique, they share an essentially negative reading of the film's love/death repetition, although the scene may carry hopeful as well as morbid implications. Just before Ursula forces her relationship with Birkin into sexuality (and she is clearly the physical instigator on screen), he tells her in a textual paraphrase that he wants "to die to our kind of life" and to "be born again in a love that is like sleep." Since these words constitute a preface to the film's *Liebestod,* perhaps it is meant to act out a realization of Birkin's wish. Since the living lovers, unlike the drowned husband and wife, do arise phoenixlike from their death postures in the mud, the film interpolation may have been inserted to show Lawrence's hopeful couple dying—not to all life but to conventional life as lived by couples like Tibby and Laura—and then as experiencing rebirth together into something better. If so, this original yet highly Lawrentian repetition and the film as a whole never succeed in clarifying what that "something better" might be. The only cinematic statement I can identify here with any assurance is negative and even somewhat anti-Lawrentian in nature. Russell and his colleagues seem, specifically, to project no faith in sexuality as offering any certainty to men and women attempting to "come through" or to "go one better" in a love relationship. Tibby and Laura Lupton are a highly erotic couple, yet their lovemaking is depicted as selfish, shallow, and ultimately fatal, since their sexual dalliance in the lake is precisely what leads to the drowning. Also, Tibby and Laura are the film's only couple who enjoy the act of love. Every other sexually explicit scene in *Women in Love,* as has been suggested earlier, emphasizes a frustrating and painful struggle far more than it emphasizes pleasure. The *Liebestod* just described exemplifies this as do all of the sexual sequences on screen involving Birkin and Hermione, Gudrun and Gerald, or Gudrun and Loerke. Near the close of the film, when Birkin and Ursula appear as man and wife in a scene implying their deepening relationship, they are shown once again reclined and intertwined—not making love but instead sleeping together in what is perhaps intended to represent their attainment of a "love that is like sleep."

The film's *Liebestod* proves unique among Russell's cinematic mirrorings because it involves no complicating imagery, only human beings or couples reflecting one another directly. Elsewhere, however, the filmmakers depend upon images, especially images drawn from the world of art, as raw material for their cinematic interpolations and as a major means of revealing character and relationship. Here, once again, it would seem that in writing *Women in Love* Lawrence has already given these filmmakers their material ready-made along with the key principle of repetition itself: Gudrun's dance of domination and, beyond it, Halliday's collection of primitive art as well as Loerke's "confessional" or self-incriminating industrial frieze and female nude on horseback. While the filmmakers have effectively adapted one of these images for the screen in Gudrun's dance, they reject or mishandle the rest. Halliday, his primitive carvings, and his hermetically sealed bohemian world disappear from the film altogether. And while Loerke remains to display his nude on horseback proudly to Gudrun and Ursula, the aesthetic image itself, so meaningful and revealing in the text, is reduced to muddled insignificance on film. In Lawrence's novel, Loerke's photograph of the statue depicts a vulnerable young girl seated upon a massive stallion, the image clearly intended as a gender-inverted repetition of Gerald astride his mare. Just as the physically powerful Gerald dominated his delicate female horse, so too has the physically insignificant yet spiritually controlling Loerke brutalized Annette von Weck, his mistress and model for the piece. "The horse is a picture of your own stock, stupid brutality," as Ursula has so clearly perceived and told the artist, "and the girl was a girl you loved and tortured and then ignored" (422). On screen, while we are allowed only a brief glimpse of Loerke's work, it is sufficient to confirm that none of Lawrence's textual repetitions survives within the image. If the film version of Loerke's horse is stiff, stupid, and brutal enough to match the original, so too is the female figure upon it. Fully clothed and almost as large as the animal itself, she seems unlikely to have been Loerke's victim—or anyone else's for that matter.

Two purely cinematic interpolations appearing late in *Women in Love* make up for this confused presentation and, by way of their effective treatment of art in repetition, confirm the principle that Russell and his associates are better off on their own, at least when it comes to deciding just what images to repeat. The two scenes are also intended as gender-inverted counterparts to one another, again faithfully applying Lawrentian technique to material not of his creation.

In the first scene Birkin attempts to convince Gerald, as in the text, that marriage isn't for everyone and that blood brotherhood, or the attainment of male love, can be as fulfilling and deep as any relationship between a man and a woman. As the two friends talk, and as Gerald moves closer to open rejection of Birkin's "offer," Russell's camera shows three female statues decorating the room and imposing their presence upon both men, but upon Gerald especially, by seeming to watch over them from above. The first figure is a bronze statuette of a young woman whose dance pose creates a visual reminder of Gudrun and her similar posturing earlier in the film. Russell's statue rests upon a shelf or mantle near a mirror, so that his camera actually shows us two female figures, although evidently in *trompe l'oeil* rather than true reflection. While visible just momentarily, the mirrored images appear to strike slightly different poses as if implying a similar discord between Gerald's vision of Gudrun and Gudrun as she really exists. While this first figure hovers above Gerald throughout the scene, the next one, another female statuette in bronze, suggests domination even more obviously by seeming to rest her outstretched hand upon his head. This too is cinematic *trompe l'oeil,* since the figure is actually several feet behind Gerald in the background. Like Russell's first statue, this one is barely shown before being replaced by another, the bust of a woman in plaster or clay. Her image is also doubled by the mirror and again implies Gudrun's influence over Gerald by framing his head (made tiny by the mirror's perspective) between her neck and breast. Their positions recall the flesh-and-blood couple in Russell's earlier "Death and Love" episode in which Gerald comes to Gudrun's bedroom more as a child seeking maternal comfort than as a lover and buries his head between her naked breasts. Russell closes this sequence by shifting his camera away from statues to focus entirely on Gerald and Birkin as they end their discussion. Here the camera alternates between views of Birkin facing his friend—so that the audience can only see the back of Gerald's head—and views which reverse the positions of the two men. The visual effect is further complicated by Russell's ever-present mirrors, which alternately reveal two Birkins confronting one Gerald, then two Geralds confronting one Birkin in response. It finally becomes impossible to determine, from the viewer's perspective, which image represents the "real" man and which the reflection.

While no actual mirrors come into play during the film's counterpart sequence, the entire scene itself is Russell's reflected image of this one. What is reversed, however, is gender rather than spatial perspective, with the two sisters replacing the failed blood brothers as the scene's principal characters. In keeping with this turnabout, Russell's art objects also reverse genders, as his triad of female statues gives way to a single masculine figure—a bust of Gerald Crich that Gudrun is sculpting in clay. As Gudrun works, she and Ursula consider Gerald's "proposal" of a two-couple excursion "high in the perfect snow." While Ursula is enthusiastic, Gudrun becomes angry—first that Gerald would discuss his plans with Birkin before speaking to her, and second that he would so casually reveal their intimate relationship to the other man, thus reducing it to a liaison with "some little type." While the sisters talk, they look down upon Gerald's clay head, in one sense inverting, yet in another sense maintaining, the vertical implications of the previous scene. The live human beings now hover over the image, rather than the other way around, yet the female figures remain above the male, preserving their position of dominance. Gudrun's statue is really a monstrous caricature of Gerald rather than a fair likeness, thereby revealing her inner vision of him much as the bronze dancing girl reveals his distorted inner vision of her. In a visual reference back to Russell's second female statue in the prior scene, Gudrun touches the top of Gerald's head as she sculpts in a gesture of anger and frustration. Finally she thrusts her sculpting tool deep into the statue's mouth in a "last blow" of sorts revealing hatred and mocking contempt for her lover. Like Russell's earlier art scene, this one also ends with a shift away from objects to human beings. The sisters' discussion is interrupted by the sound of Birkin's approaching motorbike. He motions Ursula to join him, and she quickly departs, leaving Gudrun and Gerald's repulsive clay figure to themselves.

Ursula's escape with Birkin provides an appropriate conclusion to both of Russell's mirrored art-scenes, since it graphically contrasts their living, organic relationship with one hopelessly burdened by images and thus dead and deadly in human terms. This suggestion is evident in Russell's final view of Gudrun as Ursula hurries to join Birkin—alone and confronting the ugly visage of Gerald that she has created. The earlier art scene ended on the same ominous note, since all three of its statues were covert portraits of Gudrun (inwardly if not literally Gerald's creation), now controlling him to the exclusion of Birkin and to his own complete and eventually fatal isolation. This may be why Russell closes his final, abortive love conversation between the two men by showing their potential blood brotherhood lost within a confusion of mirrors. From the viewer's visual perspective, as from Gerald's spiritual perspective, it is no longer clear who he "really" is or whether Birkin's image before him reveals a true friend or a deceptive illusion.

Seeming to avoid such dark reflections, Birkin and Ursula depart as a unified couple, moving together toward a real relationship rather than a mirage. Even their hopeful exit, however, is made slightly ambiguous by the presence of discordant if perhaps accidental imagery on the part of the filmmakers. Birkin and

Ursula drive away on an un-Lawrentian motorbike, a mechanical contrivance more suggestive of Gerald's life than of theirs. Also, this vehicle comes equipped with a sidecar. As Birkin stops beneath the sisters' window and summons Ursula to join him, it is clear from his gestures that this sidecar is where she will ride for the duration of their journey. Either the filmmakers are being ironic here by calling the happy ending into question, or they are making a substantial imagistic departure from the text as well as from their own earlier view of Birkin eventually giving in to Ursula's demand for unqualified love. Ursula's little sidecar implies no balanced partnership between lovers and fellow wanderers but rather her female status as passenger in relation to male driver or as satellite in relation to star, the very subservience she suspected Birkin of demanding all along.

With this ambiguous departure, and the close of the two sculpture sequences, Ken Russell's film shifts suddenly to the Alps and begins accelerating toward its own conclusion. As the setting changes, so too does cinematic strategy and style, with Russell seeming to abandon such complex and original repetitions as have been examined here in favor of a more linear and literal tracking of the text. Some interpolations still occur in the film's final episodes, such as the "love scene" between Gudrun and Loerke in which a pantomime-fantasy about Tchaikovsky affords him the opportunity to reveal his own homosexuality in earnest. For the most part, however, the film's last half-hour focuses on a series of brief scenes, most of which are edited versions of material drawn from the text. Much like *Sons and Lovers,* the first long Lawrence novel to reach the screen, *Women in Love* also shifts into fast-forward near the end, as if Russell had suddenly remembered that his two hours ("about all anyone can take at a sitting") were almost up.[53] Of special interest amid this rush of closing scenes, however, is the film's visual translation of Gerald's death. As he sits down and discards his cap and gloves, preparatory to final sleep, Russell's camera pulls back to show his footprints in the snow and his body at the end of them, utterly diminished by the frozen expanse of mountains in the background. The scene is absolutely static and, in its visual impression, somehow suggestive of text upon a printed page. All of the film's previously bright colors give way here to black-and-white shadow upon snow, with Gerald's tracks resembling a lengthy but linear sentence having finally come to a full stop. Also visually original, despite its exact verbal fidelity to the text, is the film's final scene in which Birkin and Ursula end on a note of discord, continuing to argue about his need for a love relationship beyond their own:

"You can't have two kinds of love. Why should you!"
"It seems as if I can't," he said. "Yet I wanted it."
"You can't have it, because it's false, impossible," she said.
"I don't believe that," he answered. (473)

But for the omission of one adjective (*false*), along with the "he saids" and "she saids," Larry Kramer's dialogue records exactly what Lawrence wrote, interpreted somewhat shrilly by Jennie Linden and in pure deadpan by Alan Bates. Although Bates's Birkin gets the last word, in keeping with the novel, Jennie Linden's Ursula gets the final and enduring image. As Birkin speaks his closing line, Russell's camera freezes on a close-up of Ursula's face that remains in view during the final screen credits. Her expression reveals pain and anger at Birkin's refusal to be satisfied with their relationship alone, and ends the film with the visual implication that many issues between the couple remain unresolved.

Except for a few such intriguing details, the film ending of *Women in Love* comes across as rushed, linear, and atypical of the production as a whole because it drops Russell's key strategy of repetition. Despite this final yet minor anticlimax, Russell and Kramer's cinematic translation remains a success, albeit one which is complicated by imperfections, contradictions, and ironies. It is a film largely stripped of Lawrence's ideas, as has been seen, despite the screenwriter's praise and defense of these ideas. At the same time, it is brought to life by inventive repetitions, this despite the director's criticism of Lawrence's commitment to the same technique. In its finest moments, *Women in Love* transcends its own paradoxes and achieves a cinematic equivalent of the "star balance" Lawrence was seeking in human terms through the love battles among his characters. The film does not blend or homogenize Kramer's reverence to Logos with Russell's visual bravado, but instead opposes them in a productive tension between Lawrentian technique and original cinematic material. The end result, when successful, achieves something close to what *The Virgin and the Gypsy* would achieve just two years later, a unique double stroke of cinematic adaptation that replicates and originates at once.

# 6

# Ken Russell's *The Rainbow:* Repetition as Regression

In the portion of *Filming Literature* devoted to D. H. Lawrence on screen, Neil Sinyard made two comments about *The Rainbow,* both speculations, since Ken Russell's film adaptation of that novel would not appear for another three years. First, Sinyard predicted correctly that on film "Ursula's encounter with the horses towards the end of *The Rainbow* . . . without the accompanying psychological analysis, would probably simply look like someone being frightened, quite reasonably, at the possibility of being stampeded."[1] Despite the unfilmability of this crucial scene in Sinyard's view, he went on to conclude his condemnation of Russell's *Women in Love* by offering the more dubious prediction that "*The Rainbow* would suit Russell better."[2]

Russell certainly shared Sinyard's opinion during the 1980s concerning the suitability of Lawrence's earlier novel to his own cinematic talents. He had a film version of *The Rainbow* in mind for at least a decade before its 1989 release. He and his second wife, Vivian, wrote the screenplay in the early 1980s, then struggled to find a producer.[3] *The Rainbow* was eventually taken on by Vestron Pictures, although with an austere budget of two million pounds, which limited filming to just over seven weeks and which also required several reductions of Russell's original plans for the project.[4]

Several cast and crew members from *Women in Love* returned to work on *The Rainbow.* Billy Williams was once again director of photography (with his work on *Gandhi* coming in between the two Lawrence projects), and Russell's close friend Luciana Arrighi was production designer. Christopher Gable, who had played Tibby, the young bridegroom, now appeared as Will Brangwen, a much older yet still immature figure. In what might be a deliberate allusion to *Women in Love,* Russell began *The Rainbow* with Gable's character saving his young daughter Ursula from drowning, thereby reversing Tibby's failure to rescue Laura and himself in the earlier film. Glenda Jackson, Russell's Oscar-winning Gudrun in *Women in Love,* now played the supporting role of Anna Brangwen. Her first appearance in *The Rainbow* shows her bathing the infant Gudrun—that is, bathing her own character of twenty years past and also, in another sense, of twenty years into the fictional future.

Newcomers included the American composer Carl Davis and actors Sammi Davis and Paul McGann as Ursula Brangwen and Anton Skrebensky, Amanda Donohoe as Winifred Inger, David Hemmings—the photographer in Michelangelo Antonioni's *Blow-Up* (1966)—as Uncle Henry, a screen modification of the younger Tom Brangwen, Judith Paris as Miss Harby, Jim Carter as Harby, and Dudley Sutton as the sadistic painter MacAllister, a character purely of Russell's creation. Even several of these "new" actors, while perhaps fresh to Lawrence filming, were by no means strangers to Russell. Paris had worked with him and Christopher Gable in numerous BBC productions. Donohoe and Davis had appeared one year earlier in Russell's screen adaptation of Bram Stoker's *The Lair of the White Worm.* Davis, who also appeared in John Boorman's *Hope and Glory* (1987), had recently lost the role of Ursula to Imogen Stubbs in Stuart Burge's three-part BBC adaptation of *The Rainbow.*

Noticeably missing from Russell's ensemble was scriptwriter Larry Kramer. While Kramer's absence may have minimized confrontations on and off the set, it may also have eliminated the productive tension and diverse perspective that fed into the artistic success of *Women in Love.* As a result, *The Rainbow* is more homogeneous, more exclusively British (with the possible exception of Carl Davis's nondescript musical contribution), and all but Russell's private project. In fact, *The Rainbow* is an example of cinematic nepotism by Russell's own admission. "I like the continuity," he told an interviewer. "I believe in the cycle of the seasons, of birth, death, and rejuvenation. My children by my first wife were in *Women in Love,* and my children by my second wife are in this [film], and there's a certain satisfaction in that."[5]

Responding to the personal and private quality of this film, Joseph Gomez describes "a curious elegiac quality to *The Rainbow* . . . [by which] various images, such as Ursula and Skrebensky on the swing boat, Ursula and Winifred in front of the fireplace, and the many walks in the Lake District, evoke scenes from other Russell films, most notably *Dante's Inferno, Clouds of Glory, Isadora,* and, of course, *Women in Love.* In fact, *The Rainbow* looks back at so much of the director's career that it provides something of a compendium of 'touchstone images.'"[6] While Gomez is correct, Russell's compendium of allusions takes in more than just his own work. *The Rainbow* is also rich with references to other Lawrence writing and to forty years of Lawrence filming, an endeavor which by 1989 had developed its own set of conventions for Russell to accept, reject, or play upon as he saw fit. A simple instance of this is the presence of Ursula's rocking horse during several of the film's early scenes, including one in which Will Brangwen, rocking his daughter upon it, attempts to "give" her the rainbow she demands by offering her a feeble substitute made of bread and jam.[7] A similar allusion, simultaneously textual and cinematic, involves Skrebensky and Ursula swinging (or again rocking) on a wooden swing boat. Based on a casual description in Lawrence's *Rainbow,* this scene more vividly recalls *Sons and Lovers* in that its visual implications are openly erotic, to the point that Sammi Davis and Paul McGann come closer in spirit to Paul Morel and Miriam Leivers than Dean Stockwell and Heather Sears did in their attempt at the original scene. A more purely cinematic allusion involves direct references to Cardiff's (but not Lawrence's) *Sons and Lovers,* to Rydell's *The Fox,* and to Miles's *The Virgin and the Gypsy.* Christopher Gable's Will, for instance, bears a close resemblance to Dean Stockwell as Paul Morel. Gable's Midlands accent is real and not Stockwell's poor imitation, but Gable's facial expressions and style of dress suggest a deliberate copy on Russell's part. Russell's much criticized ending in *The Rainbow* seems to be inspired by Cardiff's ending in *Sons and Lovers.* Both films close with their young hero/heroines, hastily packed suitcases in hand, disappearing into the distance, moving away from the camera in pursuit of their hopes and dreams.

With *The Fox* and *Virgin,* Russell's cinematic references are somewhat less direct because they relate more to theme, character development, and relationship. Like Mark Rydell, Russell has chosen to magnify the lesbian issue beyond Lawrence's original design, to the point that it becomes a major preoccupation. As Miles does to Yvette, Russell also gives his heroine two sets of parents: real parents who are overly oppressive and surrogates who are far more liberated and permissive. In Miles's *Virgin,* Yvette's benevolent parents are the Eastwoods, who sweep her away from her repressive parents in the film's closing scene. Hardly as wholesome a couple, and in fact frequently perverse, Russell's interpolated character Uncle Henry and his wife, Winifred, relate to Ursula in much the same way toward the end of the film. Unlike Ursula's biological parents, Will and Anna, Henry and Winifred are aware of her sexual relationship with Skrebensky and even encourage it by providing Winifred's country cottage for the couple's use. As Ursula sleeps with Skrebensky in an upstairs bedroom, her "new" parents drive up to greet the young lovers in what appears to be the same car the Eastwoods used to rescue Yvette—an open-topped red coupe suggestive, in the tropes of Lawrence filming at least, of mobility, freedom of spirit, and rejection of conventional standards.[8]

Among the Lawrence films, *Women in Love* is the one most frequently quoted in *The Rainbow,* as Joseph Gomez has also noted. He is correct about "Ursula and Winifred in front of the fireplace," for example, in that this sequence is a gender-reversed version of Russell's "Gladiatorial," the two women nude and intimately touching, if not wrestling, in the firelight with a white bear-skin rug for background, just as in the earlier masculine version of the scene.[9] Rabbits should be mentioned here as well, since they prove to be a major symbolic presence within *The Rainbow,* as if Russell were making amends for his decision to edit them out of *Women in Love.* As in Lawrence's *Rainbow,* Russell's Ursula assigns an essay on the rabbit to her pupils at Brinsley Street School, only now in cinematic counterpoint to Mr. Harby's lesson on the industrial revolution and the workings of a modern factory. This later scene is anticipated by several nontextual incidents intended to establish the rabbit as Ursula's personal "totem." When she learns that Uncle Henry uses ferrets to kill rabbits and protect his prize lettuce crop, Ursula becomes enraged and destroys the lettuce, thus completing the action of the rabbits herself. This incident leads Ursula to a flashback recalling her childish efforts (as in the text) to help her father plant potatoes. In Lawrence's novel, the potato planting ends with Ursula's frustration and disappointment at realizing that she is too little to be of any real help to her father. In Russell's version, however, the young Ursula seems deliberately and mischievously bent on ruining Will's seedlings by trampling them. After she's punished for this, Ursula runs away to the barn to be alone, and we see her consoling herself by cradling a large spotted rabbit in her arms.

*The Rainbow* on film seems self-consciously Blakean in its emphasis on innocence and experience in conflict, so that perhaps Russell's rabbits serve as emblems of innocence and of Ursula's innocence in particular. When she naively consents to pose nude for Winifred's friend MacAllister, for example, he decides to title his study of the two women "Experience Rewarding Innocence." In contrast to Ursula, of course, both Winifred and Mac are examples of Blakean experience,[10] with the sadistic painter emerging as another allusion on Russell's part to *Women in Love.* Mac is an extension and expansion of Loerke, as if Russell were not content with an artist describing his abuse of a young model but wanted instead to demonstrate such abuse in the flesh. In this interpolated film sequence, Ursula reluctantly agrees to pose for Mac, worrying that, like Loerke's Annette Von Weck, she'll prove to be "a bit of a fidget." Once in Mac's studio and naked, she suffers a sadistic advance from the painter who proposes to spank her, suggesting that his great satisfaction in doing so will more than make up for her pain. Ursula escapes before Mac can take action, and he is forced to vent his frustration (with a paintbrush) on the buttocks of a marble statue. Aside from the unintentional absurdity of this episode (partly because Mac possesses nothing of Loerke's sinister presence), it has the effect of turning Winifred into Ursula's betrayer, something Lawrence never intended in the text. Winifred brings Mac and Ursula together in the film certainly aware that he poses a threat. In light of this, it seems highly improbable that Ursula's affection for Winifred would survive let alone grow toward spiritual daughterhood as it does in the film.

When *The Rainbow* first appeared in 1989, critics and reviewers tended not to explore its relationship to *Women in Love* partly because cinematic memory is shorter than literary memory and the earlier film was already two decades into the past. Only G. B. Crump, writing for the *D. H. Lawrence Review,* mentioned several specific parallels between *The Rainbow* and *Women in Love,* implying that further comparative study of the two films would be worthwhile.[11] Other reviewers, working at the journalistic end of the critical spectrum, remained content to identify *The Rainbow* in relation to its predecessor as a "prequel," a term suggesting the chronological reverse of a sequel.[12] Several reviewers also noted that *Women in Love* would be a hard act for Ken Russell to follow, since that film had clearly been a "classic" or a "masterpiece."[13] They had apparently forgotten the often brutally negative reviews of twenty years earlier. They had likewise forgotten Jennie Linden and frequently mentioned in error that Glenda Jackson had played Ursula rather than Gudrun in *Women in Love.*[14]

These commentators did relate *The Rainbow* to other Ken Russell films: *Gothic* (1986), *The Lair of the White Worm* (1988), and *Salome's Last Dance* (1988). Here they tended to agree with Peter Travers, who described *The Rainbow* as a healthy departure from these bizarre efforts and, as a result, "Russell's finest work in years."[15] In a similar spirit, Kenneth Turan titled his *GQ* review of *The Rainbow* "Ken Russell Goes Straight," implying that the film achieved its success by abandoning Russell's trademark style of lurid flamboyance in favor of a more lyrical, understated approach. Even here, however, critics who acknowledged this often went on to disagree over its ultimate impact on Russell's work as a whole. Caryn James, writing for the *New York Times,* for example, praised *The Rainbow* as "Mr. Russell's most lyrical and conventional film in years," but then concluded that its "softness" constituted "both its appeal and its greatest flaw."[16] An even more extreme response to the newly reformed Ken Russell was that of Pauline Kael writing for the *New Yorker.* Perhaps forgetting that she had previously damned Russell for being much too "purple" in *Women in Love,* Kael damned him again in *The Rainbow,* by way of the perfect critical Catch-22, for seeming "to have run out of bravura."[17]

Where reviewers did agree about Russell's new Lawrence film was in identifying Sammi Davis's performance as its major weakness. Kael offered a representative opinion on this when she praised Davis for her "scrappiness" as Ursula, but observed that "nothing she says seems to have any substance: her rude, angry lines just pop into her mouth right out of the script. This Ursula is blank-faced and lightweight."[18] In a parallel but even less-tempered judgment, Tom O'Brien, reviewing for *Commonweal*, simply noted that "the lead role is too much for Sammi Davis."[19] A small number of critics did defend Davis's performance, including Stanley Kauffmann and Kenneth Turan, who described her as capturing "the archetypal questing Lawrentian aristocrat of the spirit."[20] Pro or con, all such critics writing brief reviews tended not to discuss in any detail the reasons behind their initial responses to Davis's interpretation of Ursula, something worth returning to later, since Ursula's screen persona is closely related to the substance and quality of Russell's project as a whole.

After the usual flurry of reviews, discussion of *The Rainbow* died away quickly and almost completely. This absence of attention might constitute the most damning judgment of all, especially if one considers the wealth of material that continues to be written and published about *Women in Love* even thirty years after its release. Russell himself seems to have joined the conspiracy of silence against *The Rainbow*, recalling *Women in Love* several times in his 1994 memoir, *The Lion Roars,* but remaining virtually mute on his more recent Lawrence film.[21] Only two sustained critical essays on *The Rainbow*, as distinct from standard film reviews, have been written to date: G. B. Crump's "Lawrence's *Rainbow* and Russell's *Rainbow*," and Neil Taylor's "A Woman's Love: D. H. Lawrence on Film," written as a chapter in Peter Reynolds's anthology of essays on fiction into film, *Novel Images: Literature in Performance* (1993). As its title indicates, Crump's essay is comparative and likewise analytical in its charting of the intricate imagistic designs within *The Rainbow* on screen. Taylor's chapter considers *The Rainbow* along with three other Lawrence films: *Women in Love, The Virgin and the Gypsy,* and Just Jaeckin's *Lady Chatterley's Lover* (1981). While his approach, like Crump's, also takes into account such inner workings of the film as its "homogenization" of Lawrence (by way of deletion of text and cinematic interpolation), Taylor's most interesting comments concern matters outside the body of the film relating, for example, to marketing, as when the original controversy over Lawrence's publication of *The Rainbow* is used by promoters nearly seventy years later to advertise the film, or when, in turn, the film's release becomes a new impetus for marketing the book.[22]

Any critic approaching *The Rainbow* today need not ask what remains to be said, as with *Women in Love,* but rather what should be said first to break the critical silence. For the purposes of this chapter, three points of inquiry seem most worthwhile. The first is to explore the differences in scope and chronology between Russell's film and Lawrence's novel and to pursue the cinematic implications behind these differences. Russell's *Rainbow* is, in fact, unique among the Lawrence films in its overt effort to bring only the last third of a book to the screen while omitting virtually all the rest. Russell attempts to film Ursula's story by itself and in isolation from the stories of her parents and grandparents that Lawrence tells in the text.

A second priority is to reexamine *The Rainbow* as exclusively Ursula's film or, in other words, to see it again from the standpoint of Russell's artistic intent and vision in place of Lawrence's. Such re-viewing focuses attention on two segments of *The Rainbow* into which nearly all of Ursula's story has been compressed—the extended sequence (relative to the text) detailing her relationship with Winifred Inger and the shortened but perhaps even more important sequence showing Ursula as she attempts to start her career as a teacher. "Shame" and "The Man's World" on film are especially interesting because they reveal Ken Russell's divided purposes so clearly—his efforts to hold with the original while making Ursula's experiences more familiar to contemporary audiences and more consistent with the realities of their lives. A third and last concern here is more evaluative than analytical in its attempt to explain why, to most observers, *The Rainbow* has been disappointing both in relation to its own artistic intentions and to Lawrence's—if not entirely unsuccessful, at least falling well short of what Russell achieved in *Women in Love.* Such overall judgment will require an examination of the way Ken Russell chooses to conclude his film and why Ursula Brangwen's character ultimately remains problematic—less finished and less satisfying even than her much criticized counterpart in Russell's film adaptation of *Women in Love.*[23]

Comparing his two Lawrence films during an interview with Graham Fuller, Russell makes an observation about screen time that seems significant precisely because of its distortion: "I couldn't really do justice to *Women in Love* in two hours, so it wasn't as good as it could have been. Here [in *The Rainbow*], two hours is more than ample to evoke the soul of this girl searching for freedom, breaking free from the bonds of family, and going where her spirit guides her—over the rainbow."[24] Since *The Rainbow* is no shorter or less formidable a text than *Women in Love,* Russell's ease with the standard cinematic time-frame reveals his underlying assumption that he is responsible for Ursula's story alone—for her experiences pulled from the context of family history. One effect of Russell's telescoped narrative is visual limitation and loss. By backgrounding or entirely omitting the first two-thirds of the novel, and with it the first two Brangwen generations, Russell denies himself access to some of Lawrence's most overtly cinematic writing. This will be clear to any reader of *The Rainbow* engaged in the process of inward screening—of projecting the text within the theater of imagination while reading or remembering it. Events in this novel, both large and small, seem already to have been filmed, and filmed effectively, by Lawrence working alone and without benefit of cast or crew—Tom Brangwen carried away by the flood, or, years earlier, exclaiming, "That's her," when he first

sees Lydia Lensky along the road (24), or the very young Anna Lensky commanding the geese to let her into the yard because she belongs there, "because Mr.
Brangwen's my father now. He *is*—yes he *is*. And I live here" (64), or Tom
Brangwen, again, calming Anna as her mother gives birth by carrying her to the
dark barn, to the alien yet warm world of the beasts (73–75).

These visions come to the inward eye without effort because so much natural cinema rolls through the first two major movements of Lawrence's text. Along
with such film-in-text, and intensifying it, is Lawrence's choreography within *The
Rainbow*—his dance-in-text which links the generations of Brangwen women
and which never ceases until the novel is over. One can only wonder how Russell
could have turned away from this, given his reliance on dance in *Women in Love*
and his clear effort, at least superficially, to make connections between his two
Lawrence films. Since an audience watching *The Rainbow* sees Will and Anna
Brangwen only in later married life, their troubled courtship is lost and, along
with it, the angry yet erotic rhythms of their moonlit dance:

> There was only the moving to and fro in the moonlight, engrossed,
> the swinging in the silence, that was marked only by the splash of
> sheaves, and silence, and a splash of sheaves. And ever the splash of
> his sheaves broke swifter, beating up to hers, and ever the splash of
> her sheaves recurred monotonously, unchanging, and ever the splash
> of his sheaves beat nearer.
>
> Till at last, they met at the shock, facing each other, sheaves in
> hand. And he was silvery with moonlight, with a moonlit, shadowy
> face that frightened her. She waited for him. (117)

The words upon the printed page dance along with the lovers. Also, this moving picture of Will and Anna is a study in ambivalent passion, its darkness and
light, and provides a director not so much with cinematic raw material as with
finished film. A similar observation can be made about "Anna Victrix," the later
less loving yet more triumphant counterpart to this scene in which Anna, now
pregnant with Ursula, excludes Will from her purely female dance. This dance
is also lost with the reduction of Lawrence's second generation, and even more
surprising, so too are the dances of the third generation, something which would
seem to compel inclusion in the film. In Russell's *Rainbow*, Ursula re-creates with
Anton Skrebensky neither her mother's dance with Will, also amid "great new
stacks of corn," nor her own moonlit repetition of "Anna Victrix," the final encounter with Anton by which she casts him off and dances out her emergence
into womanhood.[25]

For whatever reason, financial or directorial, Ken Russell has chosen to omit
all of Lawrence's textual dances and to substitute almost none of his own in their

place. Ursula dances briefly but in a conventional waltz, first with Anton and then with her father, at Uncle Henry and Winifred's wedding celebration. A more meaningful dance does occur during this celebration, created by the filmmakers for thematic emphasis yet falling short of Lawrence's layered and naturally cinematic choreography in the text. The film dance is Lancers, a male-initiated and male-dominated military pantomime that reverses the gender of Lawrence's dances in the text. During Lancers, Uncle Henry and Will Brangwen parody a series of marching movements and salutes, seeming to dance with one another rather than with their female partners, Anna and Winifred. Their dance eventually turns ugly and violent as Uncle Henry pretends to shoot Will Brangwen, an "enemy soldier." Will falls "wounded" to the dance floor and receives the coup de grace from Henry, who laughs as his victim pretends to die. While the ironies here are interesting because they implicate several characters at once, they are likewise relatively close to the surface of the film. Henry and Will, a most unmilitary pair of men, have turned war and violent death into a stupid game, remaining insensitive to the realities behind their charade. In words that Russell preserves from the text, they reveal their "toy-life," an immaturity and shallowness of existence, by way of their dance. Anton Skrebensky, who coins this phrase in an unintentional self-indictment, is one of the observers of Henry and Will's grotesque pantomime during Lancers. He is in uniform and about to depart for South Africa and the Boer War. Skrebensky's imminent military experience might prove more dangerous than Lancers but, by the visual symbolism of the film, it will be similarly artificial, meaningless, and ugly.

As if aware of all the visual wealth he has abandoned in Lawrence's writing, Russell makes an effort to restore parts of the early text to his film. His restoration could be called cinematic updating, a process whereby material originally related to the first or second generation of Brangwens is incorporated into the experiences of the third. In the film, for example, Will Brangwen refers to his baby daughter Gudrun as "the blackbird tuning-up," an expression originally used by the elder Tom Brangwen to describe young Tom in infancy (79). Similarly, Ursula on film repeats her insistent textual wondering about the future: "Will somebody love me . . . when I am grown up, will somebody love me?" She is answered on screen just as she was in the novel, not by her grandmother, Lydia, who is cut from the film, but by her mother, Anna: "Yes, some man will love you, child, because it's your nature. And I hope it will be somebody who will love you for what you are, and not for what he wants of you" (257). Originally, Ursula repeated her crucial question from the innocent perspective of childhood. On film, because her childhood is compressed into just a few short scenes, she asks it in late adolescence, after her romantic relationship with Skrebensky has begun. Recovered on screen, along with these brief fragments of the early novel, is Tom Brangwen's wedding speech in which he insists that every angel is created from the united souls of a married couple. In the text Tom makes this speech at his stepdaughter Anna's wedding to Will Brangwen. On film Tom's speech is given by Will himself, not at his own wedding, but years later at Uncle Henry and Winifred's. This event itself provides another example of Russell's cinematic salvage work, since it recombines two weddings from the novel: Will and Anna's, as mentioned, and Fred and Laura Brangwen's, the celebration during which Ursula loses her virginity to Anton. Language from both of these celebrations, along with specific incidents like Ursula and Anton's lovemaking, are incorporated into the on-screen wedding, which has no textual basis of its own. Lawrence writes that the younger Tom Brangwen (Henry in the film) and Winifred "continued engaged for another term. Then they married" (351). He virtually dismisses the couple with these words and never directly describes their wedding celebration in the novel at all.

It seems evident from these examples that the makers of *The Rainbow* must have felt some involvement with the early chapters of Lawrence's novel or at least some regret at their exclusion from the film. Equally evident, however, and frankly puzzling, is that what they chose to restore from the lost Brangwen saga was primarily verbal material—dialogue rather than image or scene, and for the most part minor dialogue at that. This is surprising and disappointing on several counts, one of which is Russell's reputation as a director of visions rather than words. His second Lawrentian effort appears to have dimmed and grown more language-bound than his first, despite using his own script and despite all the visual opportunities offered by the text itself. It should have been more than possible to apply the same technique of cinematic updating to visible events or scenes and not just to verbal formulations. There is no reason, for example, why an audience couldn't have watched Will Brangwen carry Ursula to the barn—with Anna giving birth to Gudrun—just as the reader inwardly watched Tom Brangwen carry Anna as her mother gave birth to young Tom. Such visual updating could have resulted in a luminous scene as in the text—creatural, human, mysterious, and cinematic all in one:

> He opened the doors, upper and lower, and they entered into the high, dry barn, that smelled warm even if it were not warm. He hung the lantern on the nail and shut the door. They were in another world now. The light shed softly on the timbered barn, on the whitewashed walls, and the great heap of hay; instruments cast their shadows largely, a ladder rose to the dark arch of a loft. Outside there was the driving rain, inside, the softly-illuminated stillness and calmness of the barn. (74)

The warm presence here of Tom Brangwen also reminds us of what, beyond scenic potential, is lost with the filmmakers' decision to focus on just one Brangwen generation. Several memorable characters are absent, along with Lawrence's major pursuit of humanity in evolution—his preoccupation with the Brangwen experience in flux from past, to present, to future age. A family history across three generations would surely prove challenging to any filmmaker, and so especially to Ken Russell and his colleagues who were working under severe budget and scheduling constraints. Beyond such general and quantitative limitations, however, it is also possible to suggest that *The Rainbow*, despite its intense visuality, might well be the most difficult Lawrence novel to film, with its earlier chapters proving the most resistant of all. The elder Tom Brangwen, in particular, while ever a vital presence, is also a figure almost without external outline or what Lawrence once referred to dismissively as "the old stable ego of the character."[26] Tom appears within Lawrence's text as if painted there by Paul Morel, all in "shimmering protoplasm" because "Only this shimmeriness is the real living. The shape is a dead crust. The shimmer is inside really."[27] As a result, it is always difficult for a reader to keep Tom Brangwen's persona sharply focused. This difficulty is made even greater because Lawrence presents Tom almost entirely in essence rather than in action. He is crucial to the text based on his being or presence alone. Who and what he is matters critically to *The Rainbow* as opposed to more familiar and filmable matters such as what he does or what he knows. That Tom Brangwen is a farmer, for example, is important to Lawrence's text because it binds him to organic process, not because it implies a body of knowledge or a series of concrete actions based upon it. In this light, perhaps Ken Russell chose wisely to leave Tom Brangwen out as cinematically the most elusive Lawrence character of all.

Will Brangwen shares Tom's remoteness from knowledge and conscious awareness, so he also seems likely to elude and frustrate the filmmaker attempting to depict a focused personality. As a character, however, Will has a somewhat more definable shape than Tom—in terms of his capacity for deep if inarticulate emotion, for example, and in terms of a spiritual and ultimately mystical urge that drives his deepest being. Such qualities, while challenging, are potentially filmable, as opposed to the organic yet amorphous heat and light of the elder Tom. One could, for instance, conceivably project Will's emotionally violent relationship with young Ursula—a dangerous paternity based on feelings so strong that they can swing from hot love to abuse in an instant. One could also film young Will and Anna in church together for the first time or at Lincoln cathedral as a married couple—physically close in both scenes yet utterly opposed in spirit. Will's single urge in the church and at the cathedral is to be swept upward toward the mystery—first by the hymn and his own powerful voice, then by the trajectory of his beloved Gothic arches. Since the Brangwen women and not the men are the logocentric members of the family, the seers and knowers, Anna's counter-urge is always to reduce Will's reverence, as vulnerable as it is profound, to mocking scrutiny. Her analytical weapons are laughter at Will's uninhibited singing in church and then deconstructive derision at Lincoln cathedral as she forces Will's attention from the arches to the gargoyles and insists that they are the faces of mocking wives or, in essence, objectifications of her own spirit (201–2).

While none of this seems easy to film, all of it seems effectively filmable. The same is true of Will Brangwen as artist, craftsman, and creator/destroyer of Adam and Eve in wood. As a compulsive maker of things, Will reveals himself in Aristotelian action and so should be more available to visual representation than the elder Tom, who reveals himself in essence alone. The cinematic challenge, however, would be to capture the relationship between Will's mysticism and his art, since the carvings are really unconscious efforts to objectify and make visible the spiritual turbulence within him. As it turns out, Russell and *The Rainbow* filmmakers have accepted none of these challenges with Will Brangwen. Unlike the elder Tom, who is omitted altogether, Will Brangwen plays a prominent role in Russell's film and is even depicted as a craftsman, a lace designer by trade and woodcarver by avocation who donates his best efforts to the church. Will's activities and works, however, are utterly marginalized on screen while Will himself is flattened and trivialized almost beyond recognition.[28] In place of mysticism, the artistic urge, and the capacity for emotional violence, Christopher Gable's Will gives us simply a doting father and, beyond this, a child himself just slightly concealed within the body of a grown man. Will Brangwen's painful conflict with Ursula in the novel is reduced to an effort to keep her with him in perpetual childhood. Will's greatest pleasure on film comes from joining the innocent games of his children—singing, playing the penny whistle, raucously enjoying a birthday party—and participating not as a parent so much as one of them, almost as Anna Brangwen's eldest son rather than her equal partner in responsibility. Should Will's children reach the adulthood that Ursula verges upon, this toy-life will end, forcing him to join his wife in sharing the burdens of maturity.

On screen Will Brangwen as child-man proves to be an absolutely static character, unchanged from his first scene with Ursula on the rocking horse until the very end. In one of the film's closing episodes, Ursula returns home nearly trampled and drowned as her unaware father sings choruses of "Row Your Boat" with his children in the next room. In contrast to this stasis, Lawrence's Will Brangwen is a character in flux to the point that his evolution across the novel becomes a highly significant shadow or background image of what his daughter Ursula is experiencing as the modern age approaches. As a married man and father, Will eventually returns to the art he had abandoned with the burning of Adam and Eve. Yet his return is also a major departure. What had been an intensely private activity now reemerges as a civic function, cultural, educational, and wholly conscious. At around the time Ursula is eight years old, "Education was in the forefront as a subject of interest. There was talk of new Swedish methods, of handwork instruction, and so on. Brangwen embraced sincerely the idea of handwork in schools. For the first time, he began to take real interest in a public affair. He had at length, from his profound sensual activity, developed a real purposive self" (235). Several years later, as Ursula is about to take her teaching post at Brinsley Street School, Lawrence once again observes that Will Brangwen's "only connection with the real outer world was through his winter evening classes, which brought him into contact with state education. About all the rest, he was oblivious and entirely indifferent—even about the [Boer] war" (355). Still later as Ursula is about to enter college, Lawrence provides Will with a professional career in parallel to his daughter's: "At last her father was going to be something socially. So long, he had been a social cypher, without form or standing. Now he was going to be Art and Handwork Instructor for the County of Nottingham. That was really a status. It was a position. He would be a specialist in his way. And he was an uncommon man. . . . Will Brangwen must become modern" (418, 421).

If Will Brangwen must become modern, so too, Lawrence implies, must the whole world. The arriving twentieth century is about to provide Will with a defining shape, the very "crust" or "stable ego" that Brangwen men had so far avoided. Will is to have an official title and role, Art and Handwork Instructor, granted him by the outside world, where previously his art had always emerged unsummoned from inside as he attempted to give shape to his inchoate urgings of spirit. In teaching arts and crafts to others, Ursula's father will now have to combine this activity with public Logos, a language which communicates, explains, and translates itself into collective mind-content.

In the text Ursula's story is quite literally an outgrowth of all this, to the point that it cannot be fully received or understood outside the context of Brangwen history and evolving Brangwen experience. She is the family's growing tip, their young and hopeful extension toward the new century, for better or for worse. In this capacity Ursula ironically and unknowingly satisfies her foremothers' age-old hunger for knowledge, for a mental life they were certain existed in the world beyond Marsh Farm. Ursula enters that world and partakes of that knowledge, attempting to build her first career upon it. At the same time, as Ursula moves toward an uncertain "modernity," along with the closing century as a whole, the vivid presences of her forefathers Tom and Will begin to grow dim as if they had existed in some distant age. The elder Tom's "shimmeriness" and heat have been extinguished by a flood twenty years earlier. One place they still flicker in the novel's later chapters is, oddly enough, in the queer little souls of Ursula's Brinsley Street pupils, most of whom resemble Tom when decades earlier he was forced against every fiber of his being to submit to school. Ironically, it is now his granddaughter's duty to impose order upon these queer little souls and prepare them for life in coming times.

School in *The Rainbow* emerges in one form or another as a key institution in the world's preparation for coming times: Will's night school, Brinsley Street School, Ursula's high school and college. It is a kind of assembly line for the human race, according to Lawrence, one which stamps out a modern shape or crust for men and women, a revised version of selfhood or identity appropriate for the new century at hand. This identity is surely no longer Tom Brangwen's organic presence, nor is it young Will Brangwen's amalgam of passion, emotion, and spiritual urge. It is far more like the stable ego that Lawrence wished to avoid in his own fictional characters, the hard external shape or crust that reforms, encloses, and regulates the protoplasm. Ironically, Ursula, Will's daughter and Tom's granddaughter, finds herself pressed into the service of this industry. She gains the knowledge she needs to do the job from her college professors, the middlemen of mind content. In turn, she applies what she knows to her work at Brinsley Street, imposing the pattern by force of will upon the children as Mr. Harby imposes an equally rigid pattern upon her. Ursula's new pattern comes with a title much like her father's—"Miss Brangwen, Fifth Form Teacher." She does finally conform to its shape as the effective "Miss Brangwen," yet at great expense to "Ursula," her former, warmer, organic self now in danger of becoming lost. It is no wonder that in college the only subject Ursula continues to enjoy, after losing her illusions about the academic wholesalers, is botany and the exact yet lovely drawing it entails of vital organisms.

Virtually all of these conflicts become obscured in Ken Russell's film of *The Rainbow* because the movie audience can no longer see, as the reader saw, where Ursula is coming from relative to the Brangwen generations in flux. With Tom's removal and Will's diminishment, viewers cannot compare their earlier experiences, based on essence or being, with Ursula's modern experience based far more firmly on doing and knowing. Nor can they compare organic identity, vitally present in Tom, Will, and the cells that Ursula loves to draw, with the mechanical roles now being imposed upon her, her students, and even her father by the same modern process. Without such evolutionary reference points, Ursula's entry into the twentieth century, by way of the man's world and a teaching career, becomes a less complex and dangerous journey than it was in the text. No longer an instance of the world's general shift from a rooted organic past toward mechanical uncertainty, Ursula's experience on screen emerges as more hopeful and more familiar to a film audience. It becomes Ken Russell's relatively optimistic demonstration of a young girl's passage from parental control, well meant yet stifling, toward independence—sexual freedom and professional self-sufficiency at the same time. This near-cliché erases Lawrence's intricate evolutionary tracing in *The Rainbow* along with his warning that human identity has been reconceived, hardened and reduced by modern times. One result of this erasure is a complete reversal of Lawrence's intent in the "Man's World" episode and, more specifically, in the "victory" Ursula wins by severely beating a student in order to regain control of her classroom and her career.

A somewhat peripheral yet related casualty of Ken Russell's erasure of two Brangwen generations is Anton Skrebensky, who, along with Ursula, takes his place on the same evolutionary continuum. Ursula is this novel's heroine in large measure because she comes to understand the process she and her age are caught up in, and then attempts to counteract it. She tries, for instance, to make room in the world for "Ursula" as well as for "Miss Brangwen," since there seems to be similar room for both "Maggie," her friend, and for "Miss Schofield," Maggie's harder and more impersonal professional self. Skrebensky, by contrast to Ursula, is one of the novel's least heroic, least effective human beings because he has completely submitted himself to modern mechanical process. Skrebensky has willingly become all of the toy roles he plays in life—socialist, aristocrat, lieutenant of engineers, and so on—so that no trace of a warm, vital, and mysterious human identity remains. In this catastrophic relinquishment of self, he emerges as the elder Tom Brangwen's opposite number, all dead crust with nothing of the living protoplasm left inside. Lawrence's presentation of Skrebensky as an instance of modern human loss is both brilliant and flawed, brilliant by way of its compression of cultural process into one individual character, yet flawed because throughout *The Rainbow* Lawrence reveals Skrebensky's failure largely by telling it rather than showing it in tangible, dramatic action. Lawrence seems not yet prepared to present Skrebensky's emptiness as he soon would the similar void within Gerald Crich, by living demonstration rather than verbal discourse. In *The Rainbow,* Lawrence informs rather than shows us that Skrebensky "seemed added up, finished." Ursula "knew him all round, not on any side did he lead into the unknown" (473). Or even more directly that "To his own intrinsic life, he was dead. And he could not rise again from the dead. His soul lay in the tomb. His life lay in the established order of things. He had his five senses too. They were to be gratified. Apart from this, he represented the great, established, extant Idea of life, and as this he was important and beyond question" (326). Perhaps as a character who has traded in his vitals for modern abstraction, Skrebensky deserves to be written about in this way. Yet such writing adds to the filmmakers' already serious problems. Without the generational contrast with men like Tom or Will Brangwen to begin with, Skrebensky's "deadness" is already going to be difficult to convey. Beyond this, without the usual help from Lawrence's own visuality, Skrebensky's character as a whole, and not just his failure, may remain unfilmable. Russell's *Rainbow* bears this out, since Paul McGann's Skrebensky is meant to be a negative character, yet it is never clear precisely why. He appears as a personable, reasonably pleasant young man, perhaps too bland and stiffly conservative for Sammi Davis's feisty Ursula. He is also a selfish and inept sex partner initially, somewhat in contrast to the textual Skrebensky, yet beyond this there is little else to hold against him. Ursula and Skrebensky simply cannot get along on screen and decide to end their relationship. The complexity of causes behind their failure, again in contrast to the text, remains invisible and unexplained.

In place of Lawrence's personal, generational, and cultural complexities, then, Ken Russell provides a radically simplified version of *The Rainbow,* yet one which still merits a second look, a focused re-viewing from the perspectives of its own cinematic strategies and goals. Russell's purposes in *The Rainbow* are wholly involved with Ursula, to the exclusion of almost all else, and with showing his audience, through her, the story of a young everywoman's struggle into maturity. For Russell, Ursula fights her battle on two familiar fronts, the sexual and the economic, attempting to gain entry into the adult worlds of love and work. To emphasize the first of these challenges, Russell reverses his usual process of telescoping Lawrence's text by expanding "Shame," one of the novel's shorter chapters, to encompass almost the entire film. Ursula's intimate but brief involvement with Winifred Inger undergoes magnification to one of two long-term and definitive love relationships in her life. Russell, unlike Lawrence, also seems intent on establishing an ongoing parallel between the two relationships, Ursula/Winifred and Ursula/Skrebensky, so that they begin almost simultaneously and end at the same time as well, very near the close of the film. As a result of this symmetry, the film's suggestion, once again departing from the text, is that Winifred and Skrebensky are competing with one another for Ursula's affections and that Ursula herself is struggling with a choice between lesbianism and heterosexuality.

Both of these cinematic interpolations are supported by the film's imagistic structure as well as by the temporal paralleling of the two love affairs. In the early courtship stages, for example, Russell's color schemes are deliberately matched for both couples with Ursula appearing in virginal white or blue (either dress, bathing suit, or fencing costume) and her suitors appearing in passionate red—with Winifred's fencing and bathing costumes, for instance, repeating the scarlet of Skrebensky's military uniform. Along the same lines, each on-screen courtship begins with a symbolic gesture of undressing. Skrebensky seductively removes Ursula's glove during their first romantic encounter in a deserted church. Immediately after, Winifred invites Ursula to her cottage and performs a variation of the same action by removing Ursula's boot. Even the cottage plays a part in Russell's imagistic symmetry by serving as love nest for both couples, once early in the film and then again very near the end. In the boot scene, the cottage offers Winifred and Ursula the privacy they need to undress completely and swim together in the rain. Later, Ursula and Skrebensky make use of it for their premarital honeymoon.

Both the parallels between these love affairs, and the suggestion of Winifred and Skrebensky as rivals, are summarized and condensed in a dream Ursula has near the close of the film. This dream is an Yvette-like vision in which Ursula views herself running naked along a wooded hillside with her two lovers—first in sunlight with Skrebensky, whom she suddenly deserts, then with Winifred in a rain shower reminiscent of their early encounter at the cottage. Ursula eventually runs off on her own, leaving both suitors behind, and climbs to the top of the hillside. Skrebensky, who has been pursuing her, reaches the summit just as she does and embraces her violently. As Ursula struggles to escape, she screams aloud and awakens to find herself at home, permanently free from both lovers, and about to pursue the future on her own.

Ursula's mirrored love relationships, and the enlargement of "Shame" in general, begin to reveal Ken Russell's conflicting loyalties and goals in *The Rainbow*—his urge to project Lawrence yet somehow to correct him and bring him up to date. Russell may have magnified the Ursula/Winifred relationship, for example, to give lesbianism equal time in the erotic arena, to remove Lawrence's embarrassing label of "Shame" and establish it as a mode of human loving neither better nor worse than all the rest. If so, this provides a clear instance of the film's attempt to improve upon the original by "contemporizing" it or replacing Lawrence's outmoded biases with views more suited to a film audience in the late twentieth century. This suggestion finds support in the film's realities as well as its dreams, since Ursula's final break with Skrebensky begins with a quarrel over Winifred. Leaving the text behind (since there Skrebensky remains unaware of Winifred), Paul McGann's character questions Ursula's friendship with her and condemns what he calls their unnatural "tendencies," thereby revealing an attitude somewhat parallel to Lawrence's own. By way of this exposure, Sammi Davis's Ursula sees Skrebensky's limitations clearly for the first time and resolves to end their relationship.

A contradiction or paradox haunts the film's enlightened rewriting, however, because deep down the filmmakers don't approve of Winifred or her "tendencies" any more than Skrebensky does. Their apparent defense of lesbianism (in part by way of Skrebensky's priggish condemnation) and their atmosphere of free sexual exploration become compromised through the figure of Winifred herself.

Amanda Donahoe's portrayal of her conveys, at the very least, crude and selfish sensuality, and at worst cold amorality to the point of danger for Ursula. The film's Winifred is, for example, a hypocrite, quite unlike her textual counterpart. Early on, she declares to Ursula that she is a worshiper of nature and condemns a miner for disrupting their mountain hike with his blasting. After meeting Uncle Henry, however, and seeing a place for herself in his affluent world, Winifred leaves her nature worship and her protests to Ursula. She jumps ship and takes Henry's side during an argument in which Ursula accuses him of destructively exploiting both nature and humankind with his mines.

Worse yet, before meeting Uncle Henry, Russell's Winifred was associated with the painter Mac, who alludes to her sexual ambiguity by calling her Fred and who carries his own erotic exploration into the darker regions of punishment and pain. As mentioned earlier, by deliberately exposing the naive Ursula to Mac's sadistic inclinations, Winifred reveals a dangerous indifference to her friend's welfare and, likewise, a fundamental interest in the girl as an experimental sex object rather than a human being. By trying to leave Lawrence behind in favor of contemporary sexual revisionism, then, the *Rainbow* filmmakers have instead collided with him full tilt. Their gesture of inclusive erotic liberalism thinly conceals a distaste for female homosexuality at least as severe as Lawrence's—likewise a value judgment as subjective as his that lesbianism is perverse while somehow male homosexuality is not. The same Ken Russell who now disapproves of Winifred had wholly celebrated Gerald and Birkin in their attempt to become lovers twenty years earlier.

As Russell seems to uphold yet also dismiss lesbianism, so too does he inadvertently undercut the larger issue of feminism in *The Rainbow,* partly by identifying it with Winifred and partly by removing it to the far corners of the film. Ursula herself, as a feminist, appears only once, literally immobilized—stiffly posed with a group of suffragettes in a still photo within the moving picture. While she surely struggles, along with her textual counterpart, for a foothold in the man's world, the film's Ursula does so far more as a young person seeking adulthood than as a woman seeking equal status with men. Feminism as an issue fades even further in *The Rainbow* because the film omits both of Ursula's adult female friends, Maggie Schofield and Dorothy Russell. It excludes them, or worse, combines and confuses them with Winifred, who emerges as the only woman in Ursula's life besides her mother. At different points in the film Winifred serves as friend, lover, confidante, and eventually surrogate parent. The thematic effect of this conflation in terms of feminism is an unaware tarnishing that deconstructs the film's surface support of women's issues. Russell's only live, walking, talking, feminist is Winifred, who replaces all three of the other women in this role and who even speaks several of Dorothy Russell's lines from the text.

Because Winifred, unlike Dorothy, Maggie, or Ursula, is tainted, her function as a spokeswoman for her gender suffers compromise and damage. As a result, and despite Russell's posture of advocacy, feminism as a serious issue in this film is cast into the shadows of Winifred's own moral ambiguity.

Rather than feminism or lesbianism, the timely social issue suggested by Winifred Inger's on-screen persona is sexual exploitation or, more precisely, sexual coercion of a subordinate (in this case a student) by a superior (in this case a teacher). While Lawrence's Ursula and Winifred are, of course, also pupil and teacher, the dynamic of their relationship and the details of its inception are very different from their updated re-emergence on screen. In the novel Ursula is attracted to Winifred and in fact falls in love with her before the older woman notices this affection and begins to return it. On film, Ursula remains unaware of Winifred until after she has been singled out for sexual attention. As Ursula's swimming class practices in the pool, Winifred (standing on a diving board) notices the girl because she is moving in the opposite direction from all the rest. Immediately interested, Winifred dives into the water, challenges her student to a race and wins, then caresses Ursula's bottom as she leaves the pool. A modern audience watching this and the rest of Ken Russell's *Rainbow* would recognize Winifred at once as a sexual predator rather than a feminist or a gay lover. The film seems to go out of its way to exaggerate Winifred's aggressive qualities, to the point that her image approximates that of a sadistic dominatrix in relation to her class of young girls. The film's teaching scenes involving Winifred turn violent at times, as when she defeats and humiliates Ursula in fencing class in order to reimpose her will upon the girl. Even when no violence is involved, Winifred's interaction with her students suggests concealed sexual arousal combined with a desire to dominate and control them. During the swimming class sequences, for example, Russell's camera shows Winifred looking down upon her girls from a diving board or balcony, either shouting orders at them from above or blowing into a shrill whistle. Such postures and actions, while having little to do with feminism or lesbian love, serve to foreshadow what Ursula will soon endure in the company of Mr. Harby at Brinsley Street School.

The "Man's World" episode on film, in fact, reveals even more clearly than "Shame" Ken Russell's divided loyalties: his efforts to mediate between the text and the contemporary preoccupations of his audience. The film succeeds visually in capturing the Victorian bleakness of work and study at Brinsley Street and Ursula's disillusionment on first encountering it, this to the point that Russell's sterile classroom scenes, with their ever-present suggestion of threat, begin to recall Dickens as well as Lawrence. Unlike the expanded film version of "Shame," "The Man's World" returns to Russell's technique of telescoping the text. Lawrence's "Man's World" chapter, well over fifty pages long, is constricted here

into two brief film episodes.[29] The first depicts Ursula's initial day of teaching at
St. Philips School (which remains unnamed on film), and ends with her double
defeat at the hands of the vicious student Richards, who injures her with a slingshot, and the equally vicious schoolmaster Harby, who uses this incident as a
pretext for a crude sexual advance of his own. The second work sequence also
depicts a single day in Ursula's teaching career, one which occurs weeks or even
months later and which ends in victory rather than defeat. By severely thrashing
Richards (the same student who wounded her, and a composite of at least two
children in Lawrence's text), Ursula reasserts control over her professional life in
relation to her rebellious group of lower-class children and also in relation to the
omnipresent and menacing Harby. Ken Russell's two classroom sequences do not
play back-to-back but are separated by Uncle Henry and Winifred's wedding.
This placement emphasizes even further Russell's interest in his heroine as lover
and worker both or, more exactly, juxtaposes her simultaneous loss of sexual and
professional virginity within these two essential spheres of human existence.

As has already been suggested, "The Man's World" allows Russell to go beyond Ursula as one individual in flux and to use its squalid circumstances toward more generalized and contemporary ends. Like "Shame," Russell's "Man's
World" is designed to reflect several social issues immediately familiar to modern film audiences in England and America. One such issue is the spiritual and
physical abuse of children, carried out here under the pretext of rigid but necessary classroom discipline. No question that this issue resonates through the text
as well, yet far less insistently than it does on film. In Russell's adaptation of "The
Man's World," his audience first sees a mass of slum children, their ages widely
varied, marshalled up like troops, prisoners, or even concentration camp victims,
all to the hideous march music of Miss Harby's piano and to the shrill sounds of
a whistle reminiscent of Winifred Inger's. Once marched in to the ordered chaos
of their classrooms, these children are immediately assailed by questions suggestive of interrogation, by sharp commands, and very soon by physical punishment.
In one early scene the camera remains focused on Ursula's face as she winces
rhythmically to the beat of Harby's cane while he thrashes Richards, the same
scruffy child whom Ursula will later beat.

If the "Man's World" episode under Russell's direction is transformed into a
contemporary outcry against child abuse, even louder and more direct than
Lawrence's, a major problem or paradox within it is that the film seems to abandon its own cause partway through—a reversal reminiscent of the backlash against
lesbianism (and feminism by guilty association) despite the film's surface gestures
of support. More specifically, the same physical abuse that causes Ursula to wince
in the first "Man's World" scene becomes her own means of salvation in the second. Her severe caning of Richards emerges as a wholly positive act, intended to

enlist the sympathy and support of Russell's audience. It becomes an "Ursula Victrix," a violent yet triumphant breakthrough that allows the heroine to assert herself effectively for the first time in the male professional world. Another source of the film's inconsistency over child abuse is the figure of Richards himself—a seemingly helpless and sickly boy who proves instead to be a formidable enemy and, quite beyond the text, a direct physical threat to Ursula. It would seem, then, that Russell either loses hold of the child-abuse question, or else consciously subverts it, by pressing Richards into conflicting duties in terms of the array of social issues reflected in the film. On one hand, Richards is a child and without question an abused one. On the other hand, he is also an immature instance of the violent male opposition, in general, to Ursula's entry into the man's world. On screen the issues of gender and child abuse eventually come into conflict, so that Richards as a feeble and mistreated boy is symbolically displaced by Richards as yet another male antagonist to Ursula. Twice, for example, he seriously fires his slingshot at her, once with bloody results. Less violent but perhaps even more telling, in their first meeting Richards corrects Ursula when she refers to him as Jimmy, insisting that she call him Jim, the adult or more manly version of his name.

Despite the surface opposition at Brinsley Street School of mature teachers versus youthful students, Jim Richards is in many ways aligned as a male with Mr. Harby against the female Ursula. Harby's punishment of the boy turns out to be part of the schoolmaster's strategy for undermining Ursula's authority in class. Also, Richards's slingshot assault, at the end of Ursula's first teaching day, inadvertently sets up Harby's sexual assault, so that Richards as a victimized child is again displaced by Richards as a threatening male and even as Harby's juvenile ally. Ursula's major battle at Brinsley Street is not with Richards but with Harby, and in moving this from text to screen Ken Russell once again reveals his attempt to adapt Lawrence to the social preoccupations of the late twentieth century. Where the issue of child abuse at least has a secure textual foundation within the "Man's World" chapter, the issue of sexual coercion does not. Lawrence's Harby, unlike Russell's, is not interested in Ursula as a woman, nor is he even aware of her sexually. He has gone beyond Skrebensky in adapting to modern mechanism, abstraction, and professional role-playing so that he appears to be neutered not just spiritually but physically. He sees Ursula not as an attractive woman but merely as a component in his educational machine, and an unreliable component at that, which will require careful maintenance and supervision:

> Ursula could not make herself a favourite with him. From the first moment she set hard against him. She set against Violet Harby also.

> Mr. Harby was, however, too much for her, he was something she
> could not come to grips with, something too strong for her. She tried
> to approach him as a young bright girl usually approaches a man,
> expecting a little chivalrous courtesy. But the fact that she was a girl,
> a woman, was ignored or used as a matter for contempt against
> her. (377)

On the other hand, Lawrence's Ursula finds Harby sexually attractive or, more
exactly, would have found him attractive had the living man not been smothered within the schoolmaster:

> She might have liked him as a man. And here he stood in some other
> capacity, bullying over such a trifle as a boy's speaking out without
> permission. Yet he was not a little, fussy man. He seemed to have
> some cruel, stubborn, evil spirit, he was imprisoned in a task too
> small and petty for him, which yet, in a servile acquiescence, he
> would fulfil, because he had to earn his living. (387)

Jim Carter's rendering of Harby creates a character in complete contrast to
Lawrence's original, even in physical appearance. Harby is huge of stature on screen,
always menacing, and decidedly ugly. Hardly ignoring Ursula's womanhood, he
begins at once to single her out sexually, just as Winifred did earlier in the film,
and to do so in ways calculated to invite immediate recognition and response from
a film audience. On Ursula's first day of work, before the children have arrived,
Harby orders her to fetch some books from a high shelf so that he can get a better look at her legs. When she drops the books and quickly bends over to recover
them, Harby studies her rear end with an expression on his face so suggestive of
a lustful leer as to approach parody. Harby's behavior is so crude and obvious
that Ursula, naive and young as she is, realizes at once what's going on.

Ursula's first day of work under Harby may begin with ogling, but it ends with
a rapid escalation into sexual aggression and blackmail—all of this beyond the
boundaries of the text. As Ursula leaves the school building, she is struck by a
stone accurately fired from Richards's slingshot. Harby appears as Ursula is tending her wound in a small washroom and, feigning concern, grasps her bleeding
hand and begins to bandage it. After mentioning Ursula's vulnerability and youth,
he tells her, "I could be very useful to you, Miss Brangwen," then, "I could make
it easier for you, so much easier, if only you'd . . ." When Ursula rejects the implications of Harby's unfinished sentence, he moves from proposition to threat.
"I could swallow you whole," he tells Ursula. "You see, Miss Brangwen, only my
cane rules this school." Harby leaves Ursula in tears, yet despite the ugliness of
his advance, the scene remains ineffective, perhaps even ludicrous. Harby's pass

at Ursula is so exaggerated and crude on film as to replace serious representation of this issue with caricature and, as a result, to diminish Harby to the proportions of a stock villain in nineteenth-century melodrama or farce. Of some interest despite this failure is the fact that Harby's behavior has been foreshadowed early in the film by Winifred Inger and her painter friend, Mac. Harby, in fact, emerges as a conflation of these two figures by incorporating several of their most unsavory qualities into his own persona. Like Winifred, he takes pleasure in the opportunities afforded him as schoolmaster to dominate his students and subordinates. Like Mac, Harby is really a sexual sadist, this to the point that the "Man's World" episodes on screen become a more dangerous replay of Ursula's first attempt to earn money on her own as Mac's model. Now at Brinsley Street, however, Mac's ineffectual pass has escalated into Harby's devouring one just as the artist's red paint, brushed across the buttocks of a statue, reemerges as Ursula's real blood and as Harby's cane applied to the living flesh of children.

Child abuse and sexual coercion are joined in "The Man's World" by a third contemporary issue. Far more than Lawrence does, Russell concerns himself with the specific content of Ursula's teaching and with teaching in general at Brinsley Street, also with the role of Logos in education—the inscribed word itself in its ambivalent potential for both clarity and confusion. As with child abuse, there is a written trace of all this within the text, as when a few missing pens provide the opportunity for punishment, transforming a tool of inscription into quantitative, economic, and political significance in place of the educational purpose it was intended to serve:

> "Not enough pens, Miss Brangwen?" . . . [Harby] said, with the smile and calm of exceeding rage against her.
> "No, we are six short," she said, quaking. . . .
> "A few days ago, there were sixty pens for this class—now there are forty eight. What is forty eight from sixty, Williams?" There was a sinister suspense in the question. (393–94)

Russell incorporates Lawrence's pen incident into his transcription of "The Man's World," then reaches beyond it by way of an original and effective screen interpolation on learning and the written word. The film's central object of inscription and education is not the pen but the blackboard, something which plays no role in Lawrence's text. During the film's school episodes, this blackboard becomes a screen-within-a-screen upon which various words and images appear in chalk, suggesting a range of possibilities and strategies for the instruction of the young. Harby makes masterful use of the blackboard as multiple instrument of quantification, social ideology, and power. He orders Richards to write the misspelled word *pinafore* correctly on the board one hundred times. This punishment replaces free discourse with repetition and rote—also with mathematical calculation (one hundred times) and gender instruction or, more precisely, with a lesson on what attire might be appropriate for Miss Brangwen but not for Richards. Interestingly enough, Richards takes pleasure in his punishment and is reluctant to leave when Ursula excuses him before he has completed his task. Once Richards does leave, Ursula picks up the chalk and finishes the assignment for him, even making an effort to imitate the boy's handwriting. In effect, Ursula has taken his place as Harby's victim and as the recipient of his dubious instruction.

In contrast to Harby's mechanical and political application of the chalk and blackboard, his young pupils make counteruse of these same objects as instruments of rebellion against the knowledge being imposed upon them. Here the film proves to be very much in accord with Lawrence's textual assertion that "Children will never naturally acquiesce to sitting in a class and submitting to knowledge. They must be compelled by a stronger, wiser will. Against which will they must always strive to revolt" (383). When the film's Ursula enters her classroom for the first time, one anonymous child has already combined inscription with rebellious image by drawing a witch on the blackboard labeled "Miss Harby." Miss Harby's response is, predictably, to erase the drawing at once. The image of teacher-as-witch is, of course, a familiar school cliché, partly because it rebels against the educational system by tacitly accepting that system's basic assumption that chalk is used to make images and words upon a blackboard. Here, Ursula's antagonist Richards proves far more of a visionary than the unknown witch-artist in that his methodology of revolt is dismissive of such normative expectations and therefore subversively effective. Richards does not write with his chalk (unless forced to do so) but instead grinds it up into dust with a *pen* knife (deconstructing both the act and the instrument of inscription simultaneously), then fills Ursula's pinafore with this dust so that when she pulls it on over her head she emerges before her class not as a witch drawn in chalk but as a living clown in whiteface.

On Ursula's first day of teaching at Brinsley Street, she employs a third approach to the chalk and blackboard distinct from either Harby's repressive application or Richards's revolutionary one. She attempts to use these tools of inscription to soften the educational process—to befriend her rough group of children and to humanize her association with them by making it personal, organic, and warm. In this spirit Ursula has drawn a large chalk-rabbit on her blackboard that presides as background image (and personal "totem") over her first day of teaching, supporting her essay-assignment on the rabbit, yet also implying the vapidity of such teaching, even though it is meant to counter Harby's mechanical lesson on the industrial revolution and the modern factory. Ursula's well-intentioned but ineffectual rabbit finally serves the film as palimpsest when the image gradually becomes obliterated by the word *pinafore* written and rewritten over it one hundred times.

Russell's second classroom episode begins with a view of Ursula at her blackboard again, seeming to have abandoned images in favor of words. She writes the syllable *Pret* on the board but is interrupted by what will become the crisis and turnabout of her young professional life: the trivial pen incident precipitated by Harby and, resulting from it, the climactic struggle with Richards that ends with his thrashing and defeat at Ursula's hands. The syllable *Pret* seems provocative because of its unrealized potential for completion into a word. Perhaps Ursula intends to build *Pret* into *Pretty* or *Pretend,* suggesting that she has not yet abandoned her effort to counter Harby's mechanism with sweetness and light. Or perhaps Ursula's *Pret* will play out as *Preterit* signaling her capitulation to the grind of grammar and the normative process of instruction at Brinsley Street School. Emotional and physical violence, however, intervene between the promising syllable and the finished word. Richards attacks another boy amid the confusion created by Harby's hunt for the lost pens. When Ursula attempts to punish him, Richards again fires his slingshot at her (missing this time), then viciously kicks at her legs as she tries to control him. Seizing Harby's cane, Ursula beats Richards to the floor with it, thrashing him so soundly that the instrument of punishment itself breaks in two across the boy's back. Symbolically, then, Ursula emerges from this petty but grim battle as "Ursula Victrix" at least twice over, having "settled" Richards and disarmed Harby (her two male tormentors) in a single stroke. Ursula returns to the blackboard after her victory and completes *Pret* into *Pretoria,* revealing that her intent before the interruption had been to carry her teaching beyond all prior expectations. She was prevented from doing so by the male intrusions of Harby and Richards, acting in subtle collusion, but now is free to carry on in the aftermath of their defeat. Ursula's inscription and underscoring of the word *Pretoria* on the board seem to announce that classroom rigor and youthful rebellion will no longer collide but converge and even lead, by way of dynamic interaction, to meaningful teaching. Ursula's new lesson on the Boer War will discard rabbits and pinafores as fit subjects for instruction in favor of race, colonialism, international conflict, and the state of the world at the dawn of the twentieth century.

Although Lawrence's heroine similarly thrashes a student-enemy into submission, she emerges as no such "Ursula Victrix" in the process, nor achieves any radical revision of her teaching by way of this act. Perhaps because of such departure from the text, critics have tended to see Russell's version of "The Man's World" as the film's most telling sequence—in terms of its own narrative structure and Ursula's difficult emergence from adolescence into independent womanhood. Michael Billington, in a *New York Times* interview with Sammi Davis, typically describes "The Man's World" as "hard [to watch] because Ursula has to mature by doing something cruel."[30] Similarly, Richard A. Blake refers to the violent climax of Russell's classroom episode as "a harrowing scene, [in which Ursula] . . . asserts her power over an unruly child in brutal hand-to-hand, foot to shin combat. Her victory is more liberating than any sexual experience she might have had."[31] The unexpected sexual reference here unintentionally yet persuasively places Ursula within the film's gallery of erotic dominators: Winifred, Mac, and even Harby himself. Such identification finds support within the film's visual structure when Sammi Davis is shown uncharacteristically wearing a man's black tie much like Harby's for the scene of Richards's defeat. Russell's own assessment of the "Man's World" sequence seems to confirm that its violent resolution intentionally signals the moment of Ursula's empowerment. In a *Manchester Guardian Weekly* interview with Derek Malcolm, Russell refers to his heroine's thrashing of Richards as "the point at which Ursula starts becoming herself." He adds, "I wouldn't be surprised if a few mothers in the audience don't get up and cheer."[32]

Lawrence, however, would most certainly not have gotten up and cheered at any of this. It is in fact surprising to realize just how far from the spirit of the text Russell's "Man's World" has strayed despite the many surface parallels of mood and situation. For Lawrence's Ursula, as for the author himself, the defeat of her child-enemy (Williams, not Richards, in the text) is no triumph at all but instead a blow struck against her own being as well as his. In order to thrash the boy into submission, she must abandon her warm and decidedly nonviolent self, her identity as "Ursula," to become fully absorbed by her newly acquired professional role as "Miss Brangwen." In doing so, and in settling Williams effectively, Ursula at least temporarily joins Skrebensky, Harby, and all of the other characters in the novel who have adapted to coming times at great expense to themselves. Lawrence writes that his Ursula, unlike Russell's, "was as if violated to death" in the aftermath of her ugly victory. "Something had broken in her; she had passed a crisis. Williams was beaten, but at a cost." And "she had paid a great price out of her own soul to do this. It seemed as if a great flame had gone through her and burnt her sensitive tissue."[33]

This opposition between text and film should really come as no surprise. With the history of the Brangwen family across three generations omitted, no cinematic trace remains of their evolution from past organic mystery toward a more familiar yet colder time-present. Ursula's professional breakthrough on film, then, can't possibly appear as a capitulation to impersonal modernity as it is in the text. Instead, it is a triumph and major moment of growth. What does prove surprising at this watershed in Russell's *Rainbow* is that his announcement of Ursula's maturity and empowerment may conflict with the spirit of his own film as well as that of Lawrence's text. Russell has devoted a great deal of effort, all through *The Rainbow*, in preparing to celebrate Ursula's passage from girlhood to womanhood and her escape from Skrebensky's toy-life. Russell implies that all or most of the characters who surround Ursula live some version of this life, either clinging to immaturity like her father or else making adulthood into a sterile game, as Skrebensky himself does. As a result of this pessimistic implication, Russell crowds his film with metaphors of play, often pairing particular toy or game images with particular boy-men or girl-women. For Will Brangwen it is a party horn, a rocking horse, and the bread-and-jam rainbow with which he attempts to pacify his daughter in the film's initial scene. For Uncle Henry it is highly detailed scale models of mining equipment that adorn the desks and shelves of his estate. For Winifred it is competitive sports and games in place of toys—swimming races and fencing matches early in the film and then croquet, very near the end, played against Ursula and won during a discussion of possible tactics in husband-hunting. At about the same late point in *The Rainbow* Russell seems to implicate several of his characters together in gamesmanship by staging a badminton match for mixed doubles—Skrebensky and Winifred against Henry and Ursula. The match takes place during a heated and somewhat incoherent political argument among the four players, implying that economic, social, and international matters merely project adult competition and gaming upon a wider field.[34]

Following Ursula's victory in the man's world, the conclusion of Russell's *Rainbow*, and its two final scenes in particular, are meant to show her decisive rejection of this toy-life and her escape from gaming and the many tedious players who have forced her to join in. Ursula's on-screen departure, presumably into mature selfhood and independence, begins as she walks away from Winifred's croquet court and Winifred herself. This departure leads to the first of two concluding episodes in the film: Ursula's encounter with the herd of horses—real and threatening horses now in place of the wooden rocking horse of her childhood. This horse scene makes sense, in relation to the girl-to-woman transition, in that Ursula's toys have now been replaced by dangerous realities. Yet, as Neil Sinyard's *Filming Literature* accurately predicted, the scene fails cinematically and proves confusing because it remains disconnected from all else that came before it. The horses suddenly appear out of a fog as Ursula rides her bicycle along a wooded pathway toward home. She's nearly trampled but saves herself by climbing a tree. The horses sweep by her and disappear as suddenly as they came. Once seemingly safe, Ursula is immediately threatened a second time. As she continues home on foot, she encounters a group of men whose identity is never precisely established, although they are most likely colliers. Large of stature and clad in brown leather, they actually resemble the horses as they pursue Ursula through a driving rainstorm. In contrast to Lawrence's colliers, who try to help Ursula at this point in the text, these men only menace her, suggesting sexual threat and bodily harm. As with the horses, these on-screen miners prove more meaningful abstractly than in the cinematic flesh. Thematically, they imply an ongoing and dangerous male presence which the now-adult Ursula must fend off on her own. In visual actuality, however, they appear and disappear entirely unexplained and are likely to leave a film audience simply puzzled.

Ursula manages to avoid these strange men by abandoning the wooded path and crossing a stream that leads her home—yet not before she stumbles in the rushing water and receives a baptismal "ducking" similar to Yvette's in *The Virgin and the Gipsy.* Ursula's arrival home marks the start of Ken Russell's final episode. As she enters the house, Ursula immediately encounters two reminders of the toy-life she is about to leave behind: the sounds of yet another children's party and a telegram from Skrebensky. Ursula does not join her family at play but takes the already opened telegram upstairs to her bedroom where, unlike Lawrence's Ursula, she reads it at once. It is at this point in the film that Ursula falls into a fever-sleep and has her dream of escape from both former lovers, Winifred and Skrebensky, in favor of independence. As she struggles to free herself from the dream Skrebensky, she awakens to see her father's face instead of his, and to replay a grown version of the childhood scene which began the film. Father and daughter appear to be in harmony again, at least for the time being. Will calls Ursula's attention to a rainbow, and she springs up at once to pursue and capture it, just as she did years before. The film concludes, and the screen credits appear, as Ursula runs full-tilt toward her rainbow, clutching a suitcase and following the same path she was prevented from taking as a little girl. While this closing sequence is clearly celebratory, its effect is to question or even belie, at the eleventh hour, Ursula's passage into adulthood. Russell's final scene seems so lyrical and fanciful as to create a toy-ending to his film, one which seems to deny all of its elaborate preparations for Ursula's entry into the mature world. It proves even less credible than Jack Cardiff's almost identical ending in *Sons and Lovers*, since the departing Paul Morel, unlike Ursula, at least has somewhere to go once he boards the train he is chasing. Rather than running toward anything definite, Russell's Ursula is simply running away or in Russell's own words enacting a fantasy-escape "over the rainbow" like Dorothy in *The Wizard of Oz.*[35]

As mentioned earlier, Russell's ending in *The Rainbow* bears some resemblance not only to Jack Cardiff's in *Sons and Lovers* but also to Christopher Miles's in *Virgin.* Here the parallels are so frequent and precise as to suggest deliberate borrowing. After immersions in baptismal waters, Yvette and Ursula seek refuge in an upstairs bedroom where a final epiphany is about to transform them both. Miles's and Russell's cameras frame the two girls identically, sitting nude on their beds, wet and shivering, trying to get warm—also traveling mentally between dream-fantasy and real experience. Certainly these endings are similar rather than exactly alike, since there is no flood in *The Rainbow* and since one heroine has a real gypsy to keep her warm while the other has only a "dear Ursula" letter from Skrebensky that she clutches tightly. Despite the differences, both Yvette and Ursula awaken on screen, after dreaming of new selves and of departures, Yvette with the Eastwoods and Ursula entirely on her own. The surprise emerging from such parallels may not only be that Ken Russell owes a visual and scenic debt to Christopher Miles. Rather, the strong likeness could suggest that Russell's Ursula emerges as closer in conception to Miles's Yvette than to Lawrence's original figure. *The Rainbow* might best be understood and appreciated as Russell's belated contribution to the cinematic literature of youth. Released in the late 1980s, *The Rainbow* may be looking backwards to the late 1960s and to Christopher Miles's *Virgin,* the quintessential Lawrentian youth film of that period.

Ironically, however, in looking back at Miles's achievements some twenty years earlier, Russell may have lost sight of his own. *Women in Love* endures as a significant film partly because of the maturity reflected in its scenic and imagistic richness and in its successful juxtaposition of several complex figures—Gudrun, Gerald, and Birkin in their evolving humanity and flux of relationships. It should be recalled that Ken Russell has complained that Jennie Linden, playing Ursula in *Women in Love,* was the weak member of his Lawrentian quartet because of her immaturity in the role, making her interpretation of Ursula too youthful and innocent to measure up to the greater intricacy of the other three. It is interesting that in *Women in Love* Russell reversed the textual age-relationship between Gudrun and Ursula, making Ursula the younger sister perhaps as a way of achieving a more plausible fit for Linden within the cast. It is equally interesting to realize that this age reversal is rectified in *The Rainbow* where Russell restores Ursula to her original position as Gudrun's older sister and as the oldest child within the Brangwen family.

Despite this correction, however, Linden's Ursula and Davis's Ursula prove limited in very similar ways as if Russell, despite his awareness of her shortcomings in *Women in Love,* managed somehow in *The Rainbow* to repeat the same mistake. Beyond bringing to the screen a far more girlish Ursula than Lawrence (or apparently even Russell) had envisioned, Linden unfortunately renders her as already complete, a static figure rather than one experiencing radical development. At the start of the film she appears as an attractive, lively, and relatively uncomplicated young woman whose major move in life is to fall in love with Birkin. Once this happens, she commits herself to him, demands an equal commitment in return, and dedicates herself, up to the film's closing freeze-frame of her face, to "perfecting" their relationship into all-powerful and all-exclusive love.

This Ursula—whether the outcome of Linden's performance, Russell's direction, or a combination of the two—offers us far less than the dynamic and ever-changing woman of Lawrence's text and less than the darker yet richer characterizations created by Linden's cinematic colleagues, Glenda Jackson, Alan Bates, and Oliver Reed.

This summary can be applied equally well to Sammi Davis's portrayal of Ursula in *The Rainbow*. No question that here she's *meant* to be immature, the same person several years earlier caught in the toils of adolescence. Despite this, Davis's interpretation of the teen-aged Ursula still makes her seem younger than her actual years—yet now, oddly enough, with Russell's full approval (and limitless praise of Davis's performance) in place of his earlier condemnation of Linden for doing the same thing. When Davis's Ursula is in buoyant and enthusiastic spirits, the performance works reasonably well, perhaps drawing strength from similar qualities in Davis's own personality, or from the efforts of a supportive director, or, as mentioned before, from the two forces working together. As a result, Davis's interpretation of Ursula succeeds in being both winning and convincing as Harby's enthusiastic novice-teacher, as Skrebensky's passionate virgin, and as Winifred's willing disciple—too hopefully innocent in all three roles to see just what lies ahead for her.

Davis's performance falters, however, once she turns Ursula's disposition dark instead of sunny or seriously angry instead of playfully scrappy. Such moments in the film are intended to represent meaningful confrontations in which Ursula asserts herself morally and spiritually against such corrupt figures as Mac, Winifred, Uncle Henry, and what they represent in the world. Here, however, Davis's youthfulness works against her, reducing Ursula's passionate rage to what seems on screen much more like the frets, pouts, and temper tantrums of a young child. This failure is nowhere more evident than in the film episode built around Ursula's condemnation of her Uncle Henry—for his comfortable capitalism, his exploitation of the colliers he depends upon, and his destructive indifference to nature. What could have provided a strong sequence emerges instead as ludicrous, largely because Ursula's outburst seems both trivial and inappropriate, as if she had suddenly regressed from adolescence to rude and unpleasant childhood. She accepts her uncle's hospitality only to insult him in his own home and before Winifred, the guest she herself invited to come along. Then in the episode's questionable climax, she destroys Henry's garden in retaliation for the trapping of wild rabbits on his estate. Ursula is shown in this scene screaming and kicking prize heads of lettuce about as if they were soccer balls, diminishing her protest and herself to juvenile proportions.

While the Uncle Henry episode presents both heroine and film at their weakest point, the truth remains that Ursula leaves the screen the same person who entered it, essentially a girl still pursuing her rainbow and her womanhood. Like Jennie Linden's Ursula twenty years earlier, this one also proves to be a static rather than a dynamic figure and, as such, a violation of Lawrence's vision of her and, unfortunately, of Ken Russell's as well. For all of Russell's foreshadowing, fanfare, and celebration, Sammi Davis's heroine never achieves the maturity he so eagerly anticipates and prepares her for. In *Women in Love,* Ursula's similar youthfulness and limited inward movement do not finally compromise that film's success. This is because she is surrounded by three figures spiritually older and deeper than herself, whose stories and fluid personalities sweep her along with them and absorb her flaws. In *The Rainbow* Ursula's immaturity and lack of growth have a wider and more detrimental effect because no similar figures appear to support and carry her through. Particularly with the disappearance of the earlier Brangwen generations, Russell's *Rainbow* remains exclusively focused on Ursula, revealing her story alone for better or for worse. If she never reaches maturity, nor ripens and develops in spirit, neither does the film as a whole.

A separate screen version of *The Rainbow* appeared on British television less than a year before Russell's film was released. This nearly simultaneous adaptation was produced by Chris Parr for Pebble Mill, the Midlands division of BBC Television, and was shown in December 1988 in three sixty-minute episodes ("Ghosts," "The Widening Circle," and "The Darkness of Paradise"). It aired again in the United States on the Arts and Entertainment Network in August 1989. Since that time the production has not been rereleased for television, nor has it been made available on commercial videotape. The screenplay for this short-lived *Rainbow* was by the Irish dramatist and fiction writer Anne Devlin, with direction by Stuart Burge, who directed the BBC version of *Sons and Lovers* seven years earlier. A casting connection of sorts exists between Russell's and Burge's *Rainbows* since, as mentioned earlier, Sammi Davis auditioned for the role of Ursula in Burge's production but was turned down in favor of Imogen Stubbs. A comparison of the two *Rainbows* reveals, clearly enough, that Burge and his colleagues made the better choice. Stubbs's Ursula (who also provides voice-over narration) seems as youthful as Davis's, yet implies, through Stubbs's effective performance, a degree of human complexity and capacity for growth beyond Davis's ability to project.

A deeper connection between the two productions is that both focus on the last third of the novel and on Ursula's story at the expense of her parents' and grandparents' stories. Here too, however, Burge, Devlin, and company seem to make more successful artistic choices than Russell does, allowing them to put back much of the material omitted from the large-screen adaptation. Ursula's grandmother Lydia Brangwen (cut from Russell's *Rainbow*) plays a small but critical role in this production as a beloved mentor to Ursula and as a source of stability. Beyond this, a favored technique in Burge's *Rainbow* is flashback, which he also used in his 1981 *Sons and Lovers* as a means of preserving early material from the novel, such as Gertrude Morel's young adulthood. In the BBC *Rainbow*, glimpses of Tom Brangwen's courtship of Lydia Lensky appear in flashbacks or, more exactly, in Ursula's clairvoyant daydreams about her ancestors, which she believes to be visions of their ghosts. In parallel to Tom's courtship of Lydia, his death is also preserved through Ursula's visions. The production begins with the flood and the drowning, also missing from Russell's film. These dramatic events are revealed to be the imaginings of a young girl, Ursula, as she lies in bed dreaming about her family's past. Ursula's vision of her grandfather's death closes as well as opens the "Ghosts" episode of Burge's *Rainbow* and becomes a workable means of unifying the production as well as preserving the text. That Ken Russell does not similarly exploit flashback in his film of *The Rainbow* seems disappointing in light of Burge's production and also surprising in light of Russell's own *Women in Love* twenty years earlier. Russell used flashback effectively in *Women in Love,* much as Burge does in *The Rainbow,* to condense and to preserve, as when he proudly saved "Class-Room" from cutting by having Ursula recall it as she watches Birkin and Hermione at the Crich wedding.

As with the two productions of *Sons and Lovers,* a comparison of the large- and small-screen versions of *The Rainbow* is both revealing and provocative. It invites speculation, for example, on the possibility of a stronger large-screen *Rainbow* had Russell's production been less his own (and his immediate family's) exclusive project. What Larry Kramer did for *Women in Love* twenty years earlier could perhaps have been achieved again by way of another dynamic and probably troubled collaboration—had Anne Devlin, for instance, or even Kramer himself written the screenplay instead of the Russells, providing not just a script for the film but a fresh artistic perspective as well.[36]

# 7
# Lady Chatterley's Lover: Filming the Unfilmable

A **Ken Russell's *Lady Chatterley* (1993)**

As the 1990s would reveal, the end of Russell's *Rainbow* was not to be the end of his involvement with D. H. Lawrence. In 1993, four years after *The Rainbow* and almost a quarter century after *Women in Love*, BBC Television carried his four-episode serialization of *Lady Chatterley's Lover*, written by Russell in collaboration with Michael Haggiag and retitled *Lady Chatterley*.[1] This third Lawrentian project established Russell as the most prolific of all the Lawrence directors to date and, for better or worse, as the individual most responsible for presenting and interpreting Lawrence to mass audiences worldwide.

Russell's most recent Lawrence production also turned out to be his most problematic, at least as measured by critical responses from media reviewers and Lawrentians alike. If such commentators recalled Russell's *Rainbow* as a retreat following *Women in Love,* they judged this latest venture to be a further loss of artistic ground and even an unintentional parody of the two earlier films. Russell's costuming and choreography, powerfully effective in the past, struck many viewers here as exaggerated to the point of absurdity. One scene in question shows Clifford being propelled into his mine in a coal cart, dressed in full military uniform (with medals) in order to intimidate his colliers into ending a strike. Another scene, after Connie and Hilda have joined their father on holiday, depicts but does not explain a costume ball during which Connie and her friends discuss serious matters while dressed as Renaissance princesses, cardinals, and kings. Russell's nepotism in casting, carried over from *The Rainbow,* was also noticed and criticized. The production predictably recycled old colleagues like Judith Paris, but then went beyond professionals, as did *The Rainbow,* to include members of the director's family. For many, this home-video effect in *Lady Chatterley* was confirmed by Russell's own appearance as "Sir Michael," a renamed version of Connie's father, Sir Malcolm Reid.

The point in mentioning these details, and including Russell's production here at all, is not to follow him from Lawrence on film to Lawrence on television, a topic deserving further treatment but beyond the scope of this study. Rather, Russell's *Lady Chatterley* is appropriate to consider here because it provides closure on one subject, Russell's Lawrentian adventure, while introducing another, Lady Chatterley on screen. Russell's 1993 *Lady Chatterley* also deserves attention because, if not successful, it remains an intriguing and informative failure to anyone surveying the fifty-year history of Lawrentian cinema. When Russell comes to frame Lawrence on the small screen, he can't help bringing with him the accumulated conventions of a five-decade effort upon the larger screen. This effort includes his own contributions as well as those of his immediate colleagues and competitors, the other Lawrence filmmakers whose work he clearly knows. Here his televised *Lady Chatterley,* regardless of its ultimate worth, functions as a review of earlier Lawrence screen productions. It also serves as an intercinematic conversation with directors like Mark Rydell and Christopher Miles, both Lawrentian filmmakers of the late 1960s and, as such, Russell's contemporaries when he directed *Women in Love.*

Allusions to what now seems to have been the golden moment of Lawrence filming proliferate within the *Lady Chatterley* production, some unobtrusive, others writ large. Clifford rides in an open white car through the ranks of his colliers, recalling Oliver Reed's Gerald in an almost identical scene. Connie and Mellors make love for the first time fully clothed and joined less in an embrace than a struggle, exactly as Alan Bates and Jennie Linden were joined early in *Women in Love.* Beyond self-reference, Russell also acknowledges Mark Rydell during the late 1960s when he decorates Mellors's hut with the pelts of dead animals and when he frames Connie in a mirror, just as Anne Heywood's March was framed in *The Fox,* nude and autoerotically aroused. By far most of Russell's allusions cite Miles's *The Virgin and the Gypsy,* as if having been quoted in that film, Russell now wishes to repay the compliment.[2] Like Miles in *Virgin,* Russell begins *Lady Chatterley* during a church service complete with organist (recalling Uncle Fred) and with voice-over provided by the opening line of the text, "Ours is essentially a tragic age," recited by the minister, inappropriately, in dull monotone.[3] Along with the film's beginning, Russell borrows a host of images from Miles's *Virgin,* most notably those used throughout the earlier film to connote sterility in Yvette's family life as well as her imaginary efforts to escape it. Like

Yvette, Russell's Connie also projects herself beyond a drab Victorian interior into nature by way of her fantasies. Also like Yvette, Connie is harshly summoned back by the ringing of a strident bell, this time by Sir Clifford. The stifling nature of daily life at Wragby is conveyed through a series of *tableaux vivants* originated by Miles for similar effect in *Virgin*. In *Lady Chatterley*, when Connie returns home from holiday she is greeted at her doorstep, much as Yvette and Lucille were as they returned from school, by family members and servants dressed in black and standing motionless as if posed for some macabre formal portrait. This scene is reinforced, in both productions, by a close-up of a particularly unattractive cut of meat about to be carved, again implying the deadly unsavoriness of all things domestic within the family. Equally in accord with Miles's *Virgin*, Russell repeatedly films key characters framed behind windows, his camera looking in at them from outside to emphasize their entrapment. Almost a decade earlier, Miles filmed Yvette this way and, acknowledging human complexity, her antagonist Aunt Cissie as well. Russell sets up a series of similar shots in *Lady Chatterley* of Connie, Mellors, Mrs. Bolton, and even Sir Clifford.

Ken Russell's *Lady Chatterley* looks backwards from another perspective as well, beyond the late 1960s trilogy and, with some intensity of focus, at its own predecessors, the earlier efforts to film Lawrence's final novel. As a result, Russell's television piece affords a useful introduction to the whole issue of *Lady Chatterley* on film, albeit one that begins at the end rather than the beginning of a chronological process. *Lady Chatterley's Lover* is in fact the most often adapted of all the Lawrence novels or, perhaps more accurately, the most often attempted. Including Russell's recent contribution, there have been three "legitimate" Lady Chatterley productions intended for general release in theaters or on television. Beyond this, and constituting one of the many ironies attending Lady Chatterley on film, Lawrence's most proper of improper novels has also generated a thriving business in pornographic knockoffs, giving rise to such hard- and soft-core titles as *Lady Chatterley's Lovers, Lady Chatterley's Passions, Young Lady Chatterley, The Loves of Lady Chatterley, The Game Keeper,* and, perhaps in the interests of cultural diversity, *Lady Chatterley in Tokyo*.

Like television, pornography remains beyond the scope of this study, so that only three of the many Lady Chatterleys will be taken up in subsequent discussion: Russell's 1993 televised serialization, Just Jaeckin's 1981 *Lady Chatterley's Lover,* and Marc Allegret's French production *L'Amant de Lady Chatterley* released in 1955. The three productions will be considered in this order, despite reversed chronology, partly because of the uniqueness of Allegret's adaptation, but primarily because of the close tie between Russell's and Jaeckin's films, specifically their mutual dependence on material drawn not from *Lady Chatterley's Lover* but from Lawrence's two earlier versions, *The First Lady Chatterley* and *John Thomas and Lady Jane.* Russell's production is really a conflation of all three texts, often relying upon dialogue unique to the more discursive *John Thomas and Lady Jane* in combination with scenes taken from the final version or from the shorter and more active *First Lady Chatterley.*[4] Should we still be keeping track of Lady Chatterley's ironies, another might now be added to the list. This complex tri-textuality is achieved by the same director and screenwriter who claimed, twenty five years earlier, not to have read *Women in Love.* Russell's new multitextual awareness may have been inspired by Just Jaeckin, whose 1981 *Lady Chatterley's Lover* provides a similar amalgam of texts, although one which relies more heavily on *The First Lady Chatterley* than on either of the two subsequent versions.

Marc Allegret's *L'Amant de Lady Chatterley* also shows some trace of Lawrence's earlier versions, although not nearly to the extent of Jaeckin's or Russell's productions. For Allegret, a different body of textual material, non-Lawrentian in origin, comes to intervene between film adaptation and original source and to act as a filtering device. *L'Amant de Lady Chatterley* is not based directly on the novel but on a French play of the same name written by Gaston Bonheur and Philippe de Rothschild. It is, in short, a film adaptation of a stage adaptation of the text. Beyond this, Allegret's production bears the intriguing burden of cultural and linguistic filtration as well. It remains unique within the Lawrentian film canon as the only non-Anglo (American, Australian, or British) production and as the only production not to be filmed in English. Among the host of questions this raises is whether or not the dialect, so crucial to all three versions of the text, can be rendered into French or into any language other than Lawrence's own.

The common element here, operating within all three films, can perhaps now be identified as some degree of distraction present in the whole effort to capture Lady Chatterley on screen. Outside material, Lawrentian or otherwise, emerges as a constant in the undertaking, always standing between film and primary text. The situation is somewhat reminiscent of Mary Shelley's *Frankenstein.* Despite being attempted again and again on screen, neither that work nor the novel Lawrence finally titled *Lady Chatterley's Lover* may ever have been filmed at all.

A separate but related universal in these films—introduced by Allegret, re-peated by Jaeckin, and exaggerated by Russell—is their sudden abandonment of text altogether at the end. None of Lawrence's Lady Chatterleys has an unequivo-cally hopeful conclusion nor even the sense of completion or finality at the close. This is because the future remains largely undetermined for Connie and Parkin and for Connie and Mellors. As if the directors could not abide such indetermi-nacy, all three end their films with the lovers united and about to begin a new life together. Here Russell does more than merely repeat or recall Allegret's and Jaeckin's romantically happy endings. He inflates them to the proportions of a grotesque yet seemingly unconscious parody of the Hollywood cliché albeit now via BBC. Russell's Mellors has decided to emigrate to Canada after leaving Wragby and is shown boarding a ship near the close of the final episode. He is not aware that after learning of his departure, Connie has raced to Southampton in her sister Hilda's car and boarded the ship as well. As Mellors leans over the railing, discussing future prospects with one of the ship's officers, a loudspeaker announces that "John Thomas" is being paged by "Lady Jane." In the closing shot, the lovers are shown reunited and embracing as the ship's wake trails behind them, fading into the distance.

While this ending constitutes one of *Lady Chatterley's* most distorted and disappointing moments, it also establishes the immediately familiar image as typical of the whole production and especially of Russell's manipulation of Lawrentian plot. Russell's characterizations do not escape such stereotyping either, particularly Joely Richardson's portrayal of Lady Chatterley, which seems a deliberate exploitation of that actress's physical resemblance to the late Princess Diana. This resemblance is carefully nurtured by Richardson's wardrobe (large picture hats especially) and aimed at satisfying the 1990s tabloid obsession with titled marriage and its discontents, particularly for the lady in question. Fortunately, something of interest and beyond cliché remains in Russell's Connie and his other characters that again sheds light on the enterprise of filming Lady Chatterley in general. Russell's title reveals this or, more precisely, his decision to shorten Lawrence's title exactly as he did. To do so implies a shift in emphasis away from Mellors and toward Connie, precisely what takes place not only in Russell's version of *Lady Chatterley* but in all three. For Jaeckin and Allegret as well, Connie's experience and awakening remain the center of focus, so that Mellors is similarly displaced in each film and similarly reduced to catalytic status—producing great change and development in Connie yet remaining essentially unchanged himself.

A consistent result of this displacement is the emergence of a simplified Mellors on screen as compared with Lawrence's and a Mellors who has been misnamed by two of the three Lady Chatterley filmmakers in exactly the same way. While all three directors call him Oliver Mellors, his name only in the final version of the text, Jaeckin and Russell actually create a character much closer to Oliver Parkin, his counterpart in *The First Lady Chatterley* and *John Thomas and Lady Jane*. All three screen versions of Mellors display a capacity for violence, just as Parkin did, yet with little of the tenderness, ultimately womanliness, which dissipates it in Mellors and sets him apart from his predecessor.

As the inward human being sheds complexity on screen, so too does the man as social entity and member of a particular class functioning within a particular community. In contrast to Parkin, the original Mellors is one of several variants of a familiar yet fascinating Lawrentian figure: the escapee who by virtue of some special quality or situation has rendered himself socially ambiguous, even classless. Rupert Birkin is such a figure, reflecting no family or class background and capable in *Women in Love* of moving comfortably from one level to another. Aaron Sisson varies yet preserves the pattern by starting from working-class origins, then transcending them by way of his "rod" or artistic gift (much as Lawrence himself did) to enter Birkin's condition of social ambivalence and flux. Oliver Mellors emerges as a third version of the same figure, yet his film counterparts do not. Jaeckin's and Russell's protagonists are both working-class men (resembling Oliver Parkin) who lack Mellors's unique powers of social and linguistic mobility. Unlike him, they can't shift from the dialect to the King's English at will, nor can they leave Tevershall, as he has done, to become officers and gentlemen before returning as gamekeepers. While Allegret's Mellors has left and returned in precisely this way, he too lacks his textual namesake's social indeterminacy because he now seems simply a middle-class person and not a working man at all.

Beyond characterization or plot, a more comprehensive question needs to be raised at the outset regarding Lady Chatterley on film. Simply put, can what Edward Garnett called "a description of the whole act" be transposed undamaged from written text to moving picture?[5] What becomes of Lawrence's sexual tenderness and touch, for instance, once made overtly visible and exposed to public viewing instead of private reading? Perhaps it approaches pornography at once by the very intrusion of theater, audience, and screen, that is, by the very nature of the medium. Or perhaps it survives the cinematic transformation with some measure of fidelity to Lawrence's own vision.

Again, Ken Russell's flawed yet instructive *Lady Chatterley* addresses such fundamental and difficult questions. As was true in *The Rainbow* and *Women in Love,* the most striking thing about Russell's sexual filming in *Lady Chatterley* is its negativity. Russell keeps his camera focused and running only when the lovemaking between Connie and Mellors seems troubled. On the other hand, when their sexual encounter threatens to approach fulfillment, Russell turns his camera away from them or else turns it off altogether.[6] Along with revealing a puzzling constant in Russell's Lawrentian filming, this observation also recapitulates the familiar options available to erotic filmmakers in general, including Allegret and Jaeckin. They can aim their cameras directly at the lovers so as to formulate a visual and auditory replication of "the whole act." Or they can choose to look away cinematically, directing the camera toward some more modest subject, perhaps one that relates implicitly or imagistically to the lovemaking. Or they can cause the mechanical eye to close altogether by way of a dissolve or fade-out, to end the erotic scene just as or just before it begins. As has been suggested, Russell employs all three techniques in his *Lady Chatterley* production, sometimes looking, sometimes looking away, sometimes not looking at all. In doing so, he again recalls the work of his predecessors, combining Allegret's visual reticence, characteristic of midcentury filming in general, with Jaeckin's more direct and practiced gaze.

If, after so many attempts, *Lady Chatterley's Lover* still resists filming, the reason for its elusiveness may be found among these very options for cinematic sexuality. Quite simply, none matches the text because all contradict or even deny Lawrence and the spirit in which he wrote it. To turn the camera away or off entirely is to repress "the whole act" rather than describe it and to convey the visual equivalent of embarrassment or shame in its presence. Yet to maintain the camera's gaze, then project its results on screen, is to embrace pornography as Lawrence insistently defined it. Each viewer watching Connie and Mellors as screen images sexually joined approaches Hermione Roddice in *Women in Love* observing her "naked animal actions in mirrors, so that . . . [she] can have it all in . . . [her] consciousness, make it all mental."[7] The movie screen holds much in common with Hermione's mirror and also with the voyeur's window through which passion can be experienced in the mind's eye, or enjoyed from a distance, dispassionately.[8] If Lady Chatterley's filmmakers are damned if they don't record "the whole act" and equally damned if they do, perhaps the text itself makes the endeavor impossible—always to be attempted, never to be achieved. This paradox, along with several more hopeful possibilities, will be taken up in the following discussion of those filmmakers who have at least made the effort to film the unfilmable.

## Just Jaeckin's *Lady Chatterley's Lover* (1981)

Released by London-Cannon Films, Ltd., this second of three attempts at Lawrence's final novel also carries the Russell signature—not Ken's but that of his first wife, Shirley, who designed the costumes for this film as she did for *Women in Love* twelve years earlier. While nominally a British production, this second cinematic Lady Chatterley was much more of an international affair than Ken Russell's televised serialization a decade later. Its script was the work of a British writer, Christopher Wicking, collaborating with a French writer, Just Jaeckin, who also directed the film. Similarly, the entire production was a cross-channel collaboration between London-Cannon and its French partner, Producteurs Associes. While Jaeckin and his colleagues worked with a nearly all-British cast, Lady Chatterley was played by a Dutch actress, Sylvia Kristel, whose command of English proved uncertain enough to require the dubbing of all her spoken lines.[9]

This same European director and leading lady had worked together seven years earlier in *Emmanuelle* (1974), a French film now typically described in movie guidebooks as "one of the classics of soft-core erotic cinema."[10] Despite such notoriety, neither *Emmanuelle* nor Jaeckin's less-famous *Lady Chatterley's Lover* remains available for purchase on commercial videotape today, a coincidence perhaps explained by the sexual tameness of both films compared with current practice on both the large and small screens.[11] At the time of its release in 1981, however, *Lady Chatterley's Lover* was marketed as erotica and largely accepted as such, based partly on Lawrence's popular image but even more strongly on Jaeckin and Kristel's reputation for *Emmanuelle*.[12] While this reputation may have helped *Lady Chatterley's Lover* at the box office, it also pigeonholed Jaeckin's Lawrence production as "soft-core pornography," a term which appears repeatedly in initial reviews of the film, whether deserved or not and despite merely an R rating in the United States. Today's standards and practices aside, Jaeckin's *Lady Chatterley's Lover* turns out to be only slightly more sexually explicit than Ken Russell's *Women in Love,* a film released over a decade earlier yet never considered pornography. My point here is not to debate the "soft core" reputation of Jaeckin's *Lady Chatterley's Lover* but to note that its effect was to remove the film from serious consideration from the start and to mute all subsequent critical response.

When *Lady Chatterley's Lover* first played in British and American theaters, the usual cluster of journalistic reviews appeared, largely mixed although leaning toward negative conclusions. By far the most favorable reaction came from David Robinson writing for the *Times* of London. Robinson described Jaeckin's film as a serious effort at presenting social issues and likewise praised its characters as at least "sharply drawn" if not particularly deep. Among the actors, Robinson singled out Nicholas Clay for being especially well cast as "a suitably rugged and enticing Mellors."[13] This judgment was echoed in several American reviews as well and even by way of the same inappropriate adjective *rugged* to describe Mellors. While the word may fit Clay's portrayal, it has little to do with the intense yet physically fragile man Lawrence created in the text. Despite praise for Clay, American reviewers tended to be harder on the film as a whole than their British counterparts with typically negative judgments expressed by Herbert Mitgang, writing for the *New York Times,* and Gary Arnold, writing for the *Washington Post.* Mitgang described Jaeckin's effort as oddly passionless or erotically cold despite the on-screen sexuality. Arnold began his review with an even more extreme condemnation: "Wedding dim-witted adaptation with half-hearted sexploitation, the pathetic film version of *Lady Chatterley's Lover* now at area theaters can scarcely fail to alienate its only potential audiences."[14] Among the initial reviewers, only one, David Robinson, pointed out that Wicking and Jaeckin's script really created a screen adaptation of Lawrence's *First Lady Chatterley* instead of *Lady Chatterley's Lover* itself.[15]

For the rest of the decade, Jaeckin's *Lady Chatterley* met with critical silence. This changed slightly in the 1990s, perhaps as a result of the film's brief appearance on videotape in 1991. Here again, however, commentators continued to be scarce. Linda Ruth Williams's book *Sex in the Head: Visions of Femininity and Film in D. H. Lawrence,* published in 1993, applies cinematic perspectives to Lawrence's texts and turns to the films from time to time as well, including two footnoted comments on Jaeckin's effort, one informational and the other judgmental. Williams mentions Shirley Russell's contribution to the film and, as a result, the similarity in costuming between *Women in Love* and *Lady Chatterley's Lover.* She also describes and dismisses the entire project in an earlier note as "Just Jaeckin's dreadful 1981 film" of *Lady Chatterley's Lover.*[16]

Less dismissive commentary on Jaeckin appeared that same year in Peter Reynolds's anthology on adaptation, *Novel Images: Literature in Performance.* One essay, Neil Taylor's "A Woman's Love," compares four Lawrence films: *Lady Chatterley's Lover, Women in Love, The Virgin and the Gypsy,* and *The Rainbow.* Taylor examines these films using several standards of measure: "homogenization" (or degree of textual condensation), reliance on film conventions, "social context," "endings," and what Taylor terms "the Laurentian"—the extent to which the films prove capable of preserving textual essence on screen. Taylor's essay is often critical of Jaeckin's results within all these categories, as when (under "social context") he describes *Lady Chatterley's Lover* as "a pretty costume-drama, in which everyone is kitted out in brand-new period outfits and Wragby Hall has been converted from the novel's long, low house of brown stone with dismal rooms into an elegant Palladian stately home." With the partial exception of Christopher Miles's *Virgin,* however, Taylor's judgments on all four films are equally critical. Also, as mentioned in the previous chapter, he directs his most incisive comments at the process of marketing the films as products. In his concluding section, Taylor discusses the intricate, shifting commercial relationship among books, films, and videotapes, and specifically how the newer product often becomes a device for reselling the original. Finally, like the lone *Times* reviewer over a decade before him, Taylor notices and mentions the connection between Jaeckin's film and Lawrence's *First Lady Chatterley* as distinct from *Lady Chatterley's Lover.*[17] This observation, however, is contained in a footnote, so the full relationship between Jaeckin's screen adaptation and Lawrence's initial version fails to receive the attention it deserves.

It is worthwhile to consider why filmmakers like Russell and Jaeckin have found Lawrence's first version of the novel attractive. One plausible reason is that, even before the adaptation process begins, it is already the most spontaneously cinematic of the three Lady Chatterley texts. Some measure of this can be found in the number of scenes in *The First Lady Chatterley,* which Lawrence eventually dropped yet which survive in both the 1981 and 1993 films largely intact. The "nailing in" episode offers an example of textual material preadapted for the screen by Lawrence himself. In a brief scene (less than a page of text), Connie and Parkin drive two nails into a large oak tree to affirm the permanence of their relationship:

> "Shall yer drive yer nail inter th' oak tree wi' mine, for good an' a'?" he asked her.
> "Yes!" she said uneasily.
> He took a large nail and with a few heavy blows drove it deep into the trunk of the tree. Then he gave another nail to her.
> "Nail it aside of mine," he said.
> She drove in her nail close beside his, and he put the hammer in his pocket.
> "Tha's done it," he said.[18]

Prior to adaptation by Russell or Jaeckin, this moment already enacts a gesture of romantic optimism recognizably cinematic; it likewise reflects a visual immediacy soon to be obscured by the complexity of discourse within both of Lawrence's later versions.

A very different incident of equal visual power occurs in Lawrence's *First Lady Chatterley* when Connie returns to England to find Clifford out of his wheelchair and on his feet, although barely so and only with the constant help of servants and crutches. Lawrence retains this scene in *John Thomas and Lady Jane,* but omits it from *Lady Chatterley's Lover.* Nonetheless, both Russell and Jaeckin preserve it in their films, probably because it proves equally unnerving for an audience, as for Connie, suddenly to *see* Clifford standing in sad parody of resurrection and cure. Here, however, the complexity of even the earliest textual version becomes lost in cinematic translation. Within *The First Lady Chatterley* Connie's vision of a grotesquely resurrected Clifford immediately follows her thoughts (or really Lawrence's authorial aside) on "the naked man, the passion and the mystery of him: the mystery of the penis! . . . the symbol of the rush of the living blood is the phallus, and the penis is the fountain of life filled with blood" (136). With this as prologue, the risen Clifford becomes not only a perversely resurrected spirit but an erect yet mechanically dead alternative to Lawrence's living phallus, like "one of the iron pillars" of the railway station which Clifford leans against as he awaits Connie's arrival (139). In Jaeckin's film this scene occurs at Wragby instead of the train station, so the mechanical association is lost. Since Lawrence's phallic aside is also omitted from the film, the likeness and the opposition between the iron column and the blood column also disappear, leaving only the visual shock, albeit still powerful, of seeing Clifford on his feet.

Two additional scenes from *The First Lady Chatterley,* cut by Lawrence in the later version yet retained by both Jaeckin and Russell, are Connie's dream of horses and, shortly afterwards, her "veiling" as she stands nude before a mirror. Here, however, the textual material is barely sketched out by Lawrence, so that the filmmakers' identical tendency is to expand or to pursue the visual potential of both scenes. In the dream sequence, Lawrence writes only that Connie "had recurrent violent dreams, of horses, of a mare which had been feeding quietly, and suddenly went mad" and later that "there was a group of horses, and a mare that would go mad and lash at the others with her heels and tear them with her teeth!" (8). In the Jaeckin film, Connie dreams of a rearing white horse and then of awakening and running outdoors clad only in her nightdress. Outside, the horse has disappeared into the foggy night, and Connie runs to a towering tree, which she leans against and embraces as the dream ends. Russell's version of the horse dream is even more exaggerated. Connie, now dressed in full riding habit, sits astride a black horse and passes through a colonnade filled with the corpses of soldiers, all bare-chested (as Mellors will be in the washing scene) and decorated with flowers (as Mellors and Connie will eventually decorate one another). The dream suddenly shifts to a scene of Clifford swimming. Connie joins him and realizes that he is really drowning. As she tries to save him, Clifford grasps her and begins to pull her under along with him. All the while, Mellors has been watching from the bank but makes no move to help.

Lawrence's veiling scene in *The First Lady Chatterley* is briefly sketched as well but probably already more cinematically realized than his dream sequence. Inspired by Clifford's reading of *Hajji Baba* that evening, Connie "put a thick veil over her face, like a Mohammedan woman, leaving only her eyes. And thus she stood naked before her mirror and looked at her slow, golden-skinned, silent body. It was beautiful too, and with a silent, sad, pure appeal. Her breasts were also eyes, and her navel was sad, closed, waiting lips. It all spoke in another, silent language, without the cheapness of words" (13). While the scene survives in both films, Lawrence's contrast between the seeing, speaking face (now covered) and the equally expressive body (now uncovered) does not. In Jaeckin's version, once Connie has veiled herself, the action moves toward autoeroticism. This might be anticipated on at least two counts, both involving intercinematic quotation. First, female masturbation and veiling likewise occurred seven years earlier in Jaeckin's *Emmanuelle,* although in two separate scenes. Also, as mentioned previously, Jaeckin may be acknowledging Mark Rydell here as well, since the image of a woman masturbating before a mirror had previously been made famous in *The Fox.* Ironically, it is an image now forever linked with Lawrence despite his extreme views on the subject and despite the fact that neither of his own heroines, March or Connie, engages in such action. In Russell's *Lady Chatterley,* the veiling incident leads to exaggeration rather than allusion. In one of the film's least effective moments, Connie decides to cover her face after first covering a nude painting on her dressing-room wall. Once veiled and naked, she bursts into Clifford's bedroom and for no explainable reason dances before the poor impotent man like a crazed latter-day Salome.

Even though these two filmmakers carry identical material to widely differing extremes, their motivation seems similar—to exploit the visuality already at hand in *The First Lady Chatterley*. One verification of this is that both Jaeckin and Russell turn away from Lawrence's first draft when later versions of the text hold out more cinematic potential. Both the 1981 and 1993 films, for example, contain the scene of Connie and Mellors's nude "baptism" together in the rain. This occurs in the final version, as well as between Connie and Parkin in *John Thomas and Lady Jane,* but not in *The First Lady Chatterley* where only a less vivid encounter by moonlight takes place.

What the Lady Chatterley filmmakers omit, then, proves just as revealing as what they include. Late in Jaeckin's adaptation, a scene occurs in which Connie, on holiday in France with Hilda, receives a letter from Clifford. Instead of reading it, she tears the letter up unopened and throws it into the sea. Beyond Connie's lack of interest in anything Clifford has to say, her gesture also acts out the film's dismissal of much that Lawrence has to write—for example, all the material in *Lady Chatterley's Lover* articulated entirely by way of letters. The wedded acts of reading and writing are important in the text to the point that it begins to resemble an epistolary novel near the end. While filming a letter surely poses a challenge, Ken Russell at least makes the imaginative effort, so that some of Lawrence's epistolary material survives within *Lady Chatterley* as voice-over. Just Jaeckin, by contrast, tends to stay with what Lawrence has previsualized and so makes no attempt to transform the more elusive and challenging text-within-text into cinema. It could be argued that this is because Jaeckin is not filming *Lady Chatterley's Lover* but *The First Lady Chatterley* instead. As it turns out, however, the earlier novel also contains an epistolary element, although less pervasive than in the final version. When Connie is away from Wragby in *The First Lady Chatterley,* she and the reader find out what is happening there through an ongoing correspondence with Clifford and Mrs. Bolton. Lawrence reveals this in a series of symmetrically paired yet radically different letters, one from each correspondent, read by Connie and the reader together. Here again, Jaeckin moves away from his primary text when its offerings are not camera-ready to begin with, so that nothing of these earlier letters survives in his film.

Partly because of the same discomfort with language, Jaeckin also excludes those portions of *The First Lady Chatterley,* beyond letters, which might also tempt the film into discourse. One instance of this is Connie's visit, late in the novel, to Blagby Street in Sheffield where Parkin has been living with the Tewson family after leaving Wragby. Connie's visit leads to a lengthy political discussion, during which Bill Tewson and Parkin's communist sympathies are revealed, and during which the issue of class conflict moves to the foreground. None of this remains in Jaeckin's adaptation, which accords with the film's logophobia and also with its tendency to simplify and depoliticize Lawrence. While his *Lady Chatterley's Lover* contains several scenes which visually display the class differences between Connie and Mellors, or Clifford and Mellors, the film consistently avoids probing past the visible contrasts and into the layered political, social, and linguistic implications beneath them. This creates a paradox worth discussing further in its impact on characterization and relationship in the Jaeckin film.

Before turning to such matters, however, a few final observations should be made on those images and scenes in Jaeckin's *Lady Chatterley's Lover* which owe no debt to Lawrence's text in any of its versions. Here, as with every other screen adaptation, textual omission and cinematic interpolation prove inseparable, so that as discursive gaps occur in *Lady Chatterley's Lover,* Jaeckin fills them with new material. The originality of this material, however, may need to be qualified, since much of it can be traced back not to Lawrence but to the earlier Lawrence films.

Two examples of such quotation involve a billiard table and the curtained windows of Sir Clifford's estate. The first comes from a scene in *Women in Love* where Oliver Reed's Gerald and Glenda Jackson's Gudrun (both formally attired) play a game of billiards at Shortlands in the early stages of their relationship. Jaeckin repeats this scene at Wragby, with Clifford and Connie similarly dressed but now with the man attempting to conduct the game, and to win control over the woman, from his wheelchair. Later in *Lady Chatterley's Lover* the billiard table appears again, although converted from object of play to instrument of cure. It now serves as Sir Clifford's exercise table, and we see him lying on it as Mrs. Bolton puts him through his therapeutic paces. Clearly the table's true function as gendered battlefield remains unchanged, only now Clifford is losing instead of winning and being transformed from Connie's master to Mrs. Bolton's pawn.

The second interpolation, involving curtains and windows, originates in Christopher Miles's *Virgin* where it functioned as a border image between entrapment and freedom. Several scenes during Jaeckin's *Lady Chatterley's Lover* begin in emulation of this with Connie waking up as a servant opens her curtains to flood the room with sunshine. The implication here is some hope of release for the imprisoned heroine, exactly as it was for Yvette. The curtained windows of Wragby are shown closing as well as opening, and in fact Jaeckin employs this as a means of closing and opening the film itself. The final sequence in *Lady Chatterley's Lover* shows Clifford at Wragby, dressed in invalid's robe and seated near a bedroom window. As an unseen figure crosses the room, Clifford looks up, smiles, and says, "Connie." The camera then moves outside the estate, and we watch the film's conclusion from some distance away. A female figure appears at the window, closes it, and draws the curtains shut, in effect entombing Clifford at Wragby. She turns out not to be Connie, however, but Mrs. Bolton, who has now taken her place. Jaeckin's initial sequence provides an exact duplication of this enclosing gesture. Although we might expect the woman at the window to be Connie in the beginning and Mrs. Bolton at the end, this is not the case. It is Mrs. Bolton in both scenes, perhaps implying that the entire film is meant as flashback.[19]

Jaeckin's interpolations involve whole episodes as well as particular scenes, and these also deserve mention because of their intercinematic content. Just after the first view of the woman at the window, *Lady Chatterley's Lover* provides an overture or prologue summarizing events from the start of the Chatterley marriage to the point of Clifford's injury. We first see Connie, recently arrived at Wragby, among the emblematic objects and activities of gentrified life. She watches Clifford riding to hounds, then racing his companions home and winning. The scene shifts to a full-dress ball, perhaps in honor of the newlyweds. Connie and Clifford dance and converse with friends (some German) about worsening conditions in Europe. As they talk, the ball is interrupted by the announcement that war has been declared. The scene shifts again—to Clifford's departure in uniform, to the trenches, and then to the explosion that paralyzes him, at which point the prologue ends. Jaeckin's *Lady Chatterley's Lover* is the only film adaptation of this text to provide an overture, yet the material within it is hardly unique. To begin among such markers of class identity as the ball and the hunt turns out to be a convention of Lawrentian filming much older than Jaeckin's 1981 contribution. It will be encountered again, and discussed further, when I take up Marc Allegret's 1955 adaptation of *Lady Chatterley's Lover*.

Another convention that Jaeckin and Russell share is to present a contrasting view of lower-class life by showing Mellors working in hellish conditions after leaving Wragby. This occurs when Connie finds Mellors after Clifford has dismissed him. She hopes for a reunion, but the effect of her visit is to anger and humiliate Mellors because of the disparity in their circumstances. In Russell's version, this sequence takes on a deliberately infernal quality, with Sean Bean's Mellors bare-chested (in an ironic reminder of the washing scene), and shoveling coal into a furnace as Joely Richardson's Connie, dressed in red Victorian finery, watches from a doorway. In Jaeckin's version, the workplace scene is less melodramatically rendered, yet clearly intended for similar effect. Nicholas Clay's Mellors has taken a job as one of Clifford's colliers and is just leaving the pit as Sylvia Kristel's Connie discovers him and disturbs his black-and-white world of men with her colorful feminine presence.

To turn from plot and situation to character is to find further reasons why *The First Lady Chatterley* might prove tempting to filmmakers like Russell and Jaeckin. Its visual immediacy is matched by an economy of characterization not present in subsequent versions. This reaches its extreme within the novel's first half where few characters intrude to complicate the interaction of Lawrence's paired couples—Mrs. Bolton and Sir Clifford/Connie and Parkin. Jaeckin embraces this economy as the basis for his streamlined or minimalist adaptation in which the same troubled quartet remains foregrounded and largely alone from beginning to end.

Because of Jaeckin's distance from Lawrence's final version, it is not surprising that so many pivotal characters from *Lady Chatterley's Lover* disappear—Tommy Dukes and the cronies, Michaelis, the Venetian gondoliers Giovanni and Daniele. Erased along with them are several figures who play critical roles in all three versions of the text (Duncan Forbes most prominently) or else who appear only in the first two. Among those erased from *The First Lady Chatterley* are the "mad musician" Connie meets in France, Albert Adam, the colonial who replaces Parkin as gamekeeper at Wragby, and the Tewson family of Blagby Street. One survivor amid all this cinematic decimation is Connie's sister Hilda, although barely so, since Jaeckin hardly allows her to speak. A second survivor is Lady Eva, who figures prominently only in Lawrence's two earlier drafts. In transferring her from text to screen, Jaeckin again relies primarily upon *The First Lady Chatterley* where she visits Wragby alone to console the paralyzed man and his wife. Lady Eva is played with remarkable effect by Elizabeth Spriggs so that her woman-to-woman conversations with Connie stand out as the most convincing sequences in the film and as its closest approach to the spirit as well as the letter of Lawrence's text.

A similar minimalism attends Jaeckin's adaptation of the four major characters, only here the stripping down affects quality instead of quantity. Each member of Lawrence's quartet is reduced to one or two essential traits with the women suffering more simplification than the men. Jaeckin's Mrs. Bolton, for instance, is interpreted convincingly by Ann Mitchell, yet presented as Sir Clifford's coldly cerebral antagonist and little else. Although he teaches her chess as in the text, she is already adept at the game's living version and resolves to defeat her master and eventually immobilize him in permanent checkmate. While Mitchell's Mrs. Bolton displays some sympathy for Connie and her situation, ultimately her covert alliance with the wife is just another move against the husband. One measure of Mrs. Bolton's reduction to Machiavellian intelligence is the film's omission of nearly all her personal history—the very material by which Lawrence reveals her warmth, her sexuality in close accord with Connie's, and her complex humanity. In Jaeckin's film, although Mrs. Bolton alludes to being widowed several years earlier, she provides no details about the pit or the accident, nor about her marriage and her feelings for her husband. In fact, she never even mentions Ted Bolton by name.

As Mrs. Bolton is limited to cold intelligence on screen, Connie is reduced to purely physical and sensual proportions. Partly because of Sylvia Kristel's performance, Connie appears less a complete character than a visible, and visibly attractive, image of female sexuality, capable of little beyond inviting our gaze. Because Jaeckin's *Lady Chatterley's Lover,* like Russell's, focuses on Connie's story, an insoluble problem arises because she proves the least interesting of all four characters. Notably missing in Jaeckin's version is most of Connie's human sympathy, a quality which predates Mellors's influence, or anyone else's, and which Lawrence reveals in his description of what she sees, hears, and feels during her ride through Tevershall. Not only is this dropped from the film but, along with it, any attempt beyond the physical to project Connie's complex rebirth into womanhood by way of her relationship with Mellors. Sylvia Kristel reduces this rebirth to a simple sexual awakening, probably revealing Jaeckin's Emmanuelle, rather than Lawrence's Connie, as the real basis for her character.

Jaeckin's Sir Clifford, as played by Shane Briant, proves more compelling than his wife, partly because his personality reflects more edges than hers (albeit cutting ones), and partly because he is in flux, evolving throughout the film unlike any of its other major figures. In Jaeckin's most complex characterization, Sir Clifford manages to reconcile this evolution with an awareness of class limits, similar to his textual counterpart's built-in restraint, which prevents him from acting or speaking in ways inappropriate to his title and station. While his evolution is interesting to observe, it proves relatively straightforward, especially in relation to the original Sir Clifford's rebirth (in grotesque contrast to Connie's) from a human being into a monster or mechanical "child-man" at once technologically empowered and helpless, essentially dead. By contrast, the on-screen Sir Clifford begins as a positive figure, capable of arousing sympathy, but then turns repulsive as he learns to enjoy the combined pleasures of self-pity, nastiness, and spite. Jaeckin's strategy early in the film for inviting compassion for Clifford is one that Ken Russell will duplicate twelve years later. Both of their Sir Cliffords are victims of post-traumatic stress syndrome, suffering similar attacks of uncontrolled panic and dreams that return them to the battlefield. While this now-familiar disorder functions overtly in both post-Vietnam productions of *Lady Chatterley's Lover,* it remains largely implicit within the text and entirely absent from Marc Allegret's 1955 screen adaptation.

Just Jaeckin singles out Sir Clifford's ride in the woods as a major turning point, an ugly encounter at which the audience's sympathy for a helpless man turns into disgust for a spiteful one. In configuring the scene for this purpose, however, the film abandons its textual source and forfeits a great deal of visually promising material. In Lawrence's novel, Clifford's ride may increase our sympathy for him because his rage and abuse of Mellors result from the unavoidable reminder of just how helpless he is. "It's obvious I'm at everybody's mercy!" he declares near the end of this episode.[20] Clifford's frustration and paralyzed anger are transformed into coldly premeditated cruelty against Connie and Mellors. By this point in the film, Clifford has begun to suspect some relationship between them and uses the ride as a pretext to become stuck in the mud in order to punish and humiliate them both. When Mellors attempts to free the wheelchair, Sir Clifford deliberately applies his brake. When Connie and then Mellors get behind the chair to push, Clifford races his engine in order to spatter them with mud. This seems noteworthy as a symbolic gesture because it acts out Clifford's textual accusation against Connie late in *Lady Chatterley's Lover* that she is "one of those half-insane, perverted women who must run after depravity, the *nostalgie de la boue*" (296). Despite this, however, more of the original is lost in this scene than preserved—most notably Lawrence's success in presenting Clifford's ambivalent humanity, destructive and pathetic at the same time, and largely unaware (as opposed to his screen counterpart) of the injury he's doing to his gamekeeper, his wife, and—most filmable of all—the flowers beneath his feet. Unfortunately, no trace of this unconscious battle between Clifford, armed with his machinery, and nature survives in the film.

Like Jaeckin's aristocrat, his gamekeeper also seems restricted to speech and action associated with a particular social class, this again partly a function of Nicholas Clay's performance. One important outcome of such restriction is that Jaeckin's gamekeeper appears as Oliver Mellors in name only, having little in common with his multilayered counterpart in the final text. The evolution of Lawrence's character from the first Parkin to the second and then to Mellors is a compelling subject in its own right. In relation to a film study of *Lady Chatterley's Lover,* it proves worthwhile as a means of separating Lawrence from his cinematic interpreters or of distinguishing between one writer's deepening ambivalence over questions of class and three filmmakers' shared need for direct and simpler visions. As Parkin evolves toward Mellors across three texts, his class identity first begins to blur, then to break down altogether. Between *The First Lady Chatterley* and *John Thomas and Lady Jane,* for example, Parkin loses much of his working-class militancy when Lawrence replaces him with Bill Tewson as the novel's Marxist spokesman. In the final version, with Mellors replacing Parkin, communist ideology gives way to utopian vision, and the original working-class man reemerges nearly classless—at home anywhere and nowhere, ever adaptable yet never comfortable, and, as suggested earlier, uniquely Lawrentian.

To observe that the hero is evolving toward his creator's social situation seems obvious. To observe as well that in erasing Parkin for Mellors Lawrence may be revealing his own class discomfort, even some measure of class betrayal, raises a more problematic issue and one that merits separate consideration beyond the subject of film. For present purposes, two examples of the hero's "declassing," as Mellors replaces Parkin in the text, prove informative in relation to Jaeckin's film and eventually all three Lady Chatterley films. First, where both Parkins serve as common soldiers during the war, Mellors eventually becomes a commissioned officer. In making this shift, Lawrence does far more than grant his hero a promotion. He allows him to leave the enlisted ranks and assume Clifford's own position as "officer and gentleman," a difficult crossing for a Tommy within the British military establishment of 1918, as for any soldier even today.

The second border that Mellors crosses and recrosses at will is linguistic—the boundary between Midlands dialect and standard English made familiar by Lawrence and by *Lady Chatterley's Lover* more than any other of his works. This discursive mobility sets up another parallel between Mellors and his lord because in at least one version of the text Sir Clifford occasionally assumes the dialect to ridicule and humiliate his gamekeeper.[21] Mellors, as distinct from Parkin, can be just as skillfully malicious with language when he wants to be, yet he goes beyond his employer in using his skill for creative and vital ends. On his tongue the dialect becomes the discourse of passion, whether ecstasy or rage, and likewise the discourse of the woods as opposed to the village or estate. When he wishes, however, Mellors can drop the dialect and return to standard English—for clarity, for convenience in daily matters, or for expressing cold hostility, as distinct from passionate rage, as when he asks Hilda "in the normal English," "Would anything that was said between you and me be quite natural, unless you said you wished me to hell before your sister ever saw me again: and unless I said something almost as unpleasant back again?" (244). The thrust of this most rhetorical of questions calls for no dialect, but for these chilling tones instead, and Mellors knows it.

On film, Jaeckin's Mellors and Russell's make few such departures from the norms, either of rank or language, and so appear more true to their class than their textual namesake. Sean Bean's Mellors, in Russell's production, has returned from the war to resume his job as gamekeeper, implying that his status in the army had been equally modest. Nicholas Clay's Mellors, in Jaeckin's film, gives no suggestion that he ever served in the war at all. The cinematic situation becomes slightly more complicated and more faithful to the original over the question of language, but only within the Jaeckin film. While neither Mellors seems capable of speaking beyond the dialect, Clay's character surprises us, but only once. In the aftermath of one of Jaeckin's love scenes, Clay's Mellors recites poetry to Kristel's Connie which he describes to her as something he has read. Clay's recitation, unlike all his other spoken lines, is carefully enunciated in standard English, revealing that the 1981 Lawrence filmmakers were aware of language as an issue within *Lady Chatterley's Lover* and were willing to represent it on screen. No further development takes place after Clay's single linguistic departure, and he returns to the dialect (or else to silence) for the remainder of the film.

All of this seems to verify the previous suggestion that both Russell and Jaeckin have re-created Oliver Parkin and simply renamed him Oliver Mellors. Both film characters prove to be simplifications even of the earlier figure, however, or approximations of him as viewed from the outside. Neither Bean's nor Clay's portrayal, for example, preserves Parkin's sense of himself above all else as a working-class man, an identity which he stubbornly protects and ultimately won't give up even for Connie. Instead of such real entanglements between class and individual identity, both films provide simple images—projections of masculine, working-class behavior and appearance that match conventional expectations and thus inadvertently present Mellors to us as Sir Clifford himself might see him. Both Bean and Clay play Mellors as especially crude, with Russell's actor exaggerating his behavior toward aggressiveness and threat, and Jaeckin's actor doing the same thing by way of appearance. This accounts for Clay's unshaven "ruggedness" during most of the film, a quality which several reviewers praised yet which conflicts with both Mellors and Parkin's appearance in the text.

On screen all four of Lawrence's major characters emerge as reduced versions of themselves regardless of which text the filmmakers may have used. A similar simplifying process affects the relationships these characters establish as they pair off into couples, with Jaeckin's film especially emphasizing the physical basis of both alliances in place of their less visible complications. For Connie and Mellors, the result is a round of sexual encounters immediately familiar to viewers of the earlier Lawrence films, as well as *Emmanuelle* (a parallel worth returning to presently). For the invalid and his nurse, the result is Sir Clifford's wholly physical rebirth at Mrs. Bolton's hands in place of the spiritual transformation she also inspires in the text. To Jaeckin's credit, however, he appreciates the symmetry between Lawrence's two couples and attempts to preserve it on film. Almost every love scene between Connie and Mellors ends with a cut to Sir Clifford and Mrs. Bolton also in bed together and bodily involved as intensely as the lovers are. While Jaeckin's passionate scenes tend to direct our gaze below the waist, his therapeutic encounters focus on the upper body and, in keeping with Lawrence, particularly on Sir Clifford's powerful shoulders and back as Mrs. Bolton labors to strengthen them.[22]

This juxtaposition of the two couples may be Jaeckin's only success in creating human relationships that remain recognizably "Laurentian," to use Neil Taylor's term. Of greatest importance here is what becomes of Connie and Mellors as Jaeckin re-creates them, not as separate individuals now but as Lawrence's crucial couple, a new living entity with a dynamic of its own. Several changes take place, in fact, one of which has already been mentioned as a function of the adaptation process itself. To project Connie and Mellors on screen as lovers, regardless of who directs or plays their parts, is to invite erotic scrutiny from a distance and by the collective gaze of an audience. As has been suggested, this approximates Lawrence's own conception of pornography and perhaps explains, in purely Lawrentian terms, why several reviewers have described the film as coldly dispassionate despite being sexually explicit.

Also in discord with Lawrence (and less the outcome of process) is Jaeckin's reversal of the gendered relationship between viewer and viewed in the text. In Lawrence, the male body remains on display most often, with male and female readers alike invited to join Connie in seeing and admiring it through feminine eyes. In Jaeckin's film, Connie's body becomes the object of display instead, made available to us at every opportunity through Mellors's aroused masculine stare. Here *Women in Love* may emerge as the single most faithful film to Lawrence's own gender-inverted gaze. Ursula is never shown nude, and Gudrun just once, but only above the waist. As in the text, the scenes of physical display are reserved for the two men: Birkin walking alone in the forest or Birkin and Gerald struggling together by the firelight. Jaeckin's one departure from his normally male viewing position is the washing scene in which Connie assumes the role of *voyeuse* and in which Mellors appears frontally nude, something which does not take place in the text or in the other two Lady Chatterley films. Despite its limited fidelity to the original, anything of potential value within Jaeckin's bathing scene becomes lost through exaggeration to the point of unintended comic relief. Connie's arousal while watching Mellors bathe reaches its climax as he draws a bucket of water by working the handle of a large, squeaking pump.[23]

Perhaps this film's most serious disharmony with Lawrence results less from such lapses, or from the adaptation process itself, than from Lawrence's own conception of the lovers. One of the film's initial reviewers stated the problem accurately when he wrote, "There are key episodes [in the original text] that probably *can't* be filmed effectively, not so much because they depict the carnal nature of a love affair but because they describe surging, mysterious, transcendent levels of feeling evoked by an overpowering physical passion that seem to defy pictorial representation. They're elusive enough when Lawrence presumes to capture them in words."[24] Although Lawrence describes "the whole act" openly and often in *Lady Chatterley's Lover,* he always does so beneath and beyond biology or along a spectrum that begins with bodies but proceeds, by involution, to sensations, feelings, ultimately mysteries. The passage describing Connie's first orgasm in unison with Mellors's affords a compelling illustration of Lawrentian sex, obscure even to his own vision let alone to any potential filmmaker's:

> And then began again the unspeakable motion that was not really motion, but pure deepening whirlpools of sensation, swirling deeper and deeper through all her tissue and consciousness, till she was one perfect concentric fluid of feeling. And she lay there crying in unconscious, inarticulate cries, the voice out of the uttermost night, the life-exclamation. And the man heard it beneath him with a kind of awe, as his life sprang out into her. And as it subsided he subsided too, and lay utterly still, unknowing, while her grip on him slowly relaxed, and she lay inert. (133–34)

Such evocations of "the whole act" in its fundamental mystery remain unfilmable. No representation of sex viewed from the outside can ever approximate it, no matter how rugged or beautiful the bodies may be. If Jaeckin's cinematic efforts most disappoint us here, perhaps the film that comes closest to capturing Lawrentian sexuality is Christopher Miles's *The Virgin and the Gypsy.* While it puts rugged and beautiful bodies on display as well, it also makes the imaginative effort to get beyond their biology. Miles's camera never allows us to be sure whether it is recording sexual consummation, inward imagining, or both at their moment of convergence.

When Jaeckin attempts something similar in *Lady Chatterley's Lover,* he also reveals a great deal about his own erotic vision—not only its departure from Lawrence's but also its real and ultimately cinematic source. Sexual fantasy occurs only once in Jaeckin's film, as Connie studies her nude body in a mirror after seeing Mellors bathe. Connie arouses herself by recalling the washing scene, only now as she reimagines it she begins to edit and revise, much like Miles's Yvette. Where the "real" scene showed Mellors alone, Connie now joins him in fantasy, so that we see her hands washing him as well as his. If Christopher Miles introduced this technique in 1970 as a visual approximation of Lawrentian writing, Jaeckin revives it a decade later in emulation not of Lawrence but of Miles. The real basis for the lovers' relationship in *Lady Chatterley's Lover*—and their sexual relationship most of all—is not Lawrence but Lawrence on film. This influence extends beyond Miles's *Virgin* to include all three films of that period along with some older sources.

The same bathing scene owes some of its inspiration to *Women in Love* and specifically to Alan Bates's walk in the woods, as a comparison of camera angles and nude male bodies filmed in profile should demonstrate. Similarly, as Ken Russell returns to *Women in Love* for the initial love scene in his *Lady Chatterley,* so too does Jaeckin, yet with less legitimate right to do so. As in Russell's tele-vised version, the first sexual meeting between Connie and Mellors in Jaeckin's film becomes a replay of the *Liebestod* from *Women in Love,* the initial love struggle between Ursula and Birkin paralleling the death struggle of the drowned newly-weds. Resembling Alan Bates and Jennie Linden, Nicholas Clay and Sylvia Kristel appear fully clothed and act out their encounter less as passionate lovers than as sexual combatants. Troubled music plays in the background as it did for Bates and Linden. The only noticeable difference between the two scenes is that Rus-sell's takes place outdoors while Jaeckin's is set inside the gamekeeper's hut. Even here, however, Jaeckin manages a reference to Russell by way of a lighted fire-place in the background reminiscent of the gladiatorial setting in *Women in Love.*

Several reminders of Mark Rydell's *The Fox* also show up in Jaeckin's produc-tion, some subtle, others immediately apparent. One involves a fantasy in which Connie visualizes herself living with Mellors in "an inexpensive little house" that she has just seen in a magazine. In Connie's fantasy, the lovers' cottage resembles the crude farmhouse in Rydell's film. Inside we see Sylvia Kristel's Connie at the piano dressed in a red gown like the one March put on to reaffirm her feminin-ity. As Connie plays, Nicholas Clay's Mellors guts the carcass of a dead animal, lifting out the creature's bloody innards with his bare hands. His actions as well as the entire fantasy form a gratuitous reminder of Paul and March in *The Fox* and as a result seem unrelated to the rest of Jaeckin's film. A more plausible bor-rowing from Rydell involves Connie's autoerotic experience—not female mas-turbation as it casually occurs in Jaeckin's *Emmanuelle* but a major scene begin-ning with a nude woman studying her sexually deprived body in the mirror as Sylvia Kristel replicates Anne Heywood's pose exactly.

This tally of debits and credits could be extended, but the principle behind it is probably clear by now. Jaeckin films Lawrence, or attempts to, through a fil-ter passed down by the Lawrentian filmmakers who preceded him: Rydell, Russell, and most of all Miles. Their influence seems strongest in Jaeckin's vision of the lovers as an erotic couple and in his choices for representing their sexuality on screen. A similar intercinematic influence extends to Jaeckin's resolution of their relationship and to his ending, which owe far more to Lawrence on film than to Lawrence regardless of which version we consult. Here, however, the source of Jaeckin's inspiration predates the late 1960s trilogy of Lawrence films by more than a decade. Marc Allegret's *L'Amant de Lady Chatterley* (1955), only the sec-ond Lawrence film ever released, began the tradition of happy endings for the lady and her gamekeeper, one that would endure until 1993 when Ken Russell came belatedly to film *Lady Chatterley* for the third time.

The dictates of this tradition are clear. Any trace of Lawrence's fondness for ambivalent endings should be erased, along with all of his more specific uncertainties about what the future holds for Connie and Mellors. In Lawrence's final version this uncertainty is expressed through their tentative situation at the end—living apart, awaiting Mellors's divorce, and communicating through the disembodied process of letter writing: "But a great deal of us is together, and we can but abide by it, and steer our courses to meet soon. John Thomas says good-night to lady Jane, a little droopingly, but with a hopeful heart" (302). At the close of the middle version, the lovers are reunited in Byron country, at least momentarily, yet face an equally uncertain future: "You'll come to me if I can't bear it?" "Yes," he said.[25] And in *The First Lady Chatterley*, which leaves us least certain of all, Lawrence's narrator simply shrugs his shoulders in print by declaring, "Ah well! The future was still to hand!" (232).

Within the cinematic tradition, however, the lovers are always reunited at the end, usually through Connie's efforts. After being apart from Mellors for a time, she resolves to leave Sir Clifford and, in all three films, searches out her lover to make their relationship permanent. The three films all close on a version of the same scene, which depicts Connie and Mellors departing together toward some unknown yet happy future. It is this ending, first created by Marc Allegret in 1955, which Ken Russell distorts to absurd proportions in 1993 as John Thomas, sailing for Canada, is paged by Lady Jane. In Jaeckin's 1981 version, Connie finds Mellors at the end of his workday in Sir Clifford's pits, then convinces him to run off with her rather than pursue his own plans for Canada. Jaeckin's closing scene seems forced and artificial, perhaps to the point of expressing doubt despite itself by insisting too strongly on the happy ever after. Nicholas Clay's Mellors declares that he won't be a kept man, then accepts Connie's offer of support in the next breath. In turn, Sylvia Kristel's Connie reveals her pregnancy to Mellors, then describes their child's future in terms so hopeful as to seem impossible. "Our child," she tells her lover, will unify "the best of you and the best of me," and thus belong to no social class at all.

## Marc Allegret's *L'Amant de Lady Chatterley* (1955)

Predating Just Jaeckin's *Lady Chatterley's Lover* by more than a quarter century, Marc Allegret's *L'Amant de Lady Chatterley* belongs to the initial black-and-white period of Lawrence filming and is only the second Lawrence production to be released, following Anthony Pelissier's *Rocking Horse Winner* by nearly six years.[26] Compared with Russell's and Jaeckin's Lady Chatterleys, this early film preserves more of Lawrence's final version of the novel, at least on the level of circumstances and events. Allegret's Mellors is the only one of the three to have a developed history, including a military promotion. *L'Amant* has gone beyond language and genre to translate *Lady Chatterley's Lover* into French in cultural and historical terms as well. A revealing clue to this can be found in the film's setting, normally a straightforward matter which in this instance becomes an apt emblem for the entire process of cultural transformation taking place. Despite French being spoken, *L'Amant* is meant to take place in England as snatches of film dialogue like "gentleman" or "M'Lady" confirm. Experientially, however, an audience is likely to remain uncertain about this because everything not only sounds French but looks French and feels profoundly French to the cultural sensibilities of even the most innocent spectator. Allegret's pubs serve *vin rouge* instead of beer, and Wragby has become a chateau. Even the automobiles seem French judging from their license tags and the location of their steering wheels.

Allegret's *L'Amant* is perhaps most noteworthy because of its cultural reconception of the text. As its geographical ambiguities reveal, the film has transported as well as translated Lawrence, ultimately in order to reflect its own spirit of place and history during the difficult years following World War II. Beyond chateaux, automobiles, and *vin rouge*, this cross-channel transformation reveals itself in the film's debt to postwar French thought, particularly to midcentury feminism, and in its parallel debt to French cinema. Here the work of Marc Allegret's compatriot Jean Renoir proves to be even more influential than that of playwrights Bonheur and de Rothschild. Renoir's *Rules of the Game* seems omnipresent within *L'Amant,* not simply quoted by Allegret so much as always faintly but clearly superimposed upon the screen. Along with these artistic and philosophical influences, traces of French popular culture reveal themselves within this film as well, sometimes in contradictory and even disruptive ways. Side-by-side with Allegret's feminist projections of the "new woman" in Constance Chatterley, for example, there survives an approved screen image of manhood in Mellors, if not specifically French certainly Latin in general and often willfully, even violently, insistent upon its own imperatives and demands. Finally, the film concludes with a sudden shift in its original social alignments and with an unmistakable movement in the direction of middle-class life. While such an ending isn't necessarily French, it certainly leaves us somewhere far from Lawrence's own closing values and ideas, perhaps not so much in another country as at another time and in the aftermath of two other wars he never lived to see.

*L'Amant de Lady Chatterley* emerges as the product of a postwar environment at least twice over. By 1955, the year of its release, occupation, resistance, and liberation were still recent experiences in France. Even more vivid, the previous year had brought a different sort of military and political watershed for France, one with tragic overtones and future implications not only for that country but for Southeast Asia and the United States as well. In May 1954, the garrison at Dienbienphu fell to the Viet Minh after two months of siege, with Joseph Laniel's government in Paris following it into defeat just a month later. In October 1954, under the new prime minister Pierre Mendes-France, French forces left Hanoi and the rest of Indochina for good.

It is likely that when Allegret's film opened in France the following year, audiences responded to its postwar story in terms of their own, an identification made easier by the film's updating of clothing and automobiles to match the 1940s and 1950s in place of Lawrence's 1920s. Reinforcing this, both Clifford and Mellors are identified as war veterans almost at once. This French Mellors tells Connie early on that he has learned a great deal from the war, then manages to resemble a soldier for the remainder of the film, wearing military-styled boots, cap, and uniform and carrying a rifle across his shoulder as he patrols Sir Clifford's estate.[27] Mellors wears this uniform until almost the film's last scene, then discards it suddenly in a gesture of self-transformation complex enough to invite further discussion below.

*L'Amant* is a film touched by war in reality as well as in fiction. Among its three leading actors, two carried with them the baggage of recent history, one as a hero, the other as an accused collaborator. Leo Genn, playing Sir Clifford, was the hero and also the film's only real Englishman. A practicing barrister before World War II, Genn served with the Royal Artillery, reaching the rank of lieutenant colonel by 1943 and receiving the French *Croix de Guerre* in 1945, a decoration for extreme valor in battle. After the war Genn became part of the British contingent investigating German atrocities at the Bergen-Belsen concentration camp and, because of his legal background, served as an assistant prosecutor in the subsequent war crimes trials. After military service and a change of careers, Genn went on to appear in dozens of stage and screen productions, including Lillian Hellman's *Another Part of the Forest* on Broadway (1946) and two successful American films, *The Snake Pit* (1948) and *Quo Vadis* (1951).

Danielle Darrieux, playing opposite Genn as Connie, also had dozens of films to her credit and was an established star who had moved from youthful, romantic roles in the early 1930s to portrayals of strong, highly sophisticated women, qualities Darrieux would carry over into her portrayal of Lady Chatterley. In strange juxtaposition to Genn's heroic status, Darrieux had been charged with entertaining German troops during the occupation and was even briefly marked for execution by the Resistance. This sentence was eventually revoked, however, and Darrieux was exonerated after the war. She resumed her film career in 1946.

Erno Crisa completed Allegret's international trio. Less established than either Genn or Darrieux, Crisa was not the director's first choice for Mellors. Allegret had planned the role for Marlon Brando, but soon discovered that he could not meet the American actor's financial demands.[28] By 1955, Brando had already achieved major screen triumphs as Stanley Kowalski in *A Streetcar Named*

*Desire,* then as Terry Malloy in *On the Waterfront,* a role which won him his first Academy Award and put him forever beyond the reach of directors of modest means like Allegret. It is interesting nevertheless to consider Brando's possible impact on this film and, by extension, on the endeavor to film Lawrence in general. Besides major star status, Brando would have added an American presence to Allegret's multinational but exclusively European production. More important, he would have lent his early energy, intensity, and existential charisma to *L'Amant,* a film with existential leanings of its own which surely would have benefited from his participation in ways now impossible to calculate. On the other hand, one can only wonder about Brando's potential linguistic effect on a film already burdened by a multilingual cast, a French script of a British book, and English subtitles translating Lawrence from French back into his native language.

This matter of linguistic multiplicity, unique to Allegret's film, is sufficiently important to deserve additional discussion, especially since language remains critically important in Lawrence's text. No two members of Allegret's central trio of actors were native speakers of the same language, and no one was dubbed as Sylvia Kristel had been in Just Jaeckin's production. All three actors deliver their lines in French with varying degrees of comfort and skill. Darrieux does so, of course, as a born Frenchwoman combining her natural eloquence with years of dramatic training and experience. Crisa, originally from Sicily, also seems fluent in French, precise yet natural and with no trace of a foreign accent. The only anomaly is his puzzling use of the masculine *mon cherie* at least twice when addressing Connie, rather than the feminine *ma cherie.* In Leo Genn's case, the problem of language is more general than this—not the occasional lapse so much as the tendency to mismanage the entire language. Genn speaks grammatically correct French, but with a heavy British accent nearly to the point of parody, and in a stilted, textbookish syntax that one early reviewer accurately described as "a lunatic 'plume de ma tante' French."[29] Most of the film's initial reviewers noticed this and condemned Genn as linguistically inept and thus as miscast in a French film. Another possibility that merits discussion is that Genn's Anglicized French is deliberate and part of a broader strategy for developing his character.

Beyond the cast, one additional source of linguistic complication in *L'Amant* is Mai Harris's English subtitles. Like Crisa's grammar, Harris's subtitles sometimes prove incorrect as when for no clear reason she censors an innocent line like "the coupling [*le couplement*] of birds" to become "the flight of birds" in English. Harris's subtitles also cause confusion when they suddenly disappear, leaving several lines of dialogue untranslated.

The man primarily responsible for this multilingual and multinational production was Marc Allegret, the film's director as well as its co-screenwriter in collaboration with Joseph Kessell. Like his leading lady, Allegret was well known and well established in film by 1955; in fact, his greatest successes were already behind him, his career having reached its peak in the 1930s. This may account for the perception among several reviewers that *L'Amant* seemed visibly dated by midcentury despite its outward trappings of postwar life.[30] Also relevant to his single effort at filming Lawrence, Allegret's cinematic career had literary and philosophic influences acting upon it from the outset. Allegret was André Gide's nephew, and his first production, *Voyage au Congo* (1927), had been a documentary account of his trip to Africa with his famous uncle. Marc's younger brother Yves also enjoyed a successful career in film that developed rapidly in the 1940s just as the older Allegret's career began to decline. Yves's initial work in cinema was as assistant to several prominent figures including Jean Renoir. The younger Allegret's association with Renoir adds further evidence, if not clear confirmation, of an intercinematic link between Renoir's *La Règle du Jeu* and the elder Allegret's *L'Amant de Lady Chatterley.*

Following its release, Allegret's Lady Chatterley became the focus of a well-known censorship case in the United States, so that early critical attention in that country was diverted from the film itself to its legal and moral considerations. Censorship continued to vex the process of filming Lawrence from its inception with *The Rocking Horse Winner* in 1949 until the end of the 1960s at least. The controversy over Allegret's *L'Amant* took place in New York State, where the film was denied a license for exhibition by State Education Department censors for presenting adultery "as a desirable, acceptable, and proper pattern of behavior."[31] This ban took place in late 1956 when the film was first released in the United States. It was upheld by the State Board of Regents, which concurred with the initial censors that *L'Amant* "glorifies adultery and presents the same as desirable, as acceptable and proper."[32] This decision was later reversed by the Appellate Division of the New York State Supreme Court but then upheld again almost immediately by the New York Court of Appeals. The case was not finally settled until 29 June 1959, when the Supreme Court, in *Kingsley International Pictures v. Board of Regents,* decided in favor of the film and against the state. While several justices based their opinions on differing legal issues, the ruling was unanimous. In writing it for the court, Justice Potter Stewart stated that the New York ban attempted to "prevent the exhibition of a motion picture because that picture advocates an idea—that adultery under certain circumstances may be proper behavior." He continued that any such prohibition violates "the First Amendment's basic guarantee . . . of freedom to advocate ideas. The State, quite simply, has thus struck at the very heart of constitutionally protected liberty. [The First Amendment] . . . protects advocacy of the opinion that adultery may sometimes be proper, no less than advocacy of socialism or the single tax."[33] In an ironic coincidence, Justice Stewart's opinion on the film predated Frederick van Pelt

Bryan's landmark opinion on the book (in *Grove Press v. Christenberry*) by just three weeks.[34]

As a result of the long court case, New York–based reviewers were unable to see and judge Allegret's 1955 film until late 1959. When they finally got their chance, most expressed disappointment at *L'Amant* and, because of its unexpected sexual timidity, wondered what all the fuss had been about. After summarizing the censorship controversy in his *New York Times* review, Bosley Crowther concluded that the film had merely turned Lawrence's powerful story into something "sterile and bland."[35] Stanley Kauffmann seconded this opinion in a *New Republic* article in more typically strident tones than Crowther's, dismissing Allegret's adaptation as "just another plodding French sex drama."[36] Arthur Knight concluded his discussion of Allegret's film for *Saturday Review* by making a direct and damning contrast between its importance as legal precedent and its insignificance as film: "The real importance of this *Lady Chatterley,* I'm afraid, lies in the law books, not in the film itself. The triumph is for freedom, not for art."[37]

In part because they were responding to *L'Amant* some years after its release, the New York critics saw several qualities in the film as anachronistic. Its datedness seemed to become even more evident to reviewers through Allegret's efforts to modernize externals such as clothing and automobiles. Leo Genn's distracting British accent posed another problem and again seemed to contradict the French quality of virtually everything else in the film. For reasons not entirely clear, however, Erno Crisa's performance as Mellors came under heavier critical attack than Genn's as Sir Clifford, with the critics tending to focus less on Crisa's acting than on his appearance and demeanor, which they found inappropriate to Mellors and unattractive in its own right. Two reviewers described Crisa as "sullen," and a third found him "sluggish."[38] Several critics even resorted to grotesque metaphors to describe Crisa's looks, much as later reviewers would for Oliver Reed as Gerald in *Women in Love.* One writer identified as J. M. described Crisa as "a blonde giant" masquerading as Mellors, while another went farther in the direction of caricature by likening him to "Johnny Weissmuller . . . as Tarzan . . . trying to make time with Lady Gray."[39]

Beyond such specific complaints, perhaps the cinematic scene itself in 1959 contributed to the American reviewers' disappointment. Foreign films were considered essentially different from American films—generally superior and intended for limited rather than widespread distribution. The success of directors like Ingmar Bergman and Federico Fellini led urbane American audiences and critics to expect European films to be artistically rather than commercially driven, thus emphasizing technique, tone, and intellectual content over action or plot. Since *L'Amant* failed, for the most part, to meet these standards, the New York reviewers may have been harsher in their judgments than they would have been over an American or even a British production.

The film's French and British reviewers, writing three or four years before the New Yorkers, reached more positive judgments, yet neither group seemed to have much to say about *L'Amant* beyond the minimum protocols of fact, summary, and opinion. One exception was Paul V. Beckley, whose 1959 review for the *New York Herald Tribune* identified some of the more provocative issues in Allegret's film if not pursuing them to conclusion. Beckley was aware, for instance, that Genn's Anglicized French may have been more than a casting mistake and instead part of a larger cultural issue involving translations beyond language alone. Beckley wrote, "Sir Clifford . . . is played by [Leo] Genn speaking French with an English accent thick enough to cut with a knife. This no doubt would add a note of authenticity for the French ear, since the Gallic viewer would regard it as a point of characterization as we might the French accent in English of [Maurice] Chevalier, but it sounded awkward to me, since all the impeccably Parisian accents around Genn's thick French are supposed to come from English throats as well as his." Beckley also pointed out the film's manipulation of gender along with nationality, noting that its consistent point of view remains feminine despite a largely male cast and crew and that Erno Crisa's Mellors is reduced and marginalized as a result, unlike Lawrence's original. "The focus is, of course, on Miss Darrieux, not the gamekeeper. It may be his ideas or ideals, if you will, that work upon her and bring about the ultimate crisis of her life, but it is the turn and twist of her conscience and passion that occupies the attention throughout."[40] Beckley's description of Mellors as Connie's catalyst unknowingly anticipates the two later Lady Chatterley productions.

After the reviews of the mid and late 1950s, critical discussion of *L'Amant de Lady Chatterley* fell away to almost nothing. This is especially surprising because several surveys of Lawrence on film appeared in the 1970s and 1980s, among them studies by Harry T. Moore, S. E. Gontarski, Gene D. Phillips, and Neil Sinyard. These writers tended to give Allegret's film second billing by confining its treatment to an isolated paragraph or in one instance (Sinyard's *Filming Literature*) a single sentence. Also puzzling, normally careful film scholars tended to be factually inaccurate about *L'Amant*, as when Gene Phillips referred to it as "the first film based on Lawrence's books" and as having been "filmed in France in the late 1950s."[41] While Phillips needs to acknowledge *The Rocking Horse Winner* as the initial Lawrence film, his blurring of dates can be explained by the gap between the film's completion in 1955 and its delayed opening in New York four years later.

To date, only two sustained treatments of *L'Amant* have appeared in print to counter what amounts to critical inattention or indifference. These essays are James F. Scott's "The Emasculation of *Lady Chatterley's Lover*," written for the premier issue of *Literature/Film Quarterly* (1973) devoted to Lawrence on film, and Lindley Hanlon's "Sensuality and Simplification," written for Michael Klein and Gillian Parker's 1981 anthology, *The English Novel and the Movies.* The Scott and Hanlon studies are interesting to compare because they reach opposite conclusions and because their judgments are often based on contradictory reactions to the same specific elements in the film. An informative instance of this is their response to Connie and Mellors's first love scene. This scene exemplifies what I have referred to earlier as averting the camera's eye in modesty, fear of the censors, or embarrassment. In *L'Amant,* Connie visits the gamekeeper's hut to see the newborn chicks hatch out at the same time Sir Clifford's workmen are clearing his forests to make way for new mines. Connie begins to cry as in the text, and Mellors escorts her into his hut. As he unbuttons her clothing, Allegret's focus shifts outdoors to the activities of Clifford's workmen. Mellors and Connie begin their sexual relationship invisible to the audience, which sees a huge tree falling to the ground instead. For James F. Scott, such imagistic substitution amounts to the worst sort of visual cliché and typifies Marc Allegret's limitations as a Lawrence filmmaker. "Connie's marital vows are thus toppled like the timber of the Chatterley estate," Scott writes.

> The analogy . . . is a very poor one. Too many cinematic heroines have lost their virtue while horses rear on their back legs or cannons boom on nearby hillsides. And there is the further point that in the case of Mellors and Connie the sexual encounter is not supposed to be considered a transgression. Rather than rupturing a living relationship (as in cutting the tree), their sexual consummation restores Connie's affective emotional life.[42]

It is tempting to second Scott here by adding that to look away, regardless of what at, seems to contradict Lawrence visually just as much as to stare directly at coupling bodies contradicts him. Also, Allegret's choice of a falling tree as sexual trope seems inappropriate not only because it implies emasculation and a blow against nature but also because Lawrence himself has already used the image for altogether different purposes in "The Fox." Despite such reservations, Lindley Hanlon sees Allegret's tree-felling image as an apt representation of Lawrentian sexuality partly because of its natural associations and partly because of its indirectness:

> The dramatic scale of the forest, its stillness and extraordinary beauty, and its use as the location of the . . . love affair set it off and encour-

age us to think of it as more than a set location which could be substituted for any other setting. The chopping down of trees becomes Allegret's symbol for the sexual act itself. Phallus-shaped trees falling to the ground as they are cut intercut between shots of the gamekeeper unbuttoning Lady Chatterley's blouse and shots of them lying together with naked shoulders visible above the blanket. In the tree-cutting image Allegret's implication is sexual fulfillment and release rather than castration which such a description might imply.[43]

Based on such conflicting perceptions, Scott and Hanlon carry their discussions to predictably opposite conclusions. For Scott, Allegret's film is overwhelmed by visual clichés like the phallic trees and by an accompanying artificiality or staginess typical of the entire production. Scott concludes by suggesting that "Lawrence's rough, agitated prose has been completely tranquilized, supplanted by the almost cloying tidiness of perfectly accented lighting and softly cushioned dolly shots. In a purely *pro forma* manner, the film does deal with adultery, but so woodenly as to relieve the theme of all its excitement or challenge."[44] Hanlon comes to praise exactly what Scott has damned, so that his conclusion redefines potential contrivance as delicacy of style and suggests that Allegret's erotic restraint becomes the appropriate cinematic equivalent of Lawrentian tenderness in sex. Hanlon writes, "Allegret's Lady Chatterley is far from . . . oozing sentimentality. The delicacy of his style and the dignity of his characters convey at least in part Lawrence's requirement that tenderness accompany carnal knowledge."[45]

Despite such divergent opinions, Scott and Hanlon remain the only writers to judge *L'Amant* as at least worthy of critical attention. While they disagree over Allegret's relationship to Lawrence, they reach common ground on the issue of cinematic rather than textual sources. Both Scott and Hanlon notice the superimposition of Jean Renoir's *La Règle du Jeu* upon *L'Amant*, again calling attention to an intervening presence or filter between text and screen as constant in the filming of *Lady Chatterley's Lover*. Here, too, Scott and Hanlon see matters differently, with Hanlon describing Allegret's relationship to Renoir in the traditional vocabulary of allusion. He refers to one of L'Amant's early sequences as the "elegant hunt episode which visually 'quotes' and in the dialogue alludes to Renoir's *Rules of the Game* (1939)."[46] Scott's description is more extreme and probably closer to the truth as a result. For him Allegret's whole effort seems "more like a remake of Renoir's *La Règle du Jeu* than an adaptation of Lawrence's novel."[47]

It's interesting to contemplate Allegret's challenge if he wished to adapt Renoir along with Lawrence and somehow reconcile their efforts. *Lady Chatterley's Lover* and *La Règle du Jeu* seem virtually incompatible so as to predict sure failure in any attempt to combine them on screen. At the same time, however, it is possible to appreciate Allegret's urge to combine Lawrence and Renoir since their works, like so many distinct chemical compounds, derive from the same elements uniquely combined. Some of these elements are a gamekeeper, a titled gentleman, his wife, and her lover. It is even conceivable that Allegret chose to film Lawrence in the first place because he saw these same elements in *Lady Chatterley's Lover,* yet with Lawrentian seriousness of intent replacing Renoir's bitter laughter.

An extreme yet intriguing suggestion about *L'Amant* is that rather than filming Lawrence through Renoir's filter, Allegret may be refilming Renoir through Lawrence's filter. The unique combination of familiar elements in *Lady Chatterley's Lover* may have invited a re-vision of *La Règle du Jeu* appropriate to Allegret's postwar world in place of Renoir's end-of-an-era in 1939. One example of such re-vision involves the issue of "rules" so critical to Renoir's ironic look at the aristocracy and, beyond it, at prewar French society on every level. Late in *La Règle du Jeu,* Robert de la Chesnaye (the titled gentleman) condenses this issue into one sentence when he says to his wife's lover, "I'm so glad she's picked someone of her own class." The game goes on with the rules unbroken so long as no class boundaries are crossed, and so long as no act, however indiscreet, disrupts the visible illusion of polite relationships. Allegret revises all of this with Lawrence's pen, since class boundaries *are* crossed in *Lady Chatterley's Lover* and since Connie and Mellors become individual human beings, beyond the limits of their station, precisely by breaking the "rules"—or troubling, indeed muddying, the all-too-placid surfaces of society. Something like this *almost* occurs in Renoir's film as well, when Christine (the wife) decides to run away with Octave (played by Renoir himself), who is neither rich nor a member of her class. Christine's astute maid, Lisette, explains all of this to Octave, telling him that her mistress will never be happy below her station. Octave, unlike Lawrence's Mellors, accepts the wisdom of this and returns Christine (along with any chance of his own happiness) to her former lover and eventually to her husband.

Because Allegret may be using Lawrence to recover Renoir (rather than the other way around), the film misses certain meaningful opportunities to engage the text. One instance of this which seems to verify Lawrence's subordinate position is Allegret's failure to exploit what little there is in *La Règle du Jeu* that could potentially lead back to *Lady Chatterley's Lover.* Specifically, Renoir ignores the Lawrentian similarity between his aristocrat, Robert de la Chesnaye, and Sir Clifford. Despite their profound differences, both men have been seduced by modern technology to the point of obsession and at the expense of any connection they may have once had with nature. For Clifford, this problem is most clearly announced by his ever-increasing preoccupation with the pits and by his addiction to the radio, which becomes his primary source of human communication. Predating both the pits and the radio is Clifford's typewriter, another mechanical image suggesting that the disease had been present early on, even when Clifford considered himself a writer of fiction rather than an industrialist. Renoir addresses the same twentieth-century problem through Robert, but by way of a unique imagery that presents it in ironic caricature. While the film also provides "serious" instances of the modern obsession with technology (the record-breaking flight, the wild airport crowd, the "live" radio report), its primary image is an appropriately absurd one—the mechanical toy. Robert de la Chesnaye collects such toys and uses them to entertain the hunting party at his country estate. While real birds are shot outside, artificial birds sing in his chambers, accompanied by musical dolls and even by a complete mechanical orchestra.

In short, Renoir's Robert seems a comic version of Lawrence's Sir Clifford, at least mechanically, or one reduced to miniature and absurd proportions. The two men are similar enough, in reflecting this clearly Lawrentian problem, so that Marc Allegret could have referenced Robert's fixation with small machines to emphasize Clifford's fixation with large ones. Something like this occurs in the 1989 production of *The Rainbow* when Ken Russell surrounds his industrialist, Uncle Henry, with miniature mining equipment, which decorates the rooms of his estate.[48] This does not occur in *L'Amant*. While Leo Genn's Clifford is a mine owner ready to sacrifice forests for pits, no sense of him as technologically preoccupied, either comically or tragically, survives in the film. He is identified with no mechanical devices, large or small, except for his wheelchair, which he detests. Even his involvement with the mines is not finally based on technological obsession, like Clifford's in the text, but on the businessman's urge for profit and the aristocrat's urge for power.

Before leaving cinematic reference and returning to the text, mention needs to be made of *L'Amant de Lady Chatterley* in relation to the other Lawrence films. First, it is possible that Allegret was looking back when he filmed *L'Amant,* not only at Renoir's work but also at Anthony Pelissier's first Lawrence film. The connection between *L'Amant* and *The Rocking Horse Winner,* based on related visions of Europe at midcentury and in the aftermath of World War II, will be taken up in subsequent discussion. Also, if Allegret looked back, he also looked ahead, albeit unknowingly. Despite the critical obscurity of his film, several of its visual tropes turn up later as unattributed quotations in the works of subsequent Lawrence filmmakers. One instance of this can be observed by watching the opening scenes of Allegret's film along with the beginning of Jack Cardiff's *Sons and Lovers.* Mining machinery intruding upon an otherwise peaceful forest, the juxtaposition of trees and smokestacks, even a fatal pit accident early on all were admired for their originality and dramatic force in Cardiff's 1960 production. All, however, prove to have originated in Allegret's opening sequences for *L'Amant,* released five years earlier.

Just Jaeckin is similarly beholden to Allegret for the opening of his 1981 film. It begins with Clifford (before his injury) riding to hounds with friends, then winning a race home to impress his new bride. The scene then shifts indoors to a formal ball at Wragby on the eve of World War I. Looking back at *L'Amant* with these opening images in mind, one suddenly realizes where they came from. The 1955 French production also begins with a hunt, horses and hounds, and then an elegant party at Wragby that evening. The only difference is that in Allegret's film the mine accident briefly intervenes between the hunt and the party. In terms of intercinematic reference, what is perhaps most noteworthy about these visions of aristocratic life is that they originate not with Marc Allegret but with Jean Renoir some seventeen years earlier. *La Règle du Jeu* is filled with similar images of the gentry at play, either hunting game outdoors or hunting each other inside the elegant drawing rooms of Robert de la Chesnaye's estate. Renoir has left his mark on at least two of the eight Lawrence film directors: first on Allegret, who borrowed knowingly from *La Règle du Jeu,* then on Jaeckin, who borrowed from Allegret, perhaps unaware of the original, highly inventive source of his material.

The remainder of this chapter will be devoted to relationships between film and text, as opposed to film and film, and to the paradox of *L'Amant de Lady Chatterley* as a screen adaptation of Lawrence. As has been suggested, despite its fidelity to the exterior of *Lady Chatterley's Lover* (especially as compared with Russell's and Jaeckin's versions), Allegret's production remains the least Lawrentian of all three Lady Chatterley films. Allegret seems able to preserve the letter of events and circumstances in the text, all the while radically revising its spirit to reflect his own age and culture and to explore essentially post-Lawrentian concerns.

Allegret's fidelity to plot results partly from a simpler relationship between text and film than in either Jaeckin's or Russell's production. Unlike the later films, *L'Amant* remains less enriched (or distracted) by material drawn from *The First Lady Chatterley* or *John Thomas and Lady Jane.*[49] One result is that Allegret's Mellors owes less to Oliver Parkin than Jaeckin's or Russell's did. As played by Erno Crisa, he avoids Parkin's crudeness, a quality brought to the role and exaggerated by Nicholas Clay and Sean Bean. Also, Crisa's Mellors seems no ordinary working man as they did but more upwardly mobile, in keeping with Lawrence's original. The film's French script informs us that Allegret's Mellors, working as Sir Clifford's gamekeeper, is *déclassé,* or displaced from a higher social position. As in the text, but not in the two other films, he becomes a worker again after having served as an officer *(un officier)* during the war. The fidelity of these details to Lawrence's original becomes somewhat blurred here, but only because of Mai Harris's English subtitles. The French word *déclassé*, for which there is no exact English equivalent, instead becomes Mellors's descent from "above his station," and his prior status as *un officier* disappears in favor of a promotion in rank. This change seriously distorts Lawrence (although through no fault of Allegret's script) because it keeps Mellors from crossing that difficult military border which separates the gentlemen from the men.

Elsewhere in *L'Amant*, Allegret remains faithful to Lawrence's plot in other ways and again in contrast to the two later films. As previously discussed, both Jaeckin and Russell make use of Lawrence's wheelchair scene, during which Clifford becomes immobilized among his flowers, as a means of demonstrating his growing nastiness. In both productions he grounds himself in the mud on purpose as a pretext for humiliating Connie and Mellors. By contrast, Leo Genn's actions and reactions in the same scene come much closer to those of the original Sir Clifford. His machinery simply fails him and at a point in the film when he has no idea of his wife's affair. He becomes angry when this happens, but not at Connie or Mellors so much as at the inescapable proof of his own helpless condition. He is rude to Mellors when calling for help but, again, not so much out of personal hostility as a rigid sense of how servants and masters should interact as they play by the rules of their particular game. Similarly, Genn's Clifford becomes annoyed with Connie (as did Lawrence's) only when she breaks these rules by helping Mellors wheel him home. "*C'est ridicule,*" he comments as she begins to push the heavy chair. "*C'est ridicule.*"

To separate these same figures from their Lawrentian gestures and circumstances, however, and to look into rather than at them, is to discover that they belong not to the novelist's world but to the filmmakers' some thirty years later. Lawrence's novel—and especially its overlapping interactions of servants and masters or servants and mistresses—allows these filmmakers the necessary framework for dramatizing their own cultural situation in place of his and for representing midcentury France in flux after a second catastrophic war and in confusion over rapidly changing alignments of gender and class.

Because they are the film's least complex figures, Sir Clifford and Mrs. Bolton provide an appropriate entry into this later reality and into the social issues that inspire and drive Allegret's Lawrentian production. As in the text, Leo Genn's Sir Clifford is the least attractive of the four major characters. On screen, however, his negativity is less a matter of individual personality than a function of social and economic position. As played by Genn, Sir Clifford emerges as a perfectly two-dimensional figure, the pure industrialist and even purer aristocrat. Lawrence's Sir Clifford takes on these identities, as well as several others: the cultivated young cynic early on, for example, then the would-be novelist, then finally the monstrous child-man who emerges at the end. In contrast to his ongoing evolution in the text, Sir Clifford in this film remains virtually what or who he is from first to last. His consistent and most obvious motive is profit, if necessary at the expense of his workers' lives. Beneath this, but equally consistent, is Clifford's need for power, perhaps to compensate for the loss of control over his own body. As his mines and profits grow, so too does his power and at least the illusion of potency in place of paralysis. Even the child that Clifford asks Connie to have by another man would provide a means of extending and prolonging this power. Clifford would impose his pseudo-paternal authority over the child and cruelly so, as he tells Connie in their last conversation together, in revenge for her liaison with a gamekeeper. Eventually this child would assume Clifford's power and extend it, along with his profits and title, beyond the grave.

As noted earlier, Leo Genn's performance, particularly his distortion of the French language, seems as unappealing and unnatural as the character he portrays—therefore probably no mistake on Marc Allegret's part as the film's reviewers had initially assumed. Instead, Genn's stilted interpretation of Clifford appears deliberate and, perhaps more important, deliberately English instead of French. Allegret's Clifford Chatterley emerges as a hostile caricature of the British lord and British businessman combined, an ugly conflation of upper-class markers like power and wealth, which the filmmakers wish to represent as foreign to their own culture and typically British instead. Genn's heavily Anglicized French also functions as a fitting objective correlative for his flawed humanity; it is always in accord with the rules, yet always hopelessly wrong. If Genn's Clifford emerges as cultural caricature, Marc Allegret shares something in common with his British contemporary Anthony Pelissier, whose *Rocking Horse Winner* began Lawrence filming just six years earlier. Pelissier's film script abounded with equally hostile anti-French stereotypes like the volatile "froggy Frenchman" Paul sees at the racetrack or the sinister dressmaker Madame Alix, who terrorizes Hester when she attempts a career. Both postwar directors seem equally anxious to reject certain values (like privilege and profit) by exporting them across the Channel or blaming them, in other words, on their closest neighbor instead of themselves.

If a perfect gentleman requires a perfect servant, Sir Clifford gets what he deserves in Allegret's version of his nurse. As played by Berthe Tissen, Mrs. Bolton becomes, among other things, a foil for Mellors, opposing his rule-breaking with strict obedience to her employer. She becomes a foil for Connie as well, replacing the wife's casual and at times erratic care with "*exactitude même,*" or a level of efficiency that better matches Clifford's rigid nature. Missing from Allegret's film is any trace of the intense, perverse intimacy that develops between the original Sir Clifford and Mrs. Bolton. Here she does not infiltrate the Chatterley household to begin a power struggle with Clifford. Nor does she win such a struggle in the end by becoming *Magna Mater* and asexual lover to her patient as in

Jaeckin's film and Lawrence's text. Late in Allegret's film, the static relationship between nurse and patient seems about to deepen into something more than polite formality. Connie has just left Wragby for good, telling Clifford that he will never see his unborn son. For a moment he appears on the verge of painful emotion, or even "male hysteria," like his namesake in the text (289). Mrs. Bolton rushes up, also visibly moved and apparently willing to offer Clifford human sympathy in place of efficiency if he will accept it. Just as suddenly as Clifford seemed about to break down, he masters his feelings, forcing both himself and Mrs. Bolton back to what they have been all through the film—a pasteboard servant and master, and Allegret's indictment of all such relationships stifled by the rules and roles of social class. "Our plans have changed," Clifford informs Mrs. Bolton as calmly as possible. "Lady Chatterley will not lunch with us today."

It is not Mrs. Bolton but Sir Clifford who reimposes this code upon them, further establishing him as Allegret's main instrument of cultural parody and protest against upper-class values and their British manifestations. For her part, Mrs. Bolton (a servant and unmistakably a Frenchwoman) is more sensitive and passionate than her master, yet keeps her feelings carefully hidden when attending to his needs. She is willing to drop the mask with Connie, however, once she realizes that the lady is less restricted by her title than the lord. In filming the brief intimacy that develops between the two women, Allegret, unlike either Russell or Jaeckin, allows Mrs. Bolton to speak warmly about her dead husband to Connie, much as in the text. Lawrence's phrase "the touch of him," which Ivy Bolton still possesses after years of widowhood, becomes transformed in French into "*La chaleur de son corps*" (the warmth of his body) (163). While the words differ from those in the text, the implications behind them seem suddenly Lawrentian, as does Connie's recognition of her own similar feelings about Mellors.

Mrs. Bolton carries her intimate conversation with Connie beyond the text when she begins to describe her marriage in metaphors newly created for the screen. She tells Connie that life with her husband and child felt natural, rather than conventionally familial or social, and that they lived as a wolf, his mate, and their cub might live ("*le loup, la louve, et le louveteau*"). While these images don't originate with Lawrence, the spirit behind them again seems to accord with his. Connie is sufficiently moved by Mrs. Bolton's words to repeat them to Mellors, leaving the impression that the lovers' own rejection of society in favor of something more primitive might conclude the film. This proves misleading, however, since the film's ending, as will be seen, removes Connie and Mellors from nature altogether and directs them toward civilization instead.

The longer Connie's affair with Mellors goes on, in fact, the less they seem like wolves—or birds, beasts, and flowers of any kind—and the more they become entangled in uniquely human questions of gender and class. Several of the film's early critics have suggested that Allegret's Connie discovers her own feminine and feminist self through her affair with Mellors and eventual separation from Sir Clifford. They observe that Connie's emerging persona closely resembles Simone de Beauvoir's "new woman" as described just six years before the film's release in *The Second Sex*.[50] In accord with de Beauvoir's landmark work, Connie moves from essence (as wife and titled lady) to existence (as woman only) by taking decisive action. Her first liberating act is not simply to have the affair, since her role permits that as long as proper discretion is maintained. Rather, it is to have the affair with a servant, thereby breaking the more difficult class barriers along with the marital vows. Connie's second important action is to leave Clifford and escape marriage altogether. Her third and final act is to defy even Mellors by refusing the ultimatum he attempts to impose upon her. Near the end of the film, Connie tells Mellors that she is returning to Wragby one last time to face Clifford honestly about her affair, her pregnancy, and her decision to leave. Mellors tries to prevent this with threats. If she goes back to Wragby for whatever reason, he says, she'll never see him again. Connie refuses to be coerced by her lover, telling Mellors that he must now learn to overcome his male pride just as, with his help, she has learned to overcome her female fear. She departs to carry out her plan, determined to act yet entirely uncertain about the consequences.

Along with her resolve, amid uncertainties and the fears they engender, Allegret's Connie owes other qualities to Simone de Beauvoir more than to Lawrence. In *The Second Sex,* de Beauvoir writes at length of woman's alterity throughout Western history, the myth of her mysterious otherness which ultimately denies her a common humanity with men. It is woman's very attraction—her sexual seductiveness, glamour, and beauty—which seems to confirm the myth of otherness, thus ironically turning her own strengths against her. De Beauvoir insists on the need for woman's demystification and for a new sexuality no longer achieved at the sacrifice of her ordinary humanity to some strange goddess of the male imagination. If Marc Allegret intended to use Lawrence's Connie to make these ideas visible and palpable, it seems at first paradoxical that he would have chosen Danielle Darrieux to play the part. Darrieux had achieved stardom during the 1930s playing women who personified the very mystery which de Beauvoir reacts against. As described in a typical film encyclopedia, Darrieux's "glorious long career in French and international films . . . saw her progress from fragile romantic ingenues to chic, elegant, sophisticated women-of-the-world roles. Throughout that long period she remained one of the screen's major stars, known and admired the world over as the embodiment and the essence of French femininity."[51]

This appears to be the Danielle Darrieux we see in the film's initial sequences—still glamorous in the mid-1950s and still playing her signature role as a sophisticated, feminine, and clearly French Constance Chatterley. During the early dinner-party scene, for instance, Connie enters dressed in a revealing black evening gown, her hair elegantly styled. Obviously worshipped by her crippled husband, Connie is pursued by other men as well, among them a French Michaelis whom she fends off decisively yet flirtatiously, without compromise to her feminine mystique. But what occurs from this point onward could be described as Marc Allegret's visual demystification of his heroine, so that by the film's conclusion nothing remains of Darrieux's earlier and more typical image. Allegret accomplishes this by way of costume changes and an accompanying simplification of hairstyle and makeup. As Connie's relationship with Mellors evolves and intensifies, her glamour diminishes, and her alluring "trademark" image fades into plainness, even to the point that one critic complains about Darrieux's "dowdy and old-maidish" appearance.[52] By the time of Connie's first sexual encounter with Mellors, her elegant coiffure has given way to a nondescript hairstyle that exaggerates an irregular profile, something never revealed in previous close-up shots. Along with this, Darrieux's elegant costumes—evening gowns and riding outfits—have given way to simple print dresses, their flowered patterns "dowdy" at best, and their loose fit concealing the lines of her body.

Deglamorized and no longer passive, Darrieux's Connie moves toward rebirth as a new woman of feminist and clearly French conception. In unintended paradox, however, the equally French Mellors turns out to be less of a partner in this development than an impediment—a macho presence contradicting and ultimately deconstructing Connie's emerging victory. Late in the film, Erno Crisa's Mellors seems to place Connie's freedom in question by revealing his own misogynist philosophy, ironically something he shares with Sir Clifford.[53] As he burns his wedding photograph, he explains to Connie that there are only two kinds of women in the world: those who detest sex and simply endure it for the sake of marriage, and those (like Bertha) who seek to know and experience everything, using men merely as the instruments of their exploration. "I don't believe in women," he tells his lover to her face, because no woman exists outside these two categories who would be capable of completing a relationship with a man—presumably not even Connie herself.

Not content with words, Mellors begins putting his beliefs into action. He is depicted in an escalating series of confrontations with women, each more threatening than the one before. The first involves Connie's sister Hilda and takes place on the eve of their trip to Venice as she drives Connie to Mellors's cottage for their final night together. Hilda and Mellors detest one another on sight and argue violently in what amounts to an accurate filming of Lawrence's original scene. As in the text, Mellors's anger at Hilda carries him almost to the point of striking her or at least of savoring the possibility if not the blow itself. "She should ha' been slapped in time," he says somewhat ambiguously in the novel (246). The line emerges even more bluntly, in Mai Harris's English subtitle, as "She deserves to be smacked." Departing from the text at this point into violence realized rather than imagined, Mellors declines to spend "a night of sensual passion" with Connie during which the lovers "Burn . . . out the shames, the deepest, oldest shames, in the most secret places" (246–47). Instead, he simply continues and intensifies the gender conflict, only now with Connie instead of Hilda. When he learns about her impending trip and the plan to bear Sir Clifford an heir, he flies into a rage that soon becomes physical. "I'm throwing you out," he tells Connie, again in Mai Harris's plain English, and pushes her roughly out the cottage door and into the night.

Soon afterwards, Mellors enjoys a second opportunity to throw a woman out: this time his estranged wife, Bertha. Unlike Russell, Jaeckin, or Lawrence, who all keep Bertha hidden as an absent yet potent force, Allegret develops her into a revealing minor character and includes a scene in which she attempts a reconciliation with Mellors by invading his cottage and his bed. This scene becomes Mellors's third and most extreme instance of hostile action against women. When he discovers Bertha in bed (with evidence that Lady Chatterley had recently preceded her there), Mellors carries out what he only wished he could do to Hilda. He strikes Bertha in the face—the phrase "slaps her around" comes to mind. He then drags her down the stairs and, in an much rougher repeat of the scene with Connie, shoves her out the door.

Perhaps more unsettling than Mellors's violent words and actions is the tacit support the film and its director give them. They are not meant to undercut Mellors but, quite the contrary, to confirm his strong image as male protagonist. While celebrating the new womanhood, Marc Allegret sets up an impossible paradox by also celebrating traditional (and traditionally Latin) manhood—the cliché of machismo which implies that male sexuality becomes all the more compelling with a dash of physical violence thrown in. One can only wonder what sort of future awaits Allegret's odd and oddly French Lawrentian couple, the feminist Connie married to the macho Latin lover Mellors.

If Connie and Mellors seem irreconcilably opposed over matters of gender, they are also worlds apart socially, yet not in the same way as Lawrence's original pair. This is partly because Allegret's Connie is portrayed in every way as Sir Clifford's social equal—a fellow aristocrat, which Lawrence's Connie was not. As the daughter of an artist (even a knighted artist), the original Connie is rooted firmly in the middle class. When Sir Clifford marries her, he not only marries down but takes on an unconventional, potentially risky partner from the start. Although Allegret tells us nothing about Connie's family, his visual portrayal of her consistently implies a woman of aristocratic background unlike her counterpart in the novel. A major means of achieving this is by way of the equestrian image, something which turns out to be a curious constant in all three Lady Chatterley films. Allegret's horses and riders, however, unlike Russell's or Jaeckin's, do not appear in Connie's dreams, nor are they film transcriptions of Lawrence's black-and-white Platonic horses from earlier versions of the text. Rather, in *L'Amant de Lady Chatterley* the horses become class emblems, serving to identify their riders as members of the gentry and as social superiors to anyone looking up at them from the ground.

This image becomes the basis for Allegret's modification of Lawrence's washing scene, for instance, to foreground its class implications in place of its erotic potential, which Jaeckin chose to emphasize instead. In Allegret's film Connie approaches the gamekeeper's cottage on horseback, dressed in boots and riding habit and carrying a whip. She dismounts and walks up to the front door to deliver her message from Sir Clifford. After receiving no response, she walks around the cottage to find Mellors bathing, clad only in trousers and unaware of her because his back is turned. On seeing him, Danielle Darrieux's Connie registers surprise, then sexual curiosity mixed with embarrassment. Her strategy for dealing with these feelings, as well as her unexpected experience of voyeurism, is to retreat, remount, and return to the scene on horseback, none of which takes place in the text. Now "above" Mellors, Connie regains control of the situation, her own feelings, and her gamekeeper. She delivers Clifford's message coldly, as mistress to servant, then departs for home to avoid an impending (and heavily symbolic) thunderstorm.

This scene leads immediately to one in which Connie's fall from the same horse predicts her eventual descent from the aristocracy to become *déclassé* like Mellors himself. When the storm breaks, Connie is forced to seek shelter at the gamekeeper's hut. As in the text, Mellors arrives and attempts to make her comfortable but becomes annoyed when she suggests returning to the hut from time to time. In Allegret's film, Darrieux's response to his annoyance is to gallop off angrily to the sound of Joseph Kosma's hopelessly melodramatic musical score. When her horse jumps a fallen tree, Connie is thrown to the ground, breaking an arm. Mellors's rescue allows the future lovers their first physical contact in this scene. Telling Connie that he has learned first aid as a soldier, he fashions a temporary sling from her scarf, lifts her onto her horse, and escorts her home. This second equestrian scene is interesting less for its symbolism or its departure from the text than for its pragmatic consequences. The injury becomes the reason for Mrs. Bolton's hiring and thus the event that begins to move Connie away from her obligations to Sir Clifford and toward her affair with Mellors.

Connie appears on horseback a third time shortly after she and Mellors become lovers. During their second sexual encounter, she experiences a reaction against the affair because Mellors has spoken "too familiarly" to her, an interesting point of protocol between carnal lovers that will be taken up shortly for its multiple implications. Connie's response is to return home at once and change her clothes, stripping off the flowered dress associated with her affair in favor of the black evening gown associated with elegant life at Wragby. The next day she appears in riding habit again, galloping her horse in circles around the estate in an effort to resume the routine patterns of her life. Connie encounters Mellors during the ride and glares at him from astride her horse. She then turns away and rides back to Wragby for one final effort at intimacy with Clifford, an effort he quickly and coldly rejects.

If Marc Allegret raises Connie Chatterley from the middle class to the gentry, he doesn't end the process of social (and textual) adjustment with her. As she moves up, so too do several of the novel's working-class figures, including the protagonist himself. Despite being a servant, for example, Berthe Tissen's Mrs. Bolton seems in all other respects a middle-class woman—well spoken, refined, delicate, and altogether different from Lawrence's original Ivy, that tough customer and collier's widow who has managed to remake herself by force of will alone. While Lawrence's Mellors has also remade himself, his roots remain, like Ivy's, firmly within the working class of Tevershall. This allows him to resume their norms of behavior and speech whenever he wishes (usually for strategic reasons). By contrast, Erno Crisa's Mellors lacks this facility and, like Mrs. Bolton, seems purely a middle-class person impersonating a servant. This comes across in his lines, which are always delivered in as careful and correct French as Darrieux's, without accent (despite Crisa's Italian origins), and always free of colloquialism or dialect. In fact, if the later pair of cinematic Olivers seem incapable of escaping the dialect (Nicholas Clay's poetry recitation aside), this one seems incapable of speaking it at all. As a result, Allegret's Mellors is denied not only his namesake's social mobility but his linguistic mobility as well, his fluency in "proper" speech, when required, along with his innate preference for the dialect, especially when heightened experience, either conflict or passion, arouses it.

The only vestige of linguistic complexity remaining in Allegret's film appears when Mellors speaks "too familiarly" to Connie during their lovemaking, thereby offending her with his words. "Too familiarly," taken verbatim from the English subtitles, represents Mai Harris's effort to translate from French what is essentially untranslatable in a single phrase. What Mellors has actually done to upset Connie is *tutoyer* her for the first time, or speak to her using the familiar rather than the polite form of address. Mellors is not expecting a visit from Connie that evening, but she manages to escape Wragby and seek him out at the hut, deliberately wearing nothing underneath her thin dress. When he first caresses her and discovers this, he is both surprised and delighted, exclaiming, "*Tu est nue,*" which instantly shocks Connie out of her passionate mood.

Several intriguing implications arise from this brief incident. It suggests, for example, that Marc Allegret may at least be glancing across the Channel toward Lawrence's Midlands where "thee" and "thou"—long dead in standard English—still survive in dialect. On the other hand, it also seems clear that most English-speaking audiences would miss this connection and instead take the subtitle simply to mean that Mellors has said something inappropriate to Connie. By contrast, French-speaking audiences would instantly respond to the issue behind Mellors's *tutoiement* and understand that Connie has taken offense because she has been addressed familiarly rather than formally by a servant, even though that servant happens to be her lover. One must assume that this second reading is correct and that it reveals Allegret's intention, since it is based on his French as opposed to Mai Harris's English translation. If so, Mellors's discourse, like so much else in the film, ultimately leads back to Connie's story rather than his and, specifically, to her struggle with class identity brought on by the affair. It was easier to go to bed with the man, it seems, than to hear him address her as "*tu*" for the first time. Far more than the deed, it is the word that offends Connie, forcing her to realize that she is now partnered with a middle-class lover (at best) and in danger of falling from her world into his.

By replacing the original Mellors with this well-spoken, middle-class substitute, Allegret avoids nearly all the linguistic intricacy that the dialect brings to the text. It is tempting to suggest that Allegret really had no choice here, since Lawrence's English, with all its layered connotations, would never have survived translation to begin with. As it turns out, however, dialect in French does play a part in *L'Amant de Lady Chatterley,* only never in the discourse of any major character. Late in the film, around the time of Connie's trip to Venice, a transitional scene occurs in which word of Mellors's affair with a lady—perhaps even Lady Chatterley herself—begins to spread through the town. Those responsible for the gossip are the working people of Tevershall (or its French equivalent), who discuss the scandal over their drinks at the village "pub." It isn't really a pub, though, but a French cafe where accordion music plays in the background and *vin rouge* is served instead of ale. The evening's customers (with Bertha herself tending bar) speculate on Mellors's sexual adventures in slangy, common French and provide the film a late moment of comic relief—in effect, what the lower classes have provided "elevated" literature for centuries. If anything, Allegret's pub scene seems more in the style of Thomas Hardy than D. H. Lawrence, reminiscent of his frequent interludes involving amusing rustics acting and speaking as chorus.

French dialect persists in a subsequent and more revealing scene between Bertha and her working-class lover, René. After Bertha's roughing up and hasty retreat from Mellors's cottage, she comes across René at a nearby pond where he is in a barge clearing weeds. He offers to help her get back at Mellors by writing an unsigned letter to Clifford revealing Connie's affair. It is clear that René and Bertha are on intimate terms. He assumes sexual privileges over her (perhaps in advance payment for his epistolary efforts), and a love scene ensues in Allegret's typically modest manner. The camera shows René as he picks Bertha up and carries her toward the woods. After a discreet fade-out, the next scene shows the lovers "some time later," lying side by side in postcoital chagrin. René raises himself up and speaks angrily to Bertha, upset that he has possessed her only physically, not emotionally or totally as Mellors had. Like the earlier pub crowd, René speaks to Bertha in coarse, slurred French ironically salted with the film's only obscenity, *merde!*

Intentionally or otherwise, Berthe and René become a distorted version of Connie and Mellors, a negative pair of lovers portrayed in caricature and condemned for their crudeness or, in effect, for the sordidness of their lower-class lives. If Sir Clifford provides Allegret with a means of rejecting the aristocracy by way of parody, Bertha, René, and the amusing pub chorus do precisely the same thing for the proletariat. This raises the fundamental questions of what remains once both high and low are dismissed from this film and what remains of Lawrence. The answers to both questions are provided, with inescapable clarity, in the film's concluding scenes.

As previously suggested, the Hollywood happy ending closes all three Lady Chatterley films with equal finality regardless of where in Europe they were produced. Marc Allegret's version speaks volumes, at least on the social questions, despite containing only two lines of dialogue and despite running for just over one minute of screen time. This final sequence opens with Connie walking along a nondescript street to find Mellors, although we can only wonder how she knows where to look. As she reaches the doorway of his apartment building, he is just coming down the stairs, suitcase in hand, about to depart for good. Connie tells Mellors (now addressing *him* as "*tu*") that she has done what she needed to do at Wragby so that now their future remains up to him. Mellors's response is to smile and speak just two words, "*Ma femme,*" at which point the lovers leave together to begin their new life, moving away from the camera hand in hand and blending in with the crowd. The setting for this final scene is itself socially revealing in that it is unlike anything previously shown. Both the estate and the woodland cottage have given way to the apartment building, suburban and middle class. Along with this, the clothing Connie and Mellors wear for their final exit blends in with this locale and again differs markedly from anything seen before.

Mellors has discarded his "military" uniform in favor of informal yet conventional male attire—open-collared shirt, slacks, and jacket. Connie wears a stylish but simple cloth coat, so the lovers now match one another. Also, a compromise has been achieved between Connie's elegant evening gowns and riding habit on one extreme and her "dowdy" flowered dress on the other.

As they walk away together, Danielle Darrieux and Erno Crisa strike us as absolutely ordinary, a middle-class couple in the middle of Europe at the middle of the twentieth century. A passer-by crosses the lovers' path and momentarily turns his head to stare, as if he had noticed something unusual about them. In a meaningful if probably unintended irony, the stranger seems to dismiss this possibility, turns away, and continues about his business. Perhaps to him, as to us, this couple now appears nondescript or far removed, to say the very least, from the pair of wolves that Mrs. Bolton urged them to become. More than Mrs. Bolton and her advice has been lost here. As Connie and Mellors disappear into the common crowd, Simone de Beauvoir and D. H. Lawrence both disappear as well.[54]

# 8

# *Kangaroo:* Taming Lawrence's Australian Beast

 If *Lady Chatterley's Lover* remains essentially unfilmed after three attempts, it is at least clear why moviemakers have continued to try. By comparison, *Kangaroo* seems not so much camera shy as downright hostile, so that it is surprising anyone has made the effort at all, even an Australian director like Tim Burstall. Toward the end of *Kangaroo*, Lawrence himself becomes embarrassed by the novel's anticinematic properties—its interminable lectures from author to reader, for instance, in place of normative dialogue and action. "Chapter follows chapter, and nothing doing," Lawrence admits, or even more frankly, "He [Somers] preached, and the record was taken down for this gramophone of a novel," or ironically, "I hope, dear reader, you like plenty of *conversation* in a novel: it makes it so much lighter and brisker."[1]

It would be easier to film conversation than the pages of monologue Lawrence offers us instead. A director attempting *Kangaroo* could always resort to voice-over to preserve the narrative, a familiar technique which Burstall for the most part refrains from using. Or he could transform monologue into dialogue by converting Lawrence's lectures into the give-and-take between characters—the very "conversations" Lawrence seems to enjoy dangling before his readers' noses, then denying them. Burstall makes such transformations with some success in *Kangaroo,* as when portions of "Harriet and Lovat at Sea in Marriage," a long parable on the subject, reemerge in a lively and amusing quarrel between husband and wife. In general, however, Burstall's strategy for coping with Lawrence's language is to surround it with images of his own making—to tell Lawrence's heavily worded story while showing us its visual objective correlative. Such a method

186

seems cinematically workable, at least in theory, and surely better than the extremes of filming the priest in his pulpit or else walking out of the temple altogether.

Nevertheless, Burstall's *Kangaroo* remains at best a qualified success, a film both difficult to fault and impossible to celebrate enthusiastically. Burstall offers us a careful production to the point of caution (both verbal and visual) and a direct-ing style in exact opposition to the risky outrageousness of Ken Russell. Such caution could be construed as the cinematic equivalent of "tameness," a quality Lawrence condemned outright in *Lady Chatterley's Lover*. At the same time, how-ever, Burstall's restraint proves ironically appropriate to *Kangaroo* in resembling a similar reluctance in the novel's own hero, Richard Lovat Somers—or at least in Somers as he comes to be viewed by his new Australian friends. Throughout *Kangaroo*, Somers remains just shy of political commitment, despite the temp-tations of Ben Cooley and Willie Struthers, and despite his own deep desire to leave some mark on the "greater" male world of causes and action. Somers, how-ever, ultimately proves unwilling to trade private imperatives for public ones, withholding himself and his talents from both causes, so that he is eventually condemned by the Australians as the worst sort of traitor—the tame sort. "You blighters from the old country are so mighty careful of risking yourselves," Jack Calcott tells him. "That's what I'm not. When I feel a thing I jump up and go for it, and damn the consequences."[2] For Jack, perhaps, Somers's reluctance typi-fies not just England but Europe and Europeans as a whole—always careful to stop just short of damning the consequences.

Tim Burstall's equally careful production of *Kangaroo* is almost exclusively an Australian product, from cast to crew to location, so that the old country can hardly be blamed for its reluctance and the impression it leaves that something always remains withheld. Ironically, Jack Calcott's indictment makes more sense when applied to the film than to Somers, who is clearly right to reject both dema-gogues in favor of his own dark gods. The film, on the other hand, could stand to take a cinematic chance now and then or to risk "doing something silly," as Birkin advises Gerald to do in *Women in Love*.[3] In those instances when this happens, by way of a particular scene or performance that damns the conse-quences, we feel the momentary urge to celebrate—not the film that Burstall made, unfortunately, so much as the one he might have made instead.[4]

By all indications, filming *Kangaroo* had been a project on Burstall's mind for years before he began working on it. Two commentators trace Burstall's interest in *Kangaroo* as far back as the early 1970s.[5] A decade later, the film was suffi-ciently under way for Burstall to discuss it in some detail with Andrew Peek in an interview. The interview reveals a number of interesting insights into *Kanga-roo*, including a connection to Ken Russell's seemingly ubiquitous *Women in Love*. Directing styles aside, it turns out that Burstall had wanted Russell's screenwriter,

Larry Kramer, to write the script for *Kangaroo,* although according to Kramer he never worked on the film because a contract agreement could not be reached.[6] Even the attempt to hire Kramer, however, offers a clear indication that Russell's film inspired Burstall, as it had several other filmmakers, to attempt a Lawrence project of his own. Less implicit, Burstall reveals to his interviewer that he wanted the openly homosexual Kramer as his screenwriter specifically to develop and clarify the relationship Lawrence explores in *Kangaroo* between political leadership and masculine love. Burstall also suggests that his interest in this relationship had less to do with the novel than with Lawrence's real-life preoccupation with it at the time he wrote *Kangaroo.*

This leads to a second, broader insight arising from the Peek interview, namely, that the director saw his version of *Kangaroo* less as a screen adaptation of Lawrence's text than as a film about Lawrence himself, a biography "very thinly disguised" as fiction, as Burstall describes it. "When I began thinking about the film . . . I thought . . . that the facts of Lawrence were just as relevant as the facts of the material in the novel. In casting Harriet, for instance, I was originally thinking of getting a German [actress]. But now, I think not."[7] Instead, Burstall got Judy Davis, his well-known compatriot, to play Harriet Somers with a German accent and at least one line of nontextual dialogue to the effect that her cousin had been a highly decorated pilot during the war. Similarly, Colin Friels, the Australian actor playing Somers, speaks with a Midlands accent and physically resembles Lawrence—or perhaps more accurately he resembles Alan Bates impersonating Lawrence as he played Birkin in *Women in Love.*

Among Burstall's largely Australian cast and crew, only Judy Davis has achieved international recognition. Before *Kangaroo,* she had appeared in prominent films such as Gillian Armstrong's *My Brilliant Career* (Australia 1979) and David Lean's *A Passage to India* (U.K. 1984), for which she received an Academy Award nomination for best actress as E. M. Forster's ambivalent heroine, Adela Quested. Davis's more recent credits include work in American films such as the Coen brothers' *Barton Fink* (1991), Woody Allen's *Husbands and Wives* (1992), and Clint Eastwood's *Absolute Power* (1997). As Harriet Somers in Burstall's *Kangaroo,* Davis won the Australian Film Institute's award for best actress in 1986. Colin Friels, Davis's husband in real life, won the award for best actor that same year for his portrayal of an enlightened fool in the title role of Nadia Tass's *Malcolm,* a film that opened simultaneously with *Kangaroo.* Among the other members of *Kangaroo's* cast, perhaps only one, Hugh Keays-Byrne (Kangaroo), has enjoyed a worldwide film audience, although briefly and dubiously, as the Toecutter in George Miller's *Mad Max* (1989), the first segment of Mel Gibson's highly successful Road Warrior trilogy.

Burstall came to the project as a veteran filmmaker whose work has remained relatively unknown outside Australia compared with the efforts of directors like Peter Weir or Gillian Armstrong. Also, Burstall's most prolific period as a director occurred more than a decade before *Kangaroo,* with his first film, *The Prize,* appearing in 1960 and gaining international attention and an award at the Venice Film Festival. Burstall's other credits include over a dozen films, among them *Two Thousand Weeks* (1969), *Stork* (1971), *Libido* (1973), *Alvin Purple* (1973), *Petersen* (1974), *End Play* (1975), *Eliza Fraser* (1976), and *The Last of the Knucklemen* (1979). Burstall's *Two Thousand Weeks* lays some claim to having helped initiate Australia's cinema renaissance because in 1969 it was that country's "first fully professional locally financed feature film in almost 20 years."[8] After *Kangaroo,* Burstall directed *Duet for Four* (1982) and a series of television productions in Australia and the United States.

As there was a Friels-Davis family connection in the cast of *Kangaroo,* there was also a Burstall connection in the crew. Tim's son Dan was the film's director of photography. Virtually the only non-Australian contributing significantly to *Kangaroo* was its scriptwriter, the British-Jamaican Evan Jones, who had also enjoyed his greatest prominence in cinema well before this film. During the 1960s Jones seems to have been Joseph Losey's screenwriter of choice, working with the American director on three major productions within four years: *The Damned* (1961), *Eva* (1962), and *King and Country* (1964).

Working together on *Kangaroo,* these filmmakers were clearly motivated by a resurgence of interest in Lawrence's life, beyond his writings, during the 1980s. This was the centennial decade of his birth, celebrated in England and around the world in 1985, also the period in which Lawrence biography reached theater and television screens for the first time. The year before *Kangaroo* was released in Europe, Peter Barber-Fleming's biography of Lawrence, *Coming Through,* appeared in England on Central Independent Television. A few years earlier, Christopher Miles's feature film *Priest of Love* opened in both Europe and America with Ian McKellen playing Lawrence and, again, reminding audiences of Alan Bates playing Birkin. If Bates, McKellen, and Friels could momentarily be seen together, through some miracle of the media, they would strike us today as cinematic triplets, looking more like one another than the real-life author they were meant to represent—identically bearded, of course, but even identically dressed in what has come to be the standard Lawrentian uniform on film, the suit and vest, always carefully wrinkled, the off-white summer hat cocked at an angle suggesting genius and freedom of spirit combined.

As first embodied in Alan Bates's Birkin, this figure accomplished, among other things, the sixtification of D. H. Lawrence on screen—his reconciliation

with, and reflection of, the radical dynamics of the 1960s. As embodied in Colin
Friels's Somers (and to a lesser extent Ian McKellen's Lorenzo), the revived visual presence twenty years later updates Lawrence inwardly, leaving his appearance unchanged yet reconfiguring his spirit to mirror the ambivalence and uncertainty of the 1980s. Friels's Somers is presented to us as a celebrated author
and thinker who nonetheless proves as fallible and confused as the rest of us.
Perhaps he is right to be politically uncertain, yet he is imaginatively uncertain
as well despite his international reputation for genius. In a deliberate confound-
ing of biography and fiction, Tim Burstall shows Colin Friels's Somers writing
*Kangaroo,* the text, all throughout *Kangaroo,* the film. His literary efforts, however, appear less an example of inspiration than of eavesdropping followed by
outright plagiarism. Whenever anyone makes an interesting remark, Somers
immediately scurries off to copy it down in his notebook.

Despite occasional lip service to Lawrentian lord-and-mastery, Somers also
proves as dependent a husband as he is a genius. Relying on Harriet for far more
than literary inspiration, he remains the passive partner in their marriage, often
intimidated by his strong-willed, dynamic wife. Similarly, Somers appears un-
decided in contrast to Harriet's resolve, slow to catch on in contrast to her sharp-
ness, and generally less possessed of Lawrentian fire than she is herself. If Ken
Russell's Birkin radicalized Lorenzo for the 1960s, Tim Burstall's Somers redo-
mesticates and tames him for the more sensitive yet far less certain 1980s and
1990s. On film Somers emerges as a man for one season—our own uneasy end
of the twentieth century.

While *Kangaroo*'s initial reviewers may not have identified Somers as a contemporary character, they have recognized his indecisiveness and, in paradoxical contrast, his biographical proximity to Lawrence. Charles Sawyer noted in
*Films in Review,* for instance, that if it were "not for the comparison to the
Lawrences of real life, it is unlikely this book would have been filmed. The Somers
are devoid of interest otherwise. He comes off a mindless wimp (when not an
actively spineless one) and she comes off a temperamental harridan."[9] Writing
for the *Washington Post,* Richard Harrington suggests, even more cuttingly, "If
watching an insecure intellectual waffle between extreme political ideologies is
your idea of excitement, *Kangaroo* may be just the film for you."[10] These same
commentators also noticed Friels's resemblance, as Somers, to Alan Bates's Birkin
and Ian McKellen's Lawrence, with their comparisons to the two earlier performances unanimously negative. Sawyer concluded, "*Kangaroo* begs comparison
with the 1981 British film *Priest of Love,* which was based on a Lawrence biography and the writings and letters of D. H. Lawrence himself. Lawrence's rather
voyeuristic nature presents a similar problem in that film, but a strong, literate
screenplay and bravura performances by Ian McKellen as Lawrence and Janet

Suzman as Frieda triumph. *Priest of Love* is a film that vanished too quickly and is a more worthy 'Lawrence effort' than *Kangaroo*."[11] In an almost identical judgment, Stanley Kauffmann observes that *Kangaroo* "is hurt further by Colin Friels's performance as Somers. Friels, who looks much like Alan Bates bearded, is adequate as a mortal, but he conveys nothing of the superhuman that Ian McKellen touched as Lawrence in the biographical *Priest of Love* (1981). Friels's lack of larger-than-life dimension helps to blunt the enterprise."[12] Other unfavorable comparisons describe "Friels as a serious, tasteful shadow of Alan Bates's Lawrence figure in the far more audacious *Women in Love*," and as bearing "an unfortunate resemblance to Alan Bates in *Women in Love* [but] muster[ing] none of Bates' internal passion."[13]

These reviewers did find internal passion and *Kangaroo*'s one larger-than-life presence in Harriet Somers, with Judy Davis's portrayal praised almost as consistently as her husband's had been damned. Sawyer's atypical "temperamental harridan" remark aside, most critics saw Davis as the film's salvation as well as its only truly Lawrentian personality. Michael Wilmington, reviewing *Kangaroo* for the *Los Angeles Times,* described her performance as "the movie's major triumph. . . . She's so superb that she begins to embody all those elements of sexuality and danger that seem missing elsewhere, that black, deep, absent vision." He concluded, "If Davis' performance were the rule here and not the exception," Burstall's film could have "carried you away."[14] Similarly, and typical of responses to the film worldwide, *Newsday* reviewer Joseph Gelmis saw "a more compelling movie played out on Davis' face than in all the words spoken by all the other characters in *Kangaroo*. Lightning crackles in her eyes."[15] Perhaps both husband and wife emerge as contemporary figures even more visibly by way of their opposition on screen. Richard Somers, the aspiring lord and master, proves to be a sensitive and sensitized male instead, gender-conscious and politically conflicted to the point of confusion and paralysis. Harriet Somers, on the other hand, if not exactly replacing her husband as lord and master, becomes the film's empowered woman, so much so that she appears passionately and paradoxically Lawrentian in the intensity of her non-Lawrentian feminism and present-day outlook in general.

While most of the reviewers' attention focused on *Kangaroo*'s central married couple and their conflicts, a few of the film's supporting figures were also noticed and, like Davis and Friels, either highly praised or else condemned. Generally, the praise went to John Walton, the film's Jack Calcott, with his strongest support coming from Amy Taubin, writing for *Village Voice,* when she suggested that Walton, "his relaxed physicality belied by feverishly glinting eyes, steals the film from its stars."[16] Taubin's opinion was closely seconded by Charles Sawyer, who described Walton as "a veteran of Australian TV and theater, [who] might well use this flimsy film as a springboard to bigger parts in better films. There's a fierceness about him that commands attention and brings to mind a more volatile Harrison Ford."[17]

The supporting actor singled out for criticism to the point of ridicule was Hugh Keays-Byrne, the film's Kangaroo. Because this role is crucial to the story, Keays-Byrne's selection for the part was identified as the film's major casting mistake. Reviewers based their judgments partly on the actor's appearance, so that their amusing, ad hominem descriptions of him recalled the similar drubbing that Oliver Reed received years before as a "miscast" Gerald in *Women in Love*. Criticism of Keays-Byrne's performance went beyond his looks, however, and was convincing in its claim that the actor had been miscast. Contrasting him with Lawrence's Ben Cooley ("Jewish, hermaphroditic . . . the projection of all the writer's fears, loathings and desires"), Amy Taubin described Keays-Byrne's version as "nothing more than a beefy, red-faced bore."[18] Other reviewers extended their frustrations to the point of recommending different actors for the part, albeit too late. Joseph Gelmis described Keays-Byrne's Kangaroo as "a comic strutting buffoon," suggesting, "What the role needs to give it credibility is a charismatic heavy, like Edward Arnold in his prime."[19] An Australian reviewer, Peter Craven, provided the most comprehensive judgment and dismissal of his countryman in the following pungent yet accurate description:

> Hugh Keays-Byrne as Kangaroo is the film's central and fatal piece of miscasting because he comes across like a teddy bear, or rather, a sort of pommified [Anglicized] koala. In the book, Lawrence manages to make Kangaroo a credible putative führer which, given the Australian context, is saying a good deal. He is the linchpin of the novel's drama and for the film to come off, it was essential that the part be played by an actor who could sustain Kangaroo's ambiguous magnetism, his beauty-in-ugliness. To me the obvious choice would have been Sam Neill and without someone of his calibre or command the film's characterization is nowhere.[20]

When the critics turned from individual performances to the film as a whole, their judgments tended to be positive but never passionate. They concluded that Tim Burstall had made an intelligent effort to film a difficult book, achieving some success but not the necessary intensity either to capture Lawrence or to leave a memorable artistic impression of his own. In place of Lawrentian intensity, Janet Maslin described her general impression of *Kangaroo* as having "something of a *Masterpiece Theater* patina."[21] Michael Wilmington concluded, "This is a tamed *Kangaroo*, one that lies too peaceably on the shelf. Yet, despite it all, the movie still has something. The dark deeps and torrential emotion, the passions, the desperate reach and reckless ambition—they all retain such potency that this *Kangaroo* . . . can take hold, despite all your objections."[22] Doris Toumarkine, a third American critic, echoed Wilmington's conclusions almost exactly in a representative assessment of the film worldwide. She called *Kangaroo* a "highly intelligent" film that "never really goes far enough in exploring its teasing political and sexual undercurrents. . . . A riot at the end . . . between the two opposing political factions provides some excitement, but the overall tone is too restrained and the pacing too sluggish. In spite of these drawbacks, *Kangaroo* should benefit from respectful reviews and positive word of mouth deriving from Davis' subtle and mesmerizing portrait of the wise German aristocrat."[23]

It is surprising that beyond such reviews *Kangaroo* engendered little discussion. Despite the perceived "intelligence" and "respectability" of Burstall's efforts, more studied commentaries on the film failed to appear, and critics remained as silent as they had been over Just Jaeckin's "unintelligent and unrespectable" *Lady Chatterley's Lover*. The closest approach to a detailed examination of Burstall's *Kangaroo* (and its relationship to the text) came from two writers, David Bradshaw in *TLS* and Harris Ross in the *D. H. Lawrence Review,* with both pieces appearing soon after the film's release. Bradshaw and Ross reached equally negative conclusions on Burstall's capacity to project Lawrence's *Kangaroo* visually, with Bradshaw often concerned with discrepancies of detail and Ross tending to take a broader view. The *TLS* critic, for instance, objected to the film's one explicit love scene as "a gratuitous indulgence" in violation of Lawrentian eroticism, yet he stopped short of comparing Burstall's scene to the similar one Lawrence provides in the text.[24] Harris Ross's concerns had less to do with particulars than with the film's governing spirit, which he regarded as a diminished version of Lawrence's, both emotionally and intellectually: "Burstall's *Kangaroo* is a respectable adaptation that lacks the literal-mindedness which made Mark Rydell's *The Fox* so appalling but that also lacks the imagination and passion that made Ken Russell's *Women in Love* so exciting. Burstall's is a respectful translation, pure and simple, or, perhaps more precisely, pure and simplified." Based on such judgments, Ross concluded that *Kangaroo* "is never completely involving because the filmmakers could find no means to translate the central character's intellectual quest into cinematic terms."[25]

In Lawrence's text, what Harris Ross identified as Somers's "intellectual quest" is really part of a larger exploration, just as *Kangaroo* itself is part of a larger literary entity, the late progression of works often labeled Lawrence's "leadership novels"—*Aaron's Rod, Kangaroo,* and *The Plumed Serpent.* This suggests that Tim Burstall's challenge, or that of any filmmaker adapting one of these novels, must involve more than the "thought adventure" and its potential representation. All three texts explore a man's capacity for preserving selfhood (including the private "thought adventure") while also maintaining two intense external relation-ships—heterosexual marriage with its ultimate and permanent commitments, and an equally final friendship with another man. Within these three novels, the Lawrentian quadrangle of two dynamic couples in flux reshapes itself into a Law-rentian triangle in no way related to the familiar triangle of romance. Here, in each of the leadership novels, a single figure deals with a triple conflict and strives for its resolution through an equilibrium in which all three imperatives are bal-anced and preserved. This is what Lawrence envisioned for "Rananim," his twen-tieth-century utopia where a man could enjoy two all-consuming relationships, final marriage and final friendship, or blood brotherhood, with no injury to the dark gods within him. This threefold quest subsumes the "intellectual quest" Ross mentioned and creates a common bond among the major male figures of the leadership novels—Richard Lovat Somers of *Kangaroo,* Aaron Sisson of *Aaron's Rod,* and both Don Cipriano and Don Ramon of *The Plumed Serpent.* Kate Leslie, the real protagonist of *The Plumed Serpent,* remains barred from Rananim's trinity by her gender and the limitations of Lawrence's vision. His utopia allows for no blood sisterhoods equal to what Ramon and Cipriano experience.

Burstall's effort to replicate Lawrence's threefold equilibrium seems admirable but limited, with only the Somers marriage achieving effective representation on film. By contrast, Somers's inwardness probably suffers the most damage, partly because of the medium itself. Burstall never mentions the "thought adventure," an implicit admission that invisible abstractions cannot easily be filmed. A re-lated obstacle to capturing selfhood on film is Colin Friels's interpretation of Somers, a problem pointed out by several reviewers. Friels's performance seldom captures introspection; instead, he offers many human qualities precisely opposed to it: congeniality in place of withdrawal, normalcy or even innocence of out-look in place of depth, and plump good health in place of consumption and the spiritual fevers it engenders. Perhaps most damaging of all, Friels's Somers comes across as too good-natured a man ever to be properly angry, as only Lawrence or one of his fictional characters could be. Without Lawrentian rage, Lawrentian selfhood and the dark gods become impossible to project.

On the elementary level of plot, it becomes even more difficult for Somers to adventure inside himself on screen because he's almost never alone. At one point, as Jack takes him to Kangaroo's military encampment, he wanders off into the woods in what could have become a clothed version of Alan Bates's forest scene in *Women in Love.* Rather than suggesting internal communion, however, Friels's moment alone in the woods suggests weakness and confusion. He becomes disoriented and lost, only to be captured by Kangaroo's militiamen and brought back to their headquarters under guard, blindfolded and humiliated. Elsewhere Somers's potential moments of privacy, during which he might reconnect with his inward spirits, always seem to occur under the watchful eye of his wife. When he walks nude into the sea to wash away his near-seduction by Kangaroo (homo-political) and Victoria Calcott (hetero-adulterous), Harriet follows closely and seductively behind him to reassert her marital rights. Similarly, when Burstall attempts to capture internal communion visually by showing Somers alone, cast-ing rocks into the sea, the camera cuts to Harriet keeping an eye on her husband from the porch of their bungalow, looking both bemused and concerned, like a mother regarding a gifted but particularly troublesome child.

Somers's quest for a male friend and a worthy masculine cause to commit to fare only a little better on screen than his need for selfhood, this again partly because of Harriet's strong presence and, eventually, her direct intervention, all of which merits further discussion. As in Lawrence's novel, Somers's first poten-tial "mate" in Australia is Jack Calcott, played impressively by John Walton. In the text, Jack provides a potential replacement for John Thomas Buryan, a like-named character present in Somers's memory of the nightmare years spent in Cornwall during the war. A farmer, and rough-spoken man's man like Jack, Buryan had been Somers's closest friend and, as his name implies, also his phal-lic "mate"—emotionally and perhaps physically. John Thomas never appears in Burstall's version of the nightmare sequence (which begins the film), thereby eliminating any foreshadowing of a potentially homoerotic "mateship" between Somers and Jack.[26] As to their relationship, little trace of sexuality remains at all. The intensity of Jack's approach to Somers may seem sexual, but it turns out to be political, the less-intimate intensity of a patriotic cause in place of personal attraction. Jack is obsessed with enlisting Somers and his talents in the service of Kangaroo. On film Jack's equally obsessive eroticism always proves heterosexual and evenly divided between his wife, Victoria, and his mate's wife, Harriet. He ap-proaches Harriet sexually twice during the film, crudely, directly, and in Somers's presence, to the point that she walks away both times, angered and insulted.

Colin Friels's mellow version of Somers seems less upset by this than Harriet and, similarly, less emotionally involved with Jack in every way as compared with Somers in the text. On film, any attraction Somers has to Jack also proves im-personal, like Jack's interest in him, only now artistically rather than politically driven. As Jack makes use of Somers (or tries to) for his cause, Somers in turn makes use of Jack for his art. He becomes fascinated with his new Australian friend's marriage, his colorful language, and his covert political activities, but fascinated at a distance as a writer would be by his subject. As Somers learns more about Jack's politics and moves closer to the Diggers, this changes, and feeling does begin to replace literary curiosity. Hardly erotic, however, this feeling turns out to be Somers's growing sense of alarm and fear for his and Harriet's personal safety. His prolonged entanglement with the Diggers and Kangaroo, or really his reluctance to give them an outright no, results partly from Jack's intimidating presence and the threat he consistently projects.

Somers's relationship with Kangaroo, Jack's general, more closely approximates the text because here the homoerotic element is clearly present. In all three leadership novels, personal male intimacy proves critical to Lawrence's vision of a perfected social and political system. Blood brotherhood—intellectual, emotional, and physical—becomes the individual unit or building block for the complete communal structure, assuming that the brother-mates love and trust one another completely and are willing to acknowledge which dark god within them is naturally superior, which naturally subservient. Burstall's adaptation accepts the challenge of examining this controversial leadership formula along with Lawrence and through the developing, although soon aborted, connection between Somers and Kangaroo. In the text, Lawrence's Kangaroo offers a corrupt version of mateship from the start. He claims insistently to love Somers, but really seems far more interested in forcing Somers to love him. Also, the potential relationship between these two men hardly seems fraternal in the novel so much as parental, with Kangaroo wishing to assume the ultimate authority of fatherhood over Somers. The original Kangaroo, Ben Cooley, projects an un-Lawrentian sort of paternity: Jewish, marsupial, and ultimately so all-encompassing as to become de facto motherhood instead of fatherhood. Lawrence's Somers eventually realizes he must break free from, and ultimately denounce, Kangaroo's male maternalism or else it will destroy him.

In Burstall's film, Hugh Keays-Byrne's Kangaroo still makes his love offering to Somers and loudly demands reciprocation, yet Lawrence's racial and parental implications in the novel become disrupted or blurred. Burstall's Kangaroo remains both nameless and raceless. He is never called Ben Cooley, never identified as Jewish, and if anything he appears purely Anglo-Saxon—even more British than Australian. This ethnic alteration accords with a larger pattern of erasure already established in discussion of the earlier Lawrence films. Every one of them, with the exception of Anthony Pelissier's *Rocking Horse Winner,* omits all reference to Jews or Jewishness and all trace of Lawrentian anti-Semitism as well.

If not Jewish, Burstall's Kangaroo doesn't seem remotely maternal either. He looks and acts more like a stern father or, in his dealings with Somers, like an elder brother, somewhat more in keeping with Lawrence's idealized vision. With these revised racial and familial associations in mind, it is possible to suggest that Burstall's Kangaroo may have been inspired by Oliver Reed's Gerald in *Women in Love,* another Anglo-Saxon elder brother attempting to control an unruly "family," his real siblings as well as a potential blood brother in Rupert Birkin. This parallel may account for Hugh Keays-Byrne's peculiar appearance and mannerisms as Kangaroo, both of which were harshly attacked by reviewers. Keays-

Byrnes's character in no way resembles Lawrence's Kangaroo, who has a long ("Jewish") face exaggerated by a pince-nez and an ample stomach resembling a pouch. Instead, like Oliver Reed, he is heavily built yet hardly soft in the middle. Both actors also wear similar mustaches and spend a good deal of time in dead-panned, brooding immobility—to an extreme in both films and at the expense of dramatic action. Keays-Byrne even appears for one or two scenes in *Kangaroo* wearing evening dress, again striking wooden poses inescapably familiar to anyone who has seen *Women in Love*. Perhaps this resemblance is meant to complete a dual parallel between the potential Friels–Keays-Byrne "mateship" in *Kangaroo* and its counterpart in *Women in Love,* the failed blood brotherhood between Alan Bates's character and Reed's.

As in Lawrence's novel, Kangaroo is put forward on film as Somers's (and Australia's) potential leader, politically and militarily, as well as his potential father, elder brother, or lover.[27] As a public figure, Kangaroo remains unconvincing, as does his private army of Diggers, so that Lawrence's leadership issue suffers diminishment, even inadvertent parody, in Burstall's adaptation. Perhaps wisely, Lawrence chose not to show too much of the Diggers in his novel, the one exception being their disruption of the Socialist rally by counting Willie Struthers out. Even the riot or "Row in Town" that follows from this incident is recounted rather than shown, as Jack Calcott describes it to Somers after the fact.

By contrast, Tim Burstall turns Somers (and the film audience) into eyewitnesses, not only to the riot but earlier to the Diggers training somewhere in the outback in preparation for civil war. Both sequences prove less than compelling, suggesting that Burstall might better have emulated Lawrence's indirection regarding military affairs. The training scenes seem "Boy Scoutish," less sinister than simply juvenile, so as to accord with Harriet's description of the Diggers as a group of children playing war. Beyond this, the riot itself, clearly intended to climax the film, fizzles rather than explodes, a little like the anarchist's bomb in the novel that "hadn't much kick in it," according to Jack, even though it did go off.[28] The street fight has been too slowly and carefully orchestrated, so that its effect is stagy and sedate. Also, the suggestion of pretense and play that blunted the training scenes compromises the battle as well. Both the Diggers and the Socialists seem unconvincing as combatants or, worse, downright silly, with Kangaroo emerging as the silliest figure of all. Leading his men into battle riding a white horse, wearing medals and a feathered hat, he makes for an easy target in more ways than one. Of all the Diggers, only John Walton as Jack projects sufficient force of personality and appearance to capture Lawrence's serious flirtation with leadership among men—its intensity, its attractiveness, its real threat of danger and death. As effective as Walton may be, however, he remains unable to bear the full weight of *Kangaroo*'s homopolitical baggage all by himself.[29]

Jack receives some unexpected help here from Judy Davis's Harriet, the film's only other fully realized and convincing character. Davis, however, hardly offers to carry this baggage so much as unpack it, perhaps even more quickly and efficiently than Lawrence does himself. It takes the whole novel for Somers to receive Kangaroo's "offer," to ponder it almost to obsession, and then finally to reject it. Davis's Harriet accomplishes all this in a single scene (not to be found in the text) where she confronts Kangaroo on her own initiative, "woman to man," explicitly questions his beliefs, and then dismisses him as a dictator and a sham. When he preaches to her on the critical importance of family in Australia, she forces him to admit that he has none of his own. Similarly, she catches him in a contradiction between political mateship and lordship—his lip service to the first as opposed to his real desire for the second. Finally, Harriet forces the issue of ideology to the film's surface (something which never happens in the text), comparing Kangaroo to Mussolini and asking him point blank if he's a fascist—a question he never answers. When Harriet returns home from her encounter, she describes Kangaroo to Somers as overripe "to the point of rotten." Her statement looks ahead less to the film's ending than to the novel's, where Kangaroo's wound reveals his inward state spiritually as well as physically. Lawrence's Ben Cooley has been shot in the guts, so his "sewers leak" as he's dying and "an unpleasant, discernible stench" fills the room.[30] Burstall's Kangaroo has been shot more politely in the chest, so despite Harriet's prophesy, no similar scene or image arises in the film.

Along with selfhood, then, Lawrence's leadership issue also fails to survive on screen. The marital issue, on the other hand, does survive and more, leaving only one-third of Lawrence's original triptych intact, or providing *Kangaroo* with an "adaptation average" of one-for-three (perhaps more impressive in baseball than in filmmaking, but perhaps not). The fact that Lawrentian marriage comes across effectively can be credited largely to Judy Davis, who like John Walton bears more than her share of the film's weight. Davis's performance gives Harriet Somers an attractive edge that nicely offsets her husband's bland, accepting nature. Together, Harriet and Somers create a couple juxtaposed by their differences, yet never to the extremes of separation or surrender. Instead, they strike an effective balance that calls for further discussion in relation to their marital counterparts in *Kangaroo,* Jack and Victoria Calcott.

Critics of Lawrence's *Kangaroo* have often mentioned that Somers and Harriet's ongoing "discussion" as husband and wife deliberately mimics the political conflict taking place just beyond their bedroom window. In the chapter called "Harriet and Lovat at Sea in Marriage," the novel's narrator speculates on what options remain available to the Somerses, or to any married couple, once the honeymoon glow of perfect love wears off. One possibility, in accord with the chapter's serio-satiric metaphor, is to steer the ship of marriage "into the rather grey Atlantic of true friendship and companionship, still keeping the flag of perfect love bravely afloat." Most wives, including Harriet, seem to favor this option—a marital comradeship not far removed from the political socialism that Willie Struthers hopes to impose on the whole of Australia. Another option proves more attractive to husbands like Somers, who remain skeptical about socialism or even democracy taken to extremes. For them, an altogether different body of marital waters, "the vast Pacific . . . of lord-and-masterdom," would allow a man to rule his wife (in theory at least) as Kangaroo hopes to rule Australia.[31]

In Tim Burstall's adaptation of *Kangaroo,* this marital analogy undergoes major modification. While Burstall retains some language from the "At Sea" chapter, he drops Lawrence's ideological comparison in favor of something less abstract. On screen, it is not the political odd couple, Struthers and Kangaroo, but the Calcotts who model opposed marital options. On film, the Calcott marriage proves even more schizophrenic than in the text, combining two mutually exclusive extremes within the same explosive relationship. On one hand, Jack remains lord and master of his domain, so that any serious infraction on Victoria's part would lead to violent consequences, and she knows it. On the other hand, this same dictatorial marriage allows a degree of freedom beyond socialism, to the point of sexual anarchy. Jack accepts no marital restraints upon his own erotic inclinations, such as the overt pursuit of his friend's wife. While otherwise fearing her husband, Victoria Calcott seems completely at ease with a similar erotic freedom—as when she offers herself to Somers, for instance, innocently as a kind of gift. Burstall develops the Calcotts' marital paradox in contrast to the Somerses' capacity to balance their own oppositions rather than explode into fragments. On film, Somers and Harriet retain their separate identities, yet never to the point of Jack and Victoria's anarchy, erotic or otherwise. This same equilibrium also suggests, however, that if any issue were sufficiently crucial to one of them, the other would give ground and in a limited sense "obey." Burstall's projection of the Somerses' marriage conveys another kind of equilibrium as well: an attractive balance between their capacity for passion as against their easy and bemused familiarity with one another after ten years together. In successfully achieving this portrait of a marriage, Burstall may have gained some advantage by selecting a real married couple to play Lawrence's fictional husband and wife.

Confined by Lawrence's three-sided story, then, *Kangaroo* on film remains effective only in fragments of the whole design. Slightly distanced from Lawrence, however, the film begins to function on its own artistic power and, oddly enough, to grow more Lawrentian in the process. Tim Burstall predicted this upturn himself during his interview with Andrew Peek while the film was still being made. Burstall was asked if he planned to film *Kangaroo* using the authentic Lawrentian locations in and around Thirroul. Burstall avoided this question and instead addressed the more difficult issue of "enforced collaboration" between a writer and a director attempting to adapt his work for the screen. "When it comes to the filming, how saturated one is in Lawrence has to be translated through one's own antennae. I might come up with a set of visual metaphors which I would hope would be [both original and] Lawrentian."[32]

Burstall's camera work, separate from his retelling of Lawrence's story, effects such a balance between fidelity and imagination, although several of *Kangaroo*'s critics would probably disagree with this. The Australian reviewer Peter Craven, for instance, has described Burstall's film as "Australia's revenge" *against* D. H. Lawrence.[33] If so, it seems a deconstructive sort of payback because Burstall's critical gaze focuses even more harshly on his own country than on the famous Pommy who visited then wrote about it. Burstall expresses his criticisms visually by filming darkness and light juxtaposed, interiors against exteriors, and by putting both to Lawrentian as well as original thematic purpose. On one hand, Burstall shows his viewers many of the predictable wide horizons—Australian seascapes deliberately overexposed and filmed along a spectrum of blues and whites. Such scenes often display tropical birds, reinforcing the suggestion of freedom and natural beauty—at least outwardly or to the innocent eye of the tourist. By contrast, a second Australia becomes visible literally within this one, as it is gradually revealed by Burstall's camera. Despite the sea and the colorful birds, indoor Australia looks for all practical purposes like Victorian England, or wartime Cornwall for that matter, from which the Somerses and the Lawrences fled as soon as they could. During Burstall's interior filming—at the Somers or the Calcott cottage, within *Kangaroo*'s fortress-estate, or at Struthers's union hall—there never seems to be enough light for a proper exposure, as if to imply that those unnaturally bright and open seascapes were only part of the truth. Because of Burstall's deliberate underexposure, many of the film's indoor scenes appear sepia-tinted and bathed in warm colors—yellow light emanating from heavily shaded lamps, often illuminating red backgrounds. Red, of course, could be the color of passion, or of "politics and red-hot treason" for that matter, yet never in this film. Instead, *Kangaroo*'s reds are the plush, ultimately stifling tones of leftover Victorian culture, its questionable values and tastes all but inescapable on screen. Harriet Somers first encounters them on the hideously painted walls of "Torestin," her new Australian home, and she is appalled. Afterwards, they appear as background in *Kangaroo* again and again, always with negative connotations: the formal flowers that decorate Kangaroo's dinner table, for instance, or the rows of heavy red volumes just behind his head as he courts Somers and preaches stale ideology. Later in the film, the specific objects change, but their colors remain the same. Kangaroo lies dying with a bloody bandage on his chest, resting on a bed heavily canopied in Victorian scarlet.

In his 1987 essay in the *D. H. Lawrence Review,* Harris Ross argued that unlike Lawrence, Tim Burstall fails to exploit Australian topography as "the objective correlative for the writer's quest to define himself."[34] In light of the above details, this may not be accurate, although it is clear that Ross was not thinking of interior topography when he made his criticism. Encountering the anachronistic inside-landscape of Australia wherever he turns, Somers on screen takes the purely Lawrentian step of escaping, as he did from Cornwall, literally trading darkness for light, enclosure for space to breathe. He seeks the bright Australian seacoast, either by himself or with Harriet, so that it may become an objective correlative in Burstall's film—for Somers's flight from suffocation in the first place, then for his celebration in privacy of Eros and individual identity.[35]

In an original twist on Lawrence's quest, Tim Burstall suggests that Somers himself brings considerable Victorian baggage with him to the beach, so that Australia is not solely responsible for hampering his quest. Somers's baggage is his clothing, literally and figuratively, causing him easily to be the most overdressed character in the film and probably the most overheated tourist ever to visit Australia in tropical winter. The man even gardens in a jacket and tie. He walks along the beach with Harriet, stubbornly attired in dark trousers, hat, tie, and suspenders—his bare feet the only concession to sunlight and warmth. While such details may be historically accurate, they also function in Burstall's film to suggest that Lawrence's protagonist is really part of the problem he seeks to solve—part Victorian-Puritan himself as he admits to Victoria, another belated and deliberately named Victorian, albeit less repressed than he is.

It is tempting to suggest that what Burstall tries to show in *Kangaroo* is Somers gradually shedding his protective coverings in bright, hot seaside Australia. Yet this may simplify what the film actually demonstrates. The stripping down of Somers on film is barely accomplished, then immediately reversed. The film contains one lighthearted and adeptly executed scene, for instance, in which the wind carries off Somers's hat, dropping it into the sea to deflate him as he preaches innate aristocracy (Kangaroo-like) to Harriet. Elsewhere, Somers does appear nude, again reminding us of Ken Russell's influential filming of Alan Bates in *Women in Love.* Colin Friels's two nude scenes in *Kangaroo* are worth examining somewhat further for a number of reasons. For one thing, they extend Russell's pattern in *Women in Love* (and Lawrence's pattern in general) of favoring male over female nudity. Like Glenda Jackson and Jennie Linden, Judy Davis never appears unclothed, not even during her most intimate scenes with her husband. More to the issue at hand, however, the two male nude scenes in *Kangaroo* are clearly intended as an interfaced pair—either as complication and catharsis or as cultural disease and potential cure. The first occurs during the "Nightmare" sequence with which Tim Burstall begins his film. Somers is ordered to strip for his military physical, which takes place in a dark, dingy room similar to those he will later encounter in Australia. Somers strips, surrounded by formally dressed doctors and officers who enjoy tormenting him. He is declared consumptive— although one would never guess by looking at Colin Friels's healthy physique— and as in the text, he is made to suffer humiliation and the sense of having been unmanned as well as unclothed. The second nude scene in *Kangaroo* is the film's objective correlative for Somers's release from all of this, at least temporarily, since he is destined to take a step backwards near the end. The scene begins with Somers walking naked into the sea and cleansing himself many times over—washing away the earlier nude scene, or at least its memory, and along with it the more recent and again tainted encounters with the Calcotts and Kangaroo.

Harriet joins her husband as he emerges from the sea, and they make love, all in keeping with the text. This love scene, which is the film's only explicitly sexual moment, has been criticized for copying a similar and more famous scene in *From Here to Eternity* showing Deborah Kerr and Burt Lancaster making love in the Hawaiian surf. This criticism may not be fully justified, however, since even if the imitation is deliberate, the resulting "flaw" remains external to the film or "incidental" in Aristotelian terms. The scene, in other words, could prove effective despite the imitation, just as Jennie Linden's performance as Ursula could succeed despite her physical resemblance to Debbie Reynolds. Thematically, the love scene seems appropriate as a climax to Somers's symbolic act of disrobing and purification, as well as a rededication to his private deities of Eros and self in place of the public agendas he has been toying with. The scene is again deliberately overexposed, in keeping with Burstall's other seascapes, becoming ever-brighter as the action becomes more passionate. Finally the camera "looks away," as it did in Marc Allegret's *L'Amant de Lady Chatterley*, but now by panning upward toward the sky as the married lovers embrace. Because of Burstall's open-apertured filming, the effect is a unique fade to white, as opposed to Allegret's more familiar fade to black.

A word seems in order here on the soundtrack that accompanies such manipulations of color and light, partly because music reinforces meaning in *Kangaroo* and partly because it helps account for the film's uncertain ending. In creating the score for *Kangaroo*, Nathan Waks depended heavily on a single work of music, Dvorak's Quartet in F major, opus 96, and particularly on its second or "Lento" movement. This musical source might not be recognized, even by a viewer familiar with the piece, because Dvorak's string quartet has been fully orchestrated for the film and played at a faster tempo than originally marked.

This musical adaptation within a literary adaptation becomes the film's celebratory leitmotif and serves as background score for all of Burstall's "oceanic" sequences including the love scene just discussed. It plays for the last time during the film's closing sequence, as Richard and Harriet leave Australia, only now the accompanying visual imagery no longer seems celebratory. Somers appears fully and formally reclothed, so that in departing he seems exactly the same as when he arrived—dark-suited, hatted, and again wearing his inescapable tie. The final color combinations prove less than hopeful as well, with the film's closing seascape shot at twilight rather than in bright sun. While evening may be appropriate for Somers's farewell to Australia, it ends the film amid some imagistic ambiguity with the vital and usually brilliant seacoast now darkly tinted in yellows and reds. Perhaps some resolution of such mixed visual and auditory signals lies in the idea of a journey and quest haltingly begun yet by no means over or abandoned. This conflation of final images, in other words, may simply suggest that what Harris Ross termed "the writer's quest to define himself" remains unfinished in Australia, yet about to be continued elsewhere.[36] That Dvorak subtitled his F major quartet "The American" provides an oblique clue as to exactly where that will be—for Richard and Harriet and for the real-life Lawrences as well.

Perhaps because of such overfine implications, critical opinions of *Kangaroo* have focused negatively on its understatement and restraint—in the *Masterpiece Theater* sense of those terms—often reaching the conclusion that it should have been a stronger, more compelling film than it became. My own assessment of *Kangaroo* accords with these judgments, especially with the idea that it promises more, or even appears capable of more, than it finally provides. The critical problem for me, however, is less a matter of caution or subtlety than of the whole remaining somehow less than the sum of its parts, especially its best parts. *Kangaroo* proves capable of transcendence, but only in flashes which are over far too soon—in a dual imagery just briefly glimpsed, for instance, which overtly conveys Tim Burstall's vision as filmmaker while implicitly preserving Lawrence's as writer. Despite such bright moments, however, *Kangaroo* on film seems unable to sustain its own best efforts or, as a result, to remain alive in memory as *Women in Love* has despite significant flaws. The phenomenon of adaptive success in glimpses, or brief moments of clarity, will be taken up again in my final chapter as typical of the fifty-year effort to capture Lawrence on film.

# 9
# *Priest of Love:* A Last Look Back, a First Look Ahead

C hristopher Miles's *Priest of Love* offers a divergent yet fitting subject for the conclusion of this study by being both unique and representative at the same time. Of the ten Lawrence feature productions released since 1949, *Priest of Love* is the only biography and the only film not grounded in a particular work of fiction.[1] All the same, Miles's *Priest* reveals close ties to the other Lawrence productions by way of their shared preoccupations and also by way of their shared writers and directors. *Priest* is the second of three Lawrence scripts by Alan Plater, for instance, following *The Virgin and the Gypsy* in 1970 and preceding *Coming Through,* an account of Lawrence's early life directed by Peter Barber-Fleming for BBC-TV in 1986.[2] In fact, if film and television can be spliced together momentarily here, *Coming Through* and *Priest* constitute Plater's rather complete screen biography of Lawrence, with the television production ending in 1912 and the film picking up in 1914, then shifting its focus to the final years of Lawrence's life. *Priest* turns out to be one of three Lawrence projects by Christopher Miles, although only two of them have been completed. Miles had been Plater's director a decade before *Priest,* when the two worked together on *Virgin.* Miles had also attempted an adaptation of *The Plumed Serpent,* a film which he was eventually forced to abandon.

*Priest of Love* belongs to another kind of trilogy as well, separate from the efforts of any single writer or director exploring his interest in Lawrence. Despite being the only large-screen biography to date, *Priest* remains part of a wider Lawrence revival that took place in the 1980s, the centennial decade of his birth. This revival (at least in the media) shifted emphasis away from his works, where it had been in the late 1960s and 1970s, and toward the man himself, attempting to probe his complex ideology, his more complex marriage, and the lifelong controversies surrounding his career as a writer. It is tempting to see this later Lawrence revival as an instance of fascination with the "mysterious other"—that is, as England and America in the 1980s looking back sixty years at a figure strikingly unlike themselves and radically opposed to their values and the drift of the century they shared. At the same time, however, this recent preoccupation with Lawrence involves reconciliation as well as curiosity. Viewed through the lens of the more recent decade, Lawrence and his beliefs have been refocused, even softened around the edges, in the interests of familiarity and contemporary comfort. Such modulation occurs in a triptych of 1980s Lawrence media-biographies if we include Peter Barber-Fleming's televised *Coming Through* and Tim Burstall's *Kangaroo*, a deliberate representation of Lawrence through Somers by the director's own admission.

If *Priest* somehow captures the spirit of Lawrence on film in the 1980s, it also captures the spirit of the whole effort, now spanning a half century, to present the artist and his works on screen. The typicality within the uniqueness of *Priest* makes it especially useful as a final point of reference for this study. Like so many of the Lawrence films, *Priest* often proves compelling, even remarkable, despite significant flaws, but only in what I have previously termed "glimpses"—brief instances of clarity ending far too soon and before they can be fully realized or examined. Also, like so many of the Lawrence films, *Priest* remains heavily reliant on the conventions of cinematic realism, in this case partly because it attempts to translate biography rather than imaginative fiction into film. Here again *Priest* seems appropriate to conclude with, since it displays both the merits and limitations of the realistic studio production. This duality allows for an overview of what has already been accomplished in Lawrence filming, as well as a glimpse of what directions still remain unexplored. Such explorations have already begun, in fact, through at least one new Lawrence film that replaces the studio ensemble with the independent filmmaker and the restrictions of realism with the possibilities of its experimental alternatives.

An insight into the realistic assumptions and intentions behind *Priest of Love* is revealed in the studio publicity that preceded the film's opening in 1981. An especially interesting press release contains two pages of photographs configured to resemble snapshots in a family album, even down to the illusion of handwritten captions and paper corners holding the photos in place. The first page shows actual photographs of Lawrence and Frieda at Mitla Temple in Oaxaca and at the Villa Mirenda near Florence, as well as posed camera portraits of Dorothy Brett, Angelo Ravagli, and Lawrence himself. The second page appears to replicate all this, only now the snapshots have been pulled from Christopher Miles's film.³ It is clear from them that Miles has avoided the studio in favor of several authentic locations (Mexico and Italy among them) where the Lawrences visited or lived. It is also clear that Miles has attempted the same degree of visual authenticity in casting, so that the real photo of Lawrence appears indistinguishable from its companion image of Ian McKellen playing him. This holds true for Dorothy Brett and the actress Penelope Keith and even beyond the principal figures to include several minor characters: Mike Gwilym's John Middleton Murry, James Faulkner's Aldous Huxley, and even Adrienne Burgess's Katherine Mansfield in little more than a walk-on appearance, albeit a photographically exact one.

Seeming to contradict this insistence on visual authenticity are several factual lapses in *Priest,* some by way of omissions, others by way of outright and often amusing mistakes. With location, for instance, Lawrence sails for America at the beginning of the film from England rather than Australia, where he actually embarked, with no mention made that he ever visited that continent at all. With casting, in among the film's many look-alikes (including Ava Gardner at the end of her career as a strikingly credible Mabel Dodge) is Tony Luhan, who is inexplicably misidentified in the press releases as a "Mexican Indian" and played by Jorge Rivero in seeming parody of countless B Westerns—an erotic Tonto to Mabel Dodge's literary Lone Ranger. My point in observing such countertendencies in *Priest of Love* toward photographic exactitude on one hand and comic cliché on the other is not to take Christopher Miles to task on scholarly grounds. Nor is it to begin a systematic comparison between his film and Lawrence's life or even Harry T. Moore's biography from which *Priest* takes its title and upon which it is partly based. Rather, the purpose of pointing out such overt unevenness is to identify inconsistency itself as the truly consistent pattern, not only within *Priest* but within the whole enterprise of screening Lawrence, which this film comes belatedly to represent.

Critics and reviewers did not focus on inconsistency when *Priest of Love* first appeared in 1981 but instead explicitly reflected it in their own writing and in their inability to agree on much of anything regarding the film. Those who weren't praising *Priest* to excess, it seems, were damning it to cinematic oblivion. Among the most extreme celebrants was Will Jones, a film reviewer who declared *Priest* to be "the best film biography" he had ever seen and also "the most successful Lawrence film of all."⁴ Only slightly less enthusiastic than Jones, Judith Crist concluded one of her two reviews of *Priest* by describing it as "a beautifully conceived and designed re-creation of literary history seen from a sophisticated and balanced perspective, touched with a humor and irony that are rare and refreshing for the genre."⁵ Gary Arnold opened his *Washington Post* review in cheerful accord with both Crist and Jones, calling the film "an unprecedented delight: a movie biography of a great writer that blends devotion and historical accuracy with tart, and ultimately stirring, character delineation. I doubt that anyone has ever filmed a more intelligent or satisfying literary bio."[6]

Among the less convinced were *Times* critic Geoff Brown, who declared *Priest* to be "irretrievably crippled by a string of misguided assumptions,"[7] and *New York Times* critic Vincent Canby, who dismissed it even more bluntly as "a foolish film."[8] Similarly harsh judgments were made by John Coleman, who concluded his *New Statesman* review by calling *Priest* "fodder for Lawrence-loathers"[9] and by Stanley Kauffmann, who questioned the need for a Lawrence screen biography at all, then ended his *New Republic* article by likening Miles's effort to "a failed TV special."[10] Kauffmann balanced his condemnation of *Priest* somewhat, however, by strongly praising Ian McKellen as Lawrence, noting that McKellen's portrayal of genius proved no less convincing than his highly successful portrayal of mediocrity as Antonio Salieri in the Broadway run of Peter Shaffer's *Amadeus*.

Here Kauffmann remained in accord with *Priest*'s more enthusiastic reviewers, who had also complimented McKellen with similar comparisons. Kauffmann split sharply with them, however, over the film's Frieda as played by Janet Suzman, whom he complained "doesn't act . . . [so much as] carries on," marring the film even further.[11] By contrast, those critics who cheered *Priest* tended to praise Suzman especially, at times even singling her out at McKellen's (or Lawrence's) expense by suggesting that the filmmakers intended her strong portrayal of a remarkable woman as their reassessment of Frieda and her influence upon her more famous husband both personally and professionally. Such observations—if accurately reflecting Miles and Plater's intent for Suzman's Frieda—link *Priest* even more closely to Peter Barber-Fleming's *Coming Through* and Tim Burstall's *Kangaroo*. Both of these productions also foreground Frieda (or her fictional surrogate, Harriet Somers) and exploit the talents of two gifted actresses, Helen Mirren and Judy Davis, to reexamine her role in Lawrence's life and work from a contemporary feminist point of view.

Reviewers like Stanley Kauffmann who criticized *Priest* often focused beyond individual performances upon broader matters such as structure or the filmmakers' governing vision of their subject. Several suggested that *Priest* had been compromised by Miles and Plater's overly "reverential" attitude toward Lawrence—a word frequently encountered among the negative reviews. Andrew Sarris, writing for the *Village Voice,* used this term to describe Miles's earlier approach in *The Virgin and the Gypsy,* then went on to complain that *Priest of Love* again "tends to take Lawrence's messianic vision at face value. As much as I admire Lawrence, I would prefer to see him treated by a moralist and an ironist than by a true believer."[12] Similarly, Ellen Pfeifer, reviewing *Priest* for the *Boston Herald American,* characterized it as an "over-reverent and pretentious treatment of Lawrence."[13]

Sheila Benson suggested in a *Los Angeles Times* article that the film   proves confusing "possibly because producer-director Christopher Miles was so reverential" toward his central character.[14] Even more dismissive, Vincent Canby commented in his *New York Times* review, "The movie may be called *Priest of Love,* but it's clear that Mr. Miles and his associates have raised . . . [Lawrence] to sainthood."[15]

Following Sheila Benson, several commentators, including many who had enjoyed *Priest,* suggested that Miles's Lawrentian zeal added needlessly to the film's convoluted plot and confusing time line. Some contended that a full appreciation and understanding of *Priest* would be impossible for audiences without prior knowledge of Lawrence's life and work. Others complained that as disciples rather than objective biographers the filmmakers attempted to include too much about Lawrence within their two-hour time frame, thereby failing to distinguish between significant matters and trivial ones. Still others found Miles's heavy dependence on flashbacks disorienting, claiming that even with prior knowledge of Lawrence it was impossible for them to follow the film's sudden and unpredictable jumps from one time and place to another. One critic suggested (correctly in my opinion) that some of Miles's flashbacks even contain flashbacks of their own.[16]

Mistakes about the film by reviewers, even normally careful reviewers like Vincent Canby and John Simon, offer tangible evidence that *Priest of Love* is not an easy film to follow. Canby and Simon both noticed the film's only reference to Lawrence's homoeroticism, for instance, yet both committed the same error in doing so. The reference occurs during *Priest*'s "bathing scene," set in Cornwall and depicting Lawrence and a male companion swimming together, then sitting nude on the beach with Lawrence drying the other man's back. The scene ends when the two are approached by the coastal police who make suggestive comments ("What a pretty picture!"), causing Lawrence's companion to retreat in embarrassment and fear of arrest. Canby and Simon both identify this shy companion as John Middleton Murry. The man does resemble Mike Gwilym who plays Murry, particularly from a distance and in the very brief glimpse of him in this scene. He's not Gwilym, however, but an actor named Graham Faulkner playing the walk-on part of William Henry Hocking, the farmer Lawrence befriended during his stay in Cornwall. As if this weren't confusing enough, particularly for a viewer unfamiliar with Lawrence's life, Hocking is never mentioned by name on screen or in the credits, and is identified only as "a Cornish farmer" in the publicity materials that describe the scene.[17]

Such vagueness may help explain why *Priest of Love* dropped from view so quickly after its release. Even if *Priest* were primarily intended for informed audiences, however, it is unusual that the *D. H. Lawrence Review* (normally a faithful reviewer of Lawrentian cinema) failed to review the film. No other serious journals, literary or cinematic, paid *Priest* much attention either, so that its only notable discussion, beyond the routine reviews, appeared in two obscure newspaper articles that intelligently discussed Miles's film within the context of Lawrence filming in general as that endeavor stood in 1981.[18] Since then, references to *Priest* have remained few and far between, although when they occasionally surface they seem just as conflicted or inconsistent as the early reviews or, really, as the film itself. A dismissive entry on *Priest of Love* in Robert A. Nowlan and Gwendolyn Wright Nowlan's *Films of the Eighties* calls it a "disappointing, aimless picture" about "the last years in the life of D. H. Lawrence."[19] By contrast, Charles Sawyer harks back to *Priest* in his 1987 review of *Kangaroo*, judging it better both cinematically and biographically, and complaining that "*Priest of Love* is a film that vanished too quickly and is a more worthy 'Lawrence effort' than *Kangaroo*."[20]

I share Sawyer's disappointment that *Priest* vanished too quickly, and without sufficient critical attention, yet for different reasons. *Priest* deserves further examination not because it is "worthy," as Sawyer suggests, but because it is typical. Rather than being remarkably better than *Kangaroo*, *Priest of Love* seems remarkably like *Kangaroo* in the way both films attempt to make sense of Lawrence from their shared 1980s perspective. Beyond the one decade, *Priest* also proves remarkably like all the Lawrence films released in the second half of the twentieth century. This similarity is most apparent in the remarkable unevenness of each film separately (even the best of them) and likewise of the whole enterprise of filming Lawrence or attempting to—matters I'll take up presently after examining *Priest*'s position within the more limited framework of its own decade.

The typicality of *Priest* as a Lawrence film of the 1980s is primarily a function of its two main characters, Lawrence and Frieda, as imagined by Christopher Miles and as interpreted by Ian McKellen and Janet Suzman. Unlike Alan Bates's sixtified Birkin/Lawrence, McKellen's main character seems much closer to Colin Friels's tamed Somers/Lawrence and to Kenneth Branagh's youthful Bert in *Coming Through*. All three emerge as instances of genius and volatility under control and of strangeness made familiar to present times. Branagh's Bert Lawrence has been softened by his youth and sense of humor so that he becomes winsome, almost puppyish in his energy and playfulness. Neither McKellen's Lawrence nor Friels's Somers shares these qualities, yet both are domesticated just the same, now as house-husbands rather than as lovable boys. Both of these "irritable geniuses" are depicted in a deliberate series of kitchen scenes, for instance, either cooking or else helping out with the chores, with McKellen's Lawrence even wearing an apron at one point, preparing a lobster dinner, and serving it waiterlike to Frieda and their assembled guests.

It is important to mention, however, that this scene moves quickly from domesticity to domestic violence when Lawrence objects to Frieda's smoking during dinner, first grabbing at her cigarette, then dousing her with water in front of everyone. By contrast, neither Branagh's young Bert nor Friels's mature Somers seems capable of such nastiness, with Somers looking less like an abusive husband, in fact, than a potential abuse victim himself. The point here is that Christopher Miles may be more honest about Lawrence than the other two biographical directors, at least when it comes to temper tantrums and domestic violence, both of which figure in at least two other important scenes in *Priest of Love*. Miles's revelations of Lawrence's darker side, however, don't go much further than this, so *Priest* remains silent about his racism, his anti-Semitism, and his eventual preoccupation with authoritarian leadership. Such silence in *Priest* demonstrates its accord, beyond the 1980s, with Lawrentian cinema as a whole. As noted elsewhere in this study, Lawrence's anti-Semitism and racism remain unacknowledged in all the Lawrence films with the single oblique exception of Anthony Pelissier's *Rocking Horse Winner.*

Before leaving Lawrence as projected in the 1980s, I should mention the challenge of representing imagination on screen, literary imagination in particular. In depicting a canonized writer like Lawrence, the need arises to demonstrate his work or at least to establish some visible basis for his reputation. During this decade of Lawrence film biographies, such a challenge bore most heavily on Burstall in *Kangaroo* and Miles in *Priest of Love,* since Barber-Fleming's *Coming Through* depicts only the promising young Lawrence, about to emerge but as yet unproven and unknown. While both Burstall and Miles devise some inventive strategies for presenting Lawrence as artist, neither *Priest* nor *Kangaroo* finally seems compelling in this regard. As mentioned in the previous chapter, Burstall shows Somers/Lawrence in the act of writing *Kangaroo* or, more accurately, in the act of plagiarizing it from fragments of other people's conversations, which he carefully records in his notebook. Miles, by contrast, develops Lawrence not as a *bricoleur* with a nice ear for dialogue but, equally unsatisfying, as a compulsive shredder of his own manuscripts. When he's not attacking Frieda in a temper tantrum, he's burning or tearing up his own works, so frequently in fact that the film contains more scenes of literary destruction than creation. The film implies that any genius as prolific as Lawrence always has enough material to spare in sacrifice to his temperamental dark gods.

More effectively, Miles also incorporates several passages from Lawrence's letters and poems into his film by way of voice-over or direct recitation. Two Lawrence poems are quoted several times during *Priest,* providing the film with a set of unifying choruses. "Bei Hennef" becomes the film's love refrain, for instance, as Lawrence and Frieda repeat it to one another often in a private ceremony of recommitment:

> You are the call and I am the answer,
> You are the wish, and I the fulfillment,
> You are the night, and I the day.
>> What else? It is perfect enough.
>> It is perfectly complete,
>> You and I,
>> What more———?

> Strange, how we suffer in spite of this![21]

In deliberate juxtaposition to "Bei Hennef," Lawrence's "Red Herring" from *Pansies* provides the film with a comic refrain, especially as Lawrence teaches it to Angelo Ravagli, then to Piero Pini, neither of whom speak English. After the landlord and the *contadino* memorize "Red Herring" (becoming firm Lawrentian disciples in the process), they recite it in heavy Italian accents to anyone willing to listen:

> My father was a working man
>> and a collier was he,
> at six in the morning they turned him down
>> and they turned him up for tea.
> My mother was a superior soul
>> a superior soul was she,
>> cut out to play a superior role
> in the god-damn bourgeoisie.[22]

Like Burstall, Miles also eventually risks losing his audience, not by including poetry but by filming Lawrence sitting down to write, and actually writing, on screen. This happens late in *Priest of Love* when Lawrence breaks a long spell of creative inactivity to begin work on *Lady Chatterley's Lover*. Approximately the final thirty minutes of Miles's film deal with the genesis of Lawrence's last novel from conception to composition at the Villa Mirenda, to laborious printing and eventual publication by Pino Orioli in Florence. Miles's *Lady Chatterley* episode is deliberately juxtaposed, through a series of cuts, to a parallel episode on Lawrence's renewed interest in painting late in life. Here again, the painting sequence takes in composition (of *Il Contadino*, with Piero Pini serving as model), then preparation for the exhibit at the Warren Gallery in London, then finally confiscation of several paintings by the censors and police, with John Gielgud's

Herbert G. Muskett in charge of the proceedings. One could argue, then, that near the end of *Priest* Miles does directly accept the challenge of presenting the artist *qua* artist on screen and of establishing some tangible evidence of his accomplishments. A problem here, however, is that Miles's emphasis distorts Lawrence's achievement in presenting it to a general audience. The impression he creates is that before 1928 Lawrence's artistic career had essentially been prologue or lengthy apprenticeship for his "masterpiece," *Lady Chatterley's Lover*, with the paintings providing a set of erotic illustrations in parallel to the text. If anything, such suggestions reinforce popular stereotypes about Lawrence's work rather than replacing them with the richer, more complicated truth.

What then becomes of Frieda Lawrence, along with her husband, in the hands of these filmmakers and through the looking glass of the 1980s? For one thing she emerges as his feminine (and feminist) equal and opposite, partly because of the strong actresses who play her part—Helen Mirren in *Coming Through*, Judy Davis (as Harriet/Frieda) in *Kangaroo*, and Janet Suzman in *Priest of Love*. All three interpretations of Frieda project a formidable woman—not just older than her gifted husband but more seasoned and more imposing than he is in many ways. All three reveal something of the mother about them in relation to Lawrence, and two of them (Davis and Suzman) eventually assume the role of his literary collaborator as well. In one of *Priest's* best moments, for instance, Lawrence hands Frieda a notebook, asking her to write down everything she knows about female sexuality so that he can "get it right" in *Lady Chatterley's Lover*. "I'll need a bigger book," she replies.

While this trio of Friedas seems to suggest the emerging woman of the 1980s— and silent creative partner as well—this is not to say that they are all alike. Each one emphasizes a different quality in Frieda so that taken together they may approach the complexities of biographical truth. Along with her maternalism toward young Bert, for example, Helen Mirren in *Coming Through* also projects a formal dignity, perhaps intended to suggest Frieda's aristocratic background. By contrast, Judy Davis lacks any trace of this, offering instead intelligence and intuition combined, perhaps making her the most interesting cinematic Frieda of all. Finally, Janet Suzman's portrayal displays neither Mirren's dignity nor Davis's insight, but an aggressiveness of temperament and behavior instead—a capacity to explode into violence or to lapse into vulgarity. While these colorful traits surely reflect the real Frieda, they also confound the screen character when taken too far. Without either Mirren's dignity or Davis's intelligence for balance, Suzman's explosive temperament seems crude, often reducing her to a nagging wife or, worse, a shrew in caricature. Partly to blame here is Suzman's weak dialogue throughout the film (her remark about the bigger book aside), seldom insightful or intelligent and never dignified. Her most frequent line in *Priest of*

*Love*, in fact, seems to be "Lorenzo!" shouted at her husband in varying tones of anger, exasperation, or complaint.

Frieda's opposite number in *Priest of Love* (and perhaps in real life as well) is Dorothy Brett, played effectively by Penelope Keith as courteous, even tempered, and always cheerfully loyal to Lawrence. When Frieda dismisses Brett in Mexico, she returns to Taos, joining Ava Gardner's Mabel in an odd coupleship that parallels and parodies the Lawrences' relationship. Gardner and Keith don't exactly steal the show, but their life together in Taos, as Lawrentian ladies-in-waiting, creates a comedic subplot easily as interesting as the major story line. This emergence of the minor figures again suggests that *Priest* is typical of the Lawrence films, so many of which feature minor characters who prove capable of overshadowing the stars. I'm thinking of John Walton's Jack Calcott in *Kangaroo*, Ronald Squire's Uncle Oscar in the 1949 *Rocking Horse Winner*, Kay Walsh and Norman Bird as Aunt Cissie and Uncle Fred in *The Virgin and the Gypsy*, Vladek Sheybal as Loerke in *Women in Love*, Jim Carter and Judith Paris as the Harbys, brother and sister schoolmasters in *The Rainbow*, and Ann Mitchell and Elizabeth Spriggs as Mrs. Bolton and Lady Eva in Just Jaeckin's *Lady Chatterley's Lover*, an otherwise lackluster production.

It is interesting that certain names on this list provide their films with small touches of humor or at least amusing departures from the serious dramatic center. While perhaps not always Lawrentian, such departures prove typical of effective Lawrence filming. In *Priest of Love*, the Mabel/Brett submotif stands out most clearly, along with several small but memorable vignettes—Piero Pini reciting "Red Herring" to the lost Huxleys in their motorcar, or the Lawrences' maid (Piero's wife) dawdling over her dusting to examine the "obscene" paintings in close detail, or Frieda cheering Lawrence up in his final illness by telling him that instead of being destroyed, his paintings are going to be deported. It is possible to suggest that a key quality identifying the best Lawrence films is their capacity to temper shadow with light and, as a result, to avoid taking themselves too seriously or treating Lawrence with too much reverence. Such avoidance helps elevate Ken Russell's *Women in Love* above *The Rainbow* and, similarly, *The Virgin and the Gypsy* above *The Fox*.

A laugh or even a wry smile, however, always proves double-edged. If responsible for several highs in Lawrence filming, humor also accounts for several unexpected dips in the roller coaster, only now the bottomings-out occur when the humor proves unintended. At certain points, several of the Lawrence filmmakers turn heavy-handed—either too serious, too symbolic, or too reverential—with the results proving inadvertently funny, at times to the point of embarrassment. In *Priest of Love* Jorge Rivero's Tony Luhan, or more aptly "Tonto" Luhan, becomes a source of such embarrassment for the filmmakers and amusement for the audience, although this example turns out to be ironically Lawrentian in the end. Tony's image and performance betray a vision of Native Americans as innocently clichéd as Lawrence's own after he had read James Fenimore Cooper but before he had encountered the real thing. In addition, the early scene in *Priest* when Lawrence embarks for America provides an instance of failed reverence with equally comic results. McKellen's Lawrence sits aboard ship signing copies of *Kangaroo.* Directly behind his head, a bright porthole creates a halo effect, transforming him from priest into saint or, even more embarrassing, into pseudo-Savior.

Looking back from the vantage point of *Priest of Love,* it is clear that similar embarrassments have occurred throughout the effort to capture Lawrence on film. One need only recall Ken Russell's *reductio ad absurdum* of Hermione Roddice and her Bible-dance—although, in fairness to Russell, the absurdity here was intended. It was not intended, however, in Franco Nero's masturbation scene (involving a whittled twig) during Miles's *Virgin* or in Marc Allegret's own erotic whittling scene, with its tall trees falling in sexual counterpoint during *L'Amant de Lady Chatterley.* Other examples of cinematic excess turning comical include Mac, the sadistic painter in *The Rainbow,* Ursula inexplicably surrounded by horses and then colliers in the fog, and Hugh Keays-Byrne as Kangaroo, riding at the head of his Diggers foolishly decked out in medals and a feathered hat.

If a laugh reveals one major source of inconsistency in Lawrence filming, so too does an exit—graceful in certain instances but utterly botched in others. The ending of *Priest* offers a revealing instance of humor gone astray and of an awkward final bow. The film's last sequence takes place in New Mexico five years after Lawrence's death. First we see Brett, Tony, Mabel, Frieda, and the now-Americanized "Angie" Ravagli frolicking together at the ranch and dancing to the same jazz music that sent Lawrence into tantrums early in the film. Frieda stops dancing and orders Ravagli to go to France, recover and cremate Lawrence's remains, and return to Taos with the ashes. This scene closes with Ravagli looking grim and with the camera focused on a barbecue fire in absurd preview of cremation.

The next scene opens with the Phoenix figure on Lawrence's gravestone in France, then shifts back to New Mexico to show Ravagli stepping off the train with an urn under his arm and his mission complete. All of Lawrence's devotees are present, yet in accord with the biographical legend, they forget him in their excitement, leaving the urn behind at the station. Frieda realizes this just as the party drives away, runs back, and embraces the urn whispering, "I'm here." As the car starts off again for the ranch, all three Lawrentian ladies place their hands on the urn, ending the film with a vision of Lorenzo literally contained and under their control. This closing image seems appropriate to *Priest* and to the general effort in the 1980s to capture and confine Lawrence on screen. At the same time, however, *Priest's* ending comes off as excessively lighthearted and trivial, especially as we watch the group drive off into the sunset singing their gay jazz tune. Awkwardly inappropriate or not, Miles's ending appears less a mistake than a deliberate attempt at irony gone wrong—at least judging from a note written in longhand across the final page of the director's shooting script. It reads, simply and accurately, "They all have their hands on him at last!"[23]

Beyond *Priest,* endings have remained troublesome throughout all five decades of Lawrence filming, often lapsing into triteness and at times compromising otherwise competent productions. We might recall Dean Stockwell as Paul Morel, for instance, chasing his London train in the final scene of *Sons and Lovers,* pursuing the dubious new beginning it seems to offer. In a less effective production with a remarkably similar conclusion, Sammi Davis's Ursula also ends her film on the run, pursuing not a train but a rainbow, Ken Russell's trope for the celluloid promises of Oz. A summary of questionable endings to D. H. Lawrence films would have to include *Lady Chatterley's Lover,* with all three versions rejecting Lawrentian indeterminacy in favor of the happy ever after, and with each successive version doing so less credibly than the one before, finally to the point of absurdity as Ken Russell's love boat sails for Canada with John Thomas being paged by Lady Jane.

While many endings to Lawrence films visibly falter, a few of them remain memorable, again underscoring the consistent pattern of inconsistency within the venture as a whole. In Ken Russell's *Women in Love,* for example, a suitably effective final scene closes an effective production, as Birkin provides the last word (verbatim from the text) while Ursula provides the last ambivalent gaze, held in freeze-frame as the credits flash across the screen. In Mark Rydell's *The Fox,* a similarly powerful final vision closes an otherwise disappointing film and proves to be one of the most compelling (and Lawrentian) moments in the production. Rydell's final shot focuses away from the characters and on the fox instead, or at least on what's left of him. We see the creature's dead muzzle and pelt nailed to the barn, ice-encrusted from the hard winter and now thawing in the spring rain. This gives the film a deliberately grotesque closing image, hardly in keeping with a Hollywood happy ending, and appropriately suggestive of the text's own uncertainty about Henry and March and their future as husband and wife.

Perhaps the most interesting cinematic endgame of all is played by Christopher Miles himself, not in *Priest of Love* but in *The Virgin and the Gypsy,* his first Lawrence film. In its closing scenes, fantasy and reality, having been opposed throughout, finally merge as Yvette breaks free from another sort of frozen image—her sterile family standing together in motionless and silent tableau—to join the Eastwoods in a real escape that plays out like a dream. Along with Russell's ending in *Women in Love,* Miles's ending in *Virgin* adeptly completes an adept production and reveals an important truth about effective Lawrence filming in general. Simply put, the Lawrence filmmakers achieve their best results in those moments when they abandon a flatly literal or realistic approach to text in favor of something other. Since Lawrence isn't fundamentally a realistic writer (although he can pass for one and often does), this otherness helps identify the cinematic "double gesture"—the visual act which, if successful, celebrates both Lawrence's text and the filmmakers' original vision superimposed upon it. Such celebrations usually involve departures from realism in these films as subtle as Lawrence's own—something which rarely occurs, unfortunately, even in the best of them and only in fleeting glimpses.

While such departures are attempted in *Priest of Love,* they fall short of realization by proving too subtle instead of not subtle enough, too timid or understated even to be noticed. John Gielgud's Herbert G. Muskett, for example, is intended more as a symbolic presence than as a specific historical figure. Miles uses him as a composite or distillation of all the censor-morons who ever harried Lawrence or, for that matter, any provocative artist. The historical Muskett figured prominently in the *Rainbow* trial (1915) and again in the suppression of Lawrence's paintings (1929), yet remained only one of many actors in a convoluted cultural drama played out over most of Lawrence's productive life.[24] Harry T. Moore's biography, upon which Miles's film is partly based, ignores Muskett almost completely, in fact, in favor of other persecutors like William Joynson-Hicks, home secretary when *Lady Chatterley's Lover* was published. In Miles's film version of *Priest,* by contrast, Muskett appears to be Lawrence's only censor, carrying on a one-man moral campaign against him. He remains ever-present as a threat, intimidating Lawrence even when he's not on screen, and always projecting the same uncompromising stance, with his deliberately monolithic personality making Gielgud's impressive acting talents unfortunately superfluous in the role.

Along with Muskett, a nameless immigration officer also appears figuratively in *Priest of Love* as the universal tool of repressive authority—perhaps decent enough as an individual human being, yet always ready to carry out his unpleasant duty and to follow the orders of his superiors without question. Played competently by Shane Rimmer, this second extrarealistic figure again fails to make an impact (at least without the hindsight of several viewings) because Miles and his colleagues present him so unremarkably that he seems actual, just another minor American official who always happens to be present at the Mexican border when the Lawrences try to cross. This misfire of intent is further complicated by a scene cut from the finished film that would have established the immigration officer's constant presence as impossible. There was to have been an encounter, near the end of the film, between this official and Angelo Ravagli as he attempted to "import" Lawrence's ashes into the United States, not from Mexico, however, but from Europe, its distant borders still somehow guarded by this same inevitable instrument of authority.[25]

Miles deserves credit for at least making the effort in *Priest* to depart from his established patterns. The film remains disappointing, however, partly because Miles's similar efforts in *Virgin,* ten years earlier, proved so much more successful. While still uneven, *Virgin* stands out as one of those few productions capable of filming against the literal grain and thereby finding an exact balance between cinematic originality and tribute to the text. We need only think of Yvette's waking fantasies here and, along with them, her Sleeping Beauty reverie beside a stone dam, imposingly Victorian yet leaking badly and requiring immediate repair. Or we might recall her similar reveries at the rectory window—Miles's demarcation line between the stifling household and the free outdoors. It is worth restating that Tim Burstall also effectively juxtaposes indoors and out as he posits two opposite, very Lawrentian Australias in *Kangaroo*: one smothered in leftover Victorian culture, the other unlimited and largely unexplored, one dim to the point of obscurity, the other bright with possibilities.

Two additional Lawrence films that stand out by way of their similar counter-filming are Ken Russell's *Women in Love* (like *Virgin* an impressive first effort followed by a disappointing second Lawrence film), and Anthony Pelissier's *Rocking Horse Winner.* Russell's best efforts come about when he achieves what Miles attempted too timidly in *Priest*—to burrow beneath the literal or else to hover slightly above it. Something like this happens late in *Women in Love* during two companion scenes, the first involving an all-male encounter between Birkin and Gerald, the second its all-female equivalent between the Brangwen sisters. Birkin and Gerald first discuss marriage (or not) surrounded by a silent audience of female statues gazing down at them from above. The conversation turns to Gerald and Birkin's friendship and its potential for something beyond the ordinary. As they begin to realize the unlikelihood of this, and as their discussion shades into dispute, the two men become lost to us and to one another in a confusion of mirrors. It proves impossible for them, and ultimately for the film audience as well, to distinguish between a potential blood brother and a misleading illusion in the glass.

No mirrors are present in the sisters' counterscene, but the sculpted image persists, now gender-reversed as a clay bust of Gerald that Gudrun models into mocking caricature. Its ugliness—made complete as she thrusts a sculpting tool into its mouth—provides the film with a most Lawrentian objective correlative, not for Gerald so much as for Gudrun—a work of art which exposes the artist who created it. Pelissier's *Rocking Horse Winner* likewise achieves its moments, amid inevitable inconsistencies, as when Paul and his mother enter a world of tempting things in an antique shop, and he gazes prophetically at a miniature horse, then through the lens of a telescope to achieve distant yet confining vision. Later Paul attends a race with his Uncle Oscar where he peers into a pair of binoculars through the wrong end, again acting out a distortion of seeing and knowing in original yet remarkably Lawrentian gestures.

A full half century has elapsed since Anthony Pelissier inaugurated the effort to bring D. H. Lawrence to the screen. As I hope I've been able to show, the results of this effort have proved inconsistent, yet at the same time consistently fascinating. While the very best Lawrence films have had their awkward lapses and embarrassments, even the worst have managed to surprise us happily at times— if not by a fine excess, at least by an unexpected departure from the predictable norms they themselves establish. It would be interesting to borrow young Paul's telescope or binoculars for a moment here and turn them from the races to the movies for a clairvoyant preview of what comes next for Lawrence on screen. While confident predictions remain impossible in film as in life, perhaps a few suggestions can still be made.

It is possible, for instance, that mainstream filmmakers have done all they can with Lawrence and all they care to do. While the 1990s have proved a remarkably productive decade for large-screen literary adaptations, Lawrence and his works have been left out of the picture. The last big Lawrence production was Ken Russell's *Rainbow,* released in 1989, since which time the larger studios have turned to other writers who seem even less likely candidates than Lawrence for cinematic transformation—Jane Austen, Henry James, E. M. Forster, and Michael Ondaatje. If their works have been adapted into artful and commercially viable cinema, we may well wonder why *The Lost Girl* or *Aaron's Rod* have not. Both of these Lawrence novels remain unfilmed, and both seem to offer at least as much cinematic promise as *Sense and Sensibility* or *A Room with a View.* Perhaps, however, such choices on the part of filmmakers and their studios turn out to be more appropriate than they appear, having been based on an accurate assessment of what can and cannot be filmed effectively and profitably. Put more broadly, mainstream filmmaking may have turned away from Lawrence, short of doing him full justice, in the implicit realization that he resists their realistic approach and their adaptation of his works into popular and profitable productions.

Should this be the case, what if anything remains ahead? One possibility is that Lawrence's works will continue to attract filmmakers as source material, but filmmakers of a different order—those whose efforts lie beyond the mainstream studios and likewise beyond the conventions and confines of realism. Some movement has already taken place in this direction, in fact, just two years prior to this writing but perhaps first predicted as far back as 1984 by a small Lawrence production that went largely unnoticed at the time. The minor but potentially prophetic work I am referring to is Robert Burgos's version of "The Horse-

Dealer's Daughter," made for television in 1984 not by any network but by the American Film Institute as part of its "Short Story Collection," which originally aired on PBS.[26]

Only thirty minutes long, Burgos's production takes several liberties with the letter of Lawrence's text but manages to preserve its essential spirit intact. For one thing, the film relocates the story from England to America but a recognizably Lawrentian America—the early-twentieth-century West, crude but vitally energetic and with its Hispanic roots still very much alive beneath the dominant Anglo culture. Burgos's *Horse Dealer's Daughter* also achieves not so much a nonrealistic as a metarealistic rendering of the text. Nothing seems unbelievable, nor even unlikely, yet the entire production takes on a coloration sufficiently strange to suggest that everything is happening in a dream. In part, Burgos achieves this coloration through actual colors. His production is saturated in shades of blue, a color both sacred and lucky to the Pueblo people who attracted Lawrence's attention so forcefully in New Mexico. Blue also served Lawrence as an emblematic color in certain of his own American works such as "The Woman Who Rode Away," where it emerges within the Chilchui mythology as the color of absence and, more to the point of that story, of death. While Lawrence never makes these same associations in "The Horse-Dealer's Daughter," they seem appropriate on screen, perhaps even to viewers unfamiliar with "The Woman Who Rode Away," as shades of blue become increasingly identified with Mabel and her ever-intensifying dance with death. Finally, the televised *Horse Dealer's Daughter* makes much of the gaze exchanged between Mabel and the doctor, often framing it in casements, possibly borrowed from Miles's *Virgin*. In an early scene, Mabel (played by Katherine Cannon) watches through a window as Jack Fergusson approaches the Pervin ranch, sold at auction and now stripped bare as the family prepares to depart. Later in the film, the same scene is repeated, only in reverse, with Jack (played by Philip Anglim) gazing at Mabel through his dispensary window as she makes ready to join her mother in death.

The point here is not to begin an extended discussion of "The Horse-Dealer's Daughter" on film, as tempting as that might be. Rather it is to suggest that Burgos's production may have provided the first step in a possible new direction. More immediately, the latest Lawrence film at the time of this writing is a new version of "The Rocking-Horse Winner," released in 1997, which in several respects carries further the experimental initiatives begun by Burgos thirteen years earlier.[27] This new "Rocking-Horse Winner" is another small film as opposed to a large studio production. It is shorter than Burgos's *Horse Dealer's Daughter*, running only twenty-three minutes, and likewise a modest venture financially. In fact, it is the effort of one independent filmmaker, Michael Almereyda, working without institutional affiliation and with a minimum of resources at his disposal.

Almereyda's cinematic medium of choice is called PXLvision, which involves filming with a toy camera and black-and-white film. While the resolution of the Fisher-Price PXL 2000 camera is sufficient to produce clear images, they always remain distorted at the same time—not blurred so much as fractured into the individual elements, or pixels, that form them. The technique's visual impact can be likened to pointillism in painting, only with the individual "points" or pixels generated electronically and sufficiently large to be evident at any distance.

It is quite remarkable, in light of this description, that after fifty years Lawrence filming seems to be breaking new ground yet coming full circle as well. The process that began at midcentury with "The Rocking-Horse Winner" ends the century with a return to that same work, although now from a radically altered cinematic perspective. Almereyda's *Rocking Horse Winner* premiered at the 1997 New York Film Festival, where it received considerable critical notice and praise. One reviewer writing for the *Village Voice* described its "out of this world look" as "perfectly matched to its subject" and concluded that the double bill in which *The Rocking Horse Winner* appeared was "the best . . . of the festival."[28]

Like Burgos's *Horse Dealer's Daughter,* Almereyda's film also resets Lawrence's work from England to the American West, only here it is present-day Los Angeles, perhaps intended to objectify the original story's materialistic issue in absolutely contemporary terms. Whatever Almereyda's intent, the atmosphere he creates is one of flimsy clapboard structures set against palm trees and of omnipresent swimming pools, convertibles, and television screens. These depressing visuals appear before us against the background noises of everyday life: machinery sounds, jet aircraft landing and taking off, helicopters hovering overhead.

Almereyda's *Rocking Horse Winner* presents even fewer significant characters than Lawrence's. Paul, the clairvoyant and doomed child, becomes Jesse on film (played by Jesse Forrestal). Like his textual counterpart he has an insatiable yet beloved mother (Paula Malcomson), although unlike Hester she remains nameless. The boy has an "unlucky" father as well, but since his mother is clearly a single parent, he never appears. Jesse also has an uncle as Paul did, not his mother's brother Oscar, but Joe (Eric Stoltz), her live-in boyfriend. Early in the film she informs the children, somewhat awkwardly, that Uncle Joe will be staying with them for a while. Almereyda's last important character is the gardener, Lawrence's Bassett now turned Hispanic, presumably the West Coast equivalent of the British domestic class. The gardener and the "uncle" share the same first name, although gardener Joe (Walter Benitez) insists on calling Uncle Joe "sir." He continues to do so even when told to stop, as if to suggest that despite California informality he clearly knows his station just as Lawrence's Bassett did.

Like every effective Lawrence filmmaker before him, Michael Almereyda finds a workable point of mediation between creative independence and artistic tribute despite his commitment to a radically experimental technique. His tribute now becomes double-edged, acknowledging not only D. H. Lawrence but also Anthony Pelissier, his cinematic predecessor. Much of Almereyda's dialogue comes verbatim from the text, and his final race (the Derby) comes metarealistically from England as the track announcer's voice intrudes an unmistakably British accent into an otherwise purely American milieu. Almereyda recognizes Pelissier by repeating his shot, almost exactly, of the servant carrying the toy horse upstairs, and likewise by showing Jesse at the racetrack, like Paul, peering into his binoculars through the wrong end.

As to Almereyda's originality, I'll mention just one additional example. With the aid of his PXL 2000 camera, he provides a rocking motion not only to Jesse's toy horse but to the entire production. Everything seems agitated to the point of convulsion, as if suffering from some *fin de siècle* disease or geological disturbance. Jesse either quivers astride his horse or else plunges furiously, merging before our eyes with the actual jockeys at the track, who seem particularly surreal, even menacing, as they race by in PXLvision. Uncle Joe "rocks" a cocktail shaker to the same disturbed rhythm of the riders and horses. In a parallel gesture, Jesse shakes a contemporary fortune-telling toy called a "Magic 8 Ball," another object like the horse for vexing the future with prophecy. This oversized, liquid-filled billiard ball contains a small triangular window in which predictions appear with every shake: "It Is Destined" when Jesse's luck is up, then ever-downward from there as in the text—"Reply Hazy, Try Again," "Cannot Predict Now," "Don't Count on It," "Not a Chance."

As with Burgos's *Horse Dealer's Daughter,* it is tempting not to end here but instead to continue discussing this recent and most intriguing adaptation. My purpose instead, however, is to close discussion of the films simply by introducing this latest effort and by suggesting that it may anticipate a new, nontraditional genre of Lawrence adaptations coming to replace or at least complicate what we have grown used to seeing over the past fifty years. Lawrence's short stories, in fact, which provide Burgos and Almereyda with their cinematic raw material, have otherwise hardly been touched by filmmakers. While both of these directors work with the stories individually, as Anthony Pelissier and Granada Television did several decades earlier, it is possible to envision a more inclusive and radical approach in the future. Lawrence's Midlands or Southwestern stories, for instance, could be interwoven into a single adaptation by innovative filmmakers, much the way Robert Altman conflated several Raymond Carver stories in his film *Short Cuts.*

Like the majority of Lawrence's shorter works, *The Plumed Serpent* also remains unfilmed, despite being a "big" novel and despite Christopher Miles's past interest in bringing it to the screen. A film of *The Plumed Serpent* in today's social climate seems even less likely than it did thirty years ago, given its strident and frequently offensive religious, cultural, and political agendas. Even its worst detractors, however, would have to admit that the novel is stunningly cinematic and clearly available to adaptation as experimental fantasy or magical realism. It would require brave as well as visionary filmmakers to take on such a project, although they might be assisted in their efforts by *Quetzalcoatl,* Lawrence's initial version of the novel, just as the Lady Chatterley filmmakers were assisted by *The First Lady Chatterley* and *John Thomas and Lady Jane.* Conflating *Quetzalcoatl* and *The Plumed Serpent* on screen might temper some of Lawrence's extremes in the final version, particularly Kate's surrender at the very end. Instead of staying in Mexico as she does in *The Plumed Serpent* and empowering Cipriano by insisting that he won't let her go, Kate closes *Quetzalcoatl* in the act of packing her bags.[29]

It is fascinating, at least for me, to preview such unfilmed Lawrence films and to anticipate what they might be like. As Jesse's "Magic 8 Ball" warns us all, however, "Don't Count on It." With the actual future, it is always a case of "Cannot Predict Now" or "Reply Hazy," although it is always tempting to "Try Again" just the same. I certainly hope the Lawrence filmmakers try again, and I look forward to their efforts, whatever direction they may take. For devotees of D. H. Lawrence, or of adaptive cinema, or both, it will be interesting to see what the twenty-first century has to offer.

It will also be interesting to look ahead toward new critical as well as creative initiatives in relation to Lawrence on film. In the past, the closest approach to a critical "boom" on the subject came in the aftermath of *The Fox* (1968), *Women in Love* (1969), and *The Virgin and the Gypsy* (1970), and probably in oblique response to those films and their considerable cultural impact. The premier issue of *Literature/Film Quarterly,* published in 1973, was devoted to Lawrence on screen. The following year Gerald R. Barrett and Thomas L. Erskine published *From Fiction to Film,* their casebook on Lawrence's "The Rocking-Horse Winner" and Pelissier's film adaptation. As previously mentioned, "The Rocking-Horse Winner" casebook remains unique in its inclusion of the only D. H. Lawrence feature film script published to date. Despite the considerable hazards of prediction, it is possible to suggest that another boom may now be developing in criticism and scholarship relating to D. H. Lawrence on film. Linda Ruth Williams's *Sex in the Head: Visions of Femininity and Film in D. H. Lawrence* needs to be acknowledged here as a foundation text for any such critical resurgence, even though it does not deal directly with the Lawrence films. Williams's study empowers other critics to do so, however, and provides them with a working vocabulary by employing film theory and cinematic perspectives to approach Lawrence's writing from a new direction.

As to new work on the films themselves, Jane Jaffe Young's *D. H. Lawrence on Screen* (1999) is only the second book to appear on the subject. Young concentrates on three films—*The Rocking Horse Winner, Sons and Lovers,* and *Women in Love*—and subjects them to a parallel, essentially formalist, examination attempting to establish a correlation between effectiveness on screen and stylistic fidelity to the text. Young contends that film adaptations of Lawrence succeed when they provide cinematic equivalents of particular formulations of syntax and diction habitual to Lawrence's prose style. Young further contends that the Lawrence filmmakers discover such equivalents more readily to the degree that they work independently, free of studio influence or the need for collaboration within the production team. While both Young and I are implicitly indebted to the Auteur Theory in our approaches to filmmaking, I see major exceptions to it that would qualify her defense of pure independence in Lawrence filmmaking. Young suggests, for example, that *Women in Love* is the most effective of the three films she examines because it was largely the creation of only one person—Ken Russell. I believe that *Women in Love* was enriched immeasurably by Larry Kramer's script and even by his ongoing artistic battles with Russell during the filming. In contrast, *The Rainbow* is a purer example of Russell's exclusive project and, in my opinion, a far less effective film.

Such debates over *Women in Love* will soon be facilitated and hopefully stimulated by the publication of Larry Kramer's film script. According to Kramer, Grove/Atlantic plans to include the script in a collection of his writings due for release in 2001.[30] The *Women in Love* screenplay will add a major and long overdue resource to the collection of readily available documents on the Lawrence films. Beyond this new development, there are broader indications that discussion over Lawrence on film is about to be sparked again, perhaps even developed into a second boom. Presently, for example, a conference is being planned by the D. H. Lawrence Study Centre at the University of Nottingham to be titled "D. H. Lawrence on Screen," and to include presentations on Lawrentian television adaptations as well as cinematic releases. While no date for this conference has yet been set, it is expected to take place in 2001 and is especially significant in light of the scant attention paid to screen adaptation by Lawrence critics and scholars in recent years. One measure of this inattention is the small number of papers devoted to film or television at international D. H. Lawrence conferences over the past decade: only one at Ottawa in 1993, one more at Nottingham in 1996, two at Taos in 1998, and, again, just one at Paris in 1999. In 2001, with a worldwide gathering of talented scholars and critics devoting all their attention to Lawrence on screen, this picture is about to change.

Filmography

■

Videography

■

Notes

■

Selected Bibliography

■

Index

# Filmography

*The Rocking Horse Winner.* Directed by Anthony Pelissier. 91 min. Two Cities Films Ltd., 1949. Producer: John Mills. Screenplay: Anthony Pelissier. Photography: Desmond Dickinson. Art Director: Carmen Dillon. Film Editor: John Seabourne. Music: William Alwyn. With Valerie Hobson (Hester), John Howard Davies (Paul), John Mills (Bassett), Ronald Squire (Uncle Oscar), and Hugh Sinclair (Paul's Father).

*L'Amant de Lady Chatterley.* Directed by Marc Allegret. 98 min. Regie du Film and Orsay Films, 1955. Producer: Gilbert Cohn-Seat. Screenplay: Marc Allegret (from the play by Gaston Bonheur and Philippe de Rothschild). Photography: Georges Perinal. Settings: Alexandre Trauner. Music: Joseph Kosma. English Subtitles: Mai Harris. With Danielle Darrieux (Connie), Leo Genn (Sir Clifford), Erno Crisa (Mellors), Berthe Tissen (Mrs. Bolton), Janine Crispin (Hilda), and Jacqueline Noelle (Bertha).

*Sons and Lovers.* Directed by Jack Cardiff. 100 min. Twentieth Century Fox, 1960. Producer: Jerry Wald. Screenplay: Gavin Lambert and T. E. B. Clarke. Photography: Freddie Francis. Art Director: Lionel Couch. Film Editor: Gordon Pilkington. Music: Mario Nascimbene. With Dean Stockwell (Paul), Wendy Hiller (Gertrude), Trevor Howard (Walter Morel), Heather Sears (Miriam), Mary Ure (Clara), Rosalie Crutchley (Mrs. Leivers), and Donald Pleasence (Pappleworth).

*The Fox.* Directed by Mark Rydell. 110 min. Claridge Pictures and Warner Brothers, 1968. Producer: Raymond Stross. Screenplay: Lewis John Carlino and Howard Koch. Photography: William Braker. Art Director: Charles Bailey. Film Editor: Thomas Stanford. Music: Lalo Schifrin. With Sandy Dennis (Banford), Keir Dullea (Paul), and Anne Heywood (March).

*Women in Love.* Directed by Ken Russell. 132 min. Brandywine Productions Ltd. and United Artists, 1969. Producers: Larry Kramer and Martin Rosen. Screenplay: Larry Kramer. Photography: Billy Williams. Art Director: Ken Jones. Sets: Luciana Arrighi. Costumes: Shirley Russell. Film Editor: Michael Bradsell. Music: Georges Delerue. With Alan Bates (Birkin), Oliver Reed (Gerald), Glenda Jackson (Gudrun), Jennie Linden (Ursula), Eleanor Bron (Hermione), Vladek Sheybal (Loerke), Alan Webb (Mr. Crich), Catherine Wilmer (Mrs. Crich), and Christopher Gable (Tibby).

*The Virgin and the Gypsy.* Directed by Christopher Miles. 92 min. Chevron Pictures, 1970. Producer: Kenneth Harper. Screenplay: Alan Plater. Photography: Bob Huke. Art Director: David Brockhurst. Film Editor: Paul Davies. Music: Patrick Gowers. With Joanna Shimkus (Yvette), Franco Nero (the gypsy), Honor Blackman (Mrs. Fawcett), Mark Burns (Major Eastwood), Maurice Denham (The Rector), Fay Compton (Granny), Kay Walsh (Aunt Cissie), and Norman Bird (Uncle Fred).

*The Rocking Horse Winner.* Directed by Peter Medak. 30 min. Highgate Pictures and Learning Corporation of America, 1977. Producer: William Dennis. Production Designer: Dilsey Jones. Music: Paul Lewis. With Nigel Rhodes (Paul), Kenneth More (Uncle Oscar), Angela Thorne (Paul's Mother), Peter Cellier (Paul's Father), and Chris Harris (Bassett).

*Lady Chatterley's Lover.* Directed by Just Jaeckin. 104 min. London-Cannon Films Ltd. and Producteurs Associes, 1981. Producers: Menahem Golan and Yoram Globus. Screenplay: Christopher Wicking and Just Jaeckin. Photography: Robert Fraisse. Costumes: Shirley Russell. Film Editor: Eunice Mountjoy. Music: Stanley Myers and Richard Harvey. With Sylvia Kristel (Connie), Shane Briant (Sir Clifford), Nicholas Clay (Mellors), Ann Mitchell (Mrs. Bolton), and Elizabeth Spriggs (Lady Eva).

*Priest of Love.* Directed by Christopher Miles. 125 min. Ronceval Inc. and Filmways Pictures, 1981. Producers: Christopher Miles and Andrew Donally. Screenplay: Alan Plater. Photography: Ted Moore. Costumes: Anthony Powell. Film Editor: Paul Davies. Music: Joseph James. With Ian McKellen (D. H. Lawrence), Janet Suzman (Frieda Lawrence), Ava Gardner (Mabel Dodge Luhan), Penelope Keith (Dorothy Brett), Jorge Rivero (Tony Luhan), John Geilgud (Herbert T. Muskett), and Maurizio Merli (Angelo Ravagli).

*Kangaroo.* Directed by Tim Burstall. 105 min. Naked Country Productions and Cineplex Odeon Films, 1986. Producer: Ross Dimsey. Screenplay: Evan Jones. Photography: Dan Burstall. Costumes: Terry Ryan. Film Editor: Edward McQueen-Mason. Music: Nathan Waks. With Colin Friels (Richard Somers), Judy Davis (Harriet Somers), John Walton (Jack Calcott), Julie Nihill (Victoria Calcott), Peter Hehir (Jaz), Peter Cummins (Willie Struthers), and Hugh Keays-Byrne (Kangaroo).

*The Rainbow.* Directed by Ken Russell. 104 min. Vestron Pictures, 1989. Producer: Ken Russell. Screenplay: Ken Russell and Vivian Russell. Photography: Billy Williams. Production Design: Luciana Arrighi. Film Editor: Peter Davies. Music: Carl Davis. With Sammi Davis (Ursula), Paul McGann (Skrebensky), Amanda Donohoe (Winifred Inger), Christopher Gable (Will Brangwen), Glenda Jackson (Anna Brangwen), David Hemmings (Uncle Henry), Dudley Sutton (Mac), Jim Carter (Mr. Harby), and Judith Paris (Miss Harby).

*The Rocking Horse Winner.* Directed by Michael Almereyda. 23 min. Spin Cycle Post, 1997. Producers: Michael Almereyda and Steve Hamilton. Screenplay: Michael Almereyda. Photography: Patrick Rousseau. Film Editor: Steve Hamilton. Sound: Nils Benson. Music: Simon Fisher Turner. With Jesse Forrestal (Jesse), Eric Stoltz (Uncle Joe), Paula Malcomson (Jesse's mother), and Walter Benitez (Joe the gardener).

# Videography

*The Widowing of Mrs. Holroyd.* Directed by Claude Watham. Granada TV, 1961. With Jennifer Wilson (Lizzie Holroyd), Edward Judd (Charlie Holroyd), Paul Daneman (Blackmore), Jimmy Ogden (Jack Holroyd), and Jennifer Quarmby (Minnie Holroyd).

*D. H. Lawrence Short Story Series.* Produced by Margaret Morris. Granada TV, 1965–1967.

> The Granada series adapted sixteen Lawrence stories for television, including "The Blind Man," "The Blue Moccasins," "Daughters of the Vicar," "In Love," "Monkey Nuts," "Mother and Daughter," "None of That," "The Prussian Officer," "Samson and Delilah," "Strike Pay," "Tickets, Please," "Two Blue Birds," and "The White Stocking."

*The Widowing of Mrs. Holroyd.* Directed by Arvin Brown. PBS-TV, 1974. With Joyce Ebert (Lizzie Holroyd), Rex Robbins (Charlie Holroyd), and Todd Jones (Blackmore).

*Sons and Lovers.* Directed by Stuart Burge. Seven 60-min. episodes. BBC-TV, 1981. Producer: Jonathan Powell. Screenplay: Trevor Griffiths. Designer: Chris Pemsel. Script Editor: Betty Willingale. Music: John Tams. With Karl Johnson (Paul), Eileen Atkins (Gertrude), Tom Bell (Walter Morel), Leonie Mellinger (Miriam), Lynn Dearth (Clara), and Jack Shepherd (Baxter Dawes).

*The Trespasser.* Directed by Colin Gregg. 90 min. Colin Gregg Film Productions Ltd. for BBC-TV, 1981. Adapted for television by Hugh Stoddart. Producer: Colin Gregg. Photography: John Metcalfe. Costumes: Monica Howe. Film Editor: Peter Delfgau. Music: Julian Dawson-Lyell. With Alan Bates (Siegmund), Pauline Moran (Helena), Dinah Stabb (Louisa), Margaret Whiting (Beatrice).

*The Captain's Doll.* Directed by Claude Watham. 110 min. BBC-TV, 1982. Screenplay: James Saunders. With Jeremy Irons (Captain Hepburn), Gila von Weitershausen (Hannele), and Jane Lapotaire (Mrs. Hepburn).

*The Rocking Horse Winner.* Directed by Robert Beirman. 1982. With Eleanor Davis (Mrs. Grahame), Charles Hathorne (Paul), Charles Keating (Uncle Oscar), and Gabriel Byrne (Bassett).

*The Boy in the Bush.* Directed by Rob Stewart. Four 50 min. episodes. British television, Channel 4, 1984. Producers: Ian Warren and Geoffrey Daniels. Screenplay: Hugh Whitemore. Photography: Peter Hendry. Costumes: Jim Murray. Film Editor: Lynn Solly. Music: Bruce Smeaton. With Kenneth Branagh (Jack Grant), Sigrid Thornton (Monica), Richard Morgan (Herbert), Lou Brown (Ross), Stephen Bisley (Esau), Jon Blake (Tom), and Celia de Burgh (Mary).

*The Horse Dealer's Daughter.* Directed by Robert Burgos. 30 min. American Film Institute for PBS-TV, 1984. Producers: Jeanne Field and Robert Burgos. Screenplay: Robert Burgos, John W. Bloch, and Robert E. Wilson. Photography: Joseph

Urbanczyk. Costumes: Stephanie Schoelzel. Film Editors: Jim Stanley and Kaja Fehr. Music: Arlon Ober. With Catherine Cannon (Mabel Pervin) and Philip Anglim (Jack Ferguson).

*Samson and Delilah.* Screenplay by Simon Gray. BBC-TV, 1984.

*Coming Through.* Directed by Peter Barber-Fleming. 80 min. British Central Independent Television, 1985. Producer: Deirdre Keir. Screenplay: Alan Plater. Costumes: Robin Fraser-Paye. Film Editor: Kevin Lester. Music: Marc Wilkinson. With Kenneth Branagh (D. H. Lawrence), Helen Mirren (Frieda Weekley), Alison Steadman (Kate), Philip Martin Brown (David), Felicity Montague (Jessie Chambers), Fiona Victory (Alice Dax), Lynn Farleigh (Lydia Lawrence), and Benjamin Whitrow (Ernest Weekley).

*The Daughter-in-Law.* Directed by Martyn Friend. BBC-TV, 1985. Producer: Carol Parks. With Sheila Hancock (Mrs. Gascoigne), Cherie Lunghi (Minnie), David Threlfall (Luther Gascoigne), and Mick Ford (Joe Gascoigne).

*The Rainbow.* Directed by Stuart Burge. Three 60 min. episodes. BBC-TV, 1988. Producer: Chris Barr. Screenplay: Anne Devlin. Photography: John Kenway. Production Design: Myles Lang. Costumes: Sue Peck. With Imogen Stubbs (Ursula), Martin Wenner (Skrebensky), Kate Buffery (Winifred Inger), Colin Tarrant (Will Brangwen), Jane Gurnett (Anna Brangwen), Jon Finch (Uncle Tom), Clare Holman (Gudrun), Tom Bell (Tom Brangwen), and Eileen Way (Lydia Brangwen).

*Lady Chatterley.* Directed by Ken Russell. Four 60 min. episodes. BBC-TV, 1993. Producer: Michael Haggiag. Screenplay: Michael Haggiag and Ken Russell. Photography: Robin Vidgeon. Production Design: James Merifield. Film Editor: Xavier Russell. Costumes: Evangeline Harrison. With Joely Richardson (Connie), Sean Bean (Mellors), James Wilby (Sir Clifford), Shirley Ann Field (Mrs. Bolton), and Hetty Baynes (Hilda).

*The Widowing of Mrs. Holroyd.* Directed by Katie Mitchell. BBC-TV, 1995. With Zoe Wanamaker (Lizzie Holroyd), Colin Firth (Charlie Holroyd), Stephen Dillane (Blackmore), Shane Fox (Jack Holroyd), and Lauren Richardson (Minnie Holroyd).

# Notes

## 1. D. H. Lawrence on Film

1. Harry T. Moore, *The Priest of Love: A Life of D. H. Lawrence,* rev. ed. (New York: Penguin Books, 1981), 572.

2. D. H. Lawrence, "When I Went to the Film," in *The Complete Poems of D. H. Lawrence,* ed. Vivian de Sola Pinto and F. Warren Roberts (New York: Viking Press, 1971), 444.

3. Lawrence, "Let Us Be Men," in *Complete Poems,* 450.

4. D. H. Lawrence, *Sons and Lovers* (New York: Viking Press, 1958), 302.

5. D. H. Lawrence, *Lady Chatterley's Lover,* ed. Michael Squires (Cambridge: Cambridge University Press, 1993), 152.

6. "D. H. Lawrence on Film," the title of this chapter, could be taken two ways— Lawrence on screen (a study of the films), or Lawrence on the topic of film (a study of his comments, attitudes, and fictional or poetic representations of the subject itself). While the first meaning provides the focal point for this study, the second meaning gives rise to a fascinating area of inquiry in itself and one which has been gaining significant critical attention in recent years. Anyone interested in pursuing the other meaning of Lawrence on film should consult San Solecki's "D. H. Lawrence's View of Film" and Nigel Morris's "Lawrence's Response to Film" as an introduction to the subject (see note 12 below). Among Lawrence's own works, two of major relevance to this second issue are *The Lost Girl,* because it is his only novel to take on the cinema and the "Picture Palace" centrally rather than marginally, and also his painting *Close Up,* which attempts to capture mechanical (and therefore pornographic) passion through image rather than inscription. Lawrence's essay "Pornography and Obscenity" may provide an oblique explication of the painting in its statement that "close-up kisses on the film . . . excite men and women to secret and separate masturbation": see *Phoenix* (New York: Viking Press, 1968), 187. For a student of Lawrence on film in its first sense, the painting *Close Up* is especially interesting because the male partner (perhaps the more grotesque of the two grotesque lovers) clearly resembles Oliver Reed as he played Gerald Crich in Ken Russell's 1969 adaptation of *Women in Love.* Finally, a major and recent contribution to the subject of Lawrence's achievement in relation to film is Linda Ruth Williams's 1993 study *Sex in the Head: Visions of Femininity and Film in D. H. Lawrence.* Here Williams suggests, among other things, that Lawrence's many overt attacks on film are belied or deconstructed by his own inherently cinematic practices. In Williams's unique vocabulary, Lawrence's self-proclaimed "scopophobia," or revulsion against looking, merely conceals a far deeper and highly productive "scopophilia," or love of the very thing he professes to hate. If so, Williams's point becomes one more among many verifications of Lawrence's familiar warning never to trust the artist (usually a damned liar) but only his tale instead.

7. Lawrence, *Lady Chatterley's Lover*, 299.

8. Richard Ellmann, *James Joyce* (New York: Oxford University Press, 1965), 310–18.

9. Brenda Maddox, *Nora: A Biography of Nora Joyce* (New York: Fawcett Columbine, 1988), 99.

10. Neil Sinyard, *Filming Literature: The Art of Screen Adaptation* (New York: St. Martin's Press, 1986), vii.

11. Harry T. Moore also makes comparisons between Lawrence and Joyce with regard to their attitudes toward film. For Moore's discussion, which reaches different conclusions from mine on the two writers, see his article "D. H. Lawrence and the Flicks," *Literature/Film Quarterly* 1 (1973): 3–11.

12. In "D. H. Lawrence's View of Film," published in *Literature/Film Quarterly* 1 (1973): 12–16, Sam Solecki provided perhaps the first summary of Lawrence's comments on the movies, made both in fictional works like *The Lost Girl* and in several essays posthumously collected in *Phoenix* and *Phoenix II*. While Solecki acknowledges Lawrence's quarrel with machinery—and therefore with film—he concludes, somewhat more hopefully than I do, that Lawrence "wasn't so much opposed to film itself as to the misuse of film he had witnessed in his society" (15). Solecki also suggests, more broadly, "that what Lawrence was primarily objecting to was the misuse of machinery, not machinery *per se*, which he felt if properly employed could free man and be beneficial to him" (15). The problem with this conclusion from my perspective is that in Lawrence's fiction there are no instances of machines—the movie camera included—being "properly employed." A recent reassessment of "Lawrence's Response to Film" by Nigel Morris appears in Paul Poplawski's *D. H. Lawrence: A Reference Companion* (Westport, Conn.: Greenwood Press, 1996), 591–603. Morris goes beyond Lawrence's overt negativity, taking into account Lawrence's own cinematic tendencies as a writer along with his more tempered comments on film, as in his review of *Manhattan Transfer*: "It is like a movie picture with an intricacy of different stories and no close-ups and no writing in between. Mr. Dos Passos leaves out the writing in between" (*Phoenix*, 364). Morris's account also points out that all of Lawrence's responses, tempered or otherwise, were directed at a medium in its artistic and technological infancy. As a result, Morris concludes, "There is every reason to assume he [Lawrence] would have approved of the best of cinema had he lived to see it reach maturity" (602).

13. It is interesting to consider what a silent film adaptation of *Women in Love* might have been like had Seltzer's Hollywood negotiations been successful. For additional details on his effort to sell the film rights, see David Ellis's *D. H. Lawrence: The Dying Game, 1922–30* (Cambridge: Cambridge University Press, 1998), 87, 93–94.

14. Moore, "D. H. Lawrence and the Flicks," provides a firsthand account of early cinematic interest in Lawrence. For additional information, see S. E. Gontarski's "Filming Lawrence" in *Modernist Studies: Literature and Culture, 1920–1940* 4 (1982): 87–95.

15. Despite its overplayed sexuality, this second attempt at *Lady Chatterley* merits critical attention, if for no other reason than because it adapts material from Lawrence's earlier versions of the text. On the other hand, Lawrence's very moral and moralistic final novel—or at least its title—has spawned a thriving cottage industry in hard-core pornographic films. If Lawrence couldn't stomach *Ben-Hur*, one can only wonder at the cosmic nausea he would have suffered with a premonition of things to come—*Young Lady Chatterley*, *Lady Chatterley's Passions*, *The Gamekeeper*, and *Lady Chatterley in Tokyo*.

16. Gerald R. Barrett and Thomas L. Erskine, eds., *From Fiction to Film: D. H. Lawrence's "The Rocking-Horse Winner"* (Encino and Belmont, Calif.: Dickenson, 1974).

17. Jane Jaffe Young, *Lawrence on Screen: Re-visioning Prose Style in the Films of "The Rocking-Horse Winner," Sons and Lovers, and Women in Love* (New York: Peter Lang, 1999).

18. George Bluestone, *Novels into Film* (Berkeley: University of California Press, 1973), x.

19. Jacques Derrida, *Positions,* trans. Alan Bass (Chicago: University of Chicago Press, 1981), 82.

20. Derrida, *Positions,* 6, 68.

21. The theory of film adaptation has been discussed from contrasting perspectives by several of the commentators already mentioned here. Among them, George Bluestone is the pioneer theoretician on the subject. He grounds his approach, in *Novels into Film,* on the assumption that the film is always a secondary work of art in relation to the text and that fiction and film are "overtly compatible, secretly hostile" (2). With respect to the "either/or" of fidelity versus artistic independence, however, Bluestone does conclude in favor of the filmmaker as an original (if minor) creator. "In the fullest sense of the word, the filmist becomes not a translator for an established author, but a new author in his own right" (62). In the introduction to their casebook on *The Rocking Horse Winner,* Barrett and Erskine also stress the primacy of the written text—to the point, in fact, of "answering" the question of fidelity far more conservatively than Bluestone does: "At this point, the basic criterion for adaptation should be kept in mind: a successful adaptation will reproduce as much of the spirit and as many of the themes of the original as possible given the limitations of the film medium" (*From Fiction to Film,* 22). Barrett and Erskine don't necessarily stress literalism as a means of doing this, but instead introduce the more flexible concept of "analogous techniques" as key to the effective film adaptation (22). A third voice in the theoretical debate is that of Joy Gould Boyum in *Double Exposure: Fiction into Film* (New York: New American Library, 1985). Boyum's book approaches film adaptation from the perspective of reader-response theory and offers a counterargument to Bluestone, Barrett, and Erskine by attempting to establish the film as at least equal in potential artistic stature to the original text. Boyum also suggests, in contrast to Bluestone, that film and narrative are far from hostile genres but, in fact, very closely related (passim, 21–40). Despite such contrasts, Boyum establishes a principle in parallel to Barrett and Erskine when she concludes that "analogous strategies" offer filmmakers their most effective tools for adapting works of literature to the screen (81). At least three other contributions to adaptation theory deserve mention in this summary. They are Geoffrey Wagner's book, *The Novel and the Cinema,* Neil Sinyard's *Filming Literature,* and Michael Klein and Gillian Parker's *The English Novel and the Movies.* The introduction to this last work, written by Michael Klein, sets up a series of adaptation categories which seem significant in relation to the present discussion. Klein lists film versions of fictional works as falling into three classes: those which achieve spiritual fidelity to the original text, those which "deconstruct . . . the source text," and those which "regard . . .the source merely as raw material, as simply the occasion for an original work" (10). Where Klein sees three mutually exclusive options here, I see a conflation—another "either/or" which becomes "and" whenever the screen adaptation transforms itself effectively into art.

22. Boyum, *Double Exposure,* 61–62.

23. Boyum, *Double Exposure,* 59.

24. Boyum, *Double Exposure,* 61.

## 2. *The Rocking Horse Winner:* Expansions and Interpolations

1. Julian Smith, "The Social Architecture of 'The Rocking-Horse Winner,'" in *From Fiction to Film,"* ed. Barrett and Erskine, 227.

2. *The Rocking Horse Winner,* originally released by Two Cities Films, is available on videocassette through Home Vision Cinema. Facets Video offered it for $39.95 in 1996. A second *Rocking Horse Winner,* not to be confused with the Pelissier film, can also be found on videotape. This is a thirty-minute version, released in 1977 by the Learning Corporation of America and intended as a classroom supplement to the teaching of Lawrence's story in secondary schools. This educational version was directed by Peter Medak and features Nigel Rhodes as Paul and Kenneth More as Uncle Oscar. "The Rocking-Horse Winner" was filmed for a third time in 1982 by Robert Bierman, for Paramount Pictures in England, and for a fourth time by independent director Michael Almereyda. His twenty-three-minute experimental version of Lawrence's story premiered at the New York Film Festival in 1997. See chapter 9 below for discussion of this latest "Rocking-Horse Winner" on film.

3. Anthony Pelissier, "The Rocking-Horse Winner: Final Shooting Script," in *From Fiction to Film,* ed. Barrett and Erskine, 200. While Pelissier's "Rocking Horse" is the only feature film script published to date, one Lawrence television script has also been published—Trevor Griffiths's *Sons and Lovers* (Nottingham: Spokesman, 1982). Griffiths's adaptation, directed by Stuart Burge, appeared in seven episodes on BBC Television in 1981.

4. D. H. Lawrence, "The Rocking-Horse Winner," in vol. 3 of *The Complete Short Stories* (New York: Viking Press, 1961), 804. Hereafter, page numbers will be cited in the text.

5. Sinyard, *Filming Literature,* 52.

6. Joan Mellen, "'The Rocking-Horse Winner' as Cinema," in *From Fiction to Film,* ed. Barrett and Erskine, 222.

7. W. D. Snodgrass, "A Rocking Horse: The Symbol, the Pattern, the Way to Live," *Hudson Review* 11 (1958): 191–200.

8. Henry Becker III, *"The Rocking Horse Winner:* Film as Parable," *Literature/Film Quarterly* 1 (1973): 56.

9. S. E. Gontarski "Filming Lawrence," *Modernist Studies: Literature and Culture, 1920–1940* 4 (1982): 89.

10. Pelissier, "Script," 143.

11. D. H. Lawrence, *Aaron's Rod,* ed. Mara Kalnins (Cambridge: Cambridge University Press, 1988), 96.

12. Lawrence, *Aaron's Rod,* 96.

13. Mellen, "'The Rocking-Horse Winner' as Cinema," 221.

14. Pelissier, "Script," 135.

15. D. H. Lawrence, *The Virgin and the Gipsy* (New York: Bantam Books, 1968), 76.

16. D. H. Lawrence, *Studies in Classic American Literature* (New York: Viking Press, 1971), 19.

17. Pelissier, "Script," 137.

18. Pelissier, "Script," 138.

19. Pelissier, "Script," 146, 148.

20. Pelissier, "Script," 155.

21. Pelissier, "Script," 156.
22. Smith, "Social Architecture," 228.
23. Smith, "Social Architecture," 227.
24. D. H. Lawrence, *Lady Chatterley's Lover,* ed. Michael Squires (Cambridge: Cambridge University Press, 1993), 196.

### 3. *Sons and Lovers:* Flight from the [S]mothering Text

1. Originally released by Fox in Great Britain, *Sons and Lovers* is not available on commercial videotape. A first-draft copy of the shooting script for *Sons and Lovers* is in the Lilly Library's collection at Indiana University in Bloomington. Also, the final shooting script with on-set revisions, dated 8 December 1959, is available at New York University's Bobst Library. The film's brush with England's censors (paralleling Anthony Pelissier's experience in filming *The Rocking Horse Winner*) occurred over a bedroom scene, not present in the text, between Dean Stockwell's Paul Morel and Mary Ure's Clara Dawes. While the couple do nothing more than kiss, their state of mind and undress imply the aftermath of lovemaking. Quite suggestive and daring by 1960 standards, the segment had to be deleted in order for the film to receive Great Britain's A rating (Adult; no unaccompanied child admitted).
2. "Lawrence: The Script . . . and the Camera," *Films and Filming,* May 1960, 9.
3. Despite Jack Cardiff's emphasis on close-up work in *Sons and Lovers,* one serious critic of the film, Dennis DeNitto, seems to have missed the effect entirely. In "All Passion Spent"—his chapter on *Sons and Lovers* in Michael Klein and Gillian Parker's *The English Novel and the Movies* (New York: Frederick Ungar, 1981)—DeNitto complains, "For some reason Cardiff has insistently kept his camera objective and distant from the characters" (246). "Occasionally the director does indulge in close-ups or close shots. . . . Generally, however, the camera is too discreet, as though embarrassed by emotional displays and tensions" (246). If an analytical film viewer like DeNitto remains unimpressed by Cardiff's close-ups or unaware of them, it is possible that moving in with the Cinemascope camera did not create the dramatic effect Cardiff had hoped for.
4. "Lawrence: The Script . . . and the Camera," 9. For further details on the making of *Sons and Lovers,* also see Jerry Wald's "Scripting 'Sons and Lovers,'" *Sight and Sound* 29 (summer 1960): 117. Wald, who produced the film, reveals that Montgomery Clift was the filmmakers' first choice to play Paul Morel. By the time production began, however, "the young actor whom we originally intended to play Paul, Montgomery Clift, grew too old, and we had to find a new Paul" (117). It is interesting to consider what *Sons and Lovers* might have become on screen had Clift's troubled and complicated qualities as an actor replaced Dean Stockwell's youthful simplicity. Despite Clift's absence, the filmmakers must have been satisfied with their final product, because they began work on another Lawrence film shortly after *Sons and Lovers* was released. T. E. B. Clarke, again working with Jerry Wald and Twentieth Century Fox, completed a final screenplay for *The Lost Girl,* dated 18 July 1961. A copy of the unpublished script remains in the hands of a private collector, and to date no film of *The Lost Girl* has ever been released.
5. Isabel Quigly, "Unlikely Lawrence," *Spectator,* July 1960, 21.
6. "The New Pictures," *Time,* 1 August 1960, 58.
7. Whitney Balliet, "An Embarrassment of Talk," *New Yorker,* 13 August 1960, 56.
8. Stanley Kauffmann, "Several Sons, Several Lovers," *New Republic,* 29 August 1960,

21–22. In an essay titled "*Sons and Lovers:* Novel to Film as a Record of Cultural Growth," Frank Baldanza includes a useful and informative summary of several reviews and early critical commentaries on Jack Cardiff's film. See *Literature/Film Quarterly* 1 (1973): 64–70.

9. Pauline Kael, *I Lost It at the Movies* (Boston: Little, Brown, 1965), 72.

10. Henry Hart, review of *Sons and Lovers* in *Films in Review* 11 (August–September 1960): 424; John Gillett, review of *Sons and Lovers* in *Film Quarterly* 14 (1960): 41.

11. Trevor Griffiths, *Sons and Lovers: Trevor Griffiths' Screenplay of the Novel by D. H. Lawrence* (Nottingham: Spokesman, 1982), 11.

12. Griffiths, *Sons and Lovers,* 11–12.

13. See Frank Baldanza, "Novel to Film," for a related discussion of the film's constrictive effect on plot in *Sons and Lovers.* Baldanza refers to this general process as "foreshortening" and contends that it takes three different forms within the film—"telescoping," "substitution," and "simplification." While Baldanza's treatment of the first of these strategies parallels my comments on condensation, his examples and conclusions differ from mine. See, for instance, Baldanza's discussion of Arthur's death, which relates it to the father's injury but not to the elder brother's death. (68)

14. John Worthen, *D. H. Lawrence: The Early Years, 1885–1912* (Cambridge: Cambridge University Press, 1991), 142.

15. D. H. Lawrence, *Sons and Lovers* (New York: Viking Press, 1958), 152. Hereafter, page numbers will be cited in text.

16. Evidence from the 8 December 1959 final shooting script for *Sons and Lovers* suggests that the filmmakers intended Paul and Miriam to be more intellectual than they turn out to be in the finished film. This quality is not conveyed by anything resembling the intensely "felt thoughts" so characteristic of their relationship in the novel. Rather it is reflected in the script much more simply by having Paul and Miriam carry on conversations about literature. One such conversation involves the entire Morel family, oddly enough, in a discussion of Browning's "Home Thoughts from the Sea" (64b–64c). Another involves Miriam and her mother in an argument about Flaubert and whether or not his writings on love accord with Christianity (40a). The only trace of such discussions surviving in the film itself is one dialogue between Paul and Miriam in which he refers to a sow in the Leivers barnyard as "The Dark Lady of the Sonnets" and "The Lady of the Lake." A moment later Paul mentions a book by Shelley which he has forgotten to bring Miriam. This leads to nothing more than a brief exchange about Mrs. Leivers's disapproval of their reading material and of Paul's influence on Miriam in general.

17. Jeffrey Meyers, *D. H. Lawrence: A Biography* (New York: Alfred A. Knopf, 1990), 18.

18. Mark Kinkead-Weekes, *D. H. Lawrence: Triumph to Exile, 1912–1922* (Cambridge: Cambridge University Press, 1996), 55.

19. One shred of interest surviving in Cardiff's swinging scene is its odd and perhaps accidental parallel to a later Lawrence work. Just after Paul's comment about being dragged down by women, he sits next to Miriam in the Leivers barn and tells her, "I've got a heart that beats. Feel it." Paul's words repeat those of another barnyard speech made by a cocksure male to his beloved: "Do you think I haven't *got* a heart?" Henry Grenfel asks Nellie March in "The Fox," "And with his hot grasp he took her hand and pressed it under his left breast. 'There's my heart,' he said, 'if you don't believe in it'" (160). The film's Miriam, like March, seems momentarily spellbound by news of the male heartbeat. Then both

women are summoned back to reality by a cry from outside the barn—Banford's in "The Fox" and Mrs. Leivers's in the *Sons and Lovers* film.

20. Paul's sketch of Clara is puzzling because it contradicts not only Lawrence's text but its own description in the script. In the film, the drawing is hastily done on the back of a leaflet Paul receives at one of Clara's suffragette rallies. It shows her exactly as she appears on the speaking platform—severe yet attractive, her hair upswept and covered by a stark black hat. The 8 December 1959 shooting script, however, describes a more openly seductive Clara in Paul's drawing, which "captures her essential femininity, as he sees it; there's a softness in her face; her hair falls to her shoulders, instead of being severely upswept" (67). What motivated the filmmakers' change here, from final script to screen, remains uncertain.

21. As opposed to the sketch of Clara, Paul's painting of his father conforms to the way the filmmakers describe it in the script: "A portrait of Morel in which his [Paul's] father, with the grime of the pit like cracks on his face, has just come up from the mine. Looking up at sudden daylight, he blinks. There is something lost yet aggressive in his expression" (21).

22. Gavin Lambert and T. E. B. Clarke, "Sons and Lovers," Final Shooting Script with On-Set Revisions, 8 December 1959, 2, Bobst Library, New York University.

23. Described in the 8 December 1959 screenplay as the "whirling spindle of [a] spiral machine" (81), this third cinematic wheel is the only one to have attracted any critical notice. In "All Passion Spent," DeNitto suggests, "Visual symbols are . . . avoided [in *Sons and Lovers* on screen] while those that do appear are either patently obvious or undeveloped. The one exception is the shot of rotating bobbins after the one of Paul and Clara embracing" (246). DeNitto does not discuss this image further, nor does he relate it to the other turning wheels in the film.

## 4. Foxes and Gypsies on Film: They Steal Chickens, Don't They?

1. John Simon, *Movies into Film: Film Criticism, 1967–1970* (New York: Dial Press, 1971), 62–63.

2. *The Fox* and *The Virgin and the Gypsy* remain unavailable commercially either on videotape or conventional film.

3. S. E. Gontarski, "Mark Rydell and the Filming of *The Fox*: An Interview," *Modernist Studies: Literature and Culture, 1920–1940*, 4 (1982): 96.

4. Simon, *Movies into Film*, 64–65.

5. Pauline Kael, "Making Lawrence More Lawrentian," in *Going Steady* (Boston: Little, Brown, 1970), 34.

6. Hollis Alpert, "Up the Rebels," *Saturday Review*, 25 July 1970, 37.

7. Penelope Gilliatt, "This England, This Past," *New Yorker*, 4 July 1970, 71.

8. Simon, *Movies into Film*, 64–65.

9. Stanley Kauffmann, review of *The Virgin and the Gypsy* in *New Republic*, 1 August 1970, 24.

10. S. E. Gontarski, "Christopher Miles on His Making of *The Virgin and the Gypsy*," *Literature/Film Quarterly* 11 (1983): 249.

11. Simon, *Movies into Film*, 137–39.

12. Kael, "Making Lawrence More Lawrentian," 30.

13. Sinyard, *Filming Literature*, vii.

14. Gontarski, "Mark Rydell," 97.

15. Gontarski, "Mark Rydell," 101–2.

16. Christopher Miles also found himself under studio pressure to alter his film, yet this amounted to censorship in reverse, another sign of changing times. Columbia Pictures (which was financing *Virgin*) did not wish to desexualize the film but, just the opposite, to magnify the erotic element by getting the gypsy on screen right away rather than "about halfway through" as in Miles's script and Lawrence's original text. (Gontarski, "Christopher Miles," 250) Like Rydell, Miles ultimately won his battle with the studio, and the film was released as he and his screenwriters had first conceived it.

17. Gontarski, "Mark Rydell," 97, 101.

18. Gontarski, "Mark Rydell," 102.

19. Kate Millett, *Sexual Politics: A Surprising Examination of Society's Most Arbitrary Folly* (Garden City, N.Y.: Doubleday, 1970), 337n.

20. "The Fox," *Playboy,* October 1967, 81–84.

21. Gontarski, "Christopher Miles," 250, 251.

22. Alan Plater, "The Virgin and the Gypsy," technical shooting script, May 1969, 105, Celeste Bartos International Film Study Center, Museum of Modern Art, New York.

23. For a treatment of what he terms "youth culture" films of the 1960s, see Geoffrey Wagner, *The Novel and the Cinema,* 39–40. Although they may belong to this genre, Wagner does not include *Virgin* or the two other Lawrence films of this period in his discussion.

24. D. H. Lawrence, "The Fox," in *D. H. Lawrence: Four Short Novels* (New York: Viking Press, 1965), 156.

25. Thomas Sobchack offers a related discussion of "externalization" in "*The Fox:* The Film and the Novel," *Western Humanities Review* 23 (1969): 73–78. He suggests that the film's heavy reliance on a purely "exterior viewpoint" is partly responsible for its failure (76). He also suggests that certain striking and effective moments in *The Fox* indicate that Mark Rydell had the capacity to make a better film than the one he actually made. Consistent with most literary critics writing on *The Fox* at the time of its release, Sobchack bases his judgments, positive and negative, largely on the issue of fidelity to the text. Relative to this issue, two additional critical studies of interest are Joan Mellen's "Outfoxing Lawrence: Novella into Film," *Literature/Film Quarterly* 1 (1973): 17–27, and Cosimo Urbano's "The Evil That Men Do: Mark Rydell's Adaptation of D. H. Lawrence's 'The Fox,'" *Literature Film Quarterly* 23 (1995): 254–61. Like Sobchack, Mellen provides a largely negative treatment of *The Fox* based for the most part on its departure from the text. Writing for the same journal more than twenty years later, Urbano by contrast defends the film and calls for its reassessment from a postmodern and feminist perspective. More specifically, he criticizes Mellen's study for focusing too narrowly on the issue of fidelity, then goes on to suggest that Rydell was using Lawrence's text as the foundation for his own cinematic defense of lesbian experimentation and protest against the patriarchal value system (as represented by Paul Grenfel), which prevents its success.

26. D. H. Lawrence, *The Virgin and the Gipsy* (New York: Bantam Books, 1968), 114. (Hereafter page numbers will be cited in the text.)

27. Christopher Miles himself does not see the deliberate indeterminacy in Lawrence's text concerning Yvette's loss of virginity. Rather, he contends that Lawrence simply had to avoid direct sexual description in deference to the sensibilities and standards of his audience. "I'm quite convinced [he tells Gontarski] that she, in fact, lost her virginity. Lawrence leaves the question politely open for the squeamish Victorian public in that

she cuts her wrists or something and this may account for the blood on the sheet. I don't take all that. She lost her virginity, and I also think that she gained her womanhood" (Gontarski, "Christopher Miles," 251). While Miles's statement allows us a clearer view of his own intentions and choices in the film, it betrays a misconception about Lawrence's readers, who can hardly be called Victorians in the mid-1920s, and about Lawrence as well, who never attempted to publish *The Virgin and the Gipsy*. Also, since Lawrence wrote *The Virgin and the Gipsy* and *Lady Chatterley's Lover* almost concurrently, his "politeness" in one text but not in the other must have been purely an artistic decision.

28. The presence of masturbation (real or symbolic) in two Lawrence film adaptations seems ironic given the author's own condemnation of the practice. Needless to say, these masturbation scenes have no textual basis in either "The Fox" or *The Virgin and the Gipsy*.

29. Alan Plater's screenplay for *The Virgin and the Gypsy* reveals that the filmmakers intended to preserve at least a hint of Major Eastwood's war experiences but nothing parallel relating to the gypsy. "During the war [Eastwood tells Yvette rather late in the script], I was buried in the snow for twenty-four hours . . . winter 1917 . . . buried alive . . . until they dug me out. None the worse for it" (Plater, "The Virgin and the Gypsy," 128). Eastwood's isolated statement in the script ends here and does not, as in the text, lead to his description of himself and the gypsy as resurrected men. Also, even this brief reference to the war was eventually cut from the finished film.

30. Lawrence, "The Fox," 121.

31. The muting of military references in *The Fox* and *Virgin* productions accords with the film industry's general silence during the late 1960s and early 1970s concerning the Vietnam War and the subject of war in general. In America, only one major studio release of the period dealt directly with the Vietnam conflict—*The Green Berets* released by Warner Brothers (along with *The Fox*) in 1968 and starring John Wayne in an anachronistic effort to apply the conventions of World War II filming to an entirely different military and political reality. Almost another decade would pass before major filmmakers began approaching the Vietnam War with a measure of artistic honesty in productions like *Coming Home* and *The Deer Hunter,* both released in 1978.

32. A detailed discussion of March's dreams remains peripheral to the purposes of this study and is readily available in several sources elsewhere. See, for example, J.-P. Naugrette's "Le Renard et les Reves: Onirisme, Ecriture, et Inconscient dans 'The Fox,'" *Etudes Anglaises,* April–June 1984, 142–55, and Louis K. Greiff's "Bittersweet Dreaming in Lawrence's 'The Fox': A Freudian Perspective," *Studies in Short Fiction* 20 (1983): 7–16. The second article reviews and summarizes several additional critical statements on March's dreams and on the text of "The Fox" in general.

33. Gontarski, "Mark Rydell," 99–100.

34. While not treating the Lawrence films directly, Laura Mulvey provides a pertinent theoretical discussion of the cinematic male gaze. See "Visual Pleasure and Narrative Cinema," in *Issues in Feminist Film Criticism,* ed. Patricia Erens (Bloomington: Indiana University Press, 1990), 28–40. Mulvey's commentary identifies "three different looks associated with cinema: that of the camera as it records the pro-filmic event, that of the audience as it watches the final product, and that of the characters at each other within the screen illusion" (39). Her emphasis is on the second kind of looking—that of the film audience, typically afforded the perspective of a concealed male voyeur, by the conventions of this medium, in relation to female images on screen. Mulvey's comments

closely accord with Kate Millett's observation in *Sexual Politics* that the March/Banford lesbian scenes in *The Fox* were conceived for the pleasure of masculine and heterosexual viewers (see Kate Millett, *Sexual Politics*, 337n.).

35. Lawrence, "The Fox," 145.

36. Lawrence, "The Fox," 146.

37. Where I see Paul's premeditated chicken-and-fox murder as a low point in the film and a spiritual violation of the text, Mark Rydell voices exactly the opposite opinion. In his 1982 interview, the director refers to this very scene as "the most Lawrentian, mystical moment in the entire film" (Gontarski, "Mark Rydell," 99).

38. D. H. Lawrence, *Women in Love* (New York: Viking Press, 1960), 27.

39. Lawrence, "The Fox," 163, 155.

40. Lawrence, *The Virgin and the Gipsy*, 7, 17.

41. Lawrence, *The Virgin and the Gipsy*, 71–72. Christopher Miles reveals his deliberate censorship of Lawrence on class and race in his 1983 interview. "I was determined to avoid those particular class clichés that Lawrence loves: the woman [Mrs. Fawcett] was a Jewess and Lawrence was very anti-Semitic. I tried to avoid the whole class thing: the Jewishness of the woman, the class of the gypsy. I wanted to avoid these for once in a British film, and I think I did it" (Gontarksi, "Christopher Miles on His Making of *The Virgin and the Gypsy*," 251).

42. Simon, *Movies into Film*, 64.

43. For Lawrence's comments on attaching a "long tail" to "The Fox," see his 16 November 1921 letter to Earl Brewster in *The Letters of D. H. Lawrence*, vol. 4, *June 1921–March 1924*, ed. Warren Roberts, James T. Boulton, Elizabeth Mansfield (Cambridge: Cambridge University Press, 1987), 124–26. This difficult conclusion for author and reader alike is also treated in Harry T. Moore's *Priest of Love* (New York: Penguin Books, 1981), 436–37, in my article on "The Fox," cited in note 32 above, and in Susan Wolkenfeld's "The Sleeping Beauty Retold: D. H. Lawrence's 'The Fox,'" *Studies in Short Fiction* 14 (1977): 345–52.

44. Lawrence, "The Fox," 175.

45. Gontarski, "Mark Rydell," 98.

46. Gontarski, "Christopher Miles," 251.

47. Gontarski, "Christopher Miles," 251.

48. It is clear from the May 1969 shooting script for *The Virgin and the Gypsy* that it was not the filmmakers' original intention to configure Yvette's escape as a fantasy and that very likely this decision was made late in the production process. In the final script scene, for example, the following exchange is recorded, involving both major and minor characters:

> *Leo:* The gipsy [*sic*] raised the alarm, first thing . . . The reservoir burst . . .
> *Yvette:* The gipsy.
> *Mary (intervening politely):* Joe Boswell, his name, sir.
> *Yvette (turning and pausing):* Joe Boswell, his name. A name, like you and me . . .
> *Rector:* Let me help you.
> *Leo:* I've got the car.
> *Yvette:* I can manage on my own.

This conversation is entirely erased from the finished film and, along with it, such textual details as the gypsy's name and an explanation for the cause of the flood (Plater, "The Virgin and the Gypsy," 149–50).

49. Kael, "Making Lawrence More Lawrentian," 30.

## 5. Ken Russell's *Women in Love:* Repetition as Revelation

1. Originally released by Brandywine Productions in 1969, *Women in Love* is currently available on videotape (MGM/UA Home Video, 1990), and can be obtained through Movies Unlimited at a 1999 catalog price of $14.95. A copy of the release script for *Women in Love,* dated July 1969, is in the holdings of Indiana University's Lilly Library at Bloomington. For the prologue scene to this film (even prior to the music and opening credits) Russell and his colleagues owe a debt to a Lawrence text separate from *Women in Love.* In this scene the audience first sees Will Brangwen at his handiwork, and hears the monotonous sound of a tapping hammer, just as Ursula and Gudrun burst in to announce their departure to watch the Crich wedding. Will looks up at them angrily because his project has been interrupted and because his daughters use any excuse to avoid remaining at home. This brief prologue takes its inspiration not from *Women in Love* but from a description in *The Rainbow* of Ursula and her father in one of their many confrontations: "She heard the tap-tap-tap of the hammer upon the metal. Her father lifted his head as the door opened. His face was ruddy and bright with instinct, as when he was a youth. . . . But there was about him an abstraction, a sort of instrumental detachment from human things. He was a worker. He watched his daughter's hard, expressionless face. A hot anger came over his breast and belly" (358–59).

2. D. H. Lawrence, *Women in Love* (New York: Viking Press, 1960), vii. Hereafter, page numbers will be cited in the text.

3. As Ken Russell puts it in an interview with biographer John Baxter, "The novel came out in 1921 [*sic*] but it had been written during the Great War, so the war was very much in . . . [Lawrence's] mind. We set the film in 1920, which was a time of disillusionment, of change. . . . I wanted to give a feeling of disillusionment right from the beginning, so I went through the archives and found that *the* popular song of that year was 'I'm Forever Blowing Bubbles,' and since the whole film is about illusion, about love and the hopes of love that aren't returned or requited or fulfilled, it seemed the choice had been made for me" (176). Although Russell is unaware of the coincidence, the film is set in the same year that Lawrence published the novel, 1920.

4. The release script of *Women in Love,* dated July 1969, reveals that this ceremony is the dedication of a memorial and not a funeral as it appears to be. The motionless soldier is not dead but completely disabled, something a film audience would scarcely realize without help from the script. The coffin-shaped box in which the soldier lies is actually an "invalid carriage," according to the script (reel 4/p. 1).

5. For other perspectives on Alan Bates's Rupert Birkin in relation to the 1960s and the hippie movement, see Richard Combs's review of *Women in Love* for *Monthly Film Bulletin* 36 (1969): 263–64, and Theodore Ross's article "Gargoyles in Motion: On the Transmigration of Character from Page to Screen and Related Questions on Literature and Film" for *College English* 39 (1977): 371–82.

6. Larry Kramer also remains vocal in the 1990s but as head of the AIDS advocacy organization "Act Up!" on issues far removed from his work on *Women in Love.*

7. Gene D. Phillips, "An Interview with Ken Russell," *Film Comment* 6 (fall 1970): 12.

8. John Baxter, *An Appalling Talent: Ken Russell* (London: Michael Joseph, 1973), 172.

9. Saul Kahan, "Ken Russell: A Director Who Respects Artists," *Los Angeles Times Calendar Magazine,* 28 March 1971, 18. A sad irony connected with the now famous Alan Bates/Oliver Reed "gladiatorial" is that when Reed died in Malta on 2 May 1999, he was working on his final film, *Gladiator.*

10. Baxter, *Russell,* 180.

11. Baxter, *Russell,* 171.

12. Baxter, *Russell,* 181–82.

13. Kahan, "Ken Russell," 18.

14. Winifred Blevins, "Lawrence's *Women in Love:* Word to Image," *Los Angeles Herald Examiner,* 12 April 1970, G4.

15. Wayne Warga, "Kramer Scripts Thinking Man's *Women in Love,*" *Los Angeles Times Calendar Magazine,* 3 May 1970, 1.

16. Warga, "Kramer Scripts," 13.

17. Baxter, *Russell,* 175.

18. For a discussion of *Women in Love* that credits Russell's work on the film (and script) as far more significant than Kramer's, see Gene D. Phillips's "Ken Russell's Two Lawrence Films: *The Rainbow* and *Women in Love,*" *Literature/Film Quarterly* 25 (1997): 68–73. Ken Hanke, even more one-sided in his approach, never mentions Kramer's contributions at all in his book *Ken Russell's Films* (Metuchen, N.J.: Scarecrow Press, 1984), 51–74.

19. Graham Fuller, "Next of Ken," *Film Comment* 25 (1989): 4.

20. Ken Russell, *The Lion Roars: Ken Russell on Film* (Boston: Faber and Faber, 1993), 73, 161.

21. Russell, *The Lion Roars,* 72.

22. Pauline Kael, "Lust for 'Art,'" *New Yorker,* 28 March 1970, 101.

23. Stephen Farber, review of *Women in Love* in *Hudson Review* 23 (1970): 322.

24. Robert F. Knoll, review of *Women in Love* in *Film Heritage* 6 (summer 1971): 5.

25. Harry T. Moore, "D. H. Lawrence and the Flicks," *Literature Film Quarterly* 1 (1973): 9.

26. As quoted in Neil Sinyard's *Filming Literature,* 52.

27. Elliott Sirkin, review of *Women in Love* in *Film Quarterly* 24 (1970): 45.

28. Simon, *Movies into Film,* 58, 60.

29. Knoll, review of *Women in Love,* 2, and Moore, "D. H. Lawrence and the Flicks," 10.

30. Knoll, review of *Women in Love,* 2.

31. Sirkin, review of *Women in Love,* 46.

32. Simon, *Movies into Film,* 62.

33. Sinyard, *Filming Literature,* 51.

34. Ross, "Gargoyles in Motion," 377.

35. G. B. Crump, "*Women in Love:* Novel and Film," *D. H. Lawrence Review* 4 (1971): 33.

36. Joseph A. Gomez, *Ken Russell: The Adaptor as Creator* (London: Frederick Muller, 1976), 81.

37. Ana Laura Zambrano, "*Women in Love:* Counterpoint on Film," *Literature/Film Quarterly* 1 (1973): 53–54.

38. Boyum, *Double Exposure,* 131.

39. D. H. Lawrence, *Lady Chatterley's Lover,* ed. Michael Squires (Cambridge: Cambridge University Press, 1993), 286.

40. Lawrence, *Studies in Classic American Literature,* 2.

41. E. M. Forster, *Aspects of the Novel* (New York: Harcourt, Brace and World, 1955), 85.

42. In his interview with John Baxter, Ken Russell reveals that a more complete version of "Rabbit" was filmed but eventually cut because he felt that it duplicated material already included in other scenes: "The chapter called 'Rabbit', for instance. Some people criticised us for leaving that out, but in essence it says the same thing as the sequence concerning the train and the horse. We did shoot the rabbit scene, in fact, but in the final cut it was obviously superfluous and ended up on the cutting room floor" (Baxter, *Russell,* 176).

43. For a discussion of Russell's "Coal-Dust" scene which describes it more positively than I do, see Linda Ruth Williams, *Sex in the Head: Visions of Femininity and Film in D. H. Lawrence* (Detroit: Wayne State University Press, 1993), 66, 83–87. Despite Williams's cinematic approach to Lawrence, her treatment of the actual Lawrence films is unfortunately limited only to a few observations. She does, however, call attention to this scene in particular "because it powerfully follows the frenetic shot/counter-shot editing of the text itself: we see the scene, we see Gudrun watching the scene, and then we see the scene again, etc." (66). Williams's reading of Lawrence's original "Coal-Dust" also differs from mine in that she emphasizes Gudrun's distancing of herself from the man on horseback (as if she were watching him on film) rather than her emotional participation in the incident and sexual arousal as a result. Williams writes that Gudrun in the text and film alike *"is represented as needing to make Gerald into a representation,* and at a proper cinematic distance. Her anger at Ursula's intervention is a protest at the betrayal of distance; Ursula's words betray the fact that they are both *there* with Gerald, and thus that he is not an 'effigy', inaccessible, existing in the 'primordial elsewhere' of Gudrun's scopic fantasy. If Ursula can shout in anger then Gerald can respond, which is exactly what Gudrun doesn't want him to do" (86). It is, however, Gudrun and not Ursula who eventually intervenes, becoming an "actress" in the scene she is watching by flinging back the crossing gates and shouting angrily at Gerald "in a strange, high voice, like a gull, or like a witch screaming out from the side of the road: 'I should think you're proud'" (Lawrence, *Women in Love,* 105).

44. For the full text of Lawrence's poem see *The Complete Poems of D. H. Lawrence,* ed. Vivian de Sola Pinto and F. Warren Roberts (New York: Viking Press, 1971), 282–84.

45. Lawrence, *Complete Poems,* 282.

46. Gerald's horseback ride also proves to be an obscure repetition of another subsequent scene related to the mines, the street-encounter between Gudrun and "Palmer." Her fastidious electrician/suitor in the text, however, remains on screen in name only, having been transformed into a loutish, drunken collier who tries to assault her before being driven off by Gerald. According to the film script, as Gerald approaches the railroad crossing during "Coal-Dust," he is "trying to get the mare to jump over or between the wagons" and urging her on by shouting "You cow!" and "you bitch" (Reel 4/Page 6). While Gerald's words remain all but inaudible over the noise of the train, they are repeated exactly by Palmer and directed at Gudrun as she fights off his clumsy attempt at seduction.

47. My thanks to Earl Ingersoll for pointing out an interesting example of film's potential for distorting perception of text if not text itself. When Anthony Burgess writes about the drowning in *Women in Love,* he mistakes Russell for Lawrence, claiming that "The young couple we meet in the first chapter, running to their wedding, we meet again drowned (Lawrence was drawing on an actual fatality in the area . . . )." See Burgess, *The Life and Work of D. H. Lawrence: Flame into Being* (New York: Arbor House, 1985), 126.

48. Joseph A. Gomez, "Russell's Images of Lawrence's Vision," in *The English Novel and the Movies,* ed. Michael Klein and Gillian Parker (New York: Frederick Ungar, 1981), 254. See also Zambrano, "Counterpoint on Film," 51, and Boyum, *Double Exposure,* 127.

49. Boyum, *Double Exposure,* 127.

50. Zambrano, "Counterpoint on Film," 51.

51. Gomez, "Russell's Images of Lawrence's Vision," 254.

52. Crump, "*Women in Love:* Novel and Film," 35.

53. Russell, *The Lion Roars,* 73.

## 6. Ken Russell's *The Rainbow:* Repetition as Regression

1. Sinyard, *Filming Literature,* 50.

2. Sinyard, *Filming Literature,* 51.

3. Russell describes the genesis of *The Rainbow* in *A British Picture: An Autobiography* (London: Heinemann, 1989), 134. "We [he and his wife, Vivian] would write a script based on *The Rainbow* by D. H. Lawrence. His *Women in Love* had been one of my greatest hits, so it seemed reasonable to assume that the earlier novel which featured the 'women' of the title as teenagers would prove to be equally successful. Given the circumstances, finding a backer should not be difficult." Russell remained optimistic after the script was completed, declaring a little later in his autobiography that he "was well pleased [with it]—mainly due to Viv's contribution." He also believed that "*The Rainbow* was a better script [than *Women in Love*] and would therefore be an even bigger hit" (141).

4. Ken Russell, *A British Picture: An Autobiography* (London: Heinemann, 1989), 275, 281. Originally released by Vestron Pictures in 1989, Russell's film adaptation of *The Rainbow* was available on commercial videotape until recently through Movies Unlimited at a purchase price of $89.99. The title was, however, dropped from the 1999 catalog. No public copy of Russell's film script for *The Rainbow* is available at the time of this writing.

5. Graham Fuller, "Next of Ken," *Film Comment* 25 (1989): 2.

6. Joseph A. Gomez, "The Elusive Gold at the End of *The Rainbow:* Russell's Adaptation of Lawrence's Novel," *Literature/Film Quarterly* 18 (1990): 136.

7. This film incident seems to have been inspired by a brief textual description of Will Brangwen's doting treatment of his daughter Ursula. "He gave her the nicest bits from his plate, putting them into her red, moist mouth. And he would make on a piece of bread-and-butter a bird, out of jam: which she ate with extraordinary relish." D. H. Lawrence, *The Rainbow* (New York: Viking Press, 1961), 212. (Hereafter, page numbers will be cited in text.) In the film version Ursula refuses even to taste her father's bread-and-jam rainbow.

8. Ken Russell borrowed several such visual tropes from Christopher Miles's *The Virgin and the Gypsy.* Early in *The Rainbow,* exactly as in that film, the camera moves from an uninspired morning in church to a close-up of Sunday dinner being carved, with both

unappetizing meals suggestive of the dreary routines of Saywell and Brangwen family life. Beyond imagery, the endings of Russell's *Rainbow* and Miles's *Virgin* are so alike as to merit separate treatment at the conclusion of this chapter.

9. Gomez, "Elusive Gold," 136.

10. During the scene in which Winifred joins Ursula in bed to reveal her plans to marry Uncle Henry, she recites the opening line of "The Clod and the Pebble" from Blake's *Songs of Experience:* "Love seeketh not Itself to please."

11. G. B. Crump, "Lawrence's *Rainbow* and Russell's *Rainbow,*" *D. H. Lawrence Review* 21 (1989): 187–201.

12. David Robinson, "The Blossoming of Love," *Times* (London), 2 November 1989, 21. See also Kenneth Turan, "Ken Russell Goes Straight," *GQ,* June 1989, 117.

13. Caryn James, "Ken Russell Goes Back to Lawrence for Love," *New York Times,* 5 May 1989, sec. 3, p. 9.

14. Tom O'Brien, "Catching Fire," *Commonweal,* 2 June 1989, 337.

15. Peter Travers, review of *The Rainbow* in *Rolling Stone,* 1 June 1989, 36. See also David Denby, "Saturday Night Special," *New York,* 29 May 1989, 64–65 and Ralph Novak, review of *The Rainbow* in *People Weekly,* 26 June 1989, 15–16.

16. James, "Ken Russell Goes Back," sec. 3, p. 9.

17. Pauline Kael, "Trampled," *New Yorker,* 29 May 1989, 103.

18. Kael, "Trampled," 102–3.

19. O'Brien, "Catching Fire," 337.

20. Turan, "Ken Russell Goes Straight," 119. See also Stanley Kauffmann, "Affairs of Love," *New Republic,* 15 May 1989, 28.

21. The director is somewhat less tight-lipped about *The Rainbow* in the autobiography he published the same year the film was released. See Russell, *A British Picture.* The two final chapters of this book provide a rambling account of filming *The Rainbow,* with comments on all of the project's setbacks and changes of plans. Many of the pre-production problems originated, according to Russell, with the studio, Vestron Pictures, which insisted that a well-known star, preferably American, appear in *The Rainbow.* According to Russell, "another major requirement of our financiers . . . [was] NAMES" (275). As a result, several "big names," both British and American, were offered parts in *The Rainbow* only to turn them down. Jeremy Irons, for example, was the studio's first choice for Will Brangwen. Also, because Glenda Jackson had not expected to be available, the part of Anna Brangwen was offered to Julie Christie, who rejected it because it was too small. The American actresses Kelly McGillis, Mariel Hemingway, and Theresa Russell all turned down the role of Winifred Inger for the same reason. Most unlikely of all, Elton John had gone as far as signing a contract to make his acting debut as Uncle Henry, but then asked to be released just as shooting was about to start. When this occurred, Russell tried to replace him with more old friends and veterans of the *Women in Love* production— Alan Bates and, after he refused, Oliver Reed. When Reed proved unavailable, Vestron had to settle for David Hemmings as Uncle Henry and Glenda Jackson (whose prior commitment had been canceled) as Anna Brangwen—both big-name stars, but of two decades earlier.

22. Neil Taylor, "A Woman's Love: D. H. Lawrence on Film," *Novel Images: Literature in Performance,* ed. Peter Reynolds (London: Routledge, 1993), 105–21.

23. An exception to this critical tendency against *The Rainbow* and in favor of *Women*

*in Love* is provided by Gene D. Phillips who sees both of Russell's Lawrence films as equally successful. See Gene D. Phillips, "Ken Russell's Two Lawrence Films: *The Rainbow* and *Women in Love*," *Literature/Film Quarterly* 25 (1997): 68–73.

24. Fuller, "Next of Ken," 4.

25. Lawrence, *The Rainbow,* 319. See also 179–81 and 478–81.

26. Lawrence to Edward Garnett, Lerici, 5 June 1914, *The Letters of D. H. Lawrence,* vol. 2, June 1913–October 1916, ed. George J. Zytaruk and James T. Boulton (Cambridge: Cambridge University Press, 1981), 182–84.

27. D. H. Lawrence, *Sons and Lovers* (New York: Viking Press, 1958), 152.

28. Will Brangwen is shown working as an artist only once on film as he carves the figure of a lion in wood on an ornate church railing. His Adam and Eve carving, an organic extension of himself in the novel burnt after his submission to Anna Victrix, becomes a baptismal font in Russell's film and the subject of a playful argument between Will and Anna Brangwen based on their more serious textual confrontation at Lincoln Cathedral. In the film, as the Brangwen family walks home from church, Will insists that the hand of God in his carving has got to be a man's hand, while his wife Anna reminds him that her own hand served as the model.

29. Russell devotes just twenty minutes of screen time to Ursula's experience as a newcomer in the man's world. Her first disastrous day of teaching takes up fifteen minutes with the remaining five devoted to her asserting herself by severely thrashing an unruly student.

30. Michael Billington, "Sammi Davis: Just Right for D. H. Lawrence," *New York Times,* 30 April 1989, sec. 2, p. 20.

31. Richard A. Blake, "Summer Fair," *America,* July 1989, 45.

32. Derek Malcolm, "Rainbow Warrior," *Manchester Guardian Weekly,* 28 August 1988, 27.

33. Lawrence, *The Rainbow,* 399, 405. Whether by design or not, the *Rainbow* filmmakers have named Ursula's unruly child-adversary after the author of the novel, David Herbert *Richards* Lawrence.

34. For additional commentary on the toy and game metaphors in this film see Crump, "Lawrence's *Rainbow* and Russell's *Rainbow,*" 195–96.

35. Fuller, "Next of Ken," 4.

36. For further discussion of Stuart Burge's adaptation of *The Rainbow,* see Howard Harper's "The BBC Television Serialization of *The Rainbow,*" *D. H. Lawrence Review* 21 (1989): 202–7.

## 7. *Lady Chatterley's Lover:* Filming the Unfilmable

1. *Lady Chatterley* is a London Films/Global Arts Production for BBC Television. Its cast includes Joely Richardson as Connie Chatterley, Sean Bean as Oliver Mellors, James Wilby as Sir Clifford, and Shirley Ann Field as Mrs. Bolton. First shown on BBC-TV in four episodes in 1993, the production was released on commercial videotape in Great Britain later that year by Pickwick Group. Since then the videotape has also been released in the United States and is listed in the 1999 Movies Unlimited catalog at a price of $89.99.

2. As noted at the outset of chapter 5, Christopher Miles opens *The Virgin and the Gypsy* with a conversation between Yvette and Lucille based, apparently, on a similar conversation between Gudrun and Ursula that began Russell's *Women in Love* two years earlier.

3. D. H. Lawrence, *Lady Chatterley's Lover,* edited by Michael Squires (Cambridge: Cambridge University Press, 1993), 5.

4. Russell's *Lady Chatterley* pays tribute to the final version of the text by incorporating Mellors's closing letter to Connie—unique to *Lady Chatterley's Lover*—in a voice-over near the end of the production. At the same time, Russell quotes material found only in Lawrence's initial version such as the scene in which Connie and Parkin drive two nails into an oak tree. Specific borrowings from *John Thomas and Lady Jane* include Clifford's mocking imitation of the dialect during an interview with Parkin about poachers and a scene in which Connie and Parkin are interrupted in an embrace by a watchful gamekeeper. In the text this incident occurs during their final meeting at Hucknall Torkard. In the television production, Russell moves the scene to Wragby and to underscore the irony makes the intruding gamekeeper Mellors's replacement.

5. For the account of Edward Garnett's remark to Lawrence, and its effect on him, see Lawrence's letter to David Garnett, 24 August 1928, *The Letters of D. H. Lawrence,* vol. 4, March 1927–November 1928, ed. James T. Boulton and Margaret H. Boulton (Cambridge: Cambridge University Press, 1991), 520.

6. As mentioned, Connie and Mellors become lovers in a scene closely resembling Russell's *Liebestod* from *Women in Love.* Here Birkin and Ursula initiate their sexual relationship in a struggle that likens them visually to the just-drowned newlyweds, Tibby and Laura Lupton. A similarly dubious beginning is followed in *Lady Chatterley* by two other explicit and disturbing love scenes. In the first, as Connie returns home after visiting Mrs. Flint, Mellors surprises her and appears to rape her against a tree. Afterwards, he threatens that if she doesn't come to his cottage he will come to Wragby instead, break in, and find her bedroom—much as Gerald found Gudrun's in *Women in Love.* When Connie comes to the cottage, she is shown enduring rather than enjoying sexual intercourse in a position suggestive of sodomy. In contrast to these early, explicit, and largely negative scenes, all of the later celebratory eroticism in the text remains unfilmed and invisible in Russell's production. When Connie spends her first night with Mellors, Russell resorts to the familiar fade-out and morning-after cliché. Similarly, in depicting their final night together, Russell cuts the sequence short with the lovers chastely embracing near a lake. Entirely omitted is any trace of Lawrence's "night of sensual passion" leading to the death of shame in Connie and, ultimately, to her rebirth (*Lady Chatterley's Lover,* 246–47).

7. D. H. Lawrence, *Women in Love* (New York: Viking Press, 1960), 36.

8. In *Sex in the Head,* Linda Ruth Williams introduces the term *scopophilia* to define such enjoyment. This love of looking, she argues, is something which Lawrence claimed to detest yet practiced to great artistic advantage (9).

9. David Robinson, "Lumet's Sophisticated View of Corruption," *Times* (London), 18 December 1981, 10.

10. James Monaco and the editors of *Baseline,* eds., *The Movie Guide* (New York: Perigee Books, 1992), 230.

11. *Lady Chatterley's Lover* (1981) is a London-Cannon Films/Producteurs Associes production, directed by Just Jaeckin with a screenplay by Christopher Wicking and Just Jaeckin, and based on the novel by D. H. Lawrence as adapted by Marc Behm. Musical score is by Stanley Myers and Richard Harvey. Photography is by Robert Fraisse.

12. The same marketing strategy was clearly in effect ten years later when the short-lived videotape of Jaeckin's *Lady Chatterley* was released. Its box-cover description reads, in part, as follows:

D. H. Lawrence's erotic novel, banned for many years, has been transformed into a sensual masterpiece of erotic cinema, starring Sylvia Kristel (*Emmanuelle*). A rich, titled, and beautiful young woman becomes bored and frustrated by a sexless marriage. She seeks emotional satisfaction in an affair with her husband's gamekeeper, oblivious of the social scandal she is creating. From the creators of *Emmanuelle* comes another high calibre classic with the emphasis on eroticism.

13. Robinson, "Lumet's Sophisticated View," 10.

14. Gary Arnold, "Shabby *Chatterley,*" *Washington Post,* 9 October 1982, C6. See also Herbert Mitgang, "Screen: Social Comment in *Lady Chatterley's Lover,*" *New York Times,* 10 May 1982, sec. 3, p. 20.

15. Robinson, "Lumet's Sophisticated View," 10. According to Gerald Pollinger, literary executor of the Lawrence estates, Wicking and Jaeckin's producers attempted to secure the film rights to *The First Lady Chatterley.* Although negotiations fell through and no contract was signed, the filmmakers went ahead with the project, drawing material from this and the later versions, without permission. The film rights to *Lady Chatterley's Lover* had been secured decades earlier, according to Pollinger, by Regie-Orsay, the French studio which released *L'Amant de Lady Chatterley* in 1955.

16. Williams, *Sex in the Head,* 162n.

17. Taylor, "A Woman's Love," 111, 121n.

18. D. H. Lawrence, *The First Lady Chatterley* (London: Heinemann, 1972), 79. Hereafter, page numbers will be cited in the text.

19. In "A Woman's Love," Neil Taylor describes the relationship between Jaeckin's opening and closing scenes as follows: the film "has begun with a slow zoom into Wragby Hall and it ends with a slow zoom out. Rather than Connie, it is Mrs. Bolton who is at the window now, and (ironically enough) closing the window, shutting in her invalid, Sir Clifford, and shutting out her rival, Connie" (113). While logic seems to support Taylor's assumption that Mrs. Bolton has replaced Connie, a careful examination of the opening sequence will verify that it is Mrs. Bolton in the window at the beginning as well as the end of the film.

20. Lawrence, *Lady Chatterley's Lover,* 190. Hereafter page numbers will be cited in the text.

21. D. H. Lawrence, *John Thomas and Lady Jane* (London: Penguin Books, 1977), 248.

22. Jaeckin's final juxtaposition appears to break the pattern by cutting from Connie and Mellors during their last night together to Sir Clifford alone as he discovers his wife's absence. The variation proves appropriate, however, so that the resulting sequence is interesting in its own right and organically related to Clifford's earlier therapeutic sessions with his nurse. Clifford wakes up suddenly, intuiting Connie's infidelity as it occurs at the gamekeeper's cottage. He drags himself out of bed and, using only his arms and shoulders now strengthened by Mrs. Bolton's ministrations, pulls himself up the staircase to Connie's bedroom. While nothing like this happens in Lawrence's novel, the scene may take its inspiration from *The First Lady Chatterley* where Connie momentarily believes that Clifford has come upstairs to find her. "She started in a shock of fear and horror. There was a noise outside. Yes! There was a knock! Had he come upstairs?" (228–29). Even though Mrs. Bolton is absent from this scene, her presence is implied through Clifford's physical efforts (simultaneously recalling his nurse and the lovers). Clifford's

crippled sexuality is also implied here through his Freudian (and cinematic) struggle up the long flight of stairs to the top.

23. Several moments in Jaeckin's *Lady Chatterley's Lover* turn eroticism into unintended comedy to the disadvantage of text and film alike. The most blatant instance of this occurs when Connie and Mellors carry on a discussion of social issues and class differences during intercourse. "You're above me!" he exclaims angrily, and inaccurately, from the top of the missionary position.

24. Arnold, "Shabby *Chatterley*," C6.

25. Lawrence, *John Thomas and Lady Jane,* 376.

26. *L'Amant de Lady Chatterley* (1955) is a Regie-Orsay film (released in the United States by Kingsley International), produced by Gilbert Cohn-Seat. It was adapted for the screen (from Lawrence's novel and the Bonheur and de Rothschild play) by director Marc Allegret. Photography by Georges Perinal, music by Joseph Kosma, and English subtitles by Mai Harris. A videotape can be purchased through Movies Unlimited at a 1999 catalog price of $19.99.

27. One of the film's early reviewers referred to Erno Crisa's costume as "the Balkan uniform he seems to be wearing." See Peter John Dyer, review of *Lady Chatterley's Lover* in *Films and Filming* 2 (September 1956): 24.

28. Rene Jordan, *Marlon Brando* (New York: Pyramid, 1973), 63.

29. Robert Hatch, review of *L'Amant de Lady Chatterley* in *Nation,* 18 July 1959, 40.

30. See, for example, Dyer, review of *Lady Chatterley's Lover,* 24; Philip T. Hartung, review of *L'Amant de Lady Chatterley* in *Commonweal,* 4 September 1959, 472; Arthur Knight, "Lady Chatterley's Lawyer," *Saturday Review,* 25 July 1959, 25.

31. Edward DeGrazia and Roger K. Newman, *Banned Films: Movies, Censors, and the First Amendment* (New York: Bowker, 1982), 98. As detailed further in Richard S. Randall, *Censorship of the Movies: The Social and Political Control of a Mass Medium* (Madison: University of Wisconsin Press, 1968), the New York authorities objected on these grounds to the following sequences in the film and ordered them deleted before its release:

> *Reel 2D:* all views of Mellors and Lady Chatterley in cabin from point where they are seen lying on cot together, in a state of undress, to end of sequence.
> *Reel 3D:* all views of Mellors caressing Lady Chatterley's buttock and all views of him unzipping her dress and caressing her bare back. Eliminate following spoken dialogue [in French] accompanying these actions:
> "But you're nude. . . . You're nude under your dress, and you didn't say so. . . . What is it?"
> Eliminate accompanying English superimposed titles:
> "You have nothing on. . . . And you didn't say so. . . . What is it?"
> *Reel 4D:* entire sequence in Mellors' bedroom showing Lady Chatterley and Mellors in bed, in a state of undress (62).

32. "Lady and the Censors," *Newsweek,* 10 December 1956, 118.

33. De Grazia and Newman, *Banned Films: Movies, Censors, and the First Amendment,* 98.

34. A detailed account of the Lady Chatterley trial in America can be found in Charles Rembar, *The End of Obscenity: The Trials of Lady Chatterley, Tropic of Cancer, and Fanny Hill* (New York: Bantam Books, 1968). While Rembar mentions the simultaneous con-

troversy in New York State involving Marc Allegret's film, a more complete treatment of this case is provided by Richard S. Randall's *Censorship of the Movies*.

35. Bosley Crowther, "Screen: 'Lady Chatterley,'" *New York Times,* 11 July 1959, 11.

36. Stanley Kauffmann, "From France, Old and New," *New Republic,* 27 July 1959, 30.

37. Arthur Knight, "Lady Chatterley's Lawyer," 25.

38. Lady Chatterley's Lover," *Filmfacts* 11 (1959): 183. See also Paul V. Beckley, "Lady Chatterley's Lover," *New York Herald Tribune,* 11 July 1959, 7, and Bosley Crowther, "Screen: 'Lady Chatterley,'" 11.

39. J. M., "Lady Chatterley's Lover," *Films in Review* 10 (August–September 1959): 423; see also John McCarten, "Laborious Love," *New Yorker,* 18 July 1959, 48.

40. Beckley, "Lady Chatterley's Lover," 7.

41. Gene D. Phillips, "Sexual Ideas in the Films of D. H. Lawrence," *Sexual Behavior* 1 (1971): 10–11.

42. James F. Scott, "The Emasculation of *Lady Chatterley's Lover,*" *Literature/Film Quarterly* 1 (1973): 43–44.

43. Lindley Hanlon, "Sensuality and Simplification," in *The English Novel and the Movies,* ed. Michael Klein and Gillian Parker (New York: Frederick Ungar, 1981), 272–73.

44. Scott, "Emasculation," 45.

45. Hanlon, "Sensuality and Simplification," 278.

46. Hanlon, "Sensuality and Simplification," 271. The words "*la règle du ju*" are, in fact, spoken twice within Allegret's dialogue, not during the hunt episode as Hanlon suggests but immediately afterwards when Clifford visits his mines because of a serious accident. He arrives at the pit on horseback, still dressed for the hunt, and is told that his workers resent the risks they must take to mine the richest vein in the district. Clifford replies that these risks come with the colliers' profession and are part of "the rules of the game," as was the shell that wounded and crippled him in the war. Mai Harris's English subtitles blur Allegret's allusion to Renoir's title by translating Clifford's reply as "It's all part of the game."

47. Scott, "Emasculation," 37.

48. As discussed in chapter 6, Ken Russell's Uncle Henry, a character of the filmmakers' own invention played by David Hemmings, is the screen equivalent of the younger Tom Brangwen in Lawrence's novel.

49. Some traces of the earlier versions survive in Allegret's production. One example involves Mellors's dog and the odd fact that in the film he's forced to shoot the animal before leaving Wragby. His new employer, as he explains to Connie over the animal's corpse, won't allow a dog. While nothing like this occurs in *Lady Chatterley's Lover,* Allegret's somewhat mawkish yet cruel moment seems an outgrowth and exaggeration of a related incident in *John Thomas and Lady Jane.* Here, short of murdering Flossie, Parkin forces her to stay with Clifford's new gamekeeper, Albert Adam, also because a dog would be impossible in his new situation at Sheffield. Parkin's rejection of Flossie is cruelly accomplished, in part because he's angry—not at the animal but at himself for caring too much about her. Like many of her human counterparts in the text, Flossie undergoes some puzzling transformations on screen, some trivial, others revealing. All of the Lady Chatterley filmmakers, for example, seem to dislike the name Flossie. In Russell's *Lady Chatterley* she becomes Bramble. In Jaeckin's *Lady Chatterley's Lover* she

loses the name entirely along with all of her personality and prominence in the text. In Allegret's *L'Amant de Lady Chatterley* she's renamed Flash, evidently relinquishing her original gender along with her name. This detail proves meaningful as an indicator of human as well as animal transformations on film. As will be discussed further, a macho gamekeeper like Allegret's Mellors (as opposed to Lawrence's) deserves a macho dog.

50. Simone de Beauvoir, *The Second Sex*, trans. H. M. Parshley (New York: Vintage Books, 1989), 725. For additional commentary on Allegret's debt to Beauvoir, see Scott, "Emasculation," 41.

51. Ephraim Katz, *The Film Encyclopedia* (New York: HarperCollins, 1994), 328.

52. Scott, "Emasculation," 40.

53. When Connie reveals Mellors as her lover in the novel, Clifford displays his misogyny by blaming her transgression on the whole gender: "My God, my God, is there any end to the beastly lowness of women!" (Lawrence, *Lady Chatterley's Lover*, 296). Leo Genn's film version of Clifford goes beyond this in his indictment, declaring that Connie, like all women, is nothing but "instinct, darkness, disorder." Genn also expands Clifford's hysterical condemnation of Connie in the text as "one of those half-insane, perverted women who must run after depravity, the *nostalgie de la boue*" (Lawrence, *Lady Chatterley's Lover*, 296). Clifford's original French remains in the film, only now broadened out to insult the entire sex. Mai Harris's English subtitles translate the insult inaccurately but with equal bluntness as "Women must crave filth."

54. Marc Allegret's ending is superficially similar to Anthony Pelissier's in *The Rocking Horse Winner*, a film made six years before *L'Amant de Lady Chatterley*. Resembling Erno Crisa's Mellors, John Mills's Bassett also appears for his final scene out of uniform, conventionally attired, and leaving with all his worldly goods in a suitcase. Both former servants are about to depart from a sterile, materialistic environment for something better. Despite their similar situations, however, the on-screen Bassett seems much closer to Lawrence (and to Beauvoir as well) than the on-screen Mellors. John Mills's character disappears existentially, moving freely and on his own toward an uncertain future with his natural vitality and sense of himself as a working-class man undiminished. By contrast, Erno Crisa's Mellors (who never seemed like a working-class man to begin with) moves out of sight complacently to the point of cinematic cliché. What lies ahead for him seems likely to include marriage, fatherhood shortly thereafter, and the prospect of a comfortable income.

## 8. *Kangaroo:* Taming Lawrence's Australian Beast

1. D. H. Lawrence, *Kangaroo* (New York: Viking Press, 1960), 286–89.

2. Lawrence, *Kangaroo*, 141–42.

3. D. H. Lawrence, *Women in Love* (New York: Viking Press, 1960), 260.

4. The film version of *Kangaroo* was released in 1986 by Ross Dimsey's Naked Country Productions with an Australian rating of M (equivalent to an American PG). The film was listed in the 1999 Movies Unlimited catalog at a price of $79.99. Copies of the film script for *Kangaroo* are available in the United States at the American Film Institute and at the Motion Picture Academy of Arts and Sciences, both in Los Angeles. Another film entitled *Kangaroo* was released in 1952. Directed by Lewis Milestone and starring Maureen O'Hara, Peter Lawford, and Richard Boone, this early *Kangaroo* is unrelated to Lawrence's and is accurately described on its videotape jacket as a "Technicolor Western set in Australia."

5. See "Love, Marriage, Life, and the Whole Damn Thing," *Cinema Papers,* March 1986, 42 (an interview with producer Ross Dimsey and director Tim Burstall); Verina Glaessner, review of *Kangaroo* in *Monthly Film Bulletin,* December 1986, 374.

6. Andrew Peek, "Tim Burstall's *Kangaroo,*" *Westerly,* December 1980, 41. Larry Kramer discussed his negotiations with the *Kangaroo* filmmakers during a phone interview with me on 14 October 1999.

7. Peek, "Tim Burstall's *Kangaroo,*" 39.

8. Brian Reis, *Australian Film: A Bibliography* (London: Mansell, 1997), 288.

9. Charles Sawyer, review of *Kangaroo* in *Films in Review,* May 1987, 295.

10. Richard Harrington, "*Kangaroo:* Politics and Prattle," *Washington Post,* 15 May 1987, D7.

11. Sawyer, review of *Kangaroo,* 296.

12. Stanley Kauffmann, "Sidney, 1922; Baltimore, 1963," *New Republic,* 30 March 1987, 24.

13. Harrington, "*Kangaroo:* Politics and Prattle." See also Janet Maslin, "Australian Politics in Lawrence's *Kangaroo,*" *New York Times,* 13 March 1987, C12.

14. Michael Wilmington, "A Tamed *Kangaroo* Plays It Safe," *Los Angeles Times Calendar Magazine,* 21 March 1987, 5.

15. Joseph Gelmis, "Adaptation of a D. H. Lawrence Novel," *Newsday,* 13 March 1997, sec. 3, p. 11.

16. Amy Taubin, "Animal Crackers," *Village Voice,* 24 March 1987, 56.

17. Sawyer, review of *Kangaroo,* 296.

18. Taubin, "Animal Crackers," 56.

19. Gelmis, "Adaptation," sec. 3, p. 11.

20. Peter Craven, review of *Kangaroo* in *Cinema Papers,* May 1987, 58.

21. Maslin, "Australian Politics," C12.

22. Wilmington, "A Tamed *Kangaroo* Plays It Safe," 5.

23. Doris Tourmarkine, review of *Kangaroo* in *Film Journal* 90 (April 1987): 29.

24. David Bradshaw, "An Absence of Strife," *Times Literary Supplement* (London), 12 December 1986, 1403.

25. Harris Ross, "*Kangaroo:* Australian Filmmakers Watching Lawrence Watching Australia," *D. H. Lawrence Review* 19 (1987): 93, 101.

26. In Burstall's film, a connection does develop between Jack Calcott and Somers's nightmare memories, yet completely unrelated to his former friend John Thomas Buryan. More ominous, Jack reminds Somers (and the audience) of the British army officer who first searches the Cornwall cottage in the opening sequence of the film. As mentioned elsewhere, Burstall's version of "The Nightmare" serves as prologue or overture to *Kangaroo* in place of Lawrence's flashback midway through the text. In the film's search scene, the officer questions Somers and Harriet, then confiscates Somers's notebook-transcription of a Cornish or Welsh folk song because he believes it to be a code. Near the end of the film, Jack Calcott repeats this action almost exactly. Believing Somers to be a spy after he rejects Kangaroo's "offer," Jack rifles through his ex-friend's papers and seizes a notebook in which he reads the words "politics and red-hot treason"—a quotation from *Kangaroo* itself, the novel that Somers has been writing throughout the film. This time Somers fights back, as he was unable to do in Cornwall, and forces Jack to retreat empty-handed.

27. Several Australian sources on *Kangaroo* mention Tim Burstall's belief that Lawrence had not grafted Italian fascism imaginatively on to Australia (as is now generally accepted),

but instead that there was a real Diggers' movement during the 1920s and a real would-be dictator. The *Cinema Papers* interview cited in note 5 above quotes Burstall as attacking "All the literary critics . . . [who] rubbished Lawrence for having invented this whole secret army bullshit because of his Italian experiences with Mussolini. . . . Kangaroo is based on a man called General Rosenthal, who was a Jewish architect, and a man interested in bringing Draconian legislation into the New South Wales parliament in order to break the unions and so on. The Secret Army did exist. It was called, of all things, the King and Empire Alliance, and its front was a patriotic organization made up of disaffected diggers." See "Love, Marriage, Life, and the Whole Damn Thing," 42.

28. Lawrence, *Kangaroo,* 326.

29. Another example of political misfire in the film involves the arrest of Jack and Somers after the Trades Hall riot. Departing from Lawrence's novel, Burstall locates Somers in the middle of the street fight as a witness to Jack's killing of at least two men. After the arrest, as it becomes clear that Jack will not be charged, Somers tells the Assistant Commissioner of Police that he wishes to make a statement, presumably to accuse Jack of murder. The film's intent here is to reveal that the Assistant Commissioner is one of the Diggers, O'Neill, the same man who warned Jack against Somers when they visited the military camp. This revelation falls flat, however, because most viewers are not likely to recognize the Assistant Commissioner as O'Neill and, as a result, to appreciate Burstall's implication of a wider fascist conspiracy. During the encampment sequence, O'Neill wears a bush hat and keeps his face averted, so that even a careful observer like Harris Ross, in his essay in the *D. H. Lawrence Review,* fails to make the connection. The *Kangaroo* film script contains an explanatory note that O'Neill and the Assistant Commissioner are the same person, suggesting that the filmmakers were aware that this might not be evident on screen. See Evan Jones, "Kangaroo," 1986, reel 10 (5B), 108–9. This unpublished U.S. version of the film script is available at the Margaret Herrick Library, Academy of Motion Picture Arts and Sciences in Los Angeles.

30. Lawrence, *Kangaroo,* 329–30.

31. Lawrence, *Kangaroo,* 171.

32. Peek, "Tim Burstall's *Kangaroo,*" 42.

33. Craven, review of *Kangaroo,* 58.

34. Ross, "*Kangaroo,*" 99.

35. Two outdoor scenes that break the celebratory pattern should be noted. The first involves Harriet's confrontation with Kangaroo, which occurs in the gardens surrounding his mansion. Here Burstall implies that Kangaroo has domesticated or colonized the outdoors so that it becomes little more than an extension of his fortress-home. Also, while the entryway may be decorated with artificial kangaroos, it is clear that their owner has entirely Europeanized his corner of Australia. Kangaroo's estate—with its flowers, trees, and fences all carefully maintained—looks remarkably like Wragby did on screen or even Shortlands in Ken Russell's *Women in Love.* The second negative outdoor scene occurs when Jack brings Somers to the Diggers' military encampment. This time the setting is a forest rather than an estate, and at first the scene appears to be developing into a Birkin-like communion with nature as Somers wanders into the woods alone while Jack converses with his comrades-in-arms. Almost immediately, however, Somers is captured by sentries who aim their rifles at him and lead him, blindfolded, back to Kangaroo's camp. The suggestion here seems to be that the Diggers and their leader are as much at odds with nature as they are with society, so that their presence in the woods constitutes an

intrusion, just as their "capture" of Somers constitutes a trespass on individual privacy and freedom.

36. Ross, "*Kangaroo,*" 99.

## 9. *Priest of Love:* A Last Look Back, a First Look Ahead

1. *Priest of Love* was produced by Christopher Miles and Andrew Donally, directed by Christopher Miles, and released by Filmways Pictures in 1981. The screenplay was by Alan Plater, based on Harry T. Moore's biography *The Priest of Love,* along with Lawrence's letters and other writings. Director of photography was Ted Moore, with costumes by Anthony Powell and music by Joseph James. It received an R rating in the United States. In 1985 a revised version of the film was released for the centennial celebration of Lawrence's birth, edited and shortened considerably from its original running time of 125 minutes. The earlier version of *Priest of Love* was released on videotape by HBO Cannon Video, but both versions were out of print at the time of this writing.

2. *Coming Through* was produced by Deirdre Keir and directed by Peter Barber-Fleming with screenplay by Alan Plater, editing by Kevin Lester, and music by Marc Wilkinson. The cast featured Kenneth Branagh as the young D. H. Lawrence. *Coming Through* was first shown on British television in 1985, Lawrence's centennial year, then released on videocassette in 1993 by BSF Video, possibly on the strength of Branagh's highly successful film career during the late 1980s and early 1990s. At the time of this writing, *Coming Through* remains available for purchase or rental and can be purchased from Movies Unlimited for $39.99.

3. This press release along with a considerable collection of publicity and review material on *Priest of Love* can be found at the Film Study Center of the Museum of Modern Art in New York City.

4. Will Jones, "D. H. Lawrence Film a Richly Layered Success," *Minneapolis Tribune,* 29 October 1981, B11.

5. Judith Crist, "D. H. Lawrence Brought to Life," *Saturday Review,* October 1981, 61. See also Crist, "When Stars Don't Shine," *50 Plus,* October 1981, 50.

6. Gary Arnold, "The 'Love' Charm: The Life and Wife of D. H. Lawrence," *Washington Post,* 16 October 1981, B1.

7. Geoff Brown, "Uncluttered but Ominous Line," *Times* (London), 19 February 1982, C13.

8. Vincent Canby, "Journeys of D. H. Lawrence," *New York Times,* 11 October 1981, 68.

9. John Coleman, "Exteriors," *New Statesman,* 19 February 1982, 30.

10. Stanley Kauffmann, "Playing a Genius," *New Republic,* 21 October 1981, 21.

11. Kauffmann, "Playing a Genius," 20.

12. Andrew Sarris, "The French Make Cinema," *Village Voice,* 14–20 October 1981, 47.

13. Ellen Pfeifer, "A Pretentious View of D. H. Lawrence," *Boston Herald American,* 16 October 1981, B6.

14. Sheila Benson, "Taking a Lawrence at Facile Value," *Los Angeles Times Calendar Magazine,* 16 October 1981, 2.

15. Canby, "Journeys of D. H. Lawrence," 68.

16. Alan Brien, "Films in the World of Real-Life Fiction," *Sunday Times* (London), 21 February 1982, 39.

17. See note 3 above. Despite the confusion it is still surprising that Canby and Simon assume Lawrence's swimming companion to be Middleton Murry, who was probably familiar with Shelley's "To a Skylark." Lawrence recites part of this poem aloud during the bathing scene, and his friend (Hocking, not Murry) asks if it is one of his own compositions.

18. See Pat Dowell, "Lawrence Joins Shadows of His Creation On-Screen," *Baltimore Sun,* 25 October 1981, D1–D2, and Nancy Mills, "Sexual Legacy of D. H. Lawrence," *San Francisco Sunday Examiner and Chronicle Datebook,* 18 October 1981, 22–23.

19. Robert A. Nowlan and Gwendolyn Wright Nowlan, *The Films of the Eighties* (Jefferson, N.C.: McFarland, 1991), 448.

20. Charles Sawyer, review of *Kangaroo* in *Films in Review,* May 1987, 296.

21. D. H. Lawrence, "Bei Hennef," in *The Complete Poems of D. H. Lawrence,* ed. Vivian de Sola Pinto and F. Warren Roberts (New York: Viking Press, 1971), 203.

22. D. H. Lawrence, "Red Herring," in *Complete Poems,* 490–91.

23. Alan Plater, "Priest of Love," director's shooting script, third draft, March 1980, 147, Film Study Center Collection, Museum of Modern Art, New York City.

24. Jeffrey Meyers discusses Lawrence's censors and speculates on their motives in his *D. H. Lawrence: A Biography* (New York: Alfred A. Knopf, 1990). See especially the account of *The Rainbow* case (182–96) in which Meyers suggests that Lawrence's eroticism gave far less offense to his enemies than did his perceived anti-patriotic and anti-military attitudes, as openly expressed in that novel during wartime.

25. Plater, "Priest of Love," scene 218, 145.

26. *The Horse Dealer's Daughter* (1984) was produced by Jeanne Field and Robert Burgos, and directed by Robert Burgos with screenplay by Robert Burgos, John W. Bloch, and Robert E. Wilson, photography by Joseph Urbanczyk, and costumes by Stephanie Schoelzel. The film was originally shown on PBS in the United States as part of the American Film Institute's "Short Story Collection." It was subsequently released on videotape by Monterey Home Video and remains available through Teacher's Video Company at a 1999 catalog price of $29.95.

27. *The Rocking Horse Winner* was produced by Michael Almereyda and Steve Hamilton. Michael Almereyda also directed the film and wrote the screenplay, with photography by Patrick Rousseau and music by Simon Fisher Turner. The film is unrated in the United States and remains commercially unavailable at the time of this writing.

28. Amy Taubin, "Short Circuit," *Village Voice,* 30 September 1997, 75.

29. D. H. Lawrence, *Quetzalcoatl,* ed. Louis L. Martz (Redding Ridge, Conn.: Black Swan Books, 1995), 326.

30. Larry Kramer discussed the forthcoming publication of his *Women in Love* film script with me in a telephone interview on 14 October 1999.

# Selected Bibliography

## General Sources on Text and Film

Baskin, Ellen, and Mandy Hicken. *Enser's Filmed Books and Plays, 1928–1991*. Aldershot, U.K.: Ashgate, 1993.

Baxter, John. *An Appalling Talent: Ken Russell*. London: Michael Joseph, 1973.

Beauvoir, Simone de. *The Second Sex*. Translated by H. M. Parshley. New York: Vintage Books, 1989.

Bluestone, George. *Novels into Film*. Berkeley: University of California Press, 1973.

Boyum, Joy Gould. *Double Exposure: Fiction into Film*. New York: New American Library, 1985.

Clancy, Jack. "The Film and the Book: D. H. Lawrence and Joseph Heller on the Screen." *Meanjin Quarterly* 30 (1971): 96–101.

Crump, G. B. "Lawrence and the Movies: *Literature/Film Quarterly*." *D. H. Lawrence Review* 6 (1973): 326–32.

DeGrazia, Edward, and Roger K. Newman. *Banned Films: Movies, Censors, and the First Amendment*. New York: Bowker, 1982.

Derrida, Jacques. *Positions*. Translated and annotated by Alan Bass. Chicago: University of Chicago Press, 1981.

Ellis, David. *D. H. Lawrence: The Dying Game, 1922–1930*. Vol. 3 of *The Cambridge Biography of D. H. Lawrence, 1885–1930*. Cambridge: Cambridge University Press, 1998.

Ellmann, Richard. *James Joyce*. New York: Oxford University Press, 1965.

Emmens, Carol A. *Short Stories on Film and Video*. 2d ed. Littleton, Colo.: Libraries Unlimited, 1985.

Forster, E. M. *Aspects of the Novel*. New York: Harcourt, Brace and World, 1955.

Fuller, Graham. "Next of Ken." *Film Comment* 25 (1989): 2, 4.
       Interview with Ken Russell.

Gomez, Joseph A. *Ken Russell: The Adaptor as Creator*. London: Frederick Muller, 1976.

Gontarski, S. E. "Filming Lawrence." *Modernist Studies: Literature and Culture, 1920–1940* 4 (1982): 87–95.

Hanke, Ken. *Ken Russell's Films*. Metuchen, N.J.: Scarecrow Press, 1984.

Haskell, Molly. *From Reverence to Rape: The Treatment of Women in the Movies*. New York: Holt, Rinehart and Winston, 1973.

Jaffe Young, Jane. *Lawrence on Screen: Re-visioning Prose Style in the Films of "The Rocking-Horse Winner," Sons and Lovers, and Women in Love*. New York: Peter Lang, 1999.

Katz, Ephraim. *The Film Encyclopedia*. New York: HarperCollins, 1994.

Kinkead-Weekes, Mark. *D. H. Lawrence: Triumph to Exile, 1912–1922*. Vol. 2 of *The*

*Cambridge Biography of D. H. Lawrence, 1885–1930.* Cambridge: Cambridge University Press, 1996.

Klein, Michael, and Gillian Parker, eds. *The English Novel and the Movies.* New York: Frederick Ungar, 1981.

Lawrence, D. H. *Aaron's Rod.* Edited by Mara Kalnins. Cambridge: Cambridge University Press, 1988.

———. *The Complete Poems of D. H. Lawrence.* Edited by Vivian de Sola Pinto and F. Warren Roberts. New York: Viking Press, 1971.

———. *The Letters of D. H. Lawrence.* 7 vols. Edited by James T. Boulton. Cambridge: Cambridge University Press, 1979–93.

———. *The Lost Girl.* Edited by John Worthen. Cambridge: Cambridge University Press, 1981.

———. *Phoenix.* Edited by Edward D. McDonald. 1936; reprint, New York: Viking Press, 1968.

———. *Phoenix II.* Edited by Warren Roberts and Harry T. Moore. New York: Viking Press, 1968.

———. *Quetzalcoatl.* Edited by Louis L. Martz. Redding Ridge, Conn.: Black Swan Books, 1995.

———. *Studies in Classic American Literature.* New York: Viking Press, 1971.

Limbacher, James L. *Feature Films on 8MM, 16MM, and Videotape.* 8th ed. New York: Bowker, 1985.

Maddox, Brenda. *Nora: A Biography of Nora Joyce.* New York: Fawcett Columbine, 1988.

McFarlane, Brian. *Novel to Film: An Introduction to the Theory of Adaptation.* Oxford: Clarendon Press, 1996.

Meyers, Jeffrey. *D. H. Lawrence: A Biography.* New York: Alfred A. Knopf, 1990.

Millett, Kate. *Sexual Politics: A Surprising Examination of Society's Most Arbitrary Folly.* Garden City, N.Y.: Doubleday, 1970.

Millett, Robert W. *The Vultures and the Phoenix: A Study of the Mandrake Press Edition of the Paintings of D. H. Lawrence.* East Brunswick, N.J.: Associated University Presses, 1983.

Monaco, James, and the editors of *Baseline,* eds. *The Movie Guide.* New York: Perigee Books, 1992.

Moore, Harry T. "D. H. Lawrence and the Flicks." *Literature/Film Quarterly* 1 (1973): 3–11.

Morris, Nigel. "Lawrence's Response to Film." In *D. H. Lawrence: A Reference Companion,* ed. Paul Poplawski, 591–603. Westport, Conn.: Greenwood Press, 1996.

———. "Screen Adaptations of Lawrence." In *D. H. Lawrence: A Reference Companion,* ed. Paul Poplawski, 604–38. Westport, Conn.: Greenwood Press, 1996.

Mulvey, Laura. "Visual Pleasure and Narrative Cinema." In *Issues in Feminist Film Criticism,* ed. Patricia Erens, 28–40. Bloomington: Indiana University Press, 1990.

Phillips, Gene D. "Ken Russell's Two Lawrence Films: *The Rainbow* and *Women in Love.*" *Literature/Film Quarterly* 25 (1997): 68–73.

———. "Sexual Ideas in the Films of D. H. Lawrence." *Sexual Behavior* 1 (1971): 10–16.

Russell, Ken. *A British Picture: An Autobiography.* London: Heinemann, 1989. Also published as *Altered States: The Autobiography of Ken Russell.* New York: Bantam Books, 1991.

———. *The Lion Roars: Ken Russell on Film.* Boston: Faber and Faber, 1993.

Sagar, Keith, ed. *A D. H. Lawrence Handbook.* New York: Barnes and Noble, 1982.

Simon, John. *Movies into Film: Film Criticism, 1967–1970.* New York: Dial Press, 1971.
   Includes Simon's film reviews of *The Fox, Women in Love,* and *The Virgin and the Gypsy.*

Sinyard, Neil. *Filming Literature: The Art of Screen Adaptation.* New York: St. Martin's Press, 1986.

Solecki, Sam. "D. H. Lawrence's View of Film." *Literature/Film Quarterly* 1 (1973): 12–16.

Stacy, Paul H. "Lawrence and Movies: A Postscript." *Literature/Film Quarterly* 2 (1974): 93–95.

Tarratt, Margaret. "An Obscene Undertaking." *Films and Filming* 17 (November 1970): 26–30.

Taylor, Neil. "A Woman's Love: D. H. Lawrence on Film." In *Novel Images: Literature in Performance,* ed. Peter Reynolds. London: Routledge, 1993.

Tibbetts, John C., and James M. Welsh, eds. *The Encyclopedia of Novels into Film.* New York: Facts on File, 1998.

Wagner, Geoffrey. *The Novel and the Cinema.* Rutherford, N.J.: Fairleigh Dickinson University Press, 1975.

Walker, John, ed. *Halliwell's Film Guide.* New York: Harper Collins, 1995.

Williams, Linda Ruth. *Sex in the Head: Visions of Femininity and Film in D. H. Lawrence.* Detroit: Wayne State University Press, 1993.

Worthen, John. *D. H. Lawrence: The Early Years, 1885–1930.* Vol. 1 of *The Cambridge Biography of D. H. Lawrence, 1885–1930.* Cambridge: Cambridge University Press, 1991.

## Sources on Individual Films

### *The Rocking Horse Winner* (1949)

Barrett, Gerald R., and Thomas L. Erskine, eds. *From Fiction to Film: D. H. Lawrence's "The Rocking-Horse Winner."* Encino and Belmont, Calif.: Dickenson, 1974.

Becker, Henry, III. "*The Rocking Horse Winner:* Film as Parable." *Literature/Film Quarterly* 1 (1973): 55–63.

Kael, Pauline. *Kiss Kiss Bang Bang.* New York: Little, Brown, 1968.

Lawrence, D. H. "The Rocking-Horse Winner." In vol. 3 of *The Complete Short Stories.* New York: Viking Press, 1961.

Mellen, Joan. "'The Rocking-Horse Winner' as Cinema." In *From Fiction to Film: D. H. Lawrence's "The Rocking-Horse Winner,"* ed. Gerald R. Barrett and Thomas L. Erskine. Encino and Belmont, Calif.: Dickenson, 1974.

Pelissier, Anthony. "Lawrence on Film: The Problem of Adapting 'Rocking-Horse Winner.'" *New York Times,* 11 June 1950, sec. 2, p. 5.

———. "The Rocking-Horse Winner: Final Shooting Script." In *From Fiction to Film: D. H. Lawrence's "The Rocking-Horse Winner,"* ed. Gerald R. Barrett and Thomas L. Erskine. Encino and Belmont, Calif.: Dickenson, 1974.

Smith, Julian. "The Social Architecture of 'The Rocking-Horse Winner.'" In *From Fiction to Film: D. H. Lawrence's "The Rocking Horse Winner,"* ed. Gerald R. Barrett and Thomas L. Erskine. Encino and Belmont, Calif.: Dickenson, 1974.

Snodgrass, W. D. "A Rocking-Horse: The Symbol, the Pattern, the Way to Live." *Hudson Review* 11 (1958): 191–200.

## L'Amant de Lady Chatterley (1955)

Balio, Tino. *The American Film Industry.* Madison: University of Wisconsin Press, 1976.
Provides a discussion of the New York State case against *L'Amant de Lady Chatterley.*

Beckley, Paul V. Review of *L'Amant de Lady Chatterley. New York Herald Tribune,* 11 July 1959, 7.

Bonheur, Gaston, and Philippe de Rothschild. *"L'Amant de Lady Chatterley."*
Stage adaptation of *Lady Chatterley's Lover* upon which the film was based.

"Court Overrules U.S. Film Censors—*Lady Chatterley's Lover." Times* (London), 30 June 1959, 8.

Crowther, Bosley. "Screen: 'Lady Chatterley.'" *New York Times,* 11 July 1959, 11.

Dyer, Peter John. Review of *Lady Chatterley's Lover. Films and Filming* 2 (September 1956): 24.

Hanlon, Lindley. "Sensuality and Simplification." In *The English Novel and the Movies,* ed. Michael Klein and Gillian Parker. New York: Frederick Ungar, 1981.

Hartung, Philip T. Review of *L'Amant de Lady Chatterley. Commonweal,* 4 September 1959, 472.

Hatch, Robert. Review of *L'Amant de Lady Chatterley. Nation,* 18 July 1959, 39–40.

Jordan, Rene. *Marlon Brando.* New York: Pyramid, 1973.
Discusses the effort to cast Brando as Mellors in *L'Amant de Lady Chatterley.*

Kauffmann, Stanley. "From France, Old and New." Review of *L'Amant de Lady Chatterley. New Republic,* 27 July 1959, 30.

Knight, Arthur. "Lady Chatterley's Lawyer." Review of *L'Amant de Lady Chatterley. Saturday Review,* 25 July 1959, 25.

"Lady and the Censors." *Newsweek,* 10 December 1956, 118.
Reports the New York State censorship case.

"Lady Chatterley on the Screen—Film of Lawrence's Novel." Review of *L'Amant de Lady Chatterley. Times* (London), 4 July 1956, 3.

"Lady Chatterley's Lover." Review of *L'Amant de Lady Chatterley. Filmfacts* 11 (1959): 183–84.

Lawrence, D. H. *Lady Chatterley's Lover.* Edited by Michael Squires. Cambridge: Cambridge University Press, 1993.

M., J. Review of *L'Amant de Lady Chatterley. Films in Review* 10 (August–September 1959): 422–23.

McCarten, John. "Laborious Love." Review of *L'Amant de Lady Chatterley. New Yorker,* 18 July 1959, 48–50.

Randall, Richard S. *Censorship of the Movies: The Social and Political Control of a Mass Medium.* Madison: University of Wisconsin Press, 1968.

Rembar, Charles. *The End of Obscenity: The Trials of Lady Chatterley, Tropic of Cancer, and Fanny Hill.* New York: Bantam Books, 1968.
Mentions the case against the film within the broader context of the case against the novel.

Scott, James F. "The Emasculation of *Lady Chatterley's Lover." Literature/Film Quarterly* 1 (1973): 37–45.

Walsh, Moira. Review of *L'Amant de Lady Chatterley. America,* 1 August 1959, 576–78.

## Sons and Lovers (1960)

Baldanza, Frank. *"Sons and Lovers:* Novel to Film as a Record of Cultural Growth." *Literature/Film Quarterly* 1 (1973): 64–70.

Balliett, Whitney. "An Embarrassment of Talk." Review of *Sons and Lovers*. *New Yorker,* 13 August 1960, 56–58.

Crowther, Bosley. "Pictorial Quality." Review of *Sons and Lovers*. *New York Times,* 14 August 1960, sec. 2, p. 1.

———. "Screen: Tepid Passions." Review of *Sons and Lovers*. *New York Times,* 3 August 1960, 35.

DeNitto, Dennis. "All Passion Spent." In *The English Novel and the Movies,* ed. Michael Klein and Gillian Parker. New York: Frederick Ungar, 1981.

Durgnat, Raymond. *A Mirror for England: British Movies from Austerity to Affluence.* New York: Praeger, 1971.

Gillett, John. Review of *Sons and Lovers*. *Film Quarterly* 14 (1960): 41–42.

Griffiths, Trevor. *Sons and Lovers: Trevor Griffiths' Screenplay of the Novel by D. H. Lawrence.* Nottingham: Spokesman, 1982.

> The film script for the seven-episode serialization of *Sons and Lovers* directed by Stuart Burge for BBC-TV in 1981.

Hart, Henry. Review of *Sons and Lovers*. *Films in Review* 11 (August–September 1960): 422–24.

Kael, Pauline. *I Lost It at the Movies.* Boston: Little, Brown, 1965.

Kauffmann, Stanley. "Several Sons, Several Lovers." Review of *Sons and Lovers* and *Psycho*. *New Republic,* 29 August 1960, 21–22.

Lambert, Gavin. "Sons and Lovers." 2 February 1959. First-draft screenplay, Lilly Library, University of Indiana, Bloomington.

Lambert, Gavin, and T. E. B. Clarke. "Sons and Lovers." 8 December 1959. Final shooting script with on-set revisions, Bobst Library, New York University, New York.

Lawrence, D. H. *Sons and Lovers.* New York: Viking Press, 1958.

"Lawrence: The Script . . . and the Camera." *Films and Filming,* May 1960, 9.

> Interviews with screenwriter Gavin Lambert and director Jack Cardiff.

"The New Pictures." Review of *Sons and Lovers*. *Time,* 1 August 1960, 58.

Quigly, Isabel. "Unlikely Lawrence." Review of *Sons and Lovers*. *Spectator,* July 1960, 21–24.

Wald, Jerry. "Scripting *Sons and Lovers*." *Sight and Sound* 29 (summer 1960): 117.

### *The Fox* (1968)

Crump, G. B. "'The Fox' on Film." *D. H. Lawrence Review* 1 (1968): 238–44.

"The Fox." *Playboy,* October 1967, 81–84.

> Photo essay emphasizing Anne Heywood's nude scenes and the film's overt eroticism.

Gontarski, S. E. "Mark Rydell and the Filming of *The Fox:* An Interview." *Modernist Studies: Literature and Culture, 1920–1940* 4 (1982): 96–104.

Greiff, Louis K. "Bittersweet Dreaming in Lawrence's 'The Fox': A Freudian Perspective." *Studies in Short Fiction* 20 (1983): 7–16.

Kael, Pauline. "Making Lawrence More Lawrentian." Review of *The Fox*. In *Going Steady.* Boston: Little, Brown, 1970.

Koch, Howard. "The Fox." Screenplay, Louis B. Mayer Library, American Film Institute, Los Angeles.

Lawrence, D. H. "The Fox." In *D. H. Lawrence: Four Short Novels.* New York: Viking Press, 1965.

Mellen, Joan. "Outfoxing Lawrence: Novella into Film." *Literature/Film Quarterly* 1 (1973): 17–27.

Naugrette, J.-P. "Le Renard et les Reves: Onirisme, Ecriture, Inconscient dans 'The Fox.'" *Etudes Anglaises,* April–June 1984, 142–55.

Sobchack, Thomas. "*The Fox:* The Film and the Novel." *Western Humanities Review* 23 (1969): 73–78.

Urbano, Cosimo. "The Evil That Men Do: Mark Rydell's Adaptation of D. H. Lawrence's 'The Fox.'" *Literature/Film Quarterly* 23 (1995): 254–61.

Wolkenfeld, Susan. "The Sleeping Beauty Retold: D. H. Lawrence's 'The Fox.'" *Studies in Short Fiction* 14 (1977): 345–52.

### *Women in Love* (1969)

Blanchard, Margaret. "Men in Charge: A Review of *Women in Love.*" *Women: A Journal of Liberation* 2 (fall 1970): 31–32.

Blevins, Winfred. "Lawrence's *Women in Love:* Word to Image." *Los Angeles Herald Examiner,* 12 April 1970, G1, G4.

Burgess, Anthony. *The Life and Work of D. H. Lawrence: Flame into Being.* New York: Arbor House, 1985.

Combs, Richard. Review of *Women in Love. Monthly Film Bulletin* 36 (1969): 263–64.

Crump, G. B. "*Women in Love*: Novel and Film." *D. H. Lawrence Review* 4 (1971): 28–41.

Farber, Stephen. Review of *Women in Love. Hudson Review* 23 (1970): 321–26.

Fisher, Jack. "Three Paintings of Sex: The Films of Ken Russell." *Film Journal* 2 (September 1972): 32–43.

Gomez, Joseph A. "Russell's Images of Lawrence's Vision." In *The English Novel and the Movies,* ed. Michael Klein and Gillian Parker. New York: Frederick Ungar, 1981.

Kael, Pauline. "Lust for 'Art.'" Review of *Women in Love. New Yorker,* 28 March 1970, 97–101.

Kahan, Saul. "Ken Russell: A Director Who Respects Artists." *Los Angeles Times Calendar Magazine,* 28 March 1971, 18.

Kauffmann, Stanley. Review of *Women in Love* and *The Boys in the Band. New Republic,* 18 April 1970, 20.

Knight, Arthur. "Liberated Classics." Review of *Women in Love. Saturday Review,* 21 March 1970, 50–53.

Knoll, Robert F. Review of *Women in Love. Film Heritage* 6 (summer 1971): 1–6.

Kramer, Larry. "Women in Love." July 1969. Script, Lilly Library, Indiana University, Bloomington.

Lawrence, D. H. *Women in Love.* New York: Viking Press, 1960.

Phillips, Gene D. "An Interview with Ken Russell." *Film Comment* 6 (fall 1970): 10–17.

———. *Ken Russell.* Boston: Twayne, 1979.

Rosen, Marjorie. "The Man Who Would Be Caine." *Film Comment* 16 (July–August 1980): 19.

> Interview with actor Michael Caine in which he reveals that Ken Russell offered him the part of Gerald in *Women in Love* and that he turned it down because of the nude wrestling scene.

Ross, Theodore. "Gargoyles in Motion: On the Transmigration of Character from Page to Screen and Related Questions on Literature and Film." *College English* 39 (1977): 371–82.

"The Secret Is Wile and Guile." *Los Angeles Herald Examiner,* 19 December 1968, C10.
    Interview with Glenda Jackson.
Sirkin, Elliott. Review of *Women in Love. Film Quarterly* 24 (1970): 43–47.
Warga, Wayne. "Kramer Scripts Thinking Man's *Women in Love.*" *Los Angeles Times Calendar Magazine,* 3 May 1970, 1, 12–13.
    Interview with Larry Kramer.
Weightman, John. "Trifling with the Dead." Review of *Women in Love. Encounter,* January 1970, 50–53.
Woodward, Ian. *Glenda Jackson: A Study in Fire and Ice.* New York: St. Martin's Press, 1985.
Zambrano, Ana Laura. "*Women in Love:* Counterpoint on Film." *Literature/Film Quarterly* 1 (1973): 46–54.

### The Virgin and the Gypsy (1970)

Alpert, Hollis. "Up the Rebels." Review of *The Virgin and the Gypsy. Saturday Review,* 25 July 1970, 37.
Crump, G. B. "Gopher Prairie or Papplewick? *The Virgin and the Gipsy* as Film." *D. H. Lawrence Review* 4 (1971): 142–53.
Gilliatt, Penelope. "This England, This Past." Review of *The Virgin and the Gypsy. New Yorker,* 4 July 1970, 71–72.
Gontarski, S. E. "Christopher Miles on His Making of *The Virgin and the Gypsy.*" *Literature/Film Quarterly* 11 (1983): 249–56.
    Interview with Christopher Miles.
———. "An English Watercolor." In *The English Novel and the Movies,* ed. Michael Klein and Gillian Parker. New York: Frederick Ungar, 1981.
Kauffmann, Stanley. Review of *The Virgin and the Gypsy* and *Two Mules for Sister Sara. New Republic,* 1 August 1970, 24, 35.
Lawrence, D. H. *The Virgin and the Gipsy.* New York: Bantam Books, 1968.
Plater, Alan. "The Virgin and the Gypsy." May 1969. Technical shooting script, Celeste Bartos International Film Study Center, Museum of Modern Art, New York.
Smith, Julian. "Vision and Revision: *The Virgin and the Gypsy* as Film." *Literature/Film Quarterly* 1 (1973): 28–36.

### The Rocking Horse Winner (1977)

Marcus, Fred. "From Story to Screen." Review of *The Garden Party* and Peter Medak's *The Rocking Horse Winner. Media and Methods* 14 (December 1977): 56–58.

### Lady Chatterley's Lover (1981)

Arnold, Gary. "Shabby *Chatterley.*" Review of *Lady Chatterley's Lover. Washington Post,* 9 October 1982, C6.
Chase, Chris. "At the Movies." *New York Times,* 14 May 1982, C8.
    Interview with Sylvia Kristel.
Coleman, John. "Pushing a Little Dope." Review of several films including *Lady Chatterley's Lover. New Statesman,* 18–25 December 1981, 51.
"Laurentiana." *D. H. Lawrence Review* 13 (1980): 285–88.
    Notice and disclaimer from Laurence Pollinger Ltd. that Cannon Films is making an unapproved version of *Lady Chatterley's Lover.*

Lawrence, D. H. *The First Lady Chatterley.* London: William Heinemann, 1972.

———. *John Thomas and Lady Jane.* London: Penguin Books, 1977.

———. *Lady Chatterley's Lover.* Edited by Michael Squires. Cambridge: Cambridge University Press, 1993.

Lefanu, Mark. Review of *Lady Chatterley's Lover. Monthly Film Bulletin,* December 1981, 248.

Len. [Lenny Borger]. Review of *Lady Chatterley's Lover. Variety,* 26 August 1981, 20.

Mitgang, Herbert. "Social Comment in *Lady Chatterley's Lover.*" Review. *New York Times,* 10 May 1982, sec. 3, p. 20.

Rickey, Carrie. "Unholy Trinity." Review of *Lady Chatterley's Lover, Roommates,* and *Memories of a French Whore. Village Voice,* 25 May 1982, 52.

Robinson, David. "Lumet's Sophisticated View of Corruption." Review of several films including *Lady Chatterley's Lover. Times* (London), 18 December 1981, 10.

## *Priest of Love* (1981)

Ansen, David. "D. H. and Frieda." Review of *Priest of Love. Newsweek,* 9 November 1981, 94.

Arnold, Gary. "The 'Love' Charm: The Life and Wife of D. H. Lawrence." Review of *Priest of Love. Washington Post,* 16 October 1981, B1, B10.

Bennetts, Leslie. "Portraying D. H. Lawrence's Wife as 'the First Hippie.'" *New York Times,* 11 October 1981, 1, 29.

    Profile of Janet Suzman as Frieda Lawrence.

Benson, Sheila. "Taking a Lawrence at Facile Value." Review of *Priest of Love. Los Angeles Times Calendar Magazine,* 16 October 1981, 2.

Brien, Alan. "Films in the World of Real-Life Fiction." Review of *Ragtime* and *Priest of Love. Sunday Times* (London), 21 February 1982, 39.

Brown, Geoff. "Uncluttered but Ominous Line." Review of *Priest of Love. Times* (London), 19 February 1982, 13.

Canby, Vincent. "Journeys of D. H. Lawrence." Review of *Priest of Love. New York Times,* 11 October 1981, 68.

Chase, Chris. "Director Talks of 'Difficult' Lawrences." *New York Times,* 16 October 1981, C8.

    Interview with Christopher Miles.

Chuta, David. "For the 'Love' of Lawrence." Review of *Priest of Love. Washington Post Weekend,* 16 October 1981, D4.

Coleman, John. "Exteriors." Review of *Priest of Love. New Statesman,* 19 February 1982, 29–30.

Crist, Judith. "D. H. Lawrence Brought to Life." Review of *Priest of Love. Saturday Review,* October 1981, 60–61.

———. "When Stars Don't Shine." Review of *Priest of Love. 50 Plus,* October 1981, 50.

Dowell, Pat. "Lawrence Joins Shadows of His Creations on Screen." *Baltimore Sun Spectator,* 25 October 1981, D1–D2.

Forbes, Jill. Review of *Priest of Love. Monthly Film Bulletin,* January 1982, 8–9.

Gelmis, Joseph. "A Biography of D. H. Lawrence." Review of *Priest of Love. Newsday,* 12 October 1981, sec. 2, p. 31.

Geng, Veronica. Review of *Beau Pere* and *Priest of Love. Soho News,* 20 October 1981, 55–57.

Jones, Will. "D. H. Lawrence Film a Richly Layered Success." Review of *Priest of Love. Minneapolis Tribune,* 29 October 1981, B11.

Kauffmann, Stanley. "Playing a Genius." Review of *Priest of Love. New Republic,* 21 October 1981, 20–21.

"Lawrence Bio-Pic: The Film Version." *D. H. Lawrence Review* 13 (1980): 191.
  Announcement that Christopher Miles's *Priest of Love* will be released in 1981.

Mills, Nancy. "Sexual Legacy of D. H. Lawrence." *San Francisco Sunday Examiner and Chronicle Datebook,* 18 October 1981, 22–23.

Moore, Harry T. *The Priest of Love: A Life of D. H. Lawrence.* Rev. ed. New York: Penguin Books, 1981.

Nowlan, Robert A., and Gwendolyn Wright Nowlan. *Films of the Eighties.* Jefferson, N.C.: McFarland, 1991.

Pfeifer, Ellen. "A Pretentious View of D. H. Lawrence." Review of *Priest of Love. Boston Herald American,* 16 October 1981, B6.

Plater, Alan. "Priest of Love." March 1980. Director's shooting script (third draft), Celeste Bartos Film Study Center, Museum of Modern Art, New York.

Powell, Dilys. "Second Time of Asking." Review of the revised and shortened version of *Priest of Love. Punch,* 13 November 1985, 84.

"Priest of Love: The Life of D. H. Lawrence, 1885–1930, Artist and Writer." Press release, Celeste Bartos Film Study Center, Museum of Modern Art, New York.

Sage, Lorna. "Revivifying Old Photographs." Review of *Priest of Love. Times Literary Supplement* (London), 26 March 1982, 340.

Sarris, Andrew. "The French Make Cinema." Review of *The Woman Next Door, The Aviator's Wife,* and *Priest of Love. Village Voice,* 14–20 October 1981, 47.

Simon, John. "Eros or Agape?" Review of *Priest of Love. National Review,* 11 December 1981, 1498.

### *Kangaroo* (1986)

Bernard, Jami. "Hopping Around Down Under with D. H. Lawrence." Review of *Kangaroo. New York Post,* 13 March 1987, 25.

Bradshaw, David. "An Absence of Strife." Review of *Kangaroo. Times Literary Supplement* (London), 12 December 1986, 1403.

Brown, Geoff. "A Certain Crazy Dignity." Review of several films including *Kangaroo. Times* (London), 5 December 1986, 14.

Conway, Ronald. "In a Deep Purple Mood." Review of several films including *Kangaroo. Quadrant* 31 (September 1987): 37–39.

Craven, Peter. Review of *Kangaroo. Cinema Papers,* May 1987, 57–58.

Gelmis, Joseph. "Adaptation of a D. H. Lawrence Novel." Review of *Kangaroo. Newsday,* 13 March 1987, sec. 3, p. 11.

Glaessner, Verina. Review of *Kangaroo. Monthly Film Bulletin,* December 1986, 373–74.

Harrington, Richard. "*Kangaroo:* Politics and Prattle." *Washington Post,* 15 May 1987, D7.

Hellman, Ian. Review of *Kangaroo. People Weekly,* 13 April 1987, 12.

Howe, Desson. "Overweight *Kangaroo* Limps." *Washington Post Weekend,* 15 May 1987, 31.

Johnstone, Iain. "Fuzzy Christmas Fear." Review of *Kangaroo. Sunday Times* (London), 7 December 1986, 46.

Jones, Evan. "Kangaroo." 1986. Film script (U.S. version), Margaret Herrick Library, Academy of Motion Picture Arts and Sciences, Los Angeles.

Kauffmann, Stanley. "Sidney, 1922; Baltimore, 1963." Review of *Kangaroo* and *Tin Men*. *New Republic,* 30 March 1987, 24–26.

Lawrence, D. H. *Kangaroo.* New York: Viking Press, 1960.

"Love, Marriage, Life, and the Whole Damn Thing." *Cinema Papers,* March 1986, 42. Interview with *Kangaroo* director Tim Burstall and producer Ross Dimsey.

Maslin, Janet. "Australian Politics in Lawrence's *Kangaroo*." *New York Times,* 13 March 1987, C12.

Minifie, Don. Review of *Kangaroo*. *Films and Filming,* November 1986, 35–36.

Nowlan, Robert A., and Gwendolyn Wright Nowlan. *Films of the Eighties*. Jefferson, N.C.: McFarland, 1991.

Peek, Andrew. "Tim Burstall's *Kangaroo*." *Westerly,* December 1980, 39–42. Interview with *Kangaroo* director Tim Burstall.

Reis, Brian. *Australian Film: A Bibliography.* London: Mansell, 1997.

Ross, Harris. "*Kangaroo:* Australian Filmmakers Watching Lawrence Watching Australia." *D. H. Lawrence Review* 19 (1987): 93–101.

Sawyer, Charles. Review of *Kangaroo*. *Films in Review,* May 1987, 295.

Slavin, John. Review of *Kangaroo*. *Filmviews* 32 (winter 1987): 37–39.

Stratton, David. Review of *Kangaroo*. *Variety,* 30 April 1986, 23, 27.

Taubin, Amy. "Animal Crackers." Review of *Kangaroo*. *Village Voice,* 24 March 1987, 56.

Tourmarkine, Doris. Review of *Kangaroo*. *Film Journal* 90 (April 1987): 28–29.

Wilmington, Michael. "A Tamed *Kangaroo* Plays It Safe." *Los Angeles Times Calendar Magazine,* 21 March 1987, 5.

## *The Rainbow* (1989)

Billington, Michael. "Sammi Davis: Just Right for D. H. Lawrence." *New York Times,* 30 April 1989, sec. 2, pp. 17, 20. Interview with Sammi Davis.

Blake, Richard A. "Summer Fair." Review of *Dead Poets Society* and *The Rainbow*. *America,* July 1989, 40, 45.

Crump, G. B. "Lawrence's *Rainbow* and Russell's *Rainbow*." *D. H. Lawrence Review* 21 (1989): 187–201.

Denby, David. "Saturday Night Special." Review of *Road House* and *The Rainbow*. *New York,* 29 May 1989, 64–65.

Gomez, Joseph A. "The Elusive Gold at the End of *The Rainbow:* Russell's Adaptation of Lawrence's Novel." *Literature/Film Quarterly* 18 (1990): 134–36.

Harper, Howard. "The BBC Television Serialization of *The Rainbow*." *D. H. Lawrence Review* 21 (1989): 202–7.

James, Caryn. "Ken Russell Goes Back to Lawrence for Love." Review of *The Rainbow*. *New York Times,* 5 May 1989, sec. 3, p. 9.

Johnstone, Iain. "Seaside Snapshot of British Madness." Review of *Chorus of Disapproval* and *The Rainbow*. *Sunday Times* (London), 5 November 1989, C5.

Kael, Pauline. "Trampled." Review of *The Rainbow* and *Miss Firecracker*. *New Yorker,* 29 May 1989, 102–4.

Kauffmann, Stanley. "Affairs of Love." Review of *The Rainbow*. *New Republic,* 15 May 1989, 28.

Kroll, Jack. "The Specter of Madness." Review of *The Rainbow. Newsweek,* 8 May 1989, 70.

Lawrence, D. H. *The Rainbow.* New York: Viking Press, 1961.

Malcolm, Derek. "Rainbow Warrior." *Manchester Guardian Weekly,* 28 August 1988, 27. Prerelease interview with Ken Russell.

*1995 Movies Unlimited Video Catalogue.* Movies Unlimited, 1994.

Novak, Ralph. Review of *The Rainbow. People Weekly,* 26 June 1989, 15–16.

Nowlan, Robert A., and Gwendolyn Wright Nowlan. *Films of the Eighties.* Jefferson, N.C.: McFarland, 1991.

O'Brien, Tom. "Catching Fire." Review of *The Rainbow. Commonweal,* 2 June 1989, 337–38.

"*The Rainbow* on Film." *D. H. Lawrence Review* 20 (1988): 358–59. Announcement that two productions of *The Rainbow* are in progress—Ken Russell's film for the large screen and a separate adaptation for BBC television.

Robinson, David. "The Blossoming of Love." Review of *The Rainbow. Times* (London), 2 November 1989, 21.

Schickel, Richard. "A Worthy Life." Review of *The Rainbow. Time,* 15 May 1989, 75.

Travers, Peter. Review of *The Rainbow. Rolling Stone,* 1 June 1989, 36.

Trotter, David. "Eco-orgasms." Review of *The Rainbow. Times Literary Supplement* (London), 10 November 1989, 1241.

Turan, Kenneth. "Ken Russell Goes Straight." Review of *The Rainbow* and *The Navigator. GQ,* June 1989, 117–20.

## *The Rocking Horse Winner* (1997)

Taubin, Amy. "Film: Short Circuit." Review of short films presented at the 1997 New York Film Festival including *The Rocking Horse Winner. Village Voice,* 30 September 1997, 75.

# Index

**Louis K. Greiff** is a professor of English at Alfred University. The present volume combines Greiff's long-standing interest in Lawrence with his more recent scholarly involvement with film and particularly with the adaptation process. His essays on these subjects and on the literature and film of the Vietnam War have appeared in the *Journal of Modern Literature, Studies in Short Fiction, Literature/Film Quarterly, Critique,* and the MLA series, Approaches to Teaching World Literature.